Fleet and Free

A HISTORY OF
BIRCHFIELD HARRIERS ATHLETICS CLUB

Fleet and Free

A HISTORY OF

BIRCHFIELD HARRIERS ATHLETICS CLUB

GARETH ROGERS
WITH WILFRED MORGAN
AND TOM McCOOK

TEMPUS

This book is dedicated to Roy Tilling
1952-2004

Front cover: Left to right: Arthur Robertson, Three-mile team race London 1908, Denise Lewis, Heptathlon Sydney 2000, Godfrey Brown, 4 x 400m Berlin 1936, Mark Lewis-Francis, 4 x 100m Athens 2004.

Back cover: Olympic gold medalist Mark Lewis-Francis with coach Steve Platt.

First published 2005

Tempus Publishing Limited
The Mill, Brimscombe Port,
Stroud, Gloucestershire, GL5 2QG
www.tempus-publishing.com

© Gareth Rogers, 2005

British Library Cataloguing in Publication Data.
A catalogue record for this book is available from the British Library.

ISBN 0 7524 3523 X

Typesetting and origination by Tempus Publishing Limited
Printed in Great Britain

Contents

Introduction	6
Prologue	6
1: Passing the Baton	8
2: Inter-city Sprinter	9
3: On your Marks!	11
4: Out of the Blocks	13
5: Anchor Leg	15
6: On the Record	16
7: Ideal Olympian	18
8: Paper Chase	19
9: Torchbearer	22
10: Second Wind	23
11: Hurdles to Clear	25
12: Onward and Upward	31
13: On the Right Track	35
14: Ladies First	40
15: Out of Darkness and into Light	43
16: Rising Stars	47
17: Local Heroes	52
18: A Family Affair	57
19: New Horizons	61
20: Raising the Bar	63
21: Life and Seoul	73
22: A Merry Dance	76
23: Pain but no Glory	82
24: Success Breeds Success	86
25: Shattered Dreams	89
26: Hammer Home	95
27: The Great Breakthrough	98
28: New Year Resolution	103
29: Ladies' Day? Ladies' Year!	108
30: Stag Party	115
31: Glory, Glory, Hallelujah!	127
32: Silver Lining	143
33: The Race of All their Lives	152
34: Daniel Canes the Opposition	163
35: Leap to Glory	173
36: High Performance	183
37: Glory Leg	189
Birchfield Harriers Records and Statistics	197
Bibliography	222
Photographs/Illustrations	222
Long Service	222
Index	223

Introduction

Most aspects of our lives – have to be developed in an available context and over a period of time. An athletics club is no exception. In developing the history of the Birchfield Harriers club of Birmingham, we must have regard to the many context: firstly, the natural human activity upon which the sport is based; secondly, the ancient games which gave form to that activity; and thirdly, in more modern times, the opportunity of leisure time and facility, which have allowed a more popular involvement by motivated and talented athletes, all without regard to income or background. (With Britain in the vanguard of the Industrial Revolution and the growth of cities, an analysis of the nation in the nineteenth century is pertinent).

In this way a full understanding of a club, which favoured a working class membership in an era when elitism bedevilled the sport, can be developed, showing the democratic means and first class administration which led to its current status as the most successful club in the history of British athletics.

Let the tale unfold!

Gareth Rogers

Prologue

The actual movements in the various events of track and field sports go back to the efforts of primitive man to survive.

With no truly effective weapons available, earliest man had to develop speed of foot; muscular power; dexterity of motion; and the ability to jump and leap in order to evade his natural enemies. When not doing this to save his own life it could be assumed that he practised with his fellows in order to improve his skills. From such practice the idea of athletic competition may have emerged.

The first trace of track and field sports goes back to various sports cultivated before the Christian era by the Egyptians and several Asian countries. Greece, of course, played a part and the Irish too. They had a great festival known as Lugnas, or the Tailtean Games, celebrated as far back as several centuries BC.

Many believe the ceremonies of the Olympic games, including some track and field events, started in the fourteenth century BC, with historical records kept from 776 BC.

The most primitive form of athletic exercise as a sport, running, has been popular from the earliest times. The simple foot race (dromos) run straight from starting point to goal – or once over the course of a stadium, being a little over 200 yards – formed an event in the Greek Olympic pentathlon or quintuple contest. There was also a race once over the course and back (diaulos) and the dolichos, a long race run many times, often as many as twelve, which was about three miles up and down the stadium. Warriors would also take part in a somewhat different event, the dromos hopliton, a short race wearing full armour whilst carrying sword and shield.

No record of these times has been handed down, but the contests must have been severe and the ancient Olympic chronicles preserve the memory of several men who fell dead at the end of the long course.

The games survived the conquest of Greece by Rome and were carried on until 394 AD, when they were abolished by order of the Roman Emperor Theodosius.

The best runners in the Middle Ages were most often found among the couriers maintained by potentates and municipalities. The Persian couriers of the Turkish Sultans often ran from Constantinople to Adrianople, and back; a distance of about 220 miles achieved in two days and two nights. In districts of India and Africa, runners were often employed to carry the mail before the age of the railways.

In all parts of Great Britain track, road, and cross-country running have been popular forms of recreation for many centuries.

Following classical times, the next record of track and field sports is not found until AD 1154 when athletic practice fields were provided in London.

Affecting the development of track and field in Medieval England was a ban against athletic events promulgated by Edward III (1327–1377) because they interfered with archery. Athletics were permitted again in the following century and were generally approved of by Henry VIII (1509–1547) who was proficient in throwing the hammer!

Henry VIII

One: Passing the Baton

Distance races for cash were flourishing in England by the start of the nineteenth century. Eventually amateur races were held at Oxford and Cambridge, in 1825, and also at Lord's Cricket Ground. Eton College originated a 100-yard hurdles race in 1837 and added sprints and steeplechase in 1843.

The first regularly organised athletics meeting of modern times in England was promoted by the Royal Military Academy, Woolwich, in 1849. A year later Exeter College, Oxford, inaugurated sports that were continued annually. At the 1850 Exeter College meeting the events were the 100, 330 and 440 yards, the 140-yard hurdles and a four-mile race. The high jump and broad jump were added in 1851. The Exeter College meeting was undoubtedly the precursor of the Cambridge sports that were begun in 1860. The Oxford and Cambridge meetings commenced in 1864 and the English Championships in 1866.

In 1852 Kensington Grammar School began to hold regular meetings. Harrow, Cheltenham College and Durham University followed a year later – and from these early meetings, athletics in English schools continued to grow. This reached its climax in the Public Schools Challenge Cup. This meeting was promoted annually by the London Athletic Club (LAC), which came into being in June 1863 under the name of the Mincing Lane Athletic Club – the majority of the founders having their business in that centre of London trade.

The Amateur Athletic Club was formed in 1866 to 'supply the want of an established ground upon which competitions in amateur athletic sports might take place between gentlemen amateurs'. The definition of 'amateur' as set out was very indicative of a social divide. 'An amateur is a person who has never competed in an open competition, or for public money, or for admission money, and who has never at any period in his life taught or assisted in the pursuit of athletic exercise as a means of livelihood, or is a mechanic, artisan, or labourer.'

The stark latter phrase obviously meant to exclude the working class athletes who raced in Scotland and the North of England.

The AAC conducted a first English Championship in the year of their formation, although the active athletes continued to ally themselves with the LAC rather than the AAC.

Meanwhile, cross-country running had its inception with the foundation of the Crick run at Rugby school in 1837, followed by many other famous schools also holding annual cross-country races. About thirty years later the Thames Hare and Hounds held cross-country runs and races (known as 'paper chases') as a winter sport; and in a few years many other 'harrier' clubs were formed throughout England.

The sport reaches new heights.

8

Two: Inter-city Sprinter

The nineteenth century was not only an era of remarkable economic progress, but also a period of social advance; a time when employers began to look at the conditions of their workers more carefully, and a time when people began to care for the poor rather than punish them.

When Victoria became Queen in 1837 most of her subjects were country dwellers. When she died sixty-four years later, most of them were townspeople and the number of large towns had doubled. This was one of history's great social and economic transformations. Britain had become the world's first predominantly urbanised industrial nation.

This unprecedented development presented the late-Victorians with a whole range of novel and pressing problems of urban living.

'A miserable region of damp, dilapidation and decay, where the deaths are twice as numerous as in the suburbs of Edgbaston. Young children die especially fast. As one of the tenants pithily put it –"There's more bugs than babies." Perfect health is unknown and decent habits almost impossible.' Such was one description of central working class Birmingham in 1875.

Birmingham was in the vanguard of provincial growth. In 1837 it had a population of about 170,000 people. By the beginning of the twentieth century that had risen threefold to 522,204. Its industrial capacity and geographical extent had expanded more than proportionately.

However, by means of parliamentary legislation, the repeated reorganisation of local government, Herculean feats of civil engineering, countless philanthropic enterprises and a great deal of Victorian paternalism – well before the end of Victoria's reign, modern city life had been made reasonable for the majority of residents. Ultimately, Birmingham overcame its twentieth Century traumas to such an extent that by 1890 an American observer could describe it as 'the best governed city in the world'.

So, a Birmingham athletics club could form, helped by those factors and the development of several others: a railway system to carry competitors to inter-club meets; a postal system to arrange fixtures; the provision of parks and recreational facilities; plus the time available to enjoy a more active life.

It was as early as 1824, even before the Stockton and Darlington line had been completed, that Birmingham businessmen had launched a project to build a railway line linking together 'the three great capitals of England'. These they identified as London, Birmingham and Liverpool. They had to wait until 1833 for parliamentary approval for the London and Birmingham railway, and also for the Grand Junction Railway Company to construct a line linking Birmingham to the existing Liverpool and Manchester railway.

By 1841 Grenville was remarking in his *Spas of England* that Birmingham had 'by fortuitous circumstances been converted into a centre of conveyance of railroad tracks to every part of the kingdom'.

Interestingly, the first travelling post office utilising the railway was established between Birmingham and Liverpool in 1838. And the new penny postage was introduced by Sir Rowland Hill in 1840, carrying circulars and pamphlets cheaply all over the country.

The newspaper post had a varied history. In 1840 newspapers were, by statute, carried free of postage. In 1870 the position was altered by act of parliament, which established a rate of a half pence for each newspaper irrespective of weight. This privilege being confined to papers published at intervals and complying with certain specified conditions. By that time reports of athletics meetings were being included in newspapers, whilst specialist athletics magazines were being published. So clubs were aware of each other and able to communicate – before and after the formation of associations.

Within Victorian Birmingham itself there were two contrasting leisure traditions. One has been labelled the 'rational recreations' and the other a 'counteracting' tradition. The latter was embodied in certain popular sports and pastimes. Many historians have interpreted it as representing the quintessential Victorian social divide between, on the one hand, those who were respectable or wanted to improve themselves; and on the other, the uncouth and feckless. The popular leisure tradition was kept under intense pressure

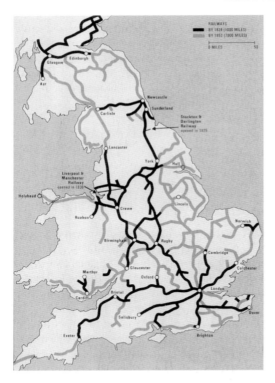

Athletics on the right lines.

throughout the Victorian era and, following national legislation in 1835, the brutal sports were to be all but eliminated.

However, the early history of public parks in Birmingham was not so smooth. It depended more on private philanthropy and voluntary effort than municipal initiative. During the 1850s the town council contemplated the purchase of 250 acres in Sutton Park, and then of Aston Hall and Park – only to abandon both projects. When the council stalled at making a realistic offer for Aston Park, forty-three acres were purchased by what might be described as a philanthropic company. By 1858 Aston Park was opened as a place of public amusement by Queen Victoria herself. The intention of the company was to recoup the investments of its shareholders out of the profits of entertainments and refreshments, and then transfer the park to the corporation.

There was progress gradually being made in the sphere of physical recreation and organised sports. In 1860 and 1862 baths were opened at Woodcock Street and Northwood Street to supplement the Kent Street baths opened in the 1850s. All were stated in a Baths Committee report to have been 'largely frequented by the working classes'.

A new trend is also identified from 1850 when the employer of 120 steel-toy makers introduced them to cricket and archery. Before long a local newspaper was reporting: 'The men possess bats, wickets and balls; bows, arrows and targets; in common. In Summer they turn out to play two or three times a week, and often sacrifice a Monday afternoon to the exercise of these sports, which at all events, is better than drinking away the Monday.'

Athletics and football were slower in gathering momentum than cricket and initially were relatively elitist pastimes. We first hear of a Birmingham Athletic Club in 1865 when it was meeting at Bingley Hall, close to what was to become Symphony Hall. The following year it opened a gymnasium in King Alfred's Place and two years later mounted Birmingham's first athletics festival.

The age profile of the Birmingham population from the end of the 1870s is pertinent to the supply of potentially fit and able sports participants. At that time the 'Great Depression' had greatly accelerated emigration from the countryside to the towns. These offered a prospect of steadier work, higher wages and greater independence as well as the attractions of social concentration. It was especially the young who were leaving the land, and young people predominated within the late-Victorian towns and cities, obviously producing a new generation of youngsters themselves.

Accompanying the energetic was the age of mass amusements following the Bank Holiday Act of 1871 and the Holiday Extension Act of 1875. Christmas Day and Good Friday were already Bank Holidays under common law. By the Act of 1871 there was added Easter Monday, the Monday of Whitsun week, the first Monday in August, and 26 December, if a weekday.

So, there was time, at last, to go running!

Three: On your Marks!

The club is assumed to owe its birth to a dispute, which arose over a cross-country race in 1876 promoted by the Excelsior Football Club. This was one of the many clubs playing on Aston Park in those days. This race had been staged annually for some years, but the last edition ended in a fiasco through a faulty trail. Prizes were awarded and this decision upset a section of participants, who claimed that these should have been withheld and the race re-run. After a stormy protest the dissatisfied competitors decided to call a meeting and form a separate cross-country club.

This meeting was held at Lozells Sunday School in Wheeler Street. It was decided to go ahead and form a club to be called the Birchfield Harriers – after the old name of the district around which their activities were centred. The first officers of the club were Thomas Bragg (President), W. Davis (Captain) and T.K. Steanes (Secretary). It is interesting to note that Tom Pank of Aston Villa was amongst those who attended the first meeting. The early days of both the Harriers and that football club saw an overlap of facilities and competitors.

In the Midlands, the centre of much sporting activity was the Aston Lower Grounds. It had been part of the grounds of Aston Hall, an impressive sixteenth century building and home of the Holte family. Birmingham City Council purchased the Hall and the surrounding park in 1864. The area was opened to the public in 1872. It was bounded by Witton Road, Witton Lane and Trinity road, making a triangle that contained about thirty-two acres. The sporting activities took place on the meadow (illustrated overpage) and it was there that three famous local clubs began their activities. The Warwickshire County Cricket Club played some of its games there before moving to Edgbaston in 1886 and when Aston Villa FC was formed

in 1874 they played on the meadow before moving to a ground in Wellington Road, Perry Barr. By 1879 Birchfield Harriers were able to stage their first track meeting there on a running track, or cinder path as it was called in those days. It was indeed a track meeting, for no field events were included in the programme. The circuit was an odd distance, 501 yards, and it sloped. However, the surface enjoyed a good reputation, so much so that in 1881 the Lower Grounds was the venue for the AAA Championship. It drew a crowd of over 10,000 spectators and made a profit of £325. An outstanding performance came from Lon Myers of the USA. He won the 440 yards in 48.6 s, the fastest recorded up to that time. However, it was not ratified because 440 yards was less than one circuit of the track. J. Ogden of Birchfield won the steeplechase to become the first club member to gain an AAA title.

However, it was primarily as a cross-country club that Birchfield achieved recognition. By February 1879 it was challenging the Moseley Harriers for the Midland

Thomas Bragg.

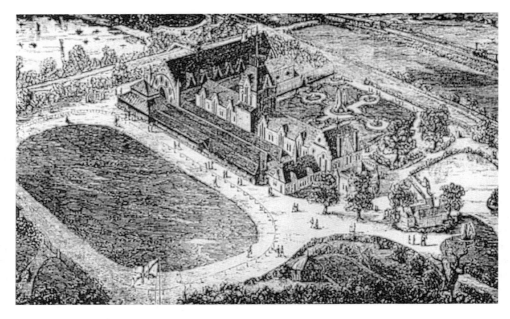

Aston Lower Grounds.

The 1880 cross-country champions.

Championship. This race ended in a similar fiasco to that which gave the club its birth. The trail of paper was lost in Sutton Park with H.M. Oliver (Moseley) and C. Beesley (Birchfield) being the only two to finish the course.

It was decided to re-run the race a month later, starting from the Calthorpe Arms, Perry Barr, and with new runners in Walter George (Moseley) and Joey Law (Birchfield) being prominent amongst a crop of good athletes added. The race was therefore worthy of the title. Moseley Harriers won, scoring 34 points to Birchfield's 47 points. The latter's team and places were as follows: J. Law 2; F. Lockyer 5; T.H. Bailey 6; W. Davies 9; G. Hibberd 10 and T. Assinder 15.

The 1879 to 1880 season was significant for the membership of W.W. Alexander. His subsequent administrative contribution to the club, and that of his family for generations to follow, is still recognised today in the name of Birmingham's major athletics stadium. His arrival coincided with the beginning of the club's real progress. That season they began to make history by beating rivals Moseley Harriers in the Midland Senior Championship, run from Moseley to Coleshill. Joey Law beat the renowned Walter George for the individual title and the team defeated Moseley by 36 points to 77. The Birchfield heroes on the day were: Joey Law 1; G. Hibberd 5; F. Lockyer 6; A.H. Hill 7; T. Lawrence 8 and J.Ogden 9.

This performance encouraged the decision to enter for the National Cross Country Championship at Roehampton. Birchfield Harriers became the first provincial club to win this prestigious event. The Stags scored 52 points with the Thames Hares and Hounds second on 74 points. The athletes' scores on this famous occasion were: Joey Law 3; A.H. Hill 4; G. Hibberd 6; T. Lawrence 8; J. Ogden 13 and F. Lockyer 18.

Four: Out of the Blocks

The club had achieved much in a short time, but found Moseley were to prevent their retention of the Midlands and National titles in 1881. In the Midland Senior at Sutton Park, Moseley scored 54 points and Birchfield scored 67 points with W.W. Alexander 4; Joey Law 5; F. Lockyer 10; A.H. Hill 12; T. Lawrence 14 and J. Ogden 22. In the National at Roehampton, Moseley finished on 41 points whilst Birchfield finished on 94 points. Running that day were: W.W. Alexander 4; J. Ogden 12; A.H. Hill 14; Joey Law 20; T. Prowse 21 and H. Horton 23. This National win by Moseley Harriers was the first of their four consecutive wins. This record stood until 1923 when Birchfield equalled it and also scored in 1924, 1925 and 1926. The record of seven successive wins in the National Championship still stands today.

As noted earlier, in 1881 J. Ogden also won the AAA two-mile steeplechase and has the distinction of being the first member to secure a title at that level.

The 1882 Midlands Senior proved ultra-competitive. Run at Four Oaks, the Moseley team provided the first man home in Walter George but Birchfield's team: Joey Law 3; T. Lawrence 7; W.W. Alexander 8; J. Ogden 11; A.H. Hill 13 and F. Lockyer 17 scored 59 points to pip Moseley by a solitary point!

However, Moseley extracted ample revenge by placing Walter George first home and scoring 41 points to Birchfield's 77 in the National Cross in which the Stags were represented by T. Lawrence 2; Joey Law 5; F. Lockyer 13; J. Ogden 17; A.H. Hill 19 and J. Chater 21.

It was about this time that the public were becoming interested in the club, which although only established for a few years had reached a high standard. Aston Villa Football Club was very supportive, especially as many members were attached to both clubs. The Villa played a friendly match with Wolverhampton Wanderers on the Old Aston Lower Grounds and the princely sum of £50 was raised for the Harriers, allowing it to clear its debts. The venue was significant as the running club's headquarters had been at the Calthorpe Arms but switched to Aston where better facilities were available.

It was at a Special General Meeting on 3 August 1882 that W.W. Alexander was first elected as Secretary and took his characteristic energy and competitiveness from the course to the committee room. The club now looked forward to the Senior at Four Oaks on 3 February 1883. They were to enjoy a double success: T. Lawrence coming home first followed by T. Thornton and the team scoring 41 points to beat Moseley by one point for the second year in succession. The team was: T. Lawrence 1; T. Thornton 2; G. Savage 6; Joey Law 7; G.A Dunning 9 and T. Crellin 16.

In the National at Roehampton, Moseley once again took their revenge by scoring 37 to Birchfield's 76. It is interesting to note that the individual winner was G.A. Dunning, who, although representing Birchfield Harriers in the Midland Seniors, competed in the race that day for Clapton Beagles. The laws governing the sport in those days apparently gave athletes freedom of choice. However, there was consolation in the victory by T. Thornton that 1883 season in his winning the AAA two-mile steeplechase: the second member to do so.

In the winter of 1883 another fascinating fact emerges. A special athletics meeting was listed for 15 December – but had to be postponed as Aston Villa needed certain members to play for them in a game against Cambridge University.

The Senior Championship, run at Four Oaks on 9 February 1884, was won by the team with H. Bate 4; G. Savage 5; T. Thornton 6; W. Etkins 7; W.W. Alexander 10 and H. Humphries 12, scoring a total of 44 points to Moseley Harrier's 72 points in second place. However, in the National, this time also at Four Oaks – Moseley sprang their usual turn with a score of 32 to Birchfield's 68. Walter George was the first man home but his input and that of several other principals in the Moseley cause was about to change. The competitive rivalry within the club between George and William Snook, which raised public interest similar to that in the performances of Steve Ovett and Sebastian Coe a century later, was ended that year when George turned professional and Snook moved across the city to join Birchfield.

In 1885, at the age of twenty-four, Snook carried all before him. He was first home in the National Cross Country at Manchester in March and in July at the AAA Championships at Southport he won the mile, four miles, ten miles and steeplechase. Not surprisingly, the winning of four titles at one AAA championship meeting is a record that has never been bettered.

In 1886, at the National held in Croydon, the club won the coveted team trophy for the second time. However, the favourite, Snook, was beaten into second place by Hickman of Coventry Godiva. Then, sensationally, although the result of the race stood, the Southern Counties, supported by the AAA, decided to suspend Snook for life from all athletics for 'not trying to win'. Without any evidence, they claimed that Snook was in league with bookmakers and was running under orders not to finish first. He was certainly heavily backed to win for bookmakers played a prominent part in athletics in those days. Snook explained that blistered feet had caused him to slow at the end of the race. As a working man he did not have the funds to take the issue to court and so Birchfield concentrated on a strong internal appeal. Sadly, the ban stood and William Snook never ran as an amateur again. The AAA was keen to be seen to be exercising influence and sending a message to athletes in general.

Snook, broken-hearted, left for France and settled in Paris. At the end of his life, in 1916, being destitute and in poor health, he wrote to W.W. Alexander about his wish to die in Birmingham. Members who knew him in his great days raised money for his fare home. He returned to Birmingham in October and died in Highcroft Hall workhouse on 9 December at the age of fifty-five. His coffin was followed to the grave in Witton Cemetery by officials of the Midland Counties AAA.

Another great athlete associated with Birchfield Harriers who was to suffer an ignominious and penniless end to his life was the multi-talented Arthur Wharton. The first major black sportsman he had the distinction of playing as goalkeeper for the Preston North End 'Invincible' team – as well as being AAA 100 yards sprint champion. Originally from the Gold Coast or Ghana, Arthur was the son of a missionary who studied for a while in a seminary at Cannock. The sprint title had been won in the vest of Cleveland College and while he was a player with Darlington FC.

William Snook.

In the summer of 1886, realising his box-office potential, the twenty-year-old Wharton took what could be described as 'career moves'. He devoted his time to Birchfield Harriers and the track at Aston Lower Grounds. He enjoyed the status of AAA 100 yards champion and his appearance at events gained a lot of advanced publicity. 'Shamateurism' was prevalent and it was possible for him to earn from appearance money and prizes, even though he was officially an amateur. The status and location of Birchfield Harriers would have improved his access to meetings and ensured a more regular income.

At Aston on 4 September the champion was said to have broken the record for the 150 yards at least twice. However, the *Darlington and Stockton Times* – from an area where there was hostility against Wharton, particularly over his transfer to Preston North End – commented: 'The fourteen and two-fifth seconds advanced on the authority of W.W. Alexander of Birchfield Harriers, who are running a series of gate-money speculations called sports, held and to be held in the Midlands… as promoter and the person most interested in procuring sensational performances he is the very last to set up as time-taker. Wharton's beating the record meant a big advertisement for the next gate-money show at Coventry.'

During the week of 11 to 18 September, Arthur ran around the Midlands with Birchfield Harriers in their 'gate-money speculations' referred to in the newspaper. The tour had been organised to 'assist in liquidating debts owing by the Midland Counties Cross Country Championship Association and the Birchfield Harriers'. It was a hectic schedule at the end of a hard season and, with his football commitments imminent, he attended six meetings, won eight races and competed in many more. In 1887 he retained the 100 yards title and spent a successful and busy summer back in the Midlands but press speculation that he would turn professional came true in April 1888 and he moved to a new base in Yorkshire. His reputation for excellence was appreciated by those who were involved with him at Birchfield and his contribution to the club's survival is noteworthy.

By this time W.W. Alexander was enjoying a move to greater prominence too and his power struggle with H.M. Oliver, the Secretary of Moseley, at club and regional level was making for compulsive viewing.

Five: Anchor Leg

Harry Oliver came from London in 1876 to work for the Birmingham Banking Company. He was a reasonable athlete and Moseley Harriers were a couple of years old. He could be described as 'a mover and shaker'. His arrival coincided with a time of creation in sport when clubs and associations were being formed. Oliver wanted to have a 'finger in every pie' and became both Secretary of Moseley Harriers and the Midland Cross Country Association when it was formed. He was a timekeeper and a handicapper for the Midland Counties Association as soon as track and field events developed. This was an important post because he could travel around the Midlands checking on the performances of various athletes. If somebody 'out in the sticks' produced a good performance then Oliver would instantly produce a membership form for Moseley Harriers! In addition he was editor and part-owner of *Midland Athlete*, which ran alongside *Sport and Play* as a leading magazine for the sport at that time.

W.W. Alexander was born on the Isle of Wight and the story related by subsequent generations relates to the death of his mother when he was fifteen. His father remarried rather too hastily for the teenager and so he left home, came to the mainland, and made his way north. Young William was keen on horses. Eventually he found a job in the Midlands looking after his favourite animals and started to take part, casually, in athletics. Again, the time to take an interest in the growth of the sport was right. Like Oliver, Alexander was a man with a lot of energy and drive. Once he had assumed a role with the Birchfield Harriers, he then wanted them to be established as the leading club. The rivalry also reflected a social divide. Oliver and his colleagues at Moseley were all white-collar people, whereas manual workers gravitated to Birchfield. Alexander himself ran a sub post office in Goole Street in Highgate, where most of the club's administration took place.

What of the relationship between these dynamic gentlemen? It is noted that at a Midlands Counties Athletics Association meeting in May 1886, a discussion took place over Small Heath Athletic Society. The 'bona fide' existence of this Society had been called into question by Mr Oliver as the MCAA Honorary

Secretary. The Society had staged a sports meeting but apparently officers had not been elected before the event took place. Mr Oliver maintained that the Society was merely a private undertaking, arranged by a small group of people who 'officiated as directors and promoters of the meeting'. He thought that they had no right to do this and suggested that any member of the Association might arrange a similar meeting and 'put the money in his pocket'.

Mr Alexander objected strongly to the fact that the Society had been brought before the Association in this manner. He stated that if the sports meeting had been a failure, then nothing more would have been heard about it. Alexander said the matter originated from the jealousy of Oliver, 'by whom he had been vilified in a most unjustifiable manner'.

It appears that the whole dispute revolved around the question of personal ill-feeling toward W.W. Alexander. Harry Oliver had written an abrasive article about the Birchfield Secretary in his publication, the *Midland Athlete*. It was considered unfair by many on the Midlands athletics scene that Oliver, as a prominent member of the MCCA, should have expressed his opinions in a manner damaging to Alexander's character. Oliver had also commented that the Small Heath event was a private spectacular and was contrary to Association rules.

So, Mr Oliver was challenged in the Association debate with the question that if he had 'the purity of the sport at heart – then why, some years ago, had he assisted at sports meetings which everyone knew were private spectaculars?'

Alexander went on to express surprise that Mr Oliver should make a 'vituperative attack' against him and thought it inconsistent for Mr Oliver to behave in this way when he himself was founder of one of the worst phases of pseudo-amateurism in the Midlands – that of exhibition running for gate receipts. The Chairman expressed concern that so much personal feeling had been 'infused into the meeting'!

Surprisingly, the next set of MCCA minutes report that 'the hatchet was buried' and that any antagonism and animosity between the two men was 'broken down'. We must doubt that such a miracle was achieved so quickly!

The magazine *Sport and Play* reported: 'Now that these outstanding differences have been overcome and peace proclaimed, let us hope that the gentlemen constituting the committee of the MCAAA will endeavour to work together in unison for the better protection of amateur sport in the Midlands. Rather than making the Association an institution for the ventilation of personal grievances amongst its members, such as it has been obviously used in the past.'

The conflict was more easily resolved by circumstances rather than platitudes when H.M. Oliver suddenly fell from grace. It was discovered by his employers that Oliver had, for some time, been taking money from the bank to pay for the printing of his magazine, which began to accrue debts. As soon as the *Midland Athlete* was published he would put the cash back before it was realised what was happening. Once caught, he was successfully prosecuted for embezzlement and sent to prison for two months. This meant he was blackballed from any sort of post in athletics and the pivotal role within the Midlands was now taken by W.W. Alexander. The new man was keen to adopt the recruitment methods of his former adversary. In his capacity as MCAA official handicapper he had access to all the athletes in the region, and many joined Birchfield. Meanwhile, with Oliver off the scene, Moseley Harriers disintegrated within three years. It was eventually resurrected but was never a force again. For W.W. Alexander and the Birchfield Harriers, the future was bright!

Six: On the Record

Reference has already been made to the fundraising initiatives of the club. At the time of William Snook's controversy, in 1886, the Harriers were already in serious financial troubles through losses at sports meeting. These had been adversely affected by poor weather. By 1887 the situation had reached the point where there were only ten runners left in the club. It was a remarkable feat for this squad to travel around England and be so competitive.

In the Midlands at Burton the team was only beaten by one point, 61 to 62, by Burton Harriers. This was a re-run Championship. The first one was declared void after an official sent the leaders around the finishing field again. This meant they were mixed up with runners just entering and it proved impossible for a count to be taken. A. Holding of Burton was first man with Arthur Mabbett second. Birchfield scored as follows: Arthur Mabbett 2; Tom Thornton 4; J.C. Cope 8; H. Humphreys 12; Sonny Morton 16 and S. Wright 20.

In the 1887 National, J.E. Hickman of Godiva was again the individual winner with Tom Thornton and Sonny Morton second and third. The team placings saw Birchfield again victorious on 37 points with Godiva second on 80 points. The club team was Tom Thornton 2; Sonny Morton 3; J.C. Cope 4; Arthur Mabbett 5; H. Humphries 10 and Tom Rudge 13.

During the 1888 season there was not a Midlands Championship staged, but in the National held at Manchester in early March the club secured their third successive team victory by scoring 77 points. Salford Harriers won the individual title with E.W. Parry being second. Scoring members for Birchfield were Tom Thornton 5; Sonny Morton 6; Tom Rudge 13; H. Humphries 14; Arthur Mabbett 17 and S. Baker 22.

The most notable performance of the track season was the victory in the AAA Two-mile Steeplechase Championship by J.C. Cope. He became the fourth member in seven years to win this particular event.

The next Midlands was run at Wolverhampton in February 1889. Birchfield took the prize with the low score of 28 points to defeat Godiva Harriers by 57 points. Amongst the top scorers were Tom Thornton 2; Tom Birch 3; J.C. Cope 4; Arthur Mabbett 5 and J. Plant 6.

In the National at Kempton Park the club was anxious to equal Moseley Harriers' record of four successive wins. After a very close struggle they were only beaten by one point by Salford Harriers, 101 to 102. E.W. Parry of Salford enjoyed a consecutive individual victory, whilst the counting team for the Birmingham club was Tom Birch 7; Tom Thornton 9; Arthur Mabbett 11; J. Plant 19; H. Humphries 22 and J.C. Cope 34.

The following season the Midlands Championship at Wolverhampton saw the club beaten 49 points to 55 by Worcester Harriers, making it only the fourth defeat in this race in the twelve years since formation. The overall record in the Senior and National Championships at this stage read:

The Senior: seven wins, four seconds and one no race.
The National: four wins, six seconds and one third.

In the National, run at Sutton Coldfield in March 1890, an exceptionally keen race was witnessed. Only three points eventually separated the first three teams with Salford on 93 points, Worcester on 95 and Birchfield on 96. The team that day was J.C. Cope 7; G.F. Boland 10; Arthur Mabbett 11; Tom Thornton 18; G.J. Hilton 19 and J. Plant 31.

In the 1891 Midlands held at Redditch in mid-February 1891, the club achieved its finest performance in this race. They won with the record low score of 26 points as follows: Charles Davies 1; Tom Birch 2; Arthur Mabbett 3; Arthur Meachams 5; Tom Thornton 7 and M. Eaton 8.

A fine win was scored in the 1891 National at Liverpool, by scoring 77 points to win by 11 points from Finchley Harriers. The scores registered were for Tom Birch 6; Charles Davies 8; Arthur Mabbett 9; M. Eaton 13; Arthur Meachams 16 and Tom Thornton 18.

The 1891 to 1892 season saw the introduction by the Midlands Cross Country Association of the Novice Championship. Although many competitors would be recognised by the current term of 'juniors', the entrance criterion was based on lack of experience rather than age. This race was won by Derby St John's with B. Ravenscroft of Small Heath Harriers as the individual victor.

In the 1892 Midlands at Northampton yet another fine win was recorded with the low score of 27 points as follows: Tom Birch 2; Charles Pierce 3: W.H. Smith 4: Charles Davies 5; Arthur Mabbett 6 and G.J. Hilton 7 to beat Godiva Harriers who finished on 78 points but had the first man home in Billy Dunkley. The wonderful packing of the whole team was a remarkable feature: ten men finished in the first seventeen home.

The 1892 National at Ockham saw a stern struggle end in a dead heat between Birchfield Harriers and Essex Beagles. Each team scored 74 points. The scoring sextet were: Tom Birch 5; W.H. Smith 8; Charles Davies 13; M. Eaton 15; Arthur Mabbett 16 and Arthur Meachams 17. In the run-off Essex Beagles were beaten 35 points to 43.

The individual highlight of the season was the victory for W.H. Smith in the AAA Two-mile Steeplechase Championship. A matter of continuity as well as celebration for the club!

No Midlands race was held in 1893 but in the National there was a reversal of fortune. Essex Beagles took revenge for the dead heat and subsequent defeat in the run-off in 1892 defeating Birchfield by 55 points to 91.

On the individual front there was another AAA Championship win for a club member. On this occasion the four-mile title going to Charles Pierce.

Again no Midlands competition was staged in 1894 but the National was run in Blackpool. Salford Harriers were emerging as a potent force in the sport and won team and individual honours with a score of 60 points with 71 points for Birchfield in second place.

For a third year running there was to be no Midlands in 1895 but the National at Wembley produced another keen struggle: Birchfield on 108, Essex Beagles on 123 and Salford on 134 being the scores of the top three teams. The club's scoring six were: Charles Davies 3; Billy Dunkley 7; Arthur Meachams 11; Tom Birch 17; M. Eaton 31 and G.J. Hilton 39.

The Midlands Championship was revived at Worcester in February 1896. The team produced a powerful performance, winning with 38 points from the host club on 67 points. The team was Billy Dunkley 3; Charles Davies 4; Arthur Meachams 5; P. Bourne 7; Charles Pierce 9 and A. Twigger 10. In the 1896 National held at Minworth, Salford again came out on top. This time by five points, 121 to 116.

By the time the summer unfolded a new influence on the sport had been introduced several thousand miles away in Greece, but there was even a Midlands background for that first Olympiad!

Seven: Ideal Olympian

If an Olympic city were chosen for proximity to the roots of the modern Games – then Birmingham would have as strong a case as Paris. Baron Pierre de Coubertin, a Frenchman, is credited with establishing the modern Olympics, but it was England that revived the ancient Greek initiative and it was in the Midlands where de Coubertin was introduced to it.

As early as 1612, Robert Dover established an English version known as 'The Olympicks' at Chipping Camden, Gloucestershire, which involved running, jumping, throwing the hammer and pitching the bar. The event continued until 1852, when it was banned by the local authority 'due to rowdiness and dangerous activities'. In 1980 'The Olympicks' were revived by local residents and are celebrated in June each year.

However, even more significant in the revival of the Olympic Games was the annual festival at Much Wenlock, Shropshire, started in 1850 by Dr William Penny Brookes. The list of events is little different from today's sports. The original objective of the Olympian Class was to promote the moral, physical and intellectual improvement of the town and neighbourhood of Wenlock. In 1860 the class separated from the reading society and was called the Wenlock Olympian Society.

Meanwhile, de Coubertin visited England several times to see how sport was developing in public schools. He found inspiration in Thomas Hughes' book *Tom Brown's Schooldays* with its depiction of education and sport. In 1886 he travelled to Rugby, the school where Hughes' novel had been set. He began to strongly embrace the belief that athletics builds character. A rower, fencer and boxer himself, he devoted his time to the study of physical education. He believed that if France were to adopt the British sporting culture, it would regain international status following its demise in the Franco-Prussian war of 1870 to 1871. In 1889 he organised the Congress of Physical Education in Paris and in the next year he made his visit to Much Wenlock to meet Brooke and observe the Olympian Society.

As a logical extension to his annual games, Brooke had formed the Shropshire Olympian Association in 1861, which led to the founding of the national Olympian Association in 1865. Brookes' aim was to create an international Olympics, primarily to promote physical education in participating countries. He did not achieve that goal but was very helpful to de Coubertin over dinner in the Gaskell Arms as they shared their mutual interest in physical education and his dream of an international Olympics.

The *Wellington Journal* of Saturday 25 October 1890 noted: 'A special or autumn festival in connection with Wenlock Olympian Society was held on Wednesday, under the presidency of Mr R.B. Benson of Lutwyche Hall. The object of the festival was chiefly to enlighten Baron Pierre de Coubertin, a French gentleman, who desires to introduce athletics more largely among his own countrymen, upon the methods adopted for the training of athletes in England. Dr Brookes, who is an untiring advocate of physical education among the young, was on this occasion largely instrumental in bringing about this meeting.'

The idea of reviving the Olympics as a true international festival grew out of that meeting. Pierre de Coubertin began proclaiming the idea in 1892, but attracted little notice. Despite repeated rebuffs at home and abroad, he persisted. On 23 June 1894 he presided over a meeting of seventy-nine delegates representing twelve countries. They unanimously voted for the restoration of the ancient Olympic Games. At first, de Coubertin gave credit to Brookes, saying 'If the Olympic Games, which modern Greece had not been able to revive, still survive today, it is not to a Greek that we are indebted, but rather to Dr W.P. Brookes.'

However, by the time the Games had been organised as an international event and Brookes had passed away, de Coubertin was taking the credit for himself. As *The Times* noted: 'If rip-offs had been in the Olympics, this one would have carried off the gold.' It has been noted that even the opening and closing ceremonies followed the Wenlock model.

The Games of the first Olympiad of the modern cycle were held under the royal patronage of the King of Greece in 1896 in a new marble stadium constructed in Athens for the purpose. Very grand, but back home in England the Birchfield Harriers had more mundane, but no less challenging, tasks in hand.

Eight: Paper Chase

In the 1897 Midlands at Northampton, the team continued its winning sequence. It is interesting to note that the club won this Championship every year it was held from 1891 to 1909. On this occasion they beat Northampton 51 points to 85 with the following team: Arthur Meachams 2; T.C. Gulliver 3; Charles Davies 9; P. Bourne 10; A. Twigger 13 and G.J. Hilton 14.

At Trafford Park, Manchester, the National produced an exceptionally close race. Only seven points divided the first four teams. Salford Harriers and Manchester Harriers experienced a dead-heat with 102 points, Warrington AC was third with 103 points, and Birchfield was fourth on 109 points.

The performance of the club's team in the 1898 Novice at Leicester was the best so far. They were placed second with 106 points to Worcester who scored 72 points. The scorers were: N.R. Day 3; A. Halfacre 14; W. Bridgeman 16; P. Shaw 18; C.A.L Burkitt 19 and T. Woolrich 36.

In the 1898 Midlands at Kettering, the team scored 50 points to win from Worcester on 78 points. The individual positions were: Arthur Meachams 3; Charles Pierce 5; N.R. Day 8; C.A.L Burkitt 9; T.C. Gulliver 12 and Charles Davies 13. The 1898 National at Northampton was won by Salford Harriers on 83 points with Birchfield fourth on 133 points.

The club secured its first victory in the Novice at Shrewsbury in February 1899 and this was a double triumph. First man home was T. Frost with the team gaining victory with 72 points to Northampton's second with 90 points. The scoring team was: T. Frost 1; C. Winterbourne 6; C. Powis 9; P. Randles 11; R. Powis 21 and T. Woolrich 24.

The 1899 Senior was held at Smethwick Cricket Ground, and in this race the Stags established a record score of 23 points to win by seventy points from Small Heath. The historic performers were: Arthur Meachams 1; W.E. Stokes 2; W.H. Tolley 3; C. Winterbourne 4; P. Randle 6 and J.N. Tolley 7.

In the 1899 National at Wembley, the team secured third place behind Haddington Harriers on 124 points and the winners Highgate Harriers on 92 points. Birchfield Harriers had a tally of 138 points. In the AAA Championships a club tradition was revived when W.E. Stokes won the two-mile steeplechase.

The 1900 Novice Championship, held at Worcester, resulted in Small Heath Harriers scoring individual and team victories. Birchfield were second with 113 points to Small Heath's 57 points.

The tide turned at the Midlands held at Halesowen in February 1900, in conjunction with a Birmingham League football match featuring Halesowen versus Wolverhampton Wanderers. The club reversed the Novice placing with Small Heath Harriers. Birchfield won with 41 points to 73 points as follows: W.E. Stokes 2; P. Randle 5; Arthur Meachams 7; B. Round 8; T. Frost 9 and C. Winterbourne 10.

In the National at Rotherham, Finchley Harriers defeated the club team by 72 points to 92. At the end of the season a team consisting of W.E. Stokes; P. Randle; W.H. Tolley and J. Tolley won the Pennefather Plate. This trophy became a permanent one for a schoolboys' team race competed for at the West Midlands Inter-District Championship and won on the basis of maximum aggregate points by any schoolboy team. It should be noted that a similar plate was donated later for schoolgirls to win.

At the 1901 Junior, held at Dunstall Park, Wolverhampton saw an individual victory for E. Bricknall, then competing as a Birchfielder. The team, however, were well beaten finishing sixth.

In the Senior Championship, also held at Dunstall Park, the team, with six men in the first ten, won with a score of 36 points to Edgbaston Harriers with 93 points. Billy Day of Derby won the individual title and he was to subsequently join Birchfield within a few years and serve them with distinction. The scorers that day were: C. Burkitt 2; W.H. Tolley 3; Arthur Meachams 5; B. Round 7; J. Thomas 9 and J.H. Tolley 10. The 1901 National at Oadby saw a close team contest: Birchfield finished fourth on 161 points with Essex Beagles in first place on 100 points.

No clear records exist for the 1902 Novice, except that the winners are known to be Leicester on 120 points with Birchfield fourth on 188 points.

In the 1902 Midlands at Derby, the club again won. The score was 53 points being made up as follows: W.E. Stokes 5; G. Scragg 7; Paul Randles 8; Arthur Meachams 9; J. Thomas 11; B. Round 13. Billy Day was again the individual winner.

The 1902 National at Lingfield witnessed a team victory for Highgate Harriers on 110 points with Birchfield fourth on 203 points.

As an end of season fixture a special three-mile match took place in September. This was W.W. Alexander and Sons against Alfred Smith and Sons, four to run in a team and three scores to count. This contest resulted in a victory for the Smith family.

With the growth of the club, and at the request of the members, branches of Birchfield Harriers were formed that season. These were based at Selly Oak and Tipton.

In the 1903 Novice Championship at Wolverhampton, Birchfield managed to enter two teams with one finishing first and the other finishing last! The winning runners on 63 points were: T. Lewis 3; William Hickman 4; W.H. Wride 11; Edwin Guest 12; Denis Lyons 16 and F.J. Reay 17.

The 1903 Senior at Oadby was won with a score of 35 points. Small Heath were second on 86 points. The club team and positions were: Paul Randles 2; James Thomas 3; Billy Day 4; William Hickman 8; T. Lewis 9 and W.E. Stokes 10.

The 1903 National at Haydock Park saw the club achieve winning honours for the first time since 1895. This was the longest period that had elapsed without the Birchfield Harriers finishing first in this race. However, they had finished second twice, third once and fourth on four occasions. The team scored 93 points to win with James Thomas 9; Paul Randles 10; T. Lewis 13; William Hickman 16; W.E. Stokes 22 and F.J. Reay 23. Salford were second with 124 points.

The season also saw individual recognition and achievement for club members. James Thomas and Paul Randles were selected for international honours and Billy Day won the Midland Counties AAA Ten-mile Championship. T. Lewis and William Hickman accomplished a record by winning Novice, Senior and National gold medals all in the same season.

Arthur Meachams maintained this high standard in the following season. He won the 1904 Midlands for the second time, at Walsall. This anchored a team victory with their finish of 39 points as follows: Arthur Meachams 1; William Hickman 3; Billy Day 4; C. Scragg 7; James Thomas 11 and S.T. Smith 13.

In the 1904 National at Wolverhampton the club finished second on 97 points to Highgate Harriers on 57 points. Recognition for club athletes continued with the selection of Arthur Meachams, Billy Day and William Hickman for the International Cross Country Championship.

In the Midland Counties AAA Championships there was a collection of individual titles: S.H. Thompson (100 yards); J.W. Morton (220 yards); J.W. Horne (440 yards); J.E. Schofield (880 yards); A. Russell in the steeplechase and mile; and Billy Day in the ten miles.

There was also club expansion off the track with additional branches being formed at Erdington, Handsworth and Worcester.

The 1905 Midlands at Cheltenham was won with 57 points, Newport Harriers being second. The team was: Billy Day 3; J. Taylor 5; T. Frost 8; James Thomas 10; T. Wall 14 and Arthur Meachams 17. The National at Lingfield in March saw the club representatives finish third with 146 points.

At the 1905 Midland Counties AAA Championships, the 100 yards and 220 yards were won by S.H. Thompson, and H. Crowther was victorious in the 440 yards; J.E. Schofield continued his success in the 880 yards, Freddie Hulford was first home in both the one and four-mile races, and F.C. Price won the high jump. S.H. Thompson is also noteworthy for defeating the world class American runner A.H. Duffey in the 100 yards scratch race before winning the MCAAA 220 yards Championship on the same day. International selection was achieved by Billy Day and Freddie Hulford.

In October 1905, Birchfield sent a team to compete in the twenty-mile road race in Paris for the Dubonnet Trophy, which was won. George Wigginton 2; Freddie Hulford 3; Billy Day 8 and J. Taylor 9 were those who scored as the counting team.

The 1906 Junior at Walsall gave the club their third team win and the third individual win. On this occasion Adam Underwood was first home and the team was Adam Underwood 1; T. Coley 3; J. Kinder 16; A. Pallett 17; M. Montgomery 19 and Edwin Guest 26 scoring 82 points to win from Derby AC who scored 105 points.

The 1906 Senior at Coventry was won with a score of 77 points to Derby second with 134 points. The places were: T. Coley 3; George Wiggington 11; James Taylor 12; A.F. Lewis 16; A. Alabaster 17 and Billy Day 18.

In the National at Haydock Park the team finished fourth with 151 points to the winners, Sutton Harriers, on 120 points.

Individual achievement was also enjoyed by Billy Day who gained international selection and Freddie Hulford who was AAA Championship winner in the four miles.

Freddie was born on 6 February 1883. He started his athletics career in 1903 with Herne Hill Harriers and found himself against the legendary Alfred Shrub, but won three consecutive one-mile MCAAA Championships. By 1905 he had joined Birchfield Harriers and ran for them in the Dubonnet Trophy and led them home in 2.4 hours. In 1907 he joined Surrey AC and later represented Great Britain in the 1912 Olympics in Stockholm at the 800m and 1,500m. After the First World War he began a second life in athletics as a starter, eventually becoming Chief Starter at the 1948 London Olympics. He kept up an active association with Birchfield Harriers and attended the annual awards dinner well past his ninetieth birthday – being revered by all Birchfielders who came to know him in that long period.

Back at the 1907 Midlands, staged in Northampton, Birchfield were showing Derby the way home, the team scoring 63 points to Derby's 117 with Billy Day 5; A. Arlablaster 16; A.F. Lewis 11; George Wiggington 12; James Taylor 13 and W.E. Stokes 15.

In the 1907 National at Colwall another convincing victory was recorded. Birchfield were first with 86 points and Highgate Harriers second with 128 points. The team to score was: Adam Underwood 3; Billy Day 9; Edward Green 15; A.F. Lewis 18; James Taylor 19 and W.B. Law 22.

Adam Underwood and Billy Day gained international selection, the former winning the international race to become the first club member to win such an individual honour. There was success too for Underwood in the AAA Championship ten-mile event.

At the MCAAA the significant name of Arthur Robertson is recorded as victor in both the four and ten-mile races; Harry Crowther won the 440 yards; Denis Lyons the 880 yards; and E.J. Negus the mile walk.

On Christmas Day 1907 an attempt was made to revive the concept of 'Christmastide Sports' by holding, at Aston, three handicaps for the 100 yards, 880 yards and three miles.

The 1908 Midlands at Derby was won. The score was 63 points to Small Heath Harriers' second with 116 points. The team was: Ernie Massey 2; Denis Lyons 5; Billy Day 9; A.F. Lewis 12; W.E. Stokes 17 and E. Waldron 18.

The 1908 National at Newbury saw Arthur Robertson first man home, being the second club member to achieve such a performance. The team, however, were narrowly beaten by Hallamshire Harriers who scored 146 points to win. Birchfield were second with 158 points.

Arthur Robertson and W.H. Day gained international selection, with the former winning the international outright to become the second club member of such distinction. He also won the MCAAA Championship in the four-mile event.

1908 was Olympic year with the event being organised in London. Arthur was about to gain a first in the history of Birchfield Harriers!

Nine: Torchbearer

Arthur Robertson was born in Sheffield in 1879. He attended King's School in Peterborough. His first recorded athletic achievement was winning the school's mile in 1894. In his teens he was attracted to cycle racing and competed with moderate success. He was twenty-five when he began to compete seriously in athletic events. In the summers of 1905 and 1906 he toured the sports meetings of the Midlands, running in handicap races from the sprints to the mile. In fifty-seven races he took thirty-two prizes.

Robertson joined Birchfield at the end of the 1906 season and took to cross-country running. He was with the club only three years but in that time enjoyed considerable success. In 1908 he was in particularly good form. He won both the National at Newbury and the International in Paris as the England team packed six into the first seven places. He was the first of three Birchfield Harriers to win these two major races in one season. Above all he became the club's first Olympian and Olympic gold medallist. He gained that distinction as a member of the British team at the London Olympics which won the three-mile race, plus Arthur took an individual silver medal in the steeplechase.

An insight into Robertson's character can be gleaned from a comment on his National victory by the magazine *Sport and Play*: 'A stampede of people from the stands to the rails gave warning of the leader's approach. It was seen that Robertson was out with a commanding lead, and we all knew his speed would get him home winner of the National Championship. Undistressed he came home, with hands down – no side, no gallery – a modest champion of the first order. Proud of his win, proud of his club.'

To the profound disappointment of his fellow Birchfielders, A.J. Robertson announced his retirement from athletics at the end of the 1909 season, this, after finishing second in the National and helping the club to win the team event for the tenth time. At the age of thirty he returned to cycle racing.

What of the development of the Olympic movement up to and including Arthur's triumph? At Athens in 1896, James Connolly of Boston, USA became the first modern Olympic Champion in the hop, step and

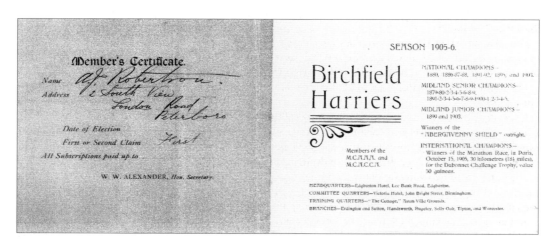

Arthur Robertson's membership card.

jump. His teammates Thomas Burke, Ellery Clark and Robert Garnett scored two victories each, as did Edwin Flack of Australia. Fittingly, a Greek, Spyros Louis won the marathon race.

The Paris Games of 1900 were held in conjunction with the Paris Exhibition, the second Olympiad proving another triumph for the United States. Roy Ewry began his outstanding Olympic career with three wins in the standing jumps and Alvin Kraendein earned four gold medals, which helped the United States to enjoy a haul of seventeen gold medals in all track and field events. A.E. Tyson, C. Bennett and J. Rimmer were successful for Great Britain.

The St Louis Games of 1904 were almost a domestic affair. There were few entries from other countries and only one non-American gold medallist, Etienne Desmarteu of Canada. Ewry again was a triple winner as were Archie Hahn, James Lightbody and Harry Hillman.

The London Games of 1908, in which Arthur Robertson competed so well, were the last to be monopolised by the USA and the British Empire. They shared twenty-two of the twenty-six track and field medals. Ewry completed his career with a double victory, which brought his gold-medal tally to eight. Mel Sheppard and Martin Sheridan of the United States were double winners as were George Larner of Britain and Erik Hemming of Sweden, who became the first Scandinavian to win at this level.

Back in Birmingham the club had a new incentive to continue their groundwork and build on the impact Robertson had made locally.

Ten: Second Wind

In the 1909 Novice at Coventry, the Birchfield youngsters finished fourth with 165 points. Small Heath took the laurels with 102 points.

The 1909 Midlands Championship at Uttoxeter was again won with a score of 63 points. Small Heath Harriers were second with 94 points. Featuring were: Ernie Massey 6; Edwin Guest 8; Billy Day 9; H. Birch 11; A. Ashby 13 and E. Waldron 16.

The National at Haydock Park was won with a score of 61 points. Hallamshire Harriers were second with 113 points. The Birchfield team was Arthur Robertson 2; Edward Green 4; Ernie Massey 5; Vic Loney 7; Billy Day 16 and Arthur Pallett 27.

That season Edward Green and Vic Loney gained selection for England, as did Ernie Massey who had previously represented Wales! As reported, Arthur Robertson enjoyed a popular 'swansong' winning the MCAAA Championship over ten miles.

In the 1910 Novice Championship at Burton, Sparkhill Harriers won with 96 points whilst Birchfield were third with 136 points.

The 1910 Midlands Championship at Coventry was noteworthy for the fact that the team was beaten for the first time since 1891. It was a very close race, as the result indicates. First were Derby AC on 82 points, second were Birchfield on 86 points and third were Thrapston AC collecting 90 points.

The National at Derby was won by Hallamshire Harriers with 83 points. Birchfield scored 135 points to finish third.

It was during the track season of 1910 that the split occurred between the AAA and the National Cyclists Union, and club members remained loyal to the AAA. The MCAAA included cycle championships in their programme and Birchfield members won several of these races. In those MCAAA Championships there were victories for C.E. Ray in the 220 and 440 yards, R.H. Golling (100 yards), T. Mason (880 yards) and S. Walker in the mile. In the two-wheel events E.W. Stanford won the 25-mile cycle championship and F. Greenway the five-mile cycle championship. The success of cycling members in the championships reminds us that in the club's early days the cycle section was a strong feature of Birchfield life.

At the annual meeting in October 1910 it was announced that the Tipton branch of the club had decided to form themselves into a separate club. The Tipton Harriers went on to develop a national reputation – particularly in cross-country racing – with first-class facilities today.

Frank Wright (front left) and Fred Hughes (front right).

Early in February 1911 a club team met the Metropolitan Club of France in Paris and won. Edward Green 2; George Wiggington 3; Ralph Stanton 4; S.L. Holmes 6; H. Birch 7 and A.F. Lewis 9 scoring 31 points to 47 by the French club.

In the 1911 Midlands at Thrapston the club team dead-heated with Thrapston AC for second place with 108 points. The winners were North Staffs Harriers on 41 points.

The National at Taplow was won by Hallamshire Harriers with a score of 54 points. Birchfield were sixth on 282 points.

The split with the NCU had continued throughout this season and as a result of this the MCAAA, for the first time, held a Championship Athletic and Cycle meeting at Villa Park over two days in June. In those MCAAA Championships there was a win for P.T. Bruhl in the 120-yard hurdles. In the cycling, E.W. Stanford was victorious in the quarter and mile events with B.L. Bird first in the ten-mile race and J. Newton enjoying success over five miles.

At the 1911 AGM, the training staff was doubled in one stroke when Frank Wright was appointed to join Fred Hughes. This represented a sign of the club's continuing ambitions.

In the 1912 Novice Championship at Derby, Thapston AC won with 97 points. Birchfield were third on 168 points.

The team for the National at Colwall also finished third with 119 points to Thrapston's winning score of 70 points.

The National at Haydock saw the team uncharacteristically well down the field, finishing eighth with 265 points.

However, there were several other interesting developments by that time. During the winter season indoor sports meetings were arranged on skating rinks at Lozells and Sparkbrook, with outstanding performances from Jimmy Murphy and Arthur Pallet, whilst the split between the AAA and the NCU had also been patched up.

In the MCAAA Championships C.E. Ray won the 220 yards and F.J. Bridge was the winner of the mile.

In Olympic year the club was honoured with the news that Frank Wright would travel to Stockholm as the trainer for the Great Britain team.

The Games are noted for the fact that originally the name of the greatest athlete in the fifth Olympiad appeared in no record books. He was Jim Thorpe, an American Indian, who won the pentathlon and decathlon, but was later disqualified for professionalism, having previously played baseball. In 1973

– twenty years after his death – the American Athletics Union restored his amateur status. This led to the IOC quashing the decision taken in 1912. He was declared 1912 Olympic Champion in both multi-events and the records amended. Even without Thorpe's victories the US was still dominant. Finland earned its first gold medals, six all told, with three of those going to Hannes Kolehmainen in the distance races.

Back home, Frank Wright was to help oversee a remarkable resurgence in Birchfield fortunes. Early 1913 witnessed the Novice, Midlands and National Championships all being won for the second time in the club's history. The Novice at Stoke was won outright by Ralph Stanton. The team won with the low score of 39 points as follows: Ralph Stanton 1; F.J. Bridge 5; S.L. Holmes 6; E. Skett 7; J.A. Fernyhough 9 and T.L. Lee 11. The Midlands at Derby was won with a score of 57 points by: S.L. Holmes 4; F.J. Bridge 6; H. Trevitt 8; Arthur Pallett 9; E. Skett 11 and T.L. Lee 19. The National at Wolverhampton provided a close race. Birchfield won by six points from Warrington AC, 120 to 126. The team was: S.L. Holmes 13; Ralph Stanton 16; E. Skett 20; S.C. Greenway 21; T.L. Lee 24 and F. Bridge 26.

During this season S.L. Holmes, E. Skett, T.L. Lee and F. Bridge gained their Novice, Midlands and National medals. In the MCAAA Championships there were titles for Ralph Stanton (mile), T. Evans (two miles walk) and J. Williamson (pole vault).

The outstanding feature of the track season was the performance of the former AAA four-mile champion Freddie Hulford. His successes at all distances from sprint up to 880 yards, in both scratch and handicap events, was noteworthy for an athlete who was originally a distance runner.

In the 1914 Midlands at Thrapston, the club were third with 110 points.

At the National at Chesham, the club team finished second with a score of 144 points to Surrey AC's 116 points.

The MCAAA Championships witnessed a double triumph for Arthur Pallett in the one-mile and four-mile races. That season Ralph Stanton also received international selection. However, minds were increasingly occupied as the year progressed on other forms of international events leading to the outbreak of the Firsrt World War.

From 1914 to 1918 all official competitions were abandoned. However, it is recorded that the interests of the sport locally were maintained by the club's President Alderman T.H. Cartwright, Vice-President H.A. Butler, Club Secretary W.W. Alexander and A.E. Machin of the MCAAA. They worked to promote sports meetings in various districts.

The club's minutes record one effort in 1914 when £132 was handed over to the Mayor of Sutton Coldfield's charity.

League cross-country races were held throughout the period of conflict and were reported to be a success both socially and athletically.

The team gained an outstanding victory in the Prince of Wales Handicap at Stamford Bridge, Chelsea, having three of the first runners home.

The cycling section also enjoyed a significant achievement. C.C. Berger rode from Leeds to London in record time. This was accomplished in 11 hours 36 minutes, beating the record for a single rider of 12 hours 49 minutes.

So, spirits remained high and the amateur flag kept flying as a new dawn approached.

Eleven: Hurdles to Clear

The 1918 to 1919 season saw the end of the First World War and the return of many members from the Army. The Championships of the Midland Cross Country Association were not revived until 1919, but Birchfield promoted jointly with the Austin Motor Company's Athletic Club, the 'Home Teams' and the Works Cross Country Championship. Great interest was taken in these contests, which were the forerunners of the Inter-Theatre of War Race at Windsor. Club members J.H. Massey, Joe Blewitt, Wal Monk, W. Gardside, A. Slim, J. Etchells and Vic Loney were included in the race. The cup was presented by King George V.

The MCAAA Championship winners were J. Quinn for the mile, Joe Blewitt for the four-mile race, Wal Monk over ten miles, Sergeant Major J. Miller over the high jump, and in the relay: F. Field, H.W. Wade, T.R. Webb and P. Saunders.

J.H. Massey won the mile in the Northern AAA Championship whilst Joe Blewitt was the AAA Championship winner in the ten miles. This latter athlete was to prove, in time, to be one of the most meritorious in club history.

C.E. or 'Joe' Blewitt was born at Upton-on-Severn in 1895. On leaving school he joined the Great Western Railway and his work took him to South Wales. There he began to take part in athletics and competed as a sprinter, but there is no record of the standard that he attained. It was during service in the Army in the First World War that he started to run distances and his achievements are recorded. In 1917 he won the Northern Command one-mile championship and in 1918 became the British Army champion at this distance. In 1919, his final year in khaki and his first year with Birchfield, he was Inter-Services Champion at the mile in 4 minutes 24 seconds and, more significantly, won the AAA ten-mile championship in 53:45. He went on to represent Great Britain at the 1920 and 1928 Olympics and would have made the 1924 Games but was forced to withdraw with injury at the last moment.

As to his performances on track, he won four AAA and nine MCAAA championships, which alone would have given him an eminent place in the club's history. However, his cross-country running was even more worthy of acclaim. In nine seasons, 1920–28, the club won the National eight times and finished second once. Blewitt was a scorer in every race, taking a record number of eight gold medals and one silver medal. He was the individual winner in 1923, finished second in 1921, and was placed in the first ten on seven occasions. In the international races he represented England five times, winning the race in 1923 and finishing fourth and fifth on other occasions.

At the end of 1928 Joe Blewitt retired from competition at the age of thirty-three. His decision took many people by surprise for he was still a capable performer. That season he had finished fifth in the National and led the club to victory in the London to Brighton.

Joe was referred to in club circles as 'A Champion of Champions' – so a Birmingham and Midland Sportsman Committee was formed and organised a testimonial on his retirement. This enabled Joe to take charge of the Saddlers Arms, eventually adjacent to the Alexander Stadium.

There was sad news early in February 1920. Fred Hughes, the club trainer for many years, passed away. He was a popular figure at events and a starter of distinction.

The Novice at Derby saw an absolute record established for this race. The club brought home five men in the first six to finish, and six in the first twelve, to win with the record score of 29 points with Tipton second on 125 points. The members to score were: Walter Freeman 1; Wal Monk 2; C.T. Clibbon 3; J. Quinn 5; Joe Blewitt 6 and J.H. Massey 12.

The Midlands at Longbridge witnessed a fierce contest between Joe Blewitt and Walter Freeman for individual honours. It was only in the last half-mile that Freeman fell back to finish sixth after a great effort to shake off Blewitt. The club team won with 42 points. North Staffs were second with 120 points. The scorers for the club were: Joe Blewitt 1; J. Quinn 3; Walter Freeman 6; A.H. Rodway 9; J. Gwillam 11 and T. Hardwick 12. The last two were juniors who competed at Derby without success, but in the Senior gained a place in the scoring six.

The National was held in Windsor Great Park and the club were particularly proud to have won on this occasion as the medals were presented to the club athletes by the King. The race itself was remarkable as it was won by Jacques Guillemot of CASG, Paris. This was the first time that a foreign national had been allowed to compete in the National. C.T. Clibbon of Birchfield was second – but this meant scoring number one for team honours. The scorers were: C.T. Clibbon 1; Joe Blewitt 3; Walter Freeman 4; A.H. Rodway 9; Wal Monk 17 and J.H. Massey 20. This totalled 54 to Surrey AC's 60 points.

The club's performance of three in the first four was outstanding. By special permission of the National Cross Country Union, the club presented to the scoring six in the National Championships the Association's gold medals in addition to the medals presented by King George V.

C.T. Clibbon, Joe Blewitt and Walter Freeman gained international selection and the latter two had also both gained Novice, Midlands and National medals in one season. This had only been previously accomplished twice, in 1903 by W.E. Hickman and T.A. Lewis and then in 1913 by E. Skett, T.L. Lee, F. Bridge and S.L. Holmes.

In the MCAAA Championships the roll of honour included: Joe Blewitt in the half mile; Jack Quinn for the mile; Wal Monk over three miles; Joe Blewitt again in the ten-mile event; T. Welch in the high jump and F.H. Roden putting the shot. At AAA Championship level Joe Blewitt won the four-mile and C.T. Clibbon the ten-mile events.

Chosen for the Olympic Games in Antwerp were: C.T. Clibbon, Joe Blewitt, Wal Monk and Walter Freeman. After an eight-year hiatus, the Olympics resumed in war-torn Belgium with the largest programme to date. These Games saw the debut of Finland's Paavo Nurmi, who was destined to be second only to Ewry in Olympic track and field victories. Nurmi won the 10,000m and cross-country races, Kolehmainen took the marathon, and five other Finnish victories in field events enabled the small Nordic nation to tie with the USA in track and field scoring. The nations had nine gold medals apiece. Twin triumphs were scored by A.G. Hill of Great Britain in the middle distances and Ugo Frigerio of Italy in the walks.

Walter Freeman had emerged through the ranks of British athletics but finished well down the field in the cross-country. However, this was only the start of an enjoyable stretch as an athlete as he settled back into the domestic racing scene.

Walter had joined the club in 1919, the same year as Joe Blewitt. Together they formed the spearhead of the cross-country team in the early '20s. Born at Astwood Bank, Worcestershire, in September 1893, he joined the Territorial Army in 1912 and the Royal Worcestershire Regiment at the outbreak of the First World War. Posted to France he spent most of the war there. The regiment alternated a week at the front with a week at rest camp, but Walter did not rest. He ran, and outstripped the opposition in any races organised. On demobilisation he returned home and decided to try his hand at cross-country racing. There can be few cases of such a rapid rise to the top. Within three seasons he was international champion – and Birchfield almost missed him. Walter began training with Sparkhill and only the jealousy of that club's top runner at seeing a novice likely to displace him encouraged him to offer his services to the Birchfield club.

The first full season of cross-country championships after the war was 1920. Walter won the Midlands Junior, was sixth in the Midlands and fourth in the National. On the strength of that came Olympic selection.

1921 was an outstanding year for Walter. He was fourth in the Midlands, and won the National and then the International at Newport, Monmouthshire. In subsequent years he was not able to recapture that golden form but remained a leading cross-country runner. He was victorious in the Midlands in the next two years and finished fourth and fifth in the National. Described as a short man with a nimble stride, Walter seems to have been ideally suited to the rigours of English cross-country courses of those days, which included many ploughed fields! His strategy was to get out in front quickly and do his best to stay there. (Walter died in October 1987, aged ninety-four. At that time he had been the club's oldest living international.)

Birchfield's
internationals, 1922.

The chief item of interest at the Annual Meeting, on 14 October 1920, was the presentation to Ralph Stanton of his 1914 International bronze plaque, which had only just been received from the National Cross Country Union!

On 16 October 1920 the club promoted the first 'Bishop of Birmingham Walk'. This was at the express wish of the Lord Bishop, Dr Russell Wakefield, who donated a cup. It started from and finished at the Cape Hill Grounds. While the walkers were away the club ran off a series of members' races. The promotion of this race was subsequently handed over to the Birmingham Walkers' Club.

An inter-club race with Cambridge University was held in November. Despite the outstanding running of Walter Freeman and J. Massey, who finished first and second, the team was soundly beaten. Sadly, Massey was seriously injured in an accident soon after and never competed again.

The Novice this season was held at Handsworth. Although the team did not score, they had the second and third runners home in E.J. Mills and R. Lowe.

In the 1921 Novice held at Wolverhampton, with a young team, the club finished fourth in a large field with a total of 188 points. In the Midlands at Derby the team scored 50 points to beat North Staffs on 89 points. Running were: Walter Freeman 4; Joe Blewitt 5; A.H. Rodway 7; Ralph Stanton 8; C.T. Clibbon 11 and H. Trevitt 15. The National at Doncaster provided the club with a brilliant double. Walter Freeman was the first man home and the team scored 48 points to easily beat Warrington AC, who scored 161 points for second position. The club positions were: Walter Freeman 1; Joe Blewitt 2; Ralph Stanton 6; C.T. Clibbon 7; Wal Monk 15 and A.H. Rodway 17. The performance of scoring 48 points had only been beaten twice since 1887, when the club scored 37 points, and in 1905 when Highgate Harriers scored 47 points.

Another notable success by the club team was a three-mile team match against The Rest of England at the London Athletics Club Sports.

Walter Freeman and Joe Blewitt were selected for the International in Wales. Walter Freeman became the third club member to win the individual honours. Joe Blewitt also counted for England's winning six.

In the MCAAA Championships there were titles as follows: C.T. Clibbon in the ten miles, F.G Wards in the four miles, Wal Monk in the mile and Pat Saunders in the half mile.

Wal Monk was the AAA champion in the four miles and second to Joe Blewitt in the England versus France 10,000 metres.

At the Annual General Meeting the balance sheet showed the strength of the club's financial position. It was during this season that the issue of providing the club with a permanent home and sports ground was first discussed.

In the Novice race, Frank Quinn, C.E. Holmes, A.T. Wall, R. Downes, E.A. Jones and A. Robinson did the best performance so far in this event. They finished third to Tipton Harriers, who won for the second year in succession.

In the 1922 Novice at Oadby the club team beat Newport Harriers by 77 points to 87 points. Scoring were: F.G. Ward 5; Jack Beman 8; E.J. Mills 11; H.J. Mealyer 12; J. Byrne 20 and L. Lawley 21.

The Midlands at Stoke provided Walter Freeman with his first win in the race and the team with an easy win. They scored 43 points with six men in the first twelve as follows: Walter Freeman 1; Jack Beman 5; E.J. Mills 7; H.J. Mealyer 8; Joe Blewitt 10 and F.G. Ward 12.

The National at Hereford saw Jacques Guillemot, who won in 1920, again successful. The team put up a very fine performance by placing six men home in the first twelve and actually finishing the scoring six before any other team had two men home. By scoring 41 points to win, the team recorded a score that had only been beaten five times in the whole series of Nationals since 1877. The scoring six were: Joe Blewitt 3; Walter Freeman 4; F.G. Ward 6; Jack Beman 7; E.J. Mills 10 and Ralph Stanton 11.

A feature of this season's cross country championships was the gaining of Novice, Midlands and National medals in one season by F.G. Ward, Jack Beman and E.J. Mills. This was a feat only previously accomplished by members in 1903, 1913 and 1920.

On 19 March 1922 a Birchfield team met several French clubs in competition in Paris. Another competitive result was achieved with Walter Freeman 3; F.G. Ward 4; Joe Blewitt 6; Jack Beman 7; G. Perry 15 and Ralph Stanton 17 scoring 53 points against the winning score by the Athletique des Sports Generaux of 45 points.

MCAAA Championship winners were: F.G. Ward in the ten miles and steeplechase; C. Treavett in the 100 and 220 yards, defeating the renowned Harold Abrahams in both events; F. Walters (880 yards); Joe Blewitt (mile); D.G. Slack (120-yard hurdles) and H.S. Rooker (440-yard hurdles).

Joe Blewitt had one of his best seasons on the track. At the AAA Championships he was second in the four miles and third in the mile. In the international four miles in Scotland he came home first and continued in good form away from home with a win over three miles in Ireland, breaking the Irish record in the process. To cap it all Joe won the Jean Bouin Memorial Race in Paris for the second year in succession.

On 3 July 1922 a special inter-club meeting was arranged with the Finland AAA at Bournville. The Birmingham public were able to watch Olympic Champions Paavo Nurmi and Hannes Kolhemainen in action on track and the world-class Finnish field athletes too. This meeting was a great success and enhanced the organisational reputation of the Birchfield Harriers club.

It should also be noted that the Ladies' Section completed their first season's efforts. So, a feature of the Annual General Meeting held in November 1922 was the presence of lady members for the first time in the history of the club.

In the 1923 Junior the club team finished a very creditable second. In fact only twenty-seven points divided the first three teams. The winners, Newport Harriers, scored 116 points, Birchfield Harriers had 125 and Sparkhill Harriers 143.

In the Midlands at Coventry, the club's achievement was near to the record for this championship. They finished with the first three men home in Walter Freeman, Joe Blewitt and Jack Beman whilst the scoring six finished in the first nine. The score was a low 27 points, completely turning the tables on Newport Harriers, the Junior winners, who scored 66 points. The scoring six were: Walter Freeman 1; Joe Blewitt 2; Jack Beman 3; Ralph Stanton 5; Eddie Webster 7 and E.J. Mills 9. Unlucky not to have gained their Senior medal in this race were: Wal Monk 11; G. Perry 18 and F.G. Ward 20.

After the wonderful form shown in the Midlands, there was much expectation about the National at Beaconsfield. Having scored in 1920, 1921 and 1922, the team was out to equal the record of four successive wins. This was held by the former Moseley Harriers and had been established as far back as 1881–84. The occasion was captured aptly by *Sport and Play* magazine.

'All who had the good fortune to witness at Beaconsfield the forty-second race for the National Cross Country Championships last Saturday will remember it as one of their prime sporting experiences. They saw the greatest performance by a club in any Championship at any time in sports history, when the Birchfield Harriers gained their fifteenth success in the race with the magic score of 36 points against the next best of 137 (Hallamshire Harriers), provided the actual champion; placed four men in the first five (excluding

Birchfield Harriers Paris team march, 1922. At unknown warriors cave, Paris.

Paris 1922. Phyllis Hall, Birchfield's first female international, wearing 21.

individual entries), and the whole six in the first twelve. Add to that the equalling of the old Moseley Harriers record of four successive wins and tell me whether a greater record could be.'

The club captain, Joe Blewitt, the individual winner, must have run the race of his career. It is reported that entering the last lap E. Harper of Hallamshire, W.M. Cotterell of Signals and Walter Freeman of Birchfield were running side-by-side in a great struggle for supremacy, with Blewitt half a mile behind. How he caught the leaders and won simply astonished all who witnessed the contest.

The team was made up as follows: Joe Blewitt 1; Walter Freeman 3; A.H. Rodway 4; Jack Beman 5; Ralph Stanton 11 and Wal Monk 12. F.G. Ward was sixteenth in the race and, as in the Midlands, was unfortunate to not obtain a winning team medal.

Members who gained international selection were Joe Blewitt, who won a brilliant race in Paris on 26 March, and Jack Beman, who finished sixteenth and counted in England's scoring six.

There were a good crop of victories in the MCAAA Championships with Jack Beman (ten miles); Joe Blewitt for the steeplechase, one mile and four miles; Harry Houghton with the 440 yards and 880 yards; W.F. Boardman (440-yard hurdles); H.S. Rooker (120-yard hurdles) and D.G. Slack for the high jump plus hop, step and jump.

The Northern Counties 440-yard hurdles champion was A.J. Boardman whilst Joe Blewitt continued his run of success with victories in the English Championship mile and the AAA Championship four miles. For the latter race Blewitt again drew the headlines as he was running level with a Frenchman in the finishing straight, was baulked by a lapped competitor and just managed to win by inches.

At a Paris meeting, held on 10 June 1923, B. McDonald beat the French record for 1,500m. At the same meeting F.G. Ward finished second in the steeplechase.

The Ladies' Section continued to make progress and won prizes and relay races in all areas of England. Overall the club was consistent, making an impact on the domestic athletics scene and recruiting new and exciting talent.

Twelve: Onward and Upward

John Edward Webster joined the club in 1923 and initially made his mark over the country. In that year he ran second in the Junior Championship and seventh in the Midland Senior. Over the next three years his running in the National was outstanding. He was second, second and then first at Wolverton.

On the track he was a force at distances from the half to ten miles, including the steeplechase. In this event he won the MCAAA Championship eleven times and was AAA champion on four occasions. Perhaps his finest achievement was at the AAA Championships of 1926 when he won the four miles and the steeplechase on the same afternoon. He succeeded Joe Blewitt as club captain in 1929.

By then he had experienced mixed emotions with respect to his Olympic aspirations. He was selected for the Paris Games in 1924 but excluded from the Stockholm Games of 1928 in contentious circumstances, when a genuine gold medal prospect. His wife had received a small gratuity because of an advertisement in which Eddie advocated the use of Phosphrogen for promoting fitness. This was deemed a sufficient infringement of the amateur status to lead to his being barred from representing Great Britain. Quite a contrast with modern athletics – but even in those days, and before, athletes received appearance money but were still eligible for the Olympics.

His running career was drawing to a close when the Second World War started but he still competed when on active service in Italy. In 1945 Eddie indicated to the club that when he returned to Birmingham from Italy he wished to take up a coaching role. Sadly, he was killed in a road traffic accident just before being demobbed.

It was in January 1924 that Eddie made his first contribution of what was to be a long and glorious time at Birchfield. He was amongst those who accompanied trainer Frank Wright on a long journey to the South of France to compete in the Aycaquer Cup at Lyons for the first time. The team of Joe Blewitt, Ralph Stanton, A.H. Rodway, Walter Freeman, Wal Monk and Eddie won the event. Ralph Stanton was first and Eddie Webster second in a field of over 300 runners. The team finished a scoring six in the first sixteen.

In the 1924 Novice at Kings Norton honours were won again with a score of 108 points to Tipton second with 116 points. The team included: A.E. Sideway 5; G. Perry 9; B. McDonald 18; S.A. Newey 22; R. Downes 26 and J. Robinson 28.

The Senior at Newport, February 1924, gave club members a pleasant surprise. Club stalwart A.H. Rodway won his first championship, and in the presence of some of the greatest athletes in the club's history. The team won as follows: A.H. Rodway 1; Ralph Stanton 3; Jack Beman 5; Eddie Webster 7; Walter Freeman 9 and A.E. Sideway 11.This gave Birchfield victory by 36 points to Newport Harriers' second place with 113 points. There was also cause for celebration over the performance of Ralph Stanton in light of the fact that he had been winning medals with and for the club since before the First World War.

In the National at Doncaster, the club, having already equalled Moseley Harriers' record, now established a fresh record by winning for the fifth year in succession. The team to accomplish this was: Eddie Webster 2; A.H. Rodway 5; Ralph Stanton 6; Joe Blewitt 8; Walter Freeman 15 and G. Perry 17, making a total of 53 points to Surrey AC with 71 points.

Eddie Webster, Ralph Stanton and Joe Blewitt were selected for international honours. They competed in England's record international team which finished 1, 2, 3, 4, 5, 6 at Newcastle-upon-Tyne (with Webster third, Blewitt fourth and Stanton sixth). An exceptional performance by Ralph Stanton, who had gained his first international vest in 1914 and for whom this was only his second international – a decade after his debut!

Birchfield Harriers again enjoyed success at the MCAAA Championships. Harry Houghton won the 440 yards and 880 yards; H.S. Rooker (120-yard hurdles); Joe Blewitt the one mile and steeplechase; Eddie Webster (ten miles); Jock Dalrymple (javelin) and D. Slack the hop, step and jump.

The English two-mile steeplechase was won by Eddie Webster while Joe Blewitt won the equivalent event in the AAA Championships. Joe had the misfortune to fall at the last water jump and sprain his ankle. He had been well within a record time but only finished with great difficulty.

There was the honour of Olympic selection to compete in France for Harry Houghton, Eddie Webster, B. McDonald, S.A. Newey, D.G. Slack and Joe Blewitt – who was named as his country's vice-captain for the Games.

In Paris, for the first time, a modern Olympiad was dominated by one man – Paavo Nurmi. In one afternoon, within two hours, Nurmi won and set Olympic records in the 1,500 metres and 5,000 metres runs. Later he added the 10,000 metres cross-country title, and also won an unofficial 3,000 metres team race. So Finland surpassed its 1920 record with ten gold medals. The USA, however, had twelve this time.

Harold Abrahams in the 100-metre dash, Eric Liddel in the 400-metre run and Douglas Lowe in the 800 metres gave Great Britain three individual victories on the track.

This was not the only international outing for the leading Birchfielders. All the Olympians gained the additional honour of selection for the British Empire v. USA at Stamford Bridge on 19 July 1924. In this match Harry Houghton and C.T. Clibbon had the distinction of being in the winning teams for their respective relays.

A week later at Huddersfield in a team challenge against the USA Olympic squad both Sparkhill and Birchfield defeated the visitors in a tight contest.

At the other end of the scale of experience the Ladies' Section was continuing to emerge. Miss Woodwooley won the first Ladies' Cross Country race held at Perry Barr. Miss Whadcote was second and Miss Bushnell was third. In the Women's 880 yards championship in London a second place was achieved by Miss Hall.

At the Annual General Meeting it was decided to hold the club's celebration dinner on 29 December 1924 to coincide with the 40th anniversary of the record established by Vice-President J.E. Fowler Dixon at the club sports on the Old Aston Lower Grounds on 29 December 1884. He was present to receive the club's Special Gold Medal to mark the occasion and it is reported that he was obviously moved by

Above left: Eddie Webster.

Above right: Contemporary kit!

the warmth of his reception. The race in question was for fifty miles and was accomplished in 6 hours 20 minutes 47 seconds. The record was still intact at the presentation all of forty years later.

On 18 January 1925, the team won the cross-country contest at Lyons for the Aycaquer Challenge Cup, for the second year in succession. Eddie Webster was second to the great French athlete Jacques Guillemot. The club team to score were: Eddie Webster 2; A.E. Sideway 9; Jack Beman 11; J.E. Morton 14; A.H. Rodway 18 and Joe Blewitt 21. This was a total of 75 points against CASG, the leading cross-country club of Paris, who were second with 88 points.

In the Midlands at Ardley, Eddie Webster 3; Joe Blewitt 5; A.E. Sideway 6; Jack Beman 8; G. Perry 10 and Frank Quinn 17, for a total of 49 points, easily beat Tipton on 102 points.

In the National at Hereford a great win was recorded. It was a fine performance to finish six men in the first twenty in a field of 245 runners. This victory was the seventeenth since 1880 and the sixth in succession. Joe Blewitt had been captain and in the scoring six in every one of this latest continuous set of races. The counting six on this occasion were: J.E. Webster 2; A.H. Rodway 10; Jack Beman 14; Joe Blewitt 15; A.E. Sideway 17 and Frank Quinn 20 to total 78 points.

Eddie Webster and A.H. Rodway gained international selection, assisting England to victory, Webster being first and Rodway eighth at Baldoyle on 28 March 1925. Webster joined the club's select band of international winners, being the fifth member to achieve this honour at that time.

Two important team races were held at Easter against the Olympique Club, Paris. The first, at the Good Friday Sports, Cape Hill, produced a keen contest. Eddie Webster was first, Joe Blewitt third and Jack Beman sixth. This made 10 points to the 11 points of the French club whose athletes finished second, fourth and fifth. The time of Webster was 9 minutes 37 seconds on a six-laps to the mile track and probably the fastest two miles ever performed on the old Cape Hill track.

The second race was held at Newport Harriers Sports, Easter Monday. Nine teams competed and produced another tight tussle, Webster winning, Blewitt second and Rodway ninth. This meant 12 points to the French club's 14 points with third, fourth and seventh places. Between the two races described, Joe Blewitt on the Easter Saturday won a fast two-mile race at Belle Vue, Manchester!

The London to Brighton Relay was organised for the first time in 1924 by the *News of the World* but the team did not compete then. However, on 20 April 1925, the team representing the club won and the order of running was: Joe Blewitt, Walter Freeman, A.E. Sideway, Frank Quinn, Jack Beman, F.G. Ward, J. Byrne, A.H. Rodway, G. Perry and Eddie Webster. The time of 4 hours 50 minutes 0.2 seconds was only 52.2 seconds slower than the previous winning team of Surrey AC but in far worse weather conditions.

The MCAAA Championships again proved worthwhile for Birchfielders. The 100 yards and 220 yards were won by A.W. Green; the quarter mile by Harry Houghton; the four miles and the two-mile steeplechase by Eddie Webster; and the amazing collection of high jump, long jump and hop, step and jump by D.G. Slack, with the javelin a victory for Jock Dalrymple.

Frank Quinn won the Irish one-mile title, whilst in the English Championship there were first places for Joe Blewitt in the four-mile event and Eddie Webster in the two-mile steeplechase.

Winners in the AAA Championships were Joe Blewitt in the four miles; Eddie Webster in the two-mile steeplechase and ten miles; and B. McDonald in the one mile. The latter athlete put up the greatest race of his career and recorded 4 minutes 18 seconds. This time had only been beaten four times since 1886.

Eddie Webster in the ten miles recorded 52 minutes 32.6 seconds, the fastest time since 1914. In this race Frank Quinn finished fourth and was mainly responsible for the fast time, cutting out the pace for the first five miles. Quinn's time of 53:30 had often been good enough to win the race in the past.

The club captain, Joe Blewitt, was the first recipient of the Leah Wright Memorial Trophy. This was presented by Frank Wright in recognition of Joe's all-round performances in flat and cross-country championships, plus his six successive national team medals.

The Ladies' Section was continuing to make progress and again scored many successes in relay races. In London they had pushed Manor Park Ladies to a new world record. Miss Oldfield, Miss Hall, Miss Wannop and Miss Parry gained standard medals in the Women's AAA Championships.

At the Annual General Meeting on 31 October, a special announcement was made with respect to Eddie Webster. It was confirmed that as winner of the AAA two-mile steeplechase and the ten-mile run the

Association had appointed him, along with Mr Osborne, an American high jumper, as joint holder of the Harvey Cup for the best championship performance of the year.

Once the social calendar wound down then serious preparations began for the Novice race in December and the Lyons trip in January. At Hednesford the team obtained second place in the Midlands Novice Championship with 214 points to the 178 points of Sutton-in-Ashfield Harriers. On 16 January 1926, the Aycaquer Trophy was won at Lyons for the third time in succession and became the property of the club. This was a remarkable feat considering that the trophy had been up for competition for twenty-five years. The team actually finished in the race as follows: A.H. Rodway 4; Frank Quinn 5; Jack Beman 6; Joe Blewitt 8; A.H. Pepper 9 and G. Perry 10. Deleting the individual runners, the actual scores for team honours were 3, 4, 5, 6, 7 and 8, making 33 points. The second team scored 120 points, and this outstanding Birchfield performance in a field of 227 runners.

In the Novice at Nuneaton in February, an excellent win was registered, with six men in the first twenty-seven in a field of 319 runners. Members to score were: W.O. Williams 3; W.A.M. Edwards 12; T. Garbett 14;m. Smith 17; F. Pearson 24 and J. Pearson 27. This made a total of 97 points with Westbury Harriers second with 213 points.

At Coventry in February, the Midland Association for the first time organised a Four Miles Youth's Race for runners aged from fifteen to eighteen. This was on the same day as the Senior Championship. It proved a real success for the club as they took both team events. The Youth's race saw R. Morgan 9; E.E. Farndon 10 and T. Philpott 11 scoring 30 points to win from Kettering Harriers who scored 31 points.

For the Midlands Championship the total of 45 points was incurred as such: Eddie Webster 2; Jack Beman 4; A.H. Rodway 7; G. Parry 8; W.O. Williams 11 and Wal Monk 13. This was achieved without Joe Blewitt and Frank Quinn who were ill at the time. Newport Harriers were second with 124 points.

The National at Wolverton was one of the finest in club history. There was a record crowd (approaching 10,000) and they witnessed a double triumph for Birchfield Harriers. Eddie Webster was first home and the team scored 43 points to the 157 points of Hallamshire Harriers in second place. The team scores were: Eddie Webster 1; A.H. Rodway 3; G. Perry 4; Walter Freeman 8; Jack Beman 12 and Joe Blewitt 15. This was the club's seventh successive win, with the club captain, Joe Blewitt, scoring in each of these – a record which still stands. A great race was enjoyed between Eddie Webster and E. Harper of Hallamshire Harriers. It was fought out from start to finish and it was only Webster's strength that gave him victory in a close run to the line.

Eddie Webster and A.H. Rodway were selected for international honours, with G. Perry nominated as a reserve. Webster, being niggled with injury, did not compete which gave Perry his chance. Rodway finished seventh and Perry twenty-third.

The London to Brighton Relay was another meritorious victory for the club. There is a prior mention that the previous year the time taken was not up to Surrey's record of 4 hours 50 but on this occasion, under better conditions, 4 minutes 26 seconds was knocked off. This established a fresh record of 4 hours 45 minutes 34.2 seconds. The team representing Birchfield was Joe Blewitt, J.E. Morton, Walter Freeman, Frank Quinn, Jack Beman, W.O. Williams, Wal Monk, G. Perry, A.E. Sideway and A.H. Rodway. Eddie Webster was, unfortunately, not well enough to compete.

The MCAAA Championships produced their usual bevy of winners. Eddie Webster won the two-mile steeplechase and the four miles; A.W. Green the 100 yards and 220 yards; Harry Houghton the 440 yards and 880 yards; B. McDonald the one mile; and Jack Beman the ten-mile event. In the mile relay the winning team was: Harry Houghton, A.W. Green, H.S. Rooker and P. Jeavons.

In the AAA Championships Eddie Webster had to compete in the two-mile steeplechase and the four-mile run with very little time between the races. His double accomplished in one afternoon indicated his outstanding ability. The club subsequently added to various awards by presenting him with the Leah Wright Trophy.

During the summer of 1926 there was increasing debate about the need to provide a first-class sports ground, not only for the Birchfield Harriers, but for Birmingham athletes in general. An offer was considered for about twelve acres of land, but it was realised that to purchase outright would absorb all the club funds. It was a serious proposition and needed careful consideration before any steps could be taken. It was not until 1927 that any decision was arrived at.

Thirteen: On the Right Track

The season 1926/27 was a most important one for the club, for during this period many important decisions were reached. On 20 September 1926, a special meeting was held: 'To consider the purchase of land for an athletic track and sports ground which will perpetuate the life work of Mr W.W. Alexander and commemorate the club's Jubilee in December 1927.' A unanimous decision to purchase was reached and it was completed on 11 November 1926. To fully realise the magnitude of the task undertaken, it should be remembered that when the club had completed that purchase they became bereft of funds. The scheme cost £20,000, which was a considerable sum in those days.

Meanwhile, the members' league races – initiated and so successful in 1925/26 – continued in the same vein. They proved the value of these races for novices as they gained the majority of medals awarded. The Novice at Harborne in December 1926 gave the club its first victory in this race. In a field of 282 runners the counting six finished as follows: L. Wheeler 8; J. Price 16; R. Morgan 19; A.E. Vernon 23; P.L. Lea 25 and W. Webster 33, a total of 124 points, beating Sutton-in-Ashfield by 75 points.

In the Novice run at Trentham Park, Stoke in February 1927, the team secured another victory by winning for the second year in succession, a feat never before accomplished as the counting six of a winning team were debarred from competing again in the Junior. The scorers were: P. Holloway 6; F.R. Bagley 12; H.C. Holloway 15; J. Sower 19; R. Smith 24 and E. Mould 28. This was a total of 104 points with Derby and County second on 142 points.

The Midlands took place at The Austin Playing Fields, Longbridge. Birchfield put up a very solid performance, placing eight men in the first sixteen to finish. They scored 46 points to win from Tipton Harriers on 89 points. Those to score were: Jack Beman 3; Joe Blewitt 4; P. Holloway 7; G. Perry 9; W.A.M. Edwards 10; and J. Robinson 13.

The National was held in Crewe Park and was a record event in a certain respect. Hallamshire Harriers defeated Birchfield Harriers handsomely by 36 points to 106 points. So came to and end the exceptional record run of seven successive National team wins.

In the London to Brighton Road Relay in April, Hallamshire Harriers were again on top form and their victory was achieved in a new record time of 4 hours 41 minutes and 48.6 seconds. On the first stage, Joe Blewitt with 23 minutes 14 seconds, and on the second B. McDonald with 24 minutes 25 seconds, established stage records for their respective legs.

Further individual distinction for club members included W.A.M. Edwards winning the Oxford v. Cambridge Inter-Varsity cross-country race; Joe Blewitt was chosen as reserve for the International at Caerleon; whilst at the MCAAA Championships there were victories for Billy Green (100 yards and 220 yards), Harry Houghton (440 yards), Cyril Ellis (half mile and mile), Jack Beman (ten miles) Eddie Webster (two-mile steeplechase) and Jock Dalrymple (javelin). The mile relay was also won by the club.

At the AAA Championships Eddie Webster won the two-mile steeplechase and Cyril Ellis the mile title. The Leah Wright Memorial Trophy, with special gold medal, was eventually awarded to Cyril Ellis for his outstanding performances across the season.

At the Four Club's Carnival at Fallowfield, Manchester in July, Ellis, in a 1,000 metres limited handicap, accomplished 2 minutes 27.6. This was a new world record, beating the previous record of 2 minutes 28.5 seconds held by the Swede, S. Lundgren. Unfortunately for Ellis, his record was overtaken by Dr O. Peltzer in Paris a month later. Peltzer recorded 2 minutes 25.8 seconds.

Lady members recorded victory in the Nottingham Cup in July. Miss Oldfield won the 50 yards dash and was second in the 100 yards. Miss Gladys Lunn won both the 440 yards and the 800 yards before switching her attentions to the long jump, where she finished second. Miss Aston won the 220 yards and was second in the 440 yards. All three ladies turned out in the relay race, which was a Birchfield victory.

The Jubilee Annual General Meeting was a great occasion in the history of the club. The report shows that an encouraging start had been made with the fund to lay out the Alexander Sports Ground, and in the first year a sum of £3,256 10s 8d had been raised. Little progress in actually laying out the ground, however, could be reported. Pending a settlement, over which the committee had no control, this work could not be undertaken.

The Jubilee dinner was held on 29 October 1927. There was a remarkable gathering of past and present notables in the athletic world to support the President, Alderman T.H. Cartwright JP. There were also representatives from football, swimming and many other sports clubs in and around Birmingham. Charlie Wood and Tom Pank, both of whom had attended the inaugural meeting of the club, were also present.

It must have been a proud and happy occasion for W.W. Alexander. Joining the club in 1880, he became the Honorary Secretary on 3 August 1882 and held the post for forty-five years. So the climax of the Jubilee proceedings was reached when the President handed to Mr Alexander a gold watch and an illuminated address, as a token of the members' appreciation of his services to the club. Mr Alexander had a wonderful ovation on rising to make his brief and modest response.

Dennis Lyons in response to the toast, 'The Club', proposed by the reigning Olympic 100 metres Champion Harold Abrahams, sounded the keynote for the future. He stated that the Jubilee by no means marked the end of the club or of the wonderful spirit prevailing amongst the members. It was a matter of grim determination that, as one man, they should go on in the future to do better and better.

As to the content of the illuminated address presented to W.W. Alexander. It stated:

'The Members, in asking your acceptance of this gold watch and address as a small token of their regard and affection for you, wish to place on record their great appreciation of your long and honourable services to the club, your unfailing courtesy to one and all, champion or novice, and the great ambitions and ideals you have infused into all members for the betterment of the club and the members themselves.

Your life's work is the admiration of all sportsmen, who as sportsmen recognise the endless sacrifices you have made not only in the interest of the club and amateur sport generally, but on behalf of the lame dog whom you have never failed.

On this great day with the club in the proud position it is, the admiration of the whole world, the foundation of which success was laid by your untiring energy and far-seeing ability, we as members are proud to be associated with you and to acknowledge you as a model leader.

Your great work may never be valued at its true worth except by those more intimately connected with you, but it has made many friends and brought much happiness to you.

Our best wishes are with you in the continuance of your good work, in which you can count on our whole-hearted support.'

Signed on behalf of members,
T.H. Cartwright, President
Henry A. Butler, Vice-President
C.E. Blewitt, Captain

The Members' League again proved a popular and beneficial feature of the early part of the cross-country season.

In December the Novice was won for the second year in succession, equalling the record held by Tipton Harriers, of two successive wins in this race. The event was held at Courthouse Green, Coventry, with a hitherto unsurpassed entry of twenty-eight clubs totalling 301 runners. The club scored 112 points to beat North Staffs Harriers by seventy-six points. Those to score were: S.G. Smith 2; H.E. Knowles 7; C.D. Smith 14; H. Allen 23; T.A. Wedgbury 27 and H.W. Fielding 39.

W.A.M. Edwards won the Inter-Varsity cross-country match for the second consecutive year in December, while, in January, Eddie Webster won the Staffs County Championship with Jack Beman as runner-up.

In the Novice at Kettering the club team again won handsomely and on this occasion had the first man in F. Light. He was the first Birchfielder to win outright since 1920. This win was the third in succession for the club. A remarkable result when it is again remembered that the winning six were debarred from further competition in the Junior. The club team was: F. Light 1; E.E. Farndon 8; S.H. Smith 9; H.J. Hackett 10; C.

Hardeman 19 and S.G. Smith 25. This made a total of 72 points, a victory over Derby and County AC who scored 144 points.

The Senior was held at Cwmbran in South Wales. The course was reported as having been one of the most demanding the event had ever been run over. The race was a chapter of accidents for the club. Eddie Webster damaged his knee when taking a water jump and retired, while J.E. Morton collapsed in the last mile. The other members rose to the occasion and nine finished in the first thirty-five. A.E. Sideway in finishing second accomplished the best performance of his career, and was well supported in the bronze medal position by Joe Blewitt. Team placings were: A.E. Sideway 2; Joe Blewitt 3; F. Light 5; H.C. Holloway 15; S.H. Smith 17 and P. Holloway 18. That made a total of 60 points, with Tipton Harriers second on 99 points.

The National at Leamington was a great triumph for the club, both individual and team honours being won. The course was described as ideal, being laid out over real hunting country with Compton Hill as a natural grandstand. It snowed during the contest but this did not deter Eddie Webster from claiming victory. The Stags packed three in the first five and half a dozen in the top fifteen: Eddie Webster 1; Jack Beman 4; Joe Blewitt 5; H.C. Holloway 11; A.E. Sideway 13 and F. Light 15. The total was 49 points, while Hallamshire Harriers scored 82 points to finish second. F. Light joined the select band of members who had gained Junior, Senior and National medals in one season.

The club won the fifth annual London to Brighton Relay in April 1928. This was the third win in four years, having been successful in 1925 and 1926. The team achieved the distinction of establishing a new course record of 4 hours 41 minutes 48.6 seconds, a time which was thirty-one seconds inside the previous best. New records were created for the first, third, fourth, sixth and eighth legs. The full team and order of running was: Joe Blewitt, W.A.M. Edwards, F. Light, Eddie Webster, A.E. Sideway, Frank Quinn, B. McDonald, W.O. Williams, H.C. Holloway and Jack Beman.

At the MCAAA Championships there were victories for the following club members: a treble for Billy Green in the 100 yards, 220 yards and 440 yards; Cyril Ellis (880 yards); Eddie Webster (two-mile steeplechase); Jack Beman in the four miles and ten miles; Cyril Ellis, Billy Green, A.W. Bridge and J.H. Hawkins in the relay; D.G. Slack in the long jump; Jock Dalrymple in the javelin and H.S. Rooker in the high jump.

At the AAA Championships, Eddie Webster won the two-mile steeplechase plus the ten-mile event whilst Cyril Ellis won the mile.

The ten miles AAA race was held outside London, at Bourneville, Birmingham for the first time for many years and produced an exceptionally fine contest. Eddie Webster's time of 52 minutes 16.2 seconds was a good effort and he was closely followed 4.2 seconds later by Jack Beman. An unusual incident occurred in this race. In rounding one of the bends Hallamshire's Ernie Harper fell, and Webster and Beman stopped and helped him to his feet, a spontaneous act of sportsmanship much appreciated by the crowd present.

To retain his mile title Cyril Ellis recorded 4:20.8 but could have gone faster if another athlete had been able to push him harder. However, Ellis enjoyed the run of his life in the British Empire v. USA 4 x one-mile relay in London. Taking the last leg, he started eight yards behind Lloyd Hahn. The American had previously broken 1 minute 52 seconds for the 800m. Producing a wonderful finish, he won for the British Empire in 17:22.6. This time was only 2.5 seconds outside the world record for this class of relay. The reception he received was well deserved.

Club members selected to represent Britain in the Olympic Games in Amsterdam were: Cyril Ellis, F. Light, Joe Blewitt, Billy Green, Harry Houghton and J.H. Hambridge. The club trainer, Frank Wright, was also selected as one of the Olympic trainers. Dennis Lyons was given the honour of acting as Chief Judge of the jumping events at the Games.

Paavo Nurmi bowed out of Olympic history with a sixth gold medal in the 10,000m. Veteran British stars Douglas Lowe and David Lord Burghley took the 800m and 400m hurdles respectively. The USA was saved from a shutout on the track when Ray Barbutt won the 400m, but did score heavily in the relays and field events. Asia appeared in the gold-medal list for the first time when Mikio Oda of Japan won the hop, step and jump. Women participated for the first time in track and field events.

As the Olympics were opening – so was the Alexander Sports Ground, but not for athletics. The Sutton Coldfield and North Birmingham Auto Club (Sunbac) staged a motorcycle dirt track meeting on the new circuit. Some 7,000 spectators turned up to watch the meeting on a sunny summer evening with music relayed from a gramophone in the enclosure to speakers on the centre green. Coloured cuffs were used to identify the riders to the crowd who, for the most part, seemed somewhat bewildered by the spectacle. Not even the colourful American rider 'Sprouts' Elder's demonstration of broadsliding captured their imagination. His new style of riding caused large amounts of dust which somewhat obscured his antics. There were those who deprecated the use of the ground for this new sport, but the financial input was welcome.

Eddie Webster, by winning one MCAAA Championship, two AAA Championships and the National Cross Country Championship was awarded the Leah Wright Memorial Trophy.

At the fifty-first Annual Meeting the announcement of the retirement of C.E. 'Joe' Blewitt, the popular club captain since October 1921, was made. Eddie Webster was then elected as the new captain of the club.

The Annual Report was an encouraging one. It stated that notwithstanding the heavy work entailed by the Alexander Sports Ground, the sporting character of the club had been maintained at its usual high standard. It had been feared by some that the possession of a sports ground might overshadow the core activities of the club. The accounts showed that during the season ending 31 August 1928, £2,550 6s 0d had been raised towards laying out the Alexander Sports Ground, making a total to date of £5,806 16s 8d.

With the cross-country season getting into full swing, the Members' League again proved popular, drawing large fields and producing some keen races.

On 17 November the club successfully visited Oxford University for the first time and proved successful. They placed the first home in Jack Beman, A.E. Sideaway and F. Light so winning team honours by 17 points to Oxford's 38 points.

The Novice in December 1928, at Sutton-in-Ashfield, saw Birchfield establish a new club record. By this win, the third in succession, the club also registered the best performance so far, a 106-point margin over second placed Dudley, 60 to 166. The team to score was: P. Southall 6; R.E. Davey 8; J.K. Gale 9; N. James 10; A. Laughton 13 and W. Morris 14.

The Midlands at Kettering provided a great race for individual honours between Eddie Webster, who was National and ex-International Champion, but had never won the Senior, J. Winfield (Derby) and G. Forryan (Nuneaton). In the end Eddie prevailed and the team scored 52 points to 113 points by Derby C & AC, who were second. The following scored for the club: Eddie Webster 1; Jack Beman 5; S.H. Smith 10; J.E. Moreton 11; A.E. Sideaway 12 and A.E. Mould 14.

The National in March 1929 at Beaconsfield saw the introduction of a new rule. Teams were limited to nine runners per race as against the twelve previously allowed. Despite Jack Beman and J.E. Moreton falling and dropping out, the team scored a fine win to record a landmark twentieth National team title. The statistics for the club now stood at twenty wins, fourteen seconds, four thirds and seven times unplaced in the forty-five National races since 1880. The scoring six were: Eddie Webster 3; F. Light 4; A.E. Sideaway 15; A.E. Mould 18.5; H.C. Holloway 22 and S.H. Smith 29 to total 91.5 points. Surrey AC was second on 184 points. A dead heat in the actual race accounts for the half point. F. Light was selected for the International in France.

The London to Brighton Relay in April 1929 witnessed an exciting duel between Hallamshire Harriers of Sheffield and the Birchfield Harriers. The times reflect this with Hallamshire winning in 4 hours 48 minutes 37 seconds, only twenty-one seconds ahead of Birchfield.

At the MCAAA Championships the usual suspects were on form! Eddie Webster won the four miles and the steeplechase; Billy Green the 100 yards and 220 yards; Cyril Ellis the half mile and one mile; P. Jeavons won the quarter mile; Jock Dalrymple both the javelin and the hammer throw and D.G. Slack tied for first place in the high jump. In the relay there was victory for Harry Houghton, Billy Green, P. Jeavons and Greg Boyles.

At the AAA Championships Cyril Ellis won the half and one mile. In doing so on the same day this Birchfielder recorded an achievement that had not been accomplished since 1884. Ellis gained further distinction by winning the half mile race in the triangular match in Ireland in July 1929.

On 8 June 1929, at Bedford, Jock Dalrymple established a new British record with a javelin throw of 185ft 1.5 inches, which stood for several decades.

Especially noteworthy in the above collection of performances was that of Billy Green in the MCAAA Championships. His victories in the 100 yards and 220 yards were his fifth successive wins in these championships. Billy Green became a member of Birchfield's Coventry branch in 1922. Initially he spread himself over a wide range of distances from the sprints to the mile. He was also encouraged to run cross-country to improve his stamina and lung capacities. He did not take long to discover that sprinting was his

Right: The first event – speedway!

Below: The National at Beaconsfield.

true forte, however, and it was in this category that he made his name and wrote himself into the records of both the Birchfield Harriers and the Midland Counties AAA. In three years he had eliminated his starting mark from ten yards to scratch for handicap events in the 100 yards.

In eleven seasons, 1925 to 1935, Billy recorded the astonishing number of twenty-four wins in Midland Championships: eleven successive wins in the 100 yards, ten victories in the 220 yards and three in the 440 yards. It is also notable that he was never able to reproduce this winning form at national level. He was only placed once in an AAA Championship final, taking second place in the 220 yards in 1929. Despite this apparent inhibition, he was an English international from 1925 to 1931, which included the 400m at the 1928 Olympic Games. His contemporaries say that he appeared to 'tighten up' on the big occasion. He later became club captain from 1929 to 1936.

It was on 27 July 1929 that the Alexander Ground was officially opened by H.A. Butler, supported by a large assembly of prominent citizens. The occasion attracted the largest crowd ever seen at Perry Barr.

At a subsequent meeting of the Amateur Athletic Association in London, the chairman declared that 'Birchfield had not only set a fine example to all other athletic clubs in the country, but had set an example to the governing body itself.'

Fourteen: Ladies First

The year 1930 was particularly important. It saw a great impetus given to women's athletics. This was mainly due to the outstanding successes of Gladys Lunn, culminating with a victory in the 880m World Championship in Prague.

The Ladies' Section, for the first time, entered a team in the Women's National Championship and finished sixth. Gladys gained the distinction of being the first to finish, a performance repeated in the Women's International Championship.

This was also the year in which the club took part for the first time in the Polytechnic Kinnaird Competition, which became one of the most prestigious events in the calendar. Invitation was restricted to twelve clubs. The best performance was in 1931 when they finished third to Achilles and Polytechnic.

W.W. Alexander was elected that year as President of the MCAAA. This was a role he decided to hold for twelve months only. Mr Alexander was the third club member to hold this distinguished position following Walter Mabbett and Denis Lyons.

April 1932 saw the advent of the club's magazine – *Stagbearer*. It was started primarily to accommodate the programmes for track league meetings and developed to place on record the club performances.

The club trainer, Frank Wright, was selected for the fifth time (1908, 1920, 1924, 1928 and 1932) to attend to the needs of the British Olympic team in Los Angeles. The great distances involved in travel and a worldwide economic depression cut the entries in half. However, the introduction of the Olympic Village marked the tenth Olympiad as another advance towards the ideal being pursued.

The USA made a strong comeback on home soil as records were beaten in almost every event. British schoolmaster Tom Hampson set a world record in the 800 metres run and his teammate Tom Green won the fifty-kilometre walk.

Meanwhile, back home, the Birchfield Ladies' Section had won the National Cross Country Championships for the first time; Gladys Lunn again being the individual winner. Birchfield were the first team to provide winning individual and team.

Apart from many fine performances by members in 1933 of greatest significance to the club was the passing of W.W. Alexander and H.A. Butler. It was also recorded with deep regret that A.H. 'Dot' Hill, one of the members of the first National team in 1880, had also died.

In 1933 A.G.K. Brown won the Public Schools Championships 880 yards and long jump. At that time he was a first claim member of the club. Upon going up to Cambridge, he became the first claim of Achilles, but remained as second claim to Birchfield.

At Himley Park in 1934 the club won the National for the twenty-fifth time. Bob Sutherland in fifth position was the first scorer for the fourth year in a row.

Ralph Kilver Brown won the 440-yard hurdles at the AAA Championships and was third in the Empire Games in London. Three javelin throwers were selected for the Games. Gladys Lunn won the women's event, while S. Wilson and J.C.W. Heath were fourth and fifth respectively in the men's competition.

Winners at the MCAAA Championships were: Billy Green in the 100 and 220 yards; Jack Fenn (880 yards); Ralph Kilver Brown for the 440-yard hurdles; J.C.W. Heath in the javelin and Jack Beman in the marathon.

The performances of Jack Beman over so many years with Birchfield Harriers suggest that here was a man of endurance. This is proven by the fact that towards the end of his athletic career, which was undoubtedly cut short by the Second World War, he ran two marathons in ten days and won both. That was in 1938 when Jack was forty-two years of age. If it had not been for his team spirit and his dedication to distance running he could have run marathons much earlier in his racing career and potentially could have achieved international honours. Marathon running in the 1930s did not have the universal appeal it enjoys today.

Jack's training methods were interesting. He was convinced that he had to make his legs strong enough to last the full twenty-six miles. In order to achieve this, much of his training consisted of long walks in heavy boots. Once a week he walked for four hours. He stated; 'You see, you've got to make sure that you walk the distance before you try to run it. In those four hours I'd do twenty miles or a bit more.'

Even in the weeks leading up to a marathon, Jack covered more miles by walking than he did by running. He walked for one to two hours on Monday, Tuesday and Wednesday. On Thursday he did his four-hour stint. He did his first run of the week on Friday, which was usually 'a fast ten miles'. Sometimes he met up with another Black Country Birchfielder, Eddie Webster, at the junction of New Road and Bilston Road, Darlaston.

The year 1935 is remembered for the record set by D.A. Currie in winning the individual title in the Everill Cup, Novice and Midlands Championships. The team also won all three competitions.

The Warwickshire County Championship was competed in for the first time as a team and won, as it was in 1936 and 1937, A. Bourton winning the individual title in 1935/36 and J.T. Richards achieving a similar distinction in 1937.

Birchfield's sequence of wins in the National Cross Country Championships was broken by Belgrave Harriers at Beaconsfield in 1935, despite fielding a strong team. However, there was a subsequent invitation to take on Belgrave at the British Games at White City, London on Whit Monday. This was eight-a-side, with six to count over three miles. Success was secured by four points with Eddie Webster in outstanding form.

In 1936 there was a change of club President following the passing of T.H. Cartwright. Into the position came the revered former club Secretary, Geoff Alexander. This was Olympic year and Frank Wright was again invited to accompany the team to Berlin as a trainer for a remarkable sixth occasion in twenty-eight years. A.G.K. Brown had already won the AAA 440 yards championship en route to selection for the Games. At Berlin he placed second in the 400m and then won a gold medal when he ran the final leg for the Great Britain team in the 4 x 400m relay.

Born on 21 February 1915, Godfrey Brown attended Warwick School. It was while he was at school that he followed older brother Ralph and sister Audrey in joining Birchfield. At school he ran all distances from the 100 yards to the mile with equal success, but settled on the 880 yards as his best event. He won this event at the Public Schools Championships in 1932, 1933 and 1934. However, he emerged as a quarter-miler of outstanding ability when he recorded a time of 48.1 in a heat at the Cambridge University Sports in 1935. He made his international debut in the match with Germany in Munich that year, finishing second in 48.4.

In 1936 he travelled to Berlin for the Olympics as the leading quarter-miler, having won the AAA title. Despite his inexperience at the distance, he performed superbly at the Games. In the semi-finals he ran a personal best of 47.7 and ninety minutes later he drew the outside lane in a six-man final. Attempting to run a fast first 200 metres, he was shocked to find himself in fourth place entering the finishing straight. A determined effort over the last fifty metres took him into second place on the line where he just failed to catch the winner, Archie Williams of the USA. His time of 46.7 was a new British record and stood for over twenty years. The photo-finish showed how remarkably close Godfrey had come and gave times of Williams 46.66, Brown 46.68. Of course, the victory of the British quartet, anchored by Godfrey, in the relay provided quite a consolation!

Brown ran the 'glory leg' in another British triumph, the 1937 match with Germany at the White City, London. The result of the match depended on the last event, a medley relay of 440–220–220–880. Godfrey was persuaded to run the 880 yards by team manager Jack Crump and took over a ten yards lead with the famous 880-metre runner, Rudolf Harbig, representing Germany. By the tactic of running what was in those days a very fast first lap of fifty-two seconds, Brown drew the sting from Harbig who tried to close the gap in the first quarter-mile. By the tape the lead had more than doubled to some twenty-five yards to win the match by two points. Around the final bend an ashen-faced Godfrey Brown had started to wobble. On completion of the race our hero leaned against a rail, completely exhausted, and was violently sick.

Away from the track he assisted Birchfield in a rather unusual way, rolling out and marking the track prior to the Waddilove Meeting in July 1936 at which Jack Lovelock set a new British record for the two miles.

The statistics for the 1937/1938 season are fulsome. The club won the Everill Cup, and the Midlands and National Championships. Then Birchfield won the Manchester to Blackpool relay, Outer Circle Relay, Warwickshire County Championship, Coventry Road Relay and the Chartres International race. There were seven firsts, eight seconds and eight thirds in the Midland Championships. This was followed by victory in the Camberley Inter-Club match and a friendly with Birmingham University. In the Midland Marathon members finished first, second, third, fifth and sixth.

The Ladies won the Midland Junior and Senior titles as well as the National Junior and Senior CC Championships. They were runners-up in the National Walking Championships and out of five events had four separate individual champions. They had international representation in sprint events in Germany and Paris.

Their leading light was, of course, Gladys Lunn. She was born on 1 June 1908, and joined Birchfield Harriers in 1926. In 1927 a motor accident interrupted her training and she did not make her mark until 1929–30. She took about two years to develop, but then became a formidable competitor. For some reason, presumably associated with the then well-known Sally Lunn teacake, she quickly became affectionately known as 'Sally'!

Despite a great interest in field events, sprinting and cross-country running, her most outstanding talent was for middle distances. At the Geneva Sports Club meeting at Stamford Bridge in 1934 she set up a world record for the 1,000m of 3:4.4. Her all-round ability was demonstrated by winning the shot with a handicap allowance of 3 feet 6 inches over Ada Fenn, who was on scratch. She announced her retirement from athletics in 1933. It was short lived and in 1934 at the Alexander Stadium she broke her own record for the 1,000m in 3:3.5 in her 'comeback' performance.

From left to right: Ralph Brown, Audrey Brown, Godfrey Brown.

In 1934 at the Empire Games in London she accomplished an unusual double victory in the javelin and 880 yards. During this period she also achieved great international status, being captain of the Women's International Cross Country team in 1932 and captain of the England team at the Empire Games, Sydney in 1938. Her running career stopped with the war, but throughout the 1930s she was captain and main inspiration to Birchfield Harriers Ladies' team, which swept all other clubs aside in the main team events of the era.

In 1947, Sally was elected president of the Midland Counties WAAA, to crown a wonderful athletics career. She became equally successful as a golfer and passed away on the tee of her favourite golf course at Great Barr in January 1988, a truly remarkable woman to the end.

Fifteen: Out of Darkness and into Light

Geoff Austin was one of the great servants of Birchfield. The bound volumes of the magazine *Stagbearer*, which he edited and published monthly from 1932 to 1953, are among the most important items in the club's archives. During the war his work was greatly appreciated by members serving in the Forces who anxiously awaited news from home, and, of course, provides a valuable source of information for the history of the club.

Soon after the outbreak of war in 1939 the Alexander Stadium was requisitioned by the Government for use by the Home Guard. The club moved its Tuesday and Thursday training nights to the Aston Manor Cricket Ground. The distance men started their road runs from the Church Tavern in Church Road. Birmingham was 'blacked out' at night and factories involved in war work required prodigious stints of overtime from workers. Meanwhile, many members were drafted into the Forces.

Throughout 1940 the *Stagbearer* recorded the fate of those involved in the fighting. Following Dunkirk, Lance Corporal Stan Allen was posted as missing in action, but then happily came the news that he had been taken prisoner. Jim Smith, a leading road relay runner, and Eddie Wright, the MCAAA long-jump champion, were also captured by the Germans. Then came news of the first fatality. A young cross-country runner, Stan Britnor, was killed when dealing with an unexploded bomb. The grim news continued. Sergeant/Pilot Len Garvey was shot down and killed at the age of twenty-six, flying in the Battle of Britain.

Gladys Lunn.

He was a member of the winning Manchester to Blackpool team in 1935 and had developed into one of the best milers in the Midlands.

France had fallen and the club was reminded of its link with the cathedral town of Chartres, south of Paris. A Birchfield team had travelled there annually since 1933 for a cross-country fixture with the top French clubs. Before the town was occupied a letter was received from Andre Filou, of the Velo Sport Chartrain, extending an invitation to return there when the war was over. The trip to Chartres, in January, had been one of the highlights of the winter season.

By 1942 the list of those posted as prisoners of war had grown to seven. Allen, Smith, Wright, plus Billy Loynes, Alan Pentland, Bill Sanders and Alan Slocombe. The club sent news to Stan Allen that he had been re-elected as Vice Captain. Sometime later the club received a letter from Allen saying that he greatly appreciated the honour bestowed in his absence and that he had celebrated by winning a 1,000 metres race at his camp in Poland. All the prisoners wrote explaining the efforts they were making to keep fit under difficult circumstances. Jim Smith asked that his spikes be sent out to him. Whether they were is not recorded.

All the championships were suspended for the duration of the war. Some athletics events were organised and factory workers joined those based locally to run in 'mob' matches, relays and inter-club competitions. Bob Reid was prominent in many of the cross-country races and the five years of war robbed him of his best years as an athlete. The same could be said of many athletes.

As the conflict turned in favour of the Allies the theatres of war changed. Ernie Davies was third in the AAA junior mile championship in 1939. In 1942 he was in North Africa chasing the retreating Germans. In their hurried departure much equipment was left behind and Ernie collected an interesting souvenir – a German Olympic vest. From the Far East the club received a cablegram from Frank Neal saying simply: 'Have made it.' It referred to his escape from Japanese occupied Singapore.

Some of Birchfield's 'old timers' passed away during the war. Charlie Wood died in 1940. He had been the oldest living member. With him went the last link with the club's foundation. He had been present at the meeting that gave birth to the Birchfield Harriers in 1876. Two of the scorers from the 1886 National, George Savage and Tom Thornton, died in 1943. Thornton's running kit had been carefully preserved for over fifty years and was buried with him. J.E. Fowler-Dixon also passed away that year, at the age of ninety-three. He was one of the founders of the AAA in 1880. In his time he had been an outstanding ultra distance man and was remembered for running forty miles in 4:46:54 at the Lower Grounds on 29 December 1884.

The later years of the war generally produced brighter news from members overseas, but there were some sickening blows. Lieutenant Geoff Wallbank was killed in North Italy in October 1944, at the age of twenty-one. Then, right at the end of the war, on 22 August 1945, Eddie Webster was killed in a traffic accident in Italy. He had been one of the great Birchfield Harriers, winner of seven AAA Championships in the 1920s and International cross-country champion in 1924.

The POWs were eventually released and all returned home safely. There was still some concern over Bill Sanders who had been a prisoner of the Japanese. Nothing had been heard of him for a long time. Then the *Stagbearer* of October 1945 reported: 'It is indeed good news to hear that Bill is in India, freed from the Japs and hopes to be home soon.'

The friends from Chartres were in touch with the club as soon as the Allies had freed the town. A letter enquired: 'How are our good friends of the Birchfield Harriers? I hope the war has not claimed too many victims from the members of your club… Many members of our club have been killed in the war.' Birchfield Harriers returned to Chartres in January 1947 for an emotional reunion. In July of that year the Velo Sport Chartrain came to Birmingham and competed in the Waddilove meeting.

The Government were slow in releasing the stadium back to the club. Weekday training took place at the North Birmingham Schools ground off Wellhead Lane. Finally, the Italian POWs, who had been occupying the stadium for eighteen months, were evacuated in January 1946. The club moved back home the following month. It was in poor shape and there was much work to be done. All at Birchfield appreciated the words of Mr Philip Noel-Baker, the Parliamentary Secretary to the Minister of Transport: 'There will be more sport than ever after the war. This must help to pull the world together, heal its wounds and eventually assist in the reconciliation of the warring nations.'

Although the ground was in a deplorable state and the club was once more in dire financial straits, the teams got back to serious training and the results during 1946 were encouraging. The cross-country men won the Warwickshire and Midland Championships and were placed second in the National at Leamington. Bob Reid was the first Birchfielder home, beaten narrowly by Jack Holden of Tipton. Belgrave Harriers took the title with 96 points against 106 points for Birchfield. Reid was first home in both the Midlands and Scottish Championships.

The women walkers were beginning to form a strong team led by Miss M. Hart who won Midland and National Road Championships. The club celebrated the glory of a National Cross Country Championship victory with Pat Sandall first home in 1946.

1947 was a disastrous year for the men's teams in the National Cross Country and the London to Brighton relay. The coach carrying the team to the National at Aspley was brought to a halt by heavy snow and never got to the course, and the relay team failed to finish. However, the ladies kept the flag flying by winning the Midlands. The four scorers were: Mary Bartlett 3; Dolly Harris 4; Ivy Kibbler 5 and Mavis Harper 6. Then the quartet packed into the first six positions as they won the National at Oxford.

There was an upturn in the fortunes of the track runners as the men ran third in the 4 x 100 yards and third also in the 4 x 440 at the AAA Championships.

The London Olympics was the major event in 1948 but as far as Birchfield was concerned the big news of the year was the victory of the ladies in the National at Sutton Park. This was the third win in succession. Ivy Kibbler won the race and she was well supported by P. Sandall 7, D. Baldero 8 and Mary Bartlett 13.

The men's victory in the Midland race was really convincing. With six in the first eighteen they totalled 54 points to that of 125 points for runners-up Godiva. Bob Reid was first home for the third successive time.

The standing of the club in these years was similar to the pre-war era. The cross-country teams were producing excellent results, but in track and field the victories at area and national level were few. Winnie Jordan won the WAAA 100 metres, and she and Gladys Clarke in the javelin, plus Sidney Cross in the triple jump, made the Olympic team. However, cross-country running and road running remained the club's strength.

In 1947 the women upheld the tradition in their National at Worsley. They won the race for the fourth consecutive year with Mary Bartleet and Zoe White in fourth and fifth respectively.

In April there was a much better showing by the men in the London to Brighton relay. Fast legs by Ted Dalton and Freddie Green took Birchfield into second place behind Belgrave. There were notable wins in the Thames Valley Relay over four stages, and the Manchester to Blackpool over eleven stages.

Shortly after the cessation of the Second World War the club had decided to allow Birmingham Speedway to hire the stadium for its matches on Saturday nights. Speedway was a booming sport and the revenue generated went a long way to providing for the upkeep of the ground. Floodlighting was installed for the motorcycle racing. The lights were mounted on stands around the track so that it could be flooded with light leaving the infield in darkness. Birchfield did not immediately see the advantage to athletics. However, at an athletics meeting in the spring of 1948 the proceedings went on into the evening and in the gathering dusk the call went out to 'put the lights on'. Then it became apparent. Athletics looked marvellous under floodlights. The idea of a floodlit meeting was born.

From a spectators' point of view the old stadium had an advantage over many new stadiums. There were no long-jump pits or pole-vault runways between the crowd and the track. The crowd was right there alongside the runner in the outside lane and under floodlights it provided an exciting atmosphere for athletes and the paying public.

The first floodlit meeting at the Alexander Stadium was staged in September 1948. It was a modest venture with local athletes taking part. The potential for a large scale, star spangled meeting was there for all to see. The following year the meeting, held on a Wednesday, featured a three cornered inter-city match, Birmingham v. London v. Manchester. However, it was the 1950 event that established the 'Floodlit' as a major meeting in the calendar.

The masterstroke was securing the entry of Fanny Blankers-Koen. The Dutch athlete was one of the superstars of her day. In the 1948 Olympics in London she had taken four gold medals. In the European Championships, this year, she had won three gold medals.

In Birmingham she was feted. At the Hercules factory she was presented with bicycles for her two children. On the track she made light work of winning the 100m and later the 80m hurdles. The meeting was a huge success and the crowd of 14,000 was said to have been the largest to have watched athletics in the Midlands, at that time.

The subsequent meetings were held on the first Saturday in October. The 1952 event brought Fanny Blankers-Koen back to the Alexander Stadium on a cold, windy night. Injury had prevented a defence of her titles in Helsinki that year but in Birmingham she took part in four events: the two sprints, high hurdles and long jump. She won them all and the long jump victory must have been particularly satisfying because she defeated the new Olympic Champion, Yvette Williams of New Zealand.

By now London had discovered the delights of floodlit athletics and Birchfield had to contend with meetings at the White City. The 1953 meeting went on without any stars. Nevertheless, the action was received with great enthusiasm by the crowd, which was estimated to have grown to 15,000. Birchfielder Fred Green had an outstanding season that year, setting a world record for the three miles at the AAA Championships. At the 'Floodlit' he ran the mile and pulled off a fine win in his best ever time of 4:08. Gordon Pirie set a new British record for the four miles at 18:35.6.

However, it was foreign stars and an international flavour that the crowd really wanted. In 1955 Birchfield were able to provide that. Seigfried Hermann from East Germany beat Ken Wood in the mile and Lang Stanley of the USA held off local boys Mike Farrell and Mike Rawson in the 880 yards.

In subsequent years it became difficult to attract the Birmingham public to the meeting. Television viewing was taking over as a national pastime and it seemed that only the true fans of athletics were prepared to attend. In the late 1950s the meeting was generally an all-British affair but still of a high standard. Birchfield had to seek a sponsor to keep the meeting afloat. The crowd was down to around 5,000.

The 1957 meeting was notable for the absence of Gordon Pirie and the presence of Derek Ibbotson. Pirie drew flak from press and spectators alike for his unexplained failure to appear. Yet Ibbotson, a glutton for competition, ran two races. He won the two miles in 8:57.4 and came back later to take the mile in 4:08.7. Peter Radford made his debut at the 'Floodlit' with a third place in the 100 yards. This did not escape the attention of a local reporter who wrote: 'I predict a great future for this eighteen year old.'

Radford began fulfilling this prediction in 1958. At the 'Floodlit', on a soft track, he won the 100 yards in a wind-assisted 9.4 and then in the last event he took the 220 yards in 21.0 to better an English native record that had stood for over forty years.

In 1960 the meeting attracted the superstar it needed. Herb Elliot, fresh from his 1,500m victory in the Rome Olympics, ran in a specially arranged three-quarter mile race. He appeared to coast to an easy win

Fanny Blankers-Koen (right) receives flowers from Mrs Geoff Austin.

in a time of 2:58.8 saying afterwards that the track was too muddy for a faster time. Muddy or not, Robbie Brightwell ran 47.5 for the 440 yards and Peter Radford 21.1 in the 220 yards.

The 1964 event had a special significance. The Tokyo Olympics were weeks away and places in the team were yet to be filled. The sprint relay squad had not been named and the 100 yards was a final trial. There was celebration for Birchfield supporters as Peter Radford sped to victory in 9.7. Other Birchfield members of the Tokyo team were also on view. Brightwell was second to Radford in the 220 yards and 400m hurdler John Cooper ran the 400m, finishing second to Adrian Metcalfe. Howard Payne won the hammer and Daphne Arden the 100 yards.

The twentieth and final floodlit meeting was staged in 1967. This featured a junior men's match, Midlands v. South, with a number of invitation events thrown in. Poor fare, perhaps, for what had been in the early years an outstanding meeting. Nevertheless, the sparse crowd were able to see three runners whose names are as prominent as any in the history of British athletics as a whole. There were two two-mile races. One was in the junior match and the other was a Senior Men's Invitation. Bruce Tulloh, the 1962 European 5,000m Champion, made his final appearance on a Midlands track, finishing second in a time of 8:41.6. In the match event, Ian Stewart won in 8:54.0 with David Bedford in fifth place.

So, with dwindling attendances the meeting was removed from the calendar. There were many athletes and spectators who bade farewell with fond memories of the Birchfield 'Floodlit'. It had had a special atmosphere.

Sixteen: Rising Stars

Birchfield was seventy-five years old in 1952, and was given the honour of promoting the National Cross Country Championship on its own course at Barr Beacon. The cross-country team, which hadn't done well for several years, showed a welcome sign of revival by coming fourth. The team followed this up by winning the London to Brighton National Relay title for the first time since 1931.

The following year it won the English Cross Country Championship at Reading, and in the Manchester to Blackpool Road Relay the club clocked up its thirteenth win in fourteen years.

The next two years saw the club placed second and third in the National Cross Country Championships but once Bob Reid retired from running and other stalwarts emigrated, unfortunately the performances deteriorated.

However, a new era was just beginning for Birchfield's fortunes on track. Freddy Green, a short, wiry, ex-paratrooper, finished second in the AAA three miles championship in 1953. This was merely a curtain raiser. The following year he broke the twelve-year-old world record for three miles, clocking 13:32.2, narrowly beating Chris Chataway who was given the same time. Birchfield's re-emergence as a great track and field force had come about.

Even when the club's fortunes were at a low ebb, it had always attracted the majority of the local athletic talent, and was a natural magnet for athletes settling or working temporarily in Birmingham. Around this time Diane Leather arrived on the scene, obviously oozing with talent. In 1955 Mike Rawson and Mike Farrell arrived, adding strength to the existing team. Peter Radford joined the club about two years later, and his sprinting ability pushed both Birchfield and British performances to the top.

Diane Leather, as was her maiden name, came to the club initially to get fit for hockey. This was not an unusual idea for dedicated sportswomen, and the sport had led to the foundation of the Ladies' Section in the early 1920s. Diane was about twenty years of age when she started attending every training session. In addition she cycled daily from her family home in Little Aston to Edgbaston to contribute to her fitness programme. Having joined in 1952, she quickly made her mark in cross-country running, being first in all the ladies' cross-country races of that year. By the end of 1953 she was involved in one world record, as the third member of a relay team running 3 x 880 yards in 6:49.0 and later she ran a mile for an English native record of 5:2.6. Her prowess over the country was shown early in 1954, when she won the Midland

and Senior Cross Country Championships and subsequently the England *v.* Scotland race. Then on 29 May, at the Midland WAAA Championships, she was the first woman in the world to break the five-minute mile in the record time of 4:59.6. This record she achieved less than an hour after winning the 800 metres in 2:14.1. A new British all-comers record recorded twenty-three days after Roger Bannister achieved the first sub-four-minute mile.

By 1955 her running had become so powerful that on, 24 June, she ran a mile in 4:58.8 at the *Daily Mirror* Cavalcade of Sport at the White City. This was a new world's best. Then, on 21 September 1955, at the Floodlit Sports, again at White City, she lowered this record to 4:45.0.

Her athletics career continued with great resolution and she ran first in most championship races from 1956 to 1958 and continued to represent England and Great Britain through to 1958. Her final two years of competition were in 1959 and 1960 and finished at club level at Brighton on 9 July 1960. That day she ran an 800m race in 2:10.0 and was selected for the 1960 Olympic Games in Rome where the event was being reintroduced to the Games. Diane was also appointed Vice-Captain.

When Mike Rawson won the 800m at the European Championships in Stockholm in 1958 he became the first Birchfielder since the war to win one of the major international championships. Mike was born in Hall Green, Birmingham in 1934 and went to Solihull School. His start in athletics was quite modest. He did not show outstanding ability as a schoolboy or youth, but he was keen and prepared to train hard. After National Service in the Army he joined the club in 1954 and came under the guidance of Lionel Pugh. His mentor was also coaching Mike Farrell. Rawson and Farrell trained together, raced against each other, and made a formidable pairing in inter-club contests.

Rawson broke through to international class quite suddenly in 1956 when he won an 800m in Turkey in 1:49.7 and followed up by winning the Midlands and AAA Championships. He had come from obscurity to the front rank of British half-milers and he was selected for matches with Czechoslovakia and Hungary. More importantly, he earned a place in the team for the Melbourne Olympics in 1956. He narrowly missed getting through to the final but his training partner, Mike Farrell, was able to go one better by qualifying and finishing fifth.

Above left: Freddy Green pips Chris Chataway.

Above right: Diane Leather.

Mike Farrell in a heat of the 880 yards, Cardiff. (right)

In the 1957 season Rawson established himself as one of the top British 800m men alongside Derek Johnson and Brian Hewson. His best time came down to 1:47.5 and he ran 47.6 for 400 metres. He took maximum points in three of the four international matches that he ran. This was a prelude to his best ever season.

His campaign for 1958 aimed at peaking for the Commonwealth and European Championships. He regained the Midland title, which he had lost to Farrell in 1957, and ran second in the AAA Championships. In this race he finished behind Hewson but ahead of Australian superstar Herb Elliot. At the Commonwealth Games in Cardiff he was third to Hewson and Elliot in a race that featured a very fast second lap. Then, a month later, came his European success, gained under extraordinary circumstances.

In those days the staggered start was not used for half-mile or 800m races. This often led to a battle for position in the early stages. This was the case in Stockholm. Rawson's semi-final was warfare for which one athlete was disqualified. Mike only just made the final in fourth place. In the final he ran superbly, producing a really tenacious effort to go past three men in the last forty metres and win the race. He then found himself disqualified for running a few strides on the infield when he was charged off the track in the scramble on the first bend. It took three hours for the jury of appeal to quash the disqualification and award him the gold medal.

Mike Rawson made a vital contribution to the club's success in 4 x 400m relays. Birchfield won the Midland title seven times between 1955 and 1961, and the AAA Championships five times in this period. After a short retirement Mike came back to win the AAA Indoor Championships at 440 yards in 1965, before moving into the family business. Mike also kept up an interest in coaching and radio sports reporting.

Birchfield had to wait a long time to produce a national men's sprint champion. From 1880 to 1956 there had been a number of MCAAA champions at 100 and 220 yards, including Billy Green with his string of victories in the 1930s. However, no one had recently taken an AAA Championship title, or indeed been the first Briton home.

The first Birchfielder to claim an AAA sprint title was John Young, when he won the 100 yards in 1956. He had an outstanding season that year, taking Midland Senior and Junior, AAA Junior, and English Schools Championships. Much was expected of him but he was never able to fulfil the promise demonstrated in 1956. After two more seasons he retired from the sport to concentrate on rugby.

The club did not have to wait long to find another outstanding young sprint prospect. Seventeen-year-old Peter Radford joined in July 1957. His rise was as spectacular as that of Young, but he went on to develop his potential. Peter became the most successful sprinter in the club's history before the current era. He competed as a Birchfielder for seven years with his most notable performances in the years 1958 to 1960.

Peter Radford was born in Walsall on 20 September 1939. As a child he had the misfortune to contract a serious kidney disease and might have been an invalid for life. Happily, he recovered completely and took up running at the age of twelve. Peter was a natural sprinter, who even then showed the makings of a champion. He ran 10.4 for 100 yards at fourteen, and took Midland Junior and English Schools Championships before joining the Birchfield Harriers. Here, he was taken on by the Midland area coach, Bill Marlow.

Peter recalls his reason for joining the club. 'Walsall had no athletics club or track. I was very ambitious at that age and wanted good competition. I also felt the need to run in good relay teams.' He was soon to find good competition in the shape of Robbie Brightwell who, although the same age, had developed physically and generally had the edge in their contests in 1957, particularly over 220 yards. The running careers of John Young and Peter Radford also overlapped. Young finished in front of Radford in the 'Floodlit' of 1957 but it was Radford first, Young second in the Inter Counties 100 yards early in the 1958 season. Comparison of their physique and style is interesting. Young, shorter and more powerful, had well-defined leg muscles, was fast out of the blocks with a short staccato stride. Radford, leaner and more fluent, was not a fast starter but came on strongly over the second half of the short sprint showing a whippy action and high knee-lift.

1958 was the year Peter Radford became British number one. His training was geared to peak performances late in the season and that is what happened. After the Inter Counties win and tests against Brightwell over 220 yards, Marlow withdrew him from the AAA Championships and concentrated his efforts on the Commonwealth Games in Cardiff in July. In this, his first international event, he reached the final of the 100 yards, finishing fourth in 9.7. He then made the semi-final of the 220 where he recorded 21.5. Peter then ran the first leg for the England team, which won the 4 x 110 yards relay. A week later he made the headlines with a win over Gardner, Robinson and Agostini – the three athletes who had finished ahead of him in the 100 yards final in Cardiff. Moving on to the European Championships in Stockholm in August, Peter was third in the 100m in a time of 10.4. He also ran in the relay team which finished second to the West Germans. All this at eighteen years of age.

In 1959 he held his ground as the top British sprinter, producing a UK record of 9.5 at the Alexander Stadium. At club level he helped Birchfield win the AAA 4 x 110 yards relay for the first time. In October there was some fine sprinting indoors in Essen, West Germany. In a series of 50m races he won the final in 5.5.

So to Olympic year, 1960: the young man was regarded as a medal prospect and his early season form endorsed that. At Aldersley Stadium, Wolverhampton, on 28 May, he not only improved his UK record for 100 yards with 9.4 but also set a new World best for the 220 yards with 20.5. Further times of 10.3 for 100m in June, and 29.9 for 300 yards in August indicated that he had peaked in time for the Olympics.

At the Rome Games, Peter made his way through the first two rounds of the 100m. He then won his semi-final and lined up for the final with the American trio of Sime, Budd and Norton as well as Figuerola of Cuba and Hary of West Germany. The race description comes from Mel Watman in *Athletics Weekly*:

'At the third attempt the field got away to a perfect start, with Radford perhaps the worst away. A gasp from the crowd as Hary's phenomenal pick-up catapulted him a yard ahead at forty, cheers as he held on to part of that lead right through to the tape... Radford coming through very well indeed for a close third... He looked crestfallen, I can't imagine why, because he ran a wonderful race and equalled his UK record of 10.3 in the process.'

The 1960 season was his last as a major force on the world scene. In subsequent years he was one of the top British sprinters but not the undoubted best that he had been. However, he was a regular selection for the British relay squad. In 1962, in Perth, Australia, he was in the English sprint relay team that retained

Peter Radford.

the title won in Cardiff. He was also a member of the Great Britain 4 x 110 yards relay team (along with another Birchfielder, Welshman Berwyn Jones), who beat the USA and equalled the world record of 40.0 on 3 August 1963.

A late selection for the Tokyo Olympics in 1964, his running in the 100m was not that of the Peter Radford of four years before. He was eliminated in the second-round heats, but he did run first leg for the relay team who lowered the UK record to 39.6. At that point he decided to retire from the track at the age of twenty-five. Knee ligament problems had bothered him for some time and that understandably made him reassess the future.

Eventually he became Professor Peter Radford, Head of the Physical Education Department at Glasgow University and Chief Executive of the British Athletic Federation. He has this to say about his time with the club:

'I look back on my Birchfield days with very great pleasure, for no athlete can have had more encouragement, support and friendship than I had from my fellow Birchfield Harriers. I trained regularly at the old Alexander Stadium on Tuesdays, Thursdays and Sunday afternoons. Some of the training sessions live vividly in my memory, and the sessions of 330s with Johnny Salisbury, Tony Shaw, Don Hitchman and others became part of Birchfield folklore.'

Seventeen: Local Heroes

Peter Radford had won the bronze medal in the 100m in Rome and both he and Welshman Nick Whitehead were in the 4 x 100m relay team which finished in the bronze-medal position. The fourth medal to be brought home was that of Carole Quinton, who finished second in the 80m hurdles.

Born in Birmingham in 1937, Carole joined Birchfield while still at school. She was spotted by Mrs Nelson-Neal, who noted her sprinting form and saw a potential hurdler. Nelson coached her in sprints and hurdles and she developed quickly into one of the best prospects in the Midlands.

Carole first caught the eye when she won the 80m hurdles at the Midland Championships in 1955. The same afternoon she was second in the 100 yards and third in the 220 yards. The following season, aged nineteen, she was taken on by the Midlands area coach, Lionel Pugh.

At 5 feet 8 inches, slim and long legged, Carole's technique was admired by the purists. She won the Midlands again in 1956 and was placed fourth in her first WAAA Championships. Then, by a series of victories over the AAA medallists, she was selected for the Melbourne Olympics. This was her first taste of international competition. She justified selection by getting through to the semi-finals and running a time of 11.4. Looking back at Melbourne, she said that the experience there had encouraged her to work much harder in training and was a major factor in her subsequent success.

Although beaten by Thelma Hopkins in the WAAA in 1957, Carole finished the season strongly. She twice equalled the English native record of 11.2. By then she was generally considered to be the top British hurdler. In 1958 Carole established herself in this position by winning the WAAA and finishing a close second in the Commonwealth Games to an Australian, Norma Thrower. Later that year she set a new British record of 10.9 in the European Championships where she was fourth in the final.

Carole had a depressing year in 1959, never hitting top form and losing regularly to Mary Bignal. However, things changed for the better in 1960. She re-established herself as the British number one and went on to achieve the best performance of her career with the silver medal in the Rome Olympics to Irena Press of the USSR. This was the highest placing by a British athlete, man or woman, in any track or field event in Rome. She retired in 1961.

Carole Quinton (centre). John Salisbury (right).

Right: Robbie Brightwell.

Below: Daphne Arden pips Mary Bignal Rand and Dorothy Hyman.

At that time there were changes in the administration of the club. Under new secretary Len Orton, assisted by Alan Stockford and Tony Shaw, a new era began. They ensured that the club was open more frequently for training, more contact was made with schools and, despite the deteriorating condition of the ground, more sports meetings were held. However, they resisted an approach to reintroduce speedway racing in 1962 – despite the potential immediate financial benefit for the club. The sport had been revived for a short season of open licence meetings on Friday nights between May and September 1960. The world's top stars were employed to contest challenge matches between Birmingham and leading National League teams of the era. Meetings were promoted by Doug Ellis, who subsequently moved from speedway into football with his acquisition of Aston Villa FC. In an interview in the *5-1* speedway magazine in 1996, Mr Ellis claimed that the city council put pressure on the club and himself to find triple the rent for the 1961 season because of the high attendances, and so the roar of the bikes was never heard again at this venue.

The ground was a real headache. There was nothing like enough money to maintain it, and although many public-spirited members formed work parties, it was clear that what had once been a great asset was fast becoming a serious liability. Many schemes were considered, but nothing came to fruition. At one time there had been negotiations between the club and Birmingham Parks' Department to develop the ground jointly and with other concerns, but these had foundered. Now the Management Committee racked their brains in an effort to solve the problem. There was a comparatively easy option. Birchfield could sell up and move further out of the city. Many felt reluctant to leave the traditional stamping ground. Also, they felt the club had a duty to remain in the area – where it could be easily reached by young and aspiring athletes from Birmingham.

Whilst everyone was concerned about the future of the ground, nothing could prevent the athletes from continuing their run of successes. In 1963 Birchfield regained the 4 x 400 yards AAA Championship title in a new record time of 3:13.

1964 brought the Tokyo Olympics and the twists and turns in the running career of Robbie Brightwell. Born in India, 27 October 1939, Robbie came to school in England immediately after the war. At school he showed up well as a sprinter and took an English Schools Championship at 220 yards. He entered Loughborough College in 1959 and there turned his attention to the 440 yards. Although he declared a dislike for the event he was, at 6 feet 2 inches and with a strong build, the archetypal quarter-miler. While at Loughborough he joined Birchfield and linked up with Mike Rawson, Mike Farrell, John Cooper and Johnny Salisbury – a most impressive 4 x 400m relay squad.

At the age of eighteen, Brightwell was blooded in two major championships: the Commonwealth Games, at which he ran the 220 yards and made the semi-finals, and the European Championships, at which he made the final. In 1960, at the age of twenty, he went to the Olympics as the leading British 400m man. He was run out in the semi-final but recorded a British record of 46.1.

In the early 1960s he vied with an Oxford student, Adrian Metcalfe, for the position as number one British quarter-miler. Robbie finished ahead of his rival in the races that mattered. In 1962 he won the European 400m Championship and finished second to George Kerr of Jamaica in the Commonwealth Games. In 1964 at the Tokyo Olympics he brought his running career to a close. He finished fourth in the 400m and ran a tremendous last leg for the British team which took the silver medals in the 4 x 400m.

This is how Mel Watman of *Athletics Weekly* concluded an article on Robbie Brightwell in March 1965. He describes the Tokyo races:

'In his semi-final he scored over Mottley and Williams on the soggy track in a majestic 45.7, while Larrabee won the other heat in 46.0.

Victory was possible the next day, but when it came to the final – the race for which he had trained so hard (three sessions daily at times), the race he must have run and re-run hundreds of times in his troubled sleep – he choked under the nervous pressure. Give or take a yard or two he ran as fast as he had ever done... but it was mechanical, passionless. On the right day that opening 200 metres of 21.7 would have paved the way to a time of about 45 seconds, but this was not the right day for Robbie and he could not handle the pace. By the time he entered the finishing straight he knew he had lost, and there was no fight left.

What a difference forty-eight hours later when Robbie ran his way into Olympic history with a relay performance of such outstanding courage that the 70,000 crowd rose to him in admiration. Racing the last

John Cooper.

lap of his career in 44.8 he carried his team from fourth to second in the final fifty metres before his legs gave way at the tape. Of such stuff are heroes made.'

In addition, John Cooper, the club captain, returned with two silver medals, one for the 400m hurdles and one for that 4 x 400m relay. Daphne Arden came home with a bronze from the 4 x 100m relay.

The club's successes in 1964 were outstanding. It competed in twenty-nine senior and junior meetings, winning twenty-seven of them, and returning with ten senior trophies. Once again it had taken the 4 x 400 yards AAA title with an excellent team consisting of John Salisbury, Mike Rawson, John Cooper and Robbie Brightwell. After this list of successes, Birchfield also won the 'Club of the Year' nomination awarded by the National Union of Track Statisticians.

The following years, 1965 and 1966, were comparatively quiet. Many of the club stalwarts of the previous decade retired. The two Mikes who had given so much to the club turned their attention to Midlands athletics' administration. Peter Radford took up a post in Canada. Tony Shaw became a football administrator and others became interested in coaching.

Plans to encourage new youngsters were made, and there was to be a special emphasis on coaching and competition. As a result of this, the juniors started to show their promise and, in 1966, the Great Britain Under-Twenty team contained eight athletes from Birchfield.

Although none of the juniors reached the 1968 Olympics in Mexico City, Birchfield was still able to provide a record number of five men and three women for the Great Britain squad. John Sherwood was the most successful of them, gaining a bronze in the 400m hurdles in a thrilling race won by David Hemery. The following year at the 1969 European Championships in Athens, John gained a silver medal in the 400m hurdles. Pat Lowe did the same in the 4 x 400m relay. Birchfield's greatest success, however, was in the 5,000m where Ian Stewart, still only twenty years old, ran like a seasoned athlete to take the gold medal. This was the beginning of Ian's great international career, and also of the remarkable Stewart family contribution to Birchfield Harriers.

In domestic competition, Birchfield's position as the leading track and field team was confirmed. The club won the first British Athletics League title after a great battle over four meetings defeating Thames Valley

Harriers by one point in the final match. The margin was so narrow that every team member could feel that it was his personal performance that had clinched it! No one would deny the role of the captain, John Cooper. He encouraged, threatened and swore his team to the title. It was a tragedy in every sense of the word when this popular athlete was killed in the Paris air crash of 1974.

John, who was born in 1940, joined the club while at Loughborough College in 1960. From then, until his death in March 1974, he was a spirited supporter of Birchfield and competed at club level more often than many athletes who attain international status.

His obituary, written by Mel Watman in *Athletics Weekly* on 16 March 1974, was a tribute to a man who is still remembered with affection by all who knew him.

'John Cooper was one of the most tenacious competitors I have ever seen and an inspiration to all around him; a man who by hard work, perseverance and grit rose to the heights of Olympic silver medallist. His rugged determination to succeed and his basically serious but jokey personality made him a valued member of the British team from 1961 to 1969. In the context of 400m hurdling history he was Britain's finest competitor since the days of Lord Burghley in the late 1920s and early 1930s and the immediate predecessor of David Hemery, John Sherwood and Alan Pascoe.'

John began at an early age as a hurdler (over 80 yards) and then achieved some success as a triple jumper. He was English Schools intermediate champion in 1957 and reached 13.81m at the age of sixteen and took up quarter-mile hurdling in 1960. Next winter while a student teacher at Loughborough, he came under the coaching influence of Geoff Gowan and in seemingly no time at all he was one of the country's leading hurdlers. He improved from 56.5 for 440 yards hurdles in 1960 to 52.0 for 400m in 1961. His next breakthrough came in 1963, when he broke the UK record with 50.5 and established himself as a competitor of the highest class – 'the scourge of Europe's hurdlers' is how one account described him at the time.

Only a comparative lack of flat speed (48.6 for 440 yards) was holding him back and during the winter of 1963/64 he worked very hard at it as he trained alongside Robbie Brightwell. The full extent of his progress was not appreciated until he ran a 400m relay leg against Olympic champion-to-be Mike Larabee at the White City in August 1964. This was a run that typified all that one admired most in John Cooper, and to quote from the *Athletics Weekly* report: 'How was Cooper (best time of 47.9) going to hold on to Larabee, a good second and a half faster than he, in order that Brightwell might stand a chance against Cassell? The only possible answer was for Cooper to hang grimly on to the American's heels for 350 metes or so, so that he could reasonably expect to maintain a forty-six-second pace and trust to guts and any luck that might be flying about for the finishing straight. Cooper clung like a leech to his man around the first bend, along the back straight and into the final turn. Now he must weaken... but no, miraculously Larabee was unable to move away from his tenacious opponent. Only that single stride's length separated them. One shudders to imagine the agony Coop must have experienced along that never ending finishing straight, but one hopes that the deafening cheers accorded him as he handed over barely three yards down were sufficient reward.'

Brightwell went on to anchor the British squad to victory, and Cooper's heroic run indicated that his goal of winning the Olympic 400m hurdles later in the season was not merely wishful thinking. The powerfully built Birchfield Harrier went to Tokyo ranked tenth for the year among the contenders with 50.6, equalled the UK record with 50.5 in his heat, improved to 50.4 in the semi-finals and placed second to Rex Cawley in the final with 50.1. John was riding on the crest of a wave; after a 45.8 relay leg in the heats he contributed a 45.6 in the final to gain, along with Tim Graham, Adrian Metcalfe and Robbie Brightwell, another silver medal, the team running a superb European record of 3:01.6 behind the USA.

Those races in Tokyo constituted the peak of John's career. The sparkle was missing in 1965 and he was injured in 1966, but he made a good comeback in 1968 to reach the Olympic semi-finals in Mexico City and clock 50.8, his best time since Tokyo. John Cooper will be remembered with admiration and affection by all of us who were privileged to have known him or simply watched him.

A letter from Tom McCook, now Club President, writing on behalf of the club was published on 23 March. It contained the following memories of 'Coop'.

'Despite his considerable fame and international successes, John went out of his way to welcome and encourage newcomers to the team irrespective of age or how talented they may have been. His good advice and words of encouragement contributed greatly in helping myself, and many others to settle in a new club, and in a new environment.

His enthusiasm was also channelled into assisting Dick Taylor of Coventry Godiva to break the UK two miles record at the Ashby Trophy Meeting at Leamington in 1967. Aware there were not enough spectators to build up atmosphere for Dick, "Coop" positioned every athlete not in the race around the track to urge Taylor on to the record.

It was, I believe, no coincidence that Birchfield enjoyed so much success in the sixties whilst John was a key member of the club. Important as his own point scoring efforts were, perhaps even more important was his enthusiasm and persuasiveness in ensuring that our top athletes turned out in the matches that mattered… John Cooper has left his friends many cherished memories.'

Eighteen: A Family Affair

Ian Stewart is regarded as one of the greatest, if not the greatest, Birchfield athlete in the club's history. He was born in Handsworth in 1949, one of the six children of John and Mary Stewart. The Stewarts were a remarkably successful family of athletes. The second child, and eldest son, Peter, who was born in Musselburgh near Edinburgh in 1947, set British records at one and two miles and won the European Indoors 3,000 metres Championship in 1971. The fourth of the line, and second eldest daughter, Mary, was born in Kings Norton in 1956. She set a world record for the 1,500m indoors (4:08.1) in 1977. Mary was the European Indoor Champion in the same year, and the Commonwealth Games Champion in Edmonton in 1978. Her record survived for twenty years.

To many, Ian is remembered for his victory in the 5,000m at the 1970 Commonwealth Games in Scotland. Here, in front of his 'home' crowd he beat Ian McCafferty and two legendary distance stars, Kip Keino and Ron Clarke, in a new European record of 13:22.8. However, this was only the tip of the iceberg in a remarkable career.

Initially with Small Heath Harriers, Ian moved to Birchfield Harriers after a short time to join his brother Peter. The brothers were coached by Geoff Warr, whom they amiably referred to as the 'Fat Man'! They both showed great potential and under Warr's guidance made rapid progress. Ian's first notable successes were over the country. He was Midland Youths Champion in 1966, runner-up in the Youths National in 1967, and both Midlands and National Champion at junior level in 1968.

In 1969, his first year as a senior, he moved straight into the front rank of top class distance runners. By then he was cutting back on cross-country races to include some indoor events. Ian announced his arrival with victory in the European Indoors 3,000m. Then, at the end of the 1969 track season, came his first major triumph, winning the European 5,000m in Athens. A title the teenager was particularly pleased to win, as nobody believed he had a chance of a medal.

Ian recalls:

'I don't think anyone expected me to get in the final, far less win it. Not even my coach and I really expected to win.

Ian Stuart wins the 1970 Commonwealth 5,000m in Edinburgh.

Peter Stewart (B22)
passes to John Potts.

I was coached at the time by Geoff Warr. I'd been with him from the age of fifteen, when I was a 5:07 miler. We both felt that I might get a medal if everything went absolutely right. It turned out to be an opportunity not to be missed. In the final, I had that winning feeling all of 600 metres from the line. That's how good I felt. Rene Jourdan from France had led through 800 in 2:12 and Mike Baxter, another of the GB men, was ahead at 1,600 but I injected some pace at 1,700.

I was worried about an East German called Bernd Diessner. He was following me all the time and I thought: "He's got to do some work", so I gave way. In fact the Soviet pair Ivan Shaopsha and Rashid Sharafutdinov, rather than the canny East German were catapulted to the front and went through 4,000 in 11:12.2.

At 600 metres I strode out just to see how the other boys were going. I was a long way out – 600 or even 800 – when I felt I could win. Sharafutdinov overtook me with 200 to go but I remained unruffled. I had a look at his face and he was just dying. I was striding along. He was sprinting.

Obviously the other runners had not done their homework, otherwise they wouldn't have run just the race I wanted. Heat and humidity never bothered me. It was just like that again when I won the World Cross in Rabat. But it was the win in Athens that changed my lifestyle. Although I ran a far superior race the following year in the Commonwealth Games in Edinburgh, everybody expected me to do well there. They hadn't given me a chance in Athens. That's why it was so special.'

That successful year set him up for 1970 and the epic race at the Meadowbank Stadium, Edinburgh. Prior to the Commonwealth Games, in April of that year, he made his debut for the club in the National Twelve-Stage Road Relay in Sutton Park. Ian ran a long leg in the record time of 25:13. He wound up his preparations for the Games with a 5,000m race in Stockholm. Stewart was pipped on the line by the German, Harald Norpoth, in a thrilling clash.

Ian Stewart was now in the public eye and with the adulation came some criticism. His detractors said that he was too motivated and too aggressive. These comments came from those who did not understand the intense competitive pressure on a top-class athlete, when anything other than victory is considered failure. His single-minded dedication to winning the big races produced an attitude that served him well and generated some magnificent performances.

In 1971 Ian ran for Scotland for the first time in the International Cross Country at San Sebastian, finishing ninth. It was generally a bad year for him. Plagued by injury and illness, most of the track season was missed. So the chance to defend his European title in Helsinki went too. However, he did put in some excellent training sessions in the winter of 1971/72 and turned his attention to the Munich Olympics. Third place in the International Cross Country in April showed that Ian was back to top form.

Peter also worked hard during that winter and his form on track in 1972 showed that he had a genuine chance of a medal in the 1,500m at Munich. He won the Elmsley Carr Mile in a new UK record of 3:55.3 and the AAA Championship at 1,500m in 3:38.2, which was also a UK record. His selection was a formality, but fate dealt him a cruel blow. In the weeks leading up to the Games he developed sciatica and was forced to withdraw, which allowed Brendan Foster, who had only finished fourth in the trials, to take his place. The problem effectively ended his ambitions to run at the highest level, a terrible disappointment for a naturally talented athlete.

Ian went to the Games with high hopes. He was in excellent physical and mental shape. In these Games the 5,000m attracted great attention from the British media and much was expected from Stewart, McCafferty and David Bedford. In a race characterised by a finishing phase of prolonged and sustained speed after a pedestrian first 3km, in which the leading group ran the last mile in just over four minutes, Ian was beaten into third place by one of the great Olympic Champions, Lasse Viren. Ian overtook the American Steve Prefontaine in the last few strides to snatch that bronze medal. He was devastated. For a man so dedicated to winning he thought it was an abject failure. Yet, Ian Stewart had achieved something that had defied some of the greatest names in British distance running such as Gordon Pirie, Chris Chataway, Derek Ibbotson, David Bedford and Brendan Foster. Ian Stewart had won medals at 5,000m in the three major events: Commonwealth, European and Olympic Games.

At club level he continued his contribution to the cause. 1973 saw him run a long leg in the National Twelve-Stage at Derby. Ian predicted that: 'The road is going to burn' and proceeded to reduce a 1:24 deficit to just four seconds on the ninth stage to ensure a Birchfield victory. Peter Stewart ran the 'glory leg' for the Stags.

In early 1974 Ian went for both the 5,000m and 10,000m at the Commonwealth Games in New Zealand. He finished fifth and sixth respectively. Afterwards Ian went through a period of introspection. Feeling stale and tired, he turned away from the track. He did not lose the need to expend energy, however, and started cycle racing. This lasted just one season before he began jogging and gradually his taste for athletics returned. In the winter of 1974/75 he recorded two very convincing wins in the Birmingham Cross Country League. Ian Stewart was back.

His form was most impressive and in April 1975 he pulled off an outstanding 'Spring double'. On 9 April in Katowice, Poland, he won the European Indoors 3,000m. A week later, in Morocco, Ian was the first man home in the newly instituted World Cross Country Championships, beating a field that included many of the world's best runners. Birchfield was well represented that day. Ray Smedley, in seventh place, was the first English representative to finish. John Graham, also representing Scotland, was fifty-first in the junior race. Mary Stewart was eighth in the ladies' race.

The Montreal Olympics dominated Ian's thoughts in 1976. He aimed to double up again but concentrated his training on the longer distance. In the event, in an obvious blunder by the selectors, he was nominated only for the 5,000m. Ian finished seventh as Lasse Viren took his fourth Olympic Gold.

In 1977 he set out to show what he could produce at 10,000m. His first showing that year was an incredibly fast ten miles on the road in the 'Michelin' on 8 May. Ian detached himself from the field within the first mile and went on widening the gap until he finished over two minutes in front of the second man in 45:13. The super-fast time caused the organisers to measure the course again! It was found to be correct.

A month later Ian became the inaugural UK 10,000m Champion at Cwmbran, South Wales. At the end of the season at the 'Coke' meeting at Crystal Palace he was sixth in what was regarded as the greatest in depth field witnessed in Britain. His time of 27:43 was a career best.

A foot injury hampered his attempt to go for the marathon at the Moscow Olympics and a glorious international career wound down.

It is quoted of Ian Stewart MBE that on his best days he was 'mean, moody and magnificent'. In Birchfield Harriers' 'Hall of Fame' he will be remembered forever.

It is reasonable to suppose that Mary, as the younger sister of two outstanding runners, should feel the pressure of comparison. She claims that she was never conscious of such pressure. Indeed, her only complaint on this score was that her triumphs were not accorded the acclaim she felt was her due, for the reaction seemed to be: 'She's a Stewart, we expect her to win.'

Mary began running, and winning, at thirteen. That winter of 1969/70 she won all the local cross-country championships. The following season she once more outstripped the local opposition and went on to become National Junior Champion.

Mary Stewart.

On the track Mary began with the 800m, which was as far as the youngsters were allowed to go in those days, at least with respect to championships. However, she managed to get in a race at 1,500m in 1970 and gave the first indication that she might be of future international calibre by recording 4:38 – a world best for a fourteen year old. In fact, her international debut at the highest level was less than two years away.

In 1971 there were victories in both the National and English Schools as an intermediate. In the summer she followed her brothers and wore the blue of Scotland as a fifteen year old in a junior international 800m race. In the winter of 1971/72 her cross-country successes continued. On 12 February she won the Scottish Championship at intermediate level and two weeks later again won the English National the day after her sixteenth birthday. The Scots rewarded her outstanding form with selection for the senior international at Cambridge. The race was won by Joyce Smith of England with Mary in seventeenth place – the second Scot to finish.

On the track that year she represented Great Britain for the first time in a junior triangular match in Sweden. She ran the 1,500m and finished third in a time of 4:33.4. Later that season Mary brought the time down to 4:27.8, a UK best for an intermediate.

Mary was still only seventeen when she went to the Commonwealth Games in Christchurch in 1974 as the only Scottish selection for the 1,500m. Her fourth place in 4:14.7 again improved the UK age record. Although still a junior she had a wealth of international experience. Her time in Christchurch was the third best by a British runner that year.

In Olympic year, 1976, she was established as the British number one at 1,500m. It was encouraging when Mary lopped seconds off her personal best in a match with the USSR in Kiev in May. Her time of 4:06.4 behind the 1972 Olympic Champion Bragina, who finished in 4:05.3, boosted her Olympic chances considerably. In the event Mary's running was disappointing. Her tactics seemed to be suspect as she was crowded out in a fast finish in her semi-final. Her forte was following a fast pace rather than accelerating off a slow one.

The indoor season of 1977 provided consolation with a couple of splendid performances. In a match against West Germany in Dortmund on 19 February she set a world record with 4:08.1 and in March at San Sebastian she won the European Indoors in 4:09.4 to complete a unique family hat-trick.

Her most notable international victory came in the Commonwealth Games in Edmonton in 1978. Mary ran for England this time and was the favourite. She ran intelligently, gradually pulling back a sizeable lead set up by Christine Benning before striding past strongly in the home straight and winning in 4:06.3, a new Commonwealth Games record that survived for twenty years.

A month later in Prague she was the victim of bad luck in the European Championships. Going into the last lap of her heat, and well placed, she tripped and fell head first to the track. With the fall went her chance of progressing, but she got up and finished the race with her nose streaming blood.

In the winter of 1979/80 Mary may have decided that there were other factors in her life and at the age of twenty-four she announced her retirement from international competition. In September of 1980 Mary married international race walker Dave Cotton. The couple live in Staffordshire and have three children.

Mary was assistant team manager at the 1996 Olympic games in Atlanta. In addition to her achievements on the track, Mary had also won a women's cross-country title in the three age categories. A unique record on behalf of a unique family.

However, the story for Ian Stewart was not complete. In May 1991 Ian made a brief but triumphant return to the sport at the age of forty-two. He finished third in the Penkridge Ten Mile road race some twenty-two years after claiming his first major title. He completed the course in 50:48 – only thirty-two seconds behind the winner, Birchfield's twenty-four-year-old Andy Symonds. A month later Ian was at it again when he won the third of his comeback races as a veteran at Stoke. He recorded the outstanding time of 49:15 to finish fourth overall in a field of 1,200 in the prestigious Michelin Ten Mile race and over two minutes in front of the second placed veteran. His time was the fastest ever recorded by a British veteran and had only been bettered at world level by regular veteran runner John Campbell of New Zealand.

His reputation as an athlete was not forgotten even into a new century. Ian Stewart was inducted into Scotland's Hall of Fame at a glittering ceremony in Edinburgh on Saint Andrews Day 2002. It was publicly confirmed that he would always have a cherished place in the memories of Scottish sporting enthusiasts for that memorable 5,000m victory in the 1970 Commonwealth Games at Edinburgh's Meadowbank Stadium when Ian defeated a world class field, one of many great memories from a remarkable 'clan'.

Nineteen: New Horizons

By the early 1970s it was clear that with changed financial fortunes, largely due to loss of any substantial revenue from sub-letting the ground for other events, the club was once again in difficulties. Although it was performing in track and field events as well as ever, it was unable to maintain a full-time groundsman, and preparing the track for running events was proving onerous on voluntary labour.

At this time, the City fathers were finally moved to build a track and stadium worthy of the City, but they were fully aware that it was highly desirable to have an active and famous athletics club in place to make full use of the facilities that were to be provided.

After some prolonged negotiations, the club yielded all its freehold land and premises and track, which had been its home since 1928. This was in exchange for a 105-year lease at the new stadium. Interestingly, there was fierce division within the club as to whether this would be of long-term benefit or not. Various options were considered, including the possibility of relocating to a green-field site near Tamworth.

In November 1974, the City Council approved proposals for the provision of a stadium to be built just off the Walsall Road and in Perry Park. The site was only half a mile away from the old ground and so preserved the connection of Birchfield with Perry Barr. The first sod was cut on 9 June 1975, by Councillor Kenneth Barton, then Chairman of the Leisure Services Committee. A little over twelve months later, the track was completed as an all weather eight-lane track with facilities and equipment up to international standards. Unfortunately, costs, the economic recession and the decision not to stage the Commonwealth Games led to a reduction in the seating and room capacity of the stadium. This, in the early days, tended to restrict the ability to attract the major international events to the new stadium and therefore limited its media profile.

Slowly, in the years 1976 to 1978, the club transferred its training and athletics meetings to the new site. When all building work was completed, the new track and stadium was named the Birmingham Alexander

Stadium and officially opened on Sunday 11 June 1978 by the Lord Mayor of Birmingham, Councillor E.F. Hanson, in the presence of a gathering of invited guests, Birchfield Harriers and young school athletes. It was fitting that the opening event was the annual sports of the West Midland Schools Athletic Association. The local schools were therefore able to compete on an international standard track. The aim was that the youngsters would be encouraged to perform well and to take up the sport when their schooldays were over.

Meanwhile, the ladies had created a new record by filling the first four places in the Midland Senior Cross Country Championship. The order of merit was: Mary Stewart 1; Sue Hassan 2; Thelwyn Bateman 3 and Gillian Dainty 4.

Mary Stewart celebrated her twenty-second birthday by taking the National Senior Cross Country title at High Wycombe at her first attempt. After a clean sweep in the Midland Championships the hopes were high for a double victory. In the event the team were squeezed out of the medals by two points.

One of the ladies' teams did, however, succeed in winning both the Midland and National team titles. The walkers Sylvia Saunders and Virginia Lovell filled the first two places in the Midlands and with Mary Brown in seventh spot took the title with ten points. The same three finished second, fifth and tenth to become the National team champions.

The highlight of the men's winter season was the youth team victory in the English National Cross Country at Leeds for the second consecutive year. The quartet was: Micky Weaver 6; Ross Copestake 17; Martin Sprason 46 and Brian Tilley 49. They ensured a twenty-two-point margin of victory over local rivals Tipton.

The senior men's track and field team in Division Two of the British Athletics League had a desperately close contest throughout the season with Daley Thompson's Essex Beagles. In the first match in Edinburgh, Tony Hadley won the 400m in 49.3 seconds and anchored the 4 x 400 squad to victory in the relay. Phil Brown was second in the 200m and the team finished runners-up.

Birchfield capitalised on their home advantage in their improved facilities and won the second fixture. Tony Hadley again won the 400m, this time in 48.8. As they were to do in every match, the 4 x 400m squad came home first. Eric McCalla in the triple jump and Peter Lewis in the 800m also won their 'A' string events. The performance of the day, however, was a new Division Two record of 3:43.3 in the 1,500m by Olympian Ray Smedley.

Essex narrowly won the third match at Southampton and guaranteed a nailbiting finish at Hendon. The result of this match was in doubt until late in the day but the 4 x 400m proved to be the difference between the two teams. Both teams finished on twenty league points but Birchfield had the edge on aggregate match points by a slender eighteen points, 979 to 959, to be crowned National Division Two Champions.

With the first two Midland League matches clashing with BAL fixtures, considerable ground had to be made up during the final two matches. A satisfactory victory in the home fixture brought Birchfield into contention. An overwhelming victory at Wolverhampton gave the club the Midland League Division One title to add to their National title.

Not to be outdone, the ladies won Division Two of the UK League and were runners-up in the Midland League Division One. In addition, two ladies who had come through the ranks from the Junior Section won gold medals in the Commonwealth Games.

Sue Reeve had started the season by winning the bronze medal in the European Indoor long jump in Milan. Her best performance of 6.48m was a mere centimetre behind the silver medal winner. Sue, appropriately, won the inaugural major meeting to be staged in her home City – the English WAAA Commonwealth Games Trials. This led to the highlight of victory in the Commonwealth Games in Edmonton, Canada with a leap of 6.59m despite a damaged knee. In an interesting reversal of fortune, she won the gold medal by one centimetre!

As noted previously, in Edmonton Mary Stewart played a waiting game in the 1,500m and did not hit the front until the start of the final straight. Such was her determination that she covered the last lap in 63.6 seconds to win by eight metres.

The third Birchfield Harrier to mount the rostrum was Aston Moore in the triple jump. Aston had earlier won the AAA triple jump in a championship best performance of 16.68m at Crystal Palace while the rain lashed down on a chilly evening. To demonstrate his versatility Aston also created a championship personal best of 7.61m in winning the Midland long-jump title. He rounded off the season in Tokyo by leading and then finishing second to his hero, the legendary Viktor Sanyeyev, with a leap of 16.76m, which equalled the UK record.

The Young Athletes League team swept all before them. The final at Crystal Palace was the highlight. There were many personal bests recorded by team members to accumulate valuable points. Event winners were Peter Weir in the boys' discus and the shot putt, Phil Brown with 21.9 in the 200m, and Dave Bennett with a new record in the 1,500m steeplechase.

In what was to prove a foretaste of the pattern for a new rivalry for the next few years, the Stags won the National Young Athletes final by fifty-five points from Haringey.

The maturing of local youngsters, supplemented by newcomers, contributed towards a successful winter season. The long serving and versatile Ray Smedley won the final two First Division Birmingham Cross Country League races. In the National Twelve-Stage Road Relay the team had the satisfaction of improving by a massive six minutes on the previous year's ninth position to push Gateshead close for the Tyneside victory.

The objective of the senior men's track and field team was to retain the status of a Division One National League team following promotion in 1978. Eventually, the squad achieved second place in two of the four matches and finished fourth overall. The improvement was reflected in the upgrading from tenth position in the UK club rankings in 1978 to fifth in 1979.

The diminutive Ainsley Bennett made his mark internationally by taking bronze medals from both sprints in the World Student Games at altitude in Mexico City with excellent times of 10.21 for 100m and 20.42 for 200m. These equalled the British records.

Robert Weir established a UK age record in the hammer at the beginning of a career of amazing longevity, while Conroy Brown climaxed a successful AAA Championship for the club by winning the triple-jump title. Phil Brown was awarded his first senior international vest and was a member of the Great Britain sprint relay squad in the European Junior Championships.

The performance of the Ladies' Section was maintained at a high level through the year and ten members represented Great Britain that season. A new name to burst on the scene was Sara Harris who took both the Midland Intermediate Cross Country title and the WAAA Senior Indoor 3,000m title.

Despite all this good news, the new decade started with the disappointment of the unexpected announcement of the retirement of Mary Stewart at the age of twenty-four. Perhaps being a top international since the age of sixteen, with the years of preparation and dedication required to compete at that level, had taken their toll and dampened her zest. The club would have to seek new heroines from within their ranks.

Twenty: Raising the Bar

The ladies immediately rose to the challenge and added to their roll of honour by winning the National Senior Cross Country Championship, at Rugeley, for the twelfth time. The team packed their four scores into the first nineteen places. The heroines were: Angela Mason 6; Gillian Dainty 8; Susan Hassan 11 and Thelwyn Bateman 19.

It was an average year for the senior men over the country, fourth in the Midlands and eleventh in the National. However, the junior team gave the club a noteworthy victory and the first since the 1953 victory in the Senior National. Five in the first thirty-five saw the club gain its first ever victory in the race. The scoring quartet was: Alan Salter 10; Neil Appleby 20; Martin Sprason 30 and Dave Ellis 31.

The ladies continued their winning ways outdoors to win every match in Division Two of the National League in addition to winning the Midland League First Division title. Sue Reeve (long jump), Gill Dainty (1,500m), Cynthia Gregory (intermediate shot) and Karen Pugh (junior discus) achieved the status of British Champions by winning their events in the WAAA Championships. The highlight of the year was the selection of Sue Reeve for the Moscow Olympics in the long jump. Thirteen years previously as a precocious fifteen-year-old schoolgirl from Hodge Hill, Sue had won her first international vest in the pentathlon. The following year, in 1968, after the withdrawal through injury of the reigning Olympic Champion, Mary Rand, Sue travelled to Mexico for her first Olympics. She fought her way back from injury problems in the early 1970s to win the 1978 Commonwealth games and again, despite injury, reached the 1980 Olympic Final. The feat earned Sue Reeve the club's premier award, the Leah Wright Trophy, for the third successive year.

The senior men's track and field team, despite some individual victories, failed to turn out full strength teams and were relegated from Division One of the National League. The problem of international athletes being developed by the club – and then not turning out at league level – was understandably contentious.

However, there were some redeeming features. The club were Midland Senior Champions and the youngsters for the third successive season won the National Young Athletes Final by seventy-nine points over nearest rivals Shaftesbury at Crystal Palace.

In front of their home crowd in the AAA Junior Championships there were triumphs for Robert Weir and Lincoln Asquith. Robert displayed his versatility by taking both the discus and hammer titles. Lincoln accomplished the more conventional double in the Youths' sprints. Phil Brown at 200m and Conroy Brown in the triple jump were champions in the junior age group.

Phil Brown's victory in the 200m contributed to a British victory against the West German junior team. Phil, Lincoln Asquith and Fenton Campbell then provided three of the successful sprint relay squad.

At the start of 1981 the club's performances in the two major cross-country championships, the Midland and the National, were as dismal as any in its long history. Birchfield were ninth in the Midland and twenty-eighth in the National. Ray Smedley finished in nineteenth place, the only Stag in the first hundred. Yet, there were signs that better times lay ahead, for several juniors and youths turned in performances that augured well for the future.

Darren Pemberton was first home in the Midland Junior. With Martin Sprason ninth, Dave Bennett fourteenth and Ross Copestake twenty-fifth, the club were second to Leicester. The Youths' race also gave cause for optimism. With John Hartigan (fifth) and David Clarke (sixth), the club took fourth place, just twelve points behind the winners, Stourport. This pair also showed up well in the English Schoolboys Championships at Wigan, Clarke finishing third and Hartigan tenth. David would represent England in the British Schools Championship in Inverness.

John Graham had emerged as an outstanding marathon prospect in 1980 with his third place in the New York race in 2:11.47. In 1981 he produced something special. Running in the Rotterdam Marathon on 23 May, he broke away from the leading group at half way. Despite an attack of the stitch around the twenty-mile mark, the Scot came home a winner by over four minutes.

Gill Dainty and Aston Moore were the stars of the indoor season. Gill ran second to Anne Wright in the 1,500m at the WAAA, was third in the West Germany match and won in the match with East Germany. In the European Indoors she was placed sixth. Aston won both long jump and triple jump at the National Indoors. He won the triple jump in the East Germany match and took the bronze in the Europeans.

Gill and Aston continued to perform well in the outdoor season and at the end of the year it was decided that they should share the Leah Wright trophy. Gill took three national titles, the 800m and 1,500m at the UK Championships and the 1,500m at the WAAA. In this race, which she won for the second year in succession, Gill improved her best time to 4:12.6. Her form earned her selection for the Great Britain team in the European Cup in Zagreb.

Aston was also selected for Zagreb and his triple jumping was among the best of his career. His five legal jumps averaged 16.64m and his top of 16.86m placed him second, only 11cm behind the reigning Olympic Champion, Uudmae of the USSR.

The senior men started their campaign to lift the club from Division Two with a convincing win at Cwmbran. The club's top performers had been persuaded to turn out this season. That achieved, the club's promotion to the top division was never be in doubt.

It was at Cwmbran that Phil Brown first took the eye as an anchor leg in the 4 x 400m. Phil gave experienced international Bill Hartley a twenty-metre start and produced a well-paced effort that brought him home first.

By the time of the fourth and final League match at Perry Barr promotion was virtually assured. The club had only to finish in the top five to go up. A comfortable third place was achieved. The ladies' team, already in Division One, took fourth place.

It was at Perry Barr that the GRE and Jubilee Cup finals were staged on 19 September. In the men's match Haringey battled with Wolverhampton & Bilston for the cup, while Birchfield took the fourth spot. The club's two event winners were Ray Smedley in the 10,000m and fifteen-year-old Byron Morrison with a two-metre-high jump. The ladies also finished fourth in the Jubilee Cup. They produced two event winners, Gill Dainty in the 1,500m and Barbara Clarke in the long jump.

At the English Schools, Lincoln Asquith won the Senior 100m, John Hartigan the Intermediate steeplechase, Cynthia Gregory the Senior girls shot and Mandy Hampton the Junior girls discus.

The club's sprinters showed up well at the AAA Junior Championships, Lincoln Asquith winning the 100m, with Fenton Campbell fourth and Trevor Henry eighth. In the 200m Phil Brown was second and Trevor Henry was fifth. John Hartigan won the youths' steeplechase and Mark Lakey the high jump. Asquith and Brown were selected for the European Junior Championships in Utrecht. Lincoln was beset with injury and went out in his heat of the 100m. Phil made the 200m final and recorded a personal best of 21.17 in fifth place.

An outstanding performance came from seasoned campaigner Ray Smedley in the Inter-Counties twenty-mile road race at Bolton on 14 June. Although this was his debut at the distance, he attacked it from the start and ran away from the field to record 1:39.58, over four minutes ahead of the runner-up.

At the end of the year the NUTS lists showed Robert Weir at the top of both discus (59.28m) and hammer (73.02m). Aston Moore had the second longest triple jump by a Briton (16.68m) and was placed third in the long jump (7.74m).

By 1982 the senior team had recovered some pride after the previous season's debacle. In the Midlands, staged at Leicester, Ray Smedley was a close second to Tony Milosorov and young Richard Partridge took some good scalps to finish sixth. The team was fourth overall. The performances of the other three teams in the championships that day were very encouraging. Darren Pemberton mounted a successful defence of his Midlands Junior title. Neil Appleby was third, and Birchfield won the team championship. Success too for the youths, led home by David Clarke in fourth place. The boys made it a treble of team victories as they totalled 47 to Wolverhampton's 72.

The Nationals at Leeds saw the club placed thirteenth, a considerable improvement. The story of the day, however, surrounded the club juniors, who won the title. This was only the club's second success in a race established in 1948.

It was the year of both the European and Commonwealth Games. A time when star performers tended to be selective about which events they would take on. To their credit most of the club's stars turned out regularly in the League matches, certainly in the men's team. This commitment was reflected in the team's third place in the final league table. The ladies did not fare so well and the season ended in relegation to Division Two. One bright spot was the move to Birchfield of Judy Livermore from Rugby.

Perhaps the season's most outstanding performance came from high jumper Mark Lakey in a Junior International match in Amsterdam on 29 August. Mark went into the match with a best of 2.15m, which on paper would have given him third place. He came out of it with a jump of 2.23m that set a new UK Youth record. It was the highest by a Briton in 1982, the highest ever by a Birchfielder, and he was still only sixteen.

There were successes at the UK Championships at Cwmbran. The victory of Aston Moore in the triple jump, with his cousin Eric McCalla second, displayed the strength of the club in this event. Phil Brown won his first National title when he beat Todd Bennett in the 400m.

The English Schools Championships were held at the Alexander Stadium in July. Lincoln Asquith had won the Senior Boys 100m in 1981. In 1982 he took the 200m in 21.2. Peter Weir won the hammer and Karen Pugh the intermediate discus.

Phil Brown and Judy Livermore were selected for the European Championships in Athens in September. Brown was appearing in his first major and he more than justified his selection. His fourth place in the 400m final in a personal best of 45.45 elevated him to the status of Britain's number one at the event. This was compounded by his performance on the last leg of the 4 x 400m relay. In a battle with new European Champion, Weber of West Germany, and the reigning Olympic Champion, Markin of the USSR, his judgement was finely tuned as he brought the team home in second place with an effort timed at 44.45.

Judy Simpson.

Judy, who had already experienced the pressure of a big championship in the Moscow Olympics two years before, took seventh place and set a new Commonwealth record with a score of 6,286 in the heptathlon. She achieved three personal bests.

An extensive track season closed with the Commonwealth Games in Brisbane in October. Seven club members were selected. They were: Judy Livermore, Gill Dainty, Robert Weir, Phil Brown, Aston Moore, Ray Smedley and John Graham. Five of them returned home with medals and John Graham ran fourth in the marathon. Regarding performance, pride of place went to Robert Weir who set a new UK record of 75.08m in winning the hammer. Robert gave generous praise to former Birchfield star thrower Howard Payne for improving his technique.

The club's other gold medallist was Phil Brown in the 4 x 400m relay. As most pundits predicted, Phil ran the last leg and took over with Maina of Kenya and Mitchell of Australia close behind. He lost the lead to Maina on the back straight and Mitchell moved in close behind him. Biding his time, Phil eased past Maina as the runners entered the home straight and held off Mitchell to bring the English team home in first place. A 'glory leg' of the highest order.

It had been a splendid year for Birchfield in many respects but the club was saddened by the death of Mrs Nelson-Neale OBE, in October. She had been a tower of strength in women's athletics for more than half a century and touching tributes were paid to her memory, the greatest, perhaps, the naming of the stand on the stadium first bend as the Nelson Stand.

That was in 1983, by which time Richard Partridge was fulfilling his potential by convincingly running away from a record size field at Wolverhampton to take the Midland Counties Cross Country title. At the tape, Richard had a twenty-one-second margin of victory over Westbury's Chris Buckley. This performance shone out in an otherwise bleak cross-country season.

In stark contrast, the road running team had an excellent campaign. Victories in the Warwickshire, Midland and Wolverhampton relays augured well for the bid to once again become 'Kings of the Road'. However, there was still fifty-four miles of hard running at Sutton Park culminating in Ross Copestake inheriting an eight-second lead courtesy of Steve Emson and stretching the margin of victory over Tipton to thirty-four seconds, the title gained for the first time since the epic race at Derby a decade before. After finishing third in Division One of the National League the previous season, Dave Lawrence's senior men's team embarked on the 1983 summer programme with high expectations of ending Wolverhampton & Bilston's reign of supremacy.

After the first fixture in London, the media were proclaiming that the league title was destined for either Haringey or Shaftsbury. However, although Birchfield had finished third they had provided six individual winners, which was more than any other club.

On two further occasions, the National League fixtures clashed with Midland League matches, with strength in depth being apparent – the club fielded two teams each time.

The stage was set for a final shoot out in mid-August at Stretford with Haringey. Both teams had sixteen match points after three fixtures. The clash with the World Championships ruled out Phil Brown and Ainsley Bennett who were key personnel in the 4 x 400m quartet in Helsinki. The club were, however, able to fly Robert Weir back after he had competed in Finland. This initiative paid a rich dividend with a double victory in the hammer and discus. On the track Simon Lane and Colin Szwed in the 800m with Alan Salter and Paul Black in the 1,500m picked up maximum points. This feat was repeated by Eric McCalla, Aston Moore and Trevor Sinclair in the long and triple jumps.

An indication of the effectiveness of the pressure being applied was that Birchfield enjoyed a thirty-two-point superiority over Haringey after only ten events. Ross Copestake and 'Biggles' Marzilius kept up the good work by being placed first and second in the 3,000m steeplechase and the task was completed by victory in the 4 x 100m relay.

The team had amassed no less than sixteen first places on that memorable day and won the match by a handsome forty-three points. This awesome performance ensured that Birchfield Harriers were League Champions of Great Britain for the first time since success in the inaugural British Athletics League in 1969. This victory earned the senior men's team the right to represent the UK in the 1984 European Club's Championship in Milan. With a late surge the ladies just passed Glasgow to secure the second promotion position for an immediate return to the UK Women's League Division One.

In the European Junior Championships held in Vienna, Lincoln Asquith destroyed a quality field to become champion in a time of 10.34. Lincoln also brought home two bronze medals in the 200m and the 4 x 100m, in which he anchored the squad to a UK junior record of 39.38.

The Walking Section continued to improve and claimed Birchfield's first ever Ladies' National Under-twenty Championship. The scorers, in appalling weather conditions at Perry Barr, were Stephanie Cooper 2; Haley Morgan 9 and Alison Gallacher 11. There was a further high note on which to end an excellent season when the Young Athletes team again successfully defended their European title in Leige.

So there was an air of positive anticipation about 1984 – which was also an Olympic year. It was particularly satisfying, in light of the club's origins, that the senior men won the Birmingham & District cross-country team title for the first time since 1953. The extent of the victory was overwhelming. For the first time since the Second World War, a club had won all four races.

It seemed the long awaited upturn in the fortunes of the seniors was at hand. The Midlands Cross Country Championship provided further evidence. Ross Copestake won the race with Alan Salter third. Birchfield logged the same points tally as Nottingham but lost the Midlands team title on countback.

The third place at the National at Newark put Birchfield into the frame for the first time since 1955. This improved form was maintained in the road relays. With John Graham achieving the fastest stage, the club won the Five-Stage Warwickshire Relay. This was followed by second in the Midland and third in the National Twelve-Stage Road Relays at Sutton Park.

The ladies also had a successful winter campaign. After her premature retirement, Mary Cotton (née Stewart) came back with a bang. She again became the Warwickshire champion before leading the club to victory in the Midland event with Gill Dainty in sixth place. Remarkably after her four-year absence from competition, Mary led England to a hard fought victory over a strong Russian squad in the Eikiden Road Relay in Japan. Indoors, the ladies successfully defended their National 4 x 200m relay title.

The splendid team effort in the final National League meeting of 1983 had catapulted the ladies' track and field team back into Division One. Unfortunately they finished sixth and were once again relegated into Division Two. There were redeeming features to the season centred around qualification for the National Cup Final. The team came within one point of being third.

The senior men's victory in the 1983 British League earned the club the honour of being the UK's representative in the cauldron of the European Club Championship in Milan. After representations to the British Amateur Athletic Board, they refused to assist Birchfield's challenge in Europe by re-scheduling any of the events in the Olympic trial or taking the performances in Milan into consideration when selecting the team to travel to Los Angeles. This was in stark contrast to the situation whereby Italy and Spain used the European Clubs as part of their selection procedure. Despite the consequential loss of five key personnel, including potential event winners such as Lincoln Asquith and Phil Brown, the team battled well in the heat to be placed sixth out of sixteen nations.

When the Olympic team was announced, four Birchfield Harriers were in the party. They were Judy Simpson (née Livermore), Phil Brown, Eric McCalla and Robert Weir.

Robert finished top Briton in ninth place in the hammer. Eric McCalla qualified for the triple jump final after breaking the 17m barrier in the qualifying round. He was unable to match this performance again and finished in eighth place. Judy Simpson had to battle against the niggling injuries with which she flew to the Games. She led by twenty points after the first day but eventually finished in a creditable fifth position, only a tantalising one point, 6,280 to 6,281, behind American Cindy Greiner.

Phil Brown started his Olympic campaign by running third behind the eventual champion, Babers of the USA, in the first round of the 400m but was eliminated in the second round. Of course Phil was to demonstrate once again that he was a completely different performer with a baton. He took over on the anchor leg in fourth place, four metres down on Australia. As ever, Phil paced his effort superbly to move into the silver medal position forty metres from the tape. The USA quartet took gold in a world 'sea level' best. The British quartet was timed at 2:59.13, which not only broke the magic three-minute barrier but created a new UK, Commonwealth and European record.

The young athletes also acquitted themselves with distinction, retaining their European title in Leige. Gary Brightwell gave evidence of his pedigree by winning the 400m, while John Hartigan achieved an excellent double in the 800m and 1,500m. The icing on the cake was provided by victories in both the 4 x 100m and 4 x 400m relays.

After a gap of several years the Waddilove Trophy was revived. The Birchfield men defeated international athletes from Scotland, Iceland and Belgium. The ladies also did well to finish second to Scotland.

For many the highlight of 1984 was the club's initial victory in the GRE Cup Final, held at Perry Barr. Wins by Lincoln Asquith (100m), Phil Brown (400m), 'Biggles' Marzillius (steeplechase) and Eric McCalla (triple jump) kept Birchfield in contention. Going into the last event, the 4 x 400m relay, the team were just two points down on Haringey.

Dave Hislop led off and Lincoln Asquith ran second. Vaughan Asprey handed over to Phil Brown third behind Garry Cook of Wolverhampton and Roy Dickens of Shaftsbury. The Olympic hero again chose the 300-metre mark as the point to make his decisive effort and surged to the front to win the race and the match for Birchfield. So, it was a year in which success was enjoyed in Asia, America – and Birmingham!

In many respects 1984 had been one of the most successful in the club's history. The results of the Senior cross-country team had improved considerably and this was maintained in 1985. In the first Birmingham & District Cross Country League at Warley Woods the team outdistanced the rest by eighteen points. Three weeks later at Coventry a victorious Ross Copestake led the team home to a resounding seventy-nine points victory, with six places out of the first eleven. Only two of that team ran in the next fixture at Perry Barr but victory was conceded by only one point. In the final race at Solihull the team demolished the opposition. Led by Neil Appleby in second place, the team packed six in the first ten to score a 35 points total.

Copestake's win at Coventry preceded his County title at Leamington, where he again led the club to victory. The Youths also excelled, taking the team competition with three wins out of four. In the National Championships at Milton Keynes, Alan Salter in nineteenth place led the team home to second place medals. This was the best performance since the 1953 triumph. Sutton Park on Easter Saturday saw the club comfortably win the MCAAA Road Relay Championship. Ashworth Laukham ran the fastest long leg.

The Ladies' team had a quieter winter, but did finish a creditable sixth in the National Road Relays. Mary Cotton had a fine season, winning both the league races that she contested, and achieving a meritorious seventh place in the National Cross Country Championships.

In a year in which there were no major games, concentration on domestic titles paid dividends. The Young Athletes League team sailed through the Midland Premier League undefeated. Individual highlights

Phil Brown triumphs again.

were David Williams' English Schools Intermediate shot putt title, and James Nixon's Youth League 200m record of 21.5.

As a team, the senior men could not have had a much better season. Never off the top of the League table, they won it with three out of four fixture victories. Contributing to the title were many superb individual performances, including Lincoln Asquith's 10.2 League record. At area level the club were Division One champions. The run of success was only halted at the end of August, when Shaftsbury relieved the men of their GRE Cup Championship.

The country called on Birchfield Harriers many times for athletes. Regulars such as Phil Brown, Eric McCalla, Lincoln Asquith and Judy Simpson were now joined by Sharon Bowie (long jump), Karen Pugh (discus), Steve Buckeridge (110m hurdles) and Derek Redmond (400m).

Phil, Eric and Judy triumphed at the UK Closed Championships in Antrim. Sadly neither Phil Brown nor Eric McCalla saw the season through; Phil, with the relatively minor problem of a hamstring injury, but Eric with the major medical challenge of kidney failure.

The new star performer in the Birchfield ranks was nineteen-year-old Derek Redmond. On 27 July in Oslo, he broke David Jenkins' ten-year-old British record for the 400m in a time of 44.82. Derek had joined Tony Hadley's squad earlier in the year, but had not at that point broken forty-six seconds! He joined Judy Simpson and Lincoln Asquith in Moscow to represent Great Britain in the Europa Cup.

The Ladies' team made a modest start to their summer campaign but improved steadily to be placed second in the final UK League Division Two fixture at Bracknell and placed third overall. They also won the final Midland League Division One at Wolverhampton, beating champions Notts AC.

Despite the further retirement of Mary Cotton in the winter of 1985/86 in preparation for the birth of her first child, the ladies enjoyed their best cross-country season since 1980. Gill Dainty won three out of four League races to claim the individual title. She was ably supported by Nicky Salisbury, who was second overall, and Allison Soar, to take the Stagbearers to second team on aggregate.

Gill Dainty won the Warwickshire Championship, and well supported by Karen McCormick and Pamela Stewart, gained second place medals. The club's strength in depth was evident in the Area Championships in which four performances count. On the frozen slopes of Great Malvern, Nicky Salisbury ran well to place second, just edging Gill Dainty into third place. Again Allison Soar provided solid support, coming in twenty-seventh, and Julie Parson's thirty-fifth place meant that the Midland title went back to Perry Barr.

The men slipped back a little after their performances of the previous year. They finished fourth overall in the Birmingham & District League. The ECCU Championships were held at Newcastle in six inches of snow. It was the youth team's turn to bring medals home. After totally dominating its section of the Birmingham & District League the team was expected to do well, and it did. Led home by Richard Schlanker in twelfth place, the Stags recorded their fourth win in ten years.

Internationals Rob Harrison in the 1,500m and Clare Summerfield in the high jump had become Birchfield members during the winter. They were joined by Alan Tapp and Steve Buckeridge in the hurdles, plus Canissus Alcindoe in the high jump, to compete for their country indoors against Spain, Hungary and the USA.

Moving off the mud onto the road, Gill Dainty held her form to become winner of the second Gaymers 3,000m road-race series. The men's form, as usual, was much better in the road relays. They won the Warwickshire Road Relay at Chelmsley Wood, and ran second in the Midland Twelve-Stage, only fifty-nine seconds behind Tipton. In the National they were again second to Tipton, but the club's time of 4:03.38 was Birchfield's fastest ever in the event.

The Young Athletes League team repeated its 1985 domination of the Midland Premier Track and Field League, with an average winning margin of nearly sixty points. Not even the most optimistic of the club's supporters would have suggested that this average could be repeated in the National Final at Perry Barr. However, the youngsters with thirty-two personal bests claimed a superb fifty-seven points victory. This was the club's fourth triumph in the thirteen-year history of the competition.

The results of the Senior Ladies' team had improved steadily over the previous two years and this continued. The Midland League was won for he first time in five years. In the UK League Division Two they pulled out all the stops in the final fixture to record an outstanding 310 points winning total, which took them to second place. Unfortunately, a pre-season change of rules denied them promotion to Division One, as only the champions were promoted.

At Cwmbran, in September, the ladies narrowly failed to wrest the Jubilee Cup from Essex Ladies. However, two weeks later, on home territory, there was the National Field Events title to celebrate.

This year at National League level the men's team relinquished its title to the runners-up in 1985, Haringey, who won all four fixtures. At the GRE final a depleted squad gained fifth spot, but the field event athletes took Birchfield to a creditable third place two weeks later in the National Field Event Championships at Perry Barr.

By far the best performance of the season was in the European Club Championships in Lisbon on 31 May and 1 June. During the winter season many Continental clubs ran a recruitment campaign, which meant they were turning out virtually the national team for summer fixtures. A massive annual budget assisted that process. So sixth place for an amateur club like Birchfield Harriers was a commendable effort. Individual winners were Lincoln Asquith, Rob Harrison and Phil Brown. Steve Buckeridge set a club record with a silver medal in the high hurdles. Bronze medals went to Aston Moore and Ainsley Bennett.

Club athletes again regularly picked up titles at area level, and, in a season that saw both Commonwealth and European Championships take place, they could look upon a valuable contribution to international athletics.

The outstanding early season form of Rob Harrison saw Peter Stewart's fourteen-year-old 1,500m and mile club records erased with marks of 3:35.74 and 3:53.85 respectively. Phil Brown posted what was then the fastest 400 metres time in Europe, 45.29, at Cwmbran to join Rob as UK Champion.

When the Commonwealth Games teams were announced there were seven Birchfield Harriers in the mix: Phil Brown (400m), Derek Redmond (400m), Aston Moore (triple jump), Lincoln Asquith (4 x 100m relay), John Graham (marathon), Karen Pugh (discus) and Judy Simpson (heptathlon). Later, Rob Harrison (1,500m) and Gill Dainty (1,500m) were added to the English team.

Phil Brown's early season form was not matched in Edinburgh, but he took a bronze behind Roger Black and Darren Clarke, before anchoring the England relay squad to victory in a repeat of his gold medal performance in Brisbane. Karen Pugh exceeded expectations by gaining a bronze in the discus, and Lincoln Asquith led off the 4 x 100m squad to silver medals.

Judy Simpson's heptathlon gold was one of the best performances of the Championships. After six events she was lying second to Jane Flemming of Australia, and needed to be nearly two seconds in front at the end of the 800m to win. She was, at 1.91 seconds, to win the championship by four points in a new Games record of 6,282 points.

Judy was to surpass even this performance at the European Championships in Stuttgart. She reeled off a succession of personal bests and going into the last event led the competition by twenty-one points. The gold, however, was not a likely proposition against women whose 800m times were so much better than hers. She ran sensibly to finish in 2:11.70 and take the bronze medal. Her score of 6,623 set a new Commonwealth record. On her way to this total Judy set club records in the 100m hurdles and the high jump. Her hurdles time of 13.05 had only been bettered by one British hurdler – Shirley Strong. She high jumped 1.92m – within touch of the British record of 1.95m. In the seven disciplines she recorded five personal bests.

In the final analysis 1986 produced a 'mixed bag' for the club. Waging a European campaign and having on occasions to field three senior men's teams on the same day meant that the National League title was lost. There was also relegation to Division Two of the Midland League.

The ladies, meanwhile, had partially fulfilled their promise of 1985 and won the Midland League. Success came to the club in varying forms. At one end of the spectrum Judy Simpson took women's multi-events into world class, and at the other end an excellent race walking squad were age-group champions, with Zoe Hollier as National Champion.

The ladies got off to an even better start in 1987 than they had the previous year by winning the Midland Women's Cross Country League. Three victories out of four fixtures were achieved. Gill Dainty went on to retain her Midland title. The senior men's cross-country team finished third overall after a tight battle with Wolverhampton for second place.

By comparison the youths dominated their section of the league, even more so than in 1985, winning every fixture. They went on to secure the Midland Counties Boys title with the successful Youth League team placing second.

The club travelled expectantly to Luton for the ECCU Championships and although it performed well, the only trophy brought back to Perry Barr was the Centenary Trophy. The seniors were close to being in the frame, finishing fifteen points behind third-placed Tipton.

Early in the year Eric McCalla made a welcome return to competition with second place in the AAA Indoor Championships in January. Claire Summerfield also made the podium with third in the high jump, and Tim Blakeway went even better than both of them by winning the Youths' high jump.

The ladies showed the men that they could also perform well on the road, with Gill Dainty running the fastest leg of the day to bring home silver medals in the Midland Counties Road Relay. The men also weighed in with second place in their equivalent championship, after lying fifth at the end of the tenth leg.

In the National Twelve-Stage the team were in fifteenth position after the first long leg, by leg four they had moved up to third. That is where the Stags remained, ending up 1 minute 16 seconds down on their 1986 time.

The club travelled to Portsmouth for the first British League match with a team well below full strength, but surprisingly finished second. It was becoming clear that the club's ability to place well in the 'B' string events was proving an important factor. There were nine 'B' string wins in this match.

In the last match at Plaistow, Haringey gave Birchfield a hard time but could not quite overcome a team whose spirit was running high. Black vests again dominated, and with maximum points in the steeplechase, the Championship went back to Perry Barr for the third time in five years.

On the first Sunday in August, a thirty points victory in the semi-final of the GRE Cup put Birchfield in the final, to be held a fortnight later. Haringey won the Cup by nineteen points, but the margin would have been reduced. The 4 x 400m squad crossed the line first in a new club record but were sadly disqualified for an illegal takeover.

At area level the Midland League Division Two team ran out champions, and the Division Five outfit gained promotion to Division Four. The greatest reward for the senior men was the honour of representing the UK at the following year's European Clubs' Championships in Paris.

In spite of losing so many of its top athletes to higher age groups, the Young Athletes team maintained its remarkable record in the Midlands Premier Division of the National League. Birchfield and Wolverhampton & Bilston both went into the fifth and final fixture unbeaten. Once more a depleted young squad rose to the occasion and between them registered eight personal bests to snatch victory by just one point – after a recount! For the third year in succession the youngsters had taken the area title, with a marvellous record of played fifteen and won fifteen.

The ladies' team enjoyed an outstanding season in various competitions. They started with an emphatic win in the first Midland League at Nottingham in April. In the second match at Coventry at the end of May, they produced an even more decisive victory. The ladies retained the Midland League title with a win in the final fixture at Perry Barr in August, the table showing a winning margin of 159 points, much greater than in 1986.

At national level, in the UK Women's League Division Two, the competition was perhaps a little easier with Essex Ladies now in Division One. In the first fixture at Grangemouth in May they had a comfortable forty-three points victory. Another forty-three points victory at Wolverhampton at the end of June doubled their lead at the top of the table. Victory was expected in the final fixture at Hounslow in late August but what was surprising was the margin of 115 points. On the track there were only three events in which the girls did not score maximum points.

With Midland and National League titles secured, and morale running high, the next objective was the Jubilee Cup. They qualified for the final at Perry Barr with a thirty-one points win at Cwmbran.

Essex Ladies provided the main opposition in mid-August. In a competition restricted to one per event, it was a close and exciting battle throughout, but the ladies lost out to Essex by just three points. Birchfield won two events: Karen Pugh in the discus and the 4 x 400m relay. Despite the disappointment, it had been a fine season for the track team.

As in previous years, many athletes were selected for international fixtures and major championships. Stewart Faulkner, in the long jump, emerged as an outstanding prospect, winning the UK Senior title at Derby in May with 7.68m, a distance just four centimetres short of Daley Thompson's UK Junior record. He vowed to break it before the end of the season was finished and achieved his goal with 7.86m at the National Junior Championships at Perry Barr in July. Stewart then took the silver medal in the European Junior Championships.

Perhaps the biggest disappointment of the season was Judy Simpson's withdrawal from the World Championships. Although selected, a knee injury prevented her from high jumping. The other female internationals, Karen Pugh, Suzanne Guise, Claire Summerfield, Jacqui Zaslona and Sharon Bowe, performed well for their country.

Eric McCalla showed surprisingly good form following a kidney transplant operation. He won the UK Triple Jump title with 16.46m and was first in an international match at Gateshead with 16.45m. It was a considerable blow both to Eric and the club that he was not selected for the World Championships. Those who did make it to Rome were Lincoln Asquith, Phil Brown and Derek Redmond.

Lincoln's hopes were dashed when the team were disqualified for an illegal takeover at the end of the first leg. Phil, true to his form in championships, ran poorly in the 400m, but very well on the last leg of the relay! In the final he held off Hernandez of Cuba and Schmidt of West Germany to bring the team home in the silver medal position, a fine performance by the British quartet – who included Derek Redmond – in a new European and Commonwealth record of 2:58.86.

Derek went to the World Championships as the British number one. He won his first and second-round heats and then the semi-final where in complete control he stopped the clock at 44.50 – a new UK record. In the final Derek finished fifth in 45.06, appearing to tighten up towards the end. However, it was the highest placing by a Birchfielder in a World Championship and at the end of the 1987 season Derek was the recipient of the Leah Wright Trophy.

Twenty-One: Life and Seoul

As a new Olympic year dawned so Birchfield's leading lights were conducting a personal health check.

'I cannot remember what it is like to run round a track without my left knee hurting', revealed the club and country's top heptathlete Judy Simpson. The problem that had bedevilled her was eventually diagnosed as a cyst, for which she had surgery in November of that year. 'I have had trouble for two years with my left knee and didn't realise what it was', she stated. 'The cyst must have been growing all that time but now it has been removed I know I won't have the problem again. That was the only injury that was stopping me, so hopefully I am right. I can lay the foundation for this year and for Seoul.'

The injury had prevented Judy competing in Rome at the World Championships and the whole of the 1987 season had been a bitter letdown after her achievements in 1986.

South Korea was obviously a world away from those club athletes tackling more traditional January fare in pursuit of their athletics. In the Midland Counties Cross Country Championships at Burton the youths' race was a tense and tight situation. At three-quarters-of-a-mile Birchfield's Mark Burdiss and Sutton's Alistair O'Connor had opened a lead of fifteen metres on Leicester's Neil Allen. This pair, rivals of old from neighbouring clubs, played 'cat and mouse' with each other over the testing long course. They stayed closely glued together with the issue wide open. Then, with 600 metres to go, Burdiss struck for home. The first reaction was that he had gone too early, as O'Connor responded and matched his move. However, the young Stag was full of running and poured on the pace to win by fourteen seconds.

The next month Shireen Samy showed a welcome return to form when she scored a fine runaway win in the Midland Women's Cross Country Championship at Blaise Castle, Bristol. Shireen, Nicky Salisbury and Charnwood's Eileen Foster pulled clear early on – before Samy took command after just a mile. From then on she cruised to a comfortable and confident victory. Club colleague Nicky Salisbury continued her good winter form with an encouraging second placing. Despite that impressive one–two and Lisa Cox finishing ninth, Birchfield suffered the frustration of no fourth scorer so team victory went to local club Westbury Harriers.

The fourth and final fixture of the Birmingham & District Cross Country League, Division One, produced a real cracker at Perry Park. Three laps of firm parkland provided a fast course ideal for the track men. On the final circuit Craig Mochrie of Loughborough unleashed an impressive piece of aggressive running and ensured the race was his. Birchfield's John Hartigan, having at one time looked in danger of falling apart, held on well and on the third circuit he tracked his training partner Bill Bedell of Telford before outkicking him for third place. Fellow Stag Neil Appleby kept out fast finishing Alan Jackson of Stourbridge for fifth place. The Birchfield boys ran well overall. Starting the day in third and thirty-six points behind leaders Wolverhampton they virtually halved everyone else's score to take the fixture and regain the League title.

So to indoor events – and at the National Under-Twenty Indoor Championships at Cosford, the form and confidence suggested the top juniors were set to make a major impact that year – perhaps all the way to Seoul. Nineteen-year-old Birchfield Harrier Stewart Faulkner was both European Junior Long Jump Champion and UK Senior Champion. He had Olympic ambitions. However, Stewart was to be severely tested by Shaftesbury Barnet's Jason Canning, who had set a UK indoor record of 7.52m the previous month. The seventeen-year-old Londoner advanced that record in the first round with a 7.62m leap. Faulkner responded with 7.40m. Both fouled in the second round but in the third Birchfield's man cleared a championship winning jump with a junior indoor record of 7.81m – six centimetres short of his own outdoor career best.

The most thrilling final of the championships was the junior girls' 60m. Multi-talented Katharine Merry concentrated her energies at just this event in these championships and began as favourite. In the heats and semi-finals her times were only marginally faster than Haslemere's Renate Chinyou, who made the better start. Merry fought back and caught her rival on the line, but it was a long agonising wait before Katharine was declared champion – with both girls clocked at 7.70.

Previously, the young Birchfield athlete had been named as the January Rotary Watches/Sportsmail Female Athlete of the Month. She had proved a brilliant all-rounder in 1987. Katharine topped the under-thirteen age group rankings at 100m, 200m and long jump whilst also setting records at 75m hurdles (11.3) and high jump (1.69m). This was the beginning of a great career – as time would prove.

Also in March and with only four weeks to go to the London Marathon, Birchfiield's Sally Ellis gained a psychological advantage over two of her main rivals for Britain's Olympic marathon team. This was running against the Leeds pair of Veronique Marot and Angela Pain in the Adidas Half Marathon. Ellis and Marot were neck and neck throughout most of the race and the outcome was only decided in the last mile when Sally's race sharpness prevailed as she smashed her personal best by over two minutes.

As the track season began to open there was a lot of interest in a Birchfield sprinter who had only taken up the sport recently. It was already felt that twenty-three-year-old Michael Rosswess was on the threshold of the 'big time'. His personal bests were 10.7 for the 100m and 21.7 for the 200, but his stunning indoor form in the winter suggested those would be very short lived. In January, Michael had been a surprise 60m bronze medallist at the Omron Games at Cosford. He clocked 6.80 – after a semi-final 6.79 – finishing third behind Barrington Williams and Ernest Obeng, but edging out the double Olympic Decathlon Champion Daley Thompson. Rosswess also improved his indoor 200m personal best to 21.3. However, his most memorable achievement was a win in the England v. USA international in March. 'That was my most pleasing performance because it was such a big event', recalled Michael, who stormed to a 6.87 victory after a terrible start. He admitted: 'Starting is my weakness because I am so tall. My strongest part, like Linford Christies's, is the end of the race.' His coach, Michael Oluban, believed he had a remarkable talent on his hands stating: 'I would call him a cat – very skinny but with phenomenal speed!' The local lad became so dedicated that he gave up work to concentrate on his sprinting and the training involved.

The month of June witnessed a number of issues both on and off track. Television coverage had forced the eight champion clubs in the European Clubs Final in Venice – including Birchfield Harriers – to split the event over two days. The influence of Italian television was so great that the first day's competition on the Saturday lasted just over one-and-a-half hours. The second day's competition was not much longer and all packed into two-and-a-half hours. It was a problem the organisers could do little about. The finals were very expensive to host and the TV coverage with its resulting demands were a necessary by-product. Birchfield team manager Dave Lawrence would have preferred just one day's programme stating: 'The event has to be financed through television but because of that there is a lot of time being wasted for the athletes.' It is interesting to study the club's financial commitment at the time. The six-day trip was costing Birchfield about £16,000, with about £9,000 being donated by the GRE British Athletics League and Sports Council. Some of the remainder was met by the club's sponsor Glynwed International. The club had to find the balance and it was a problem Dave Lawrence believed needed attention in the future.

At the same time and back home the Midland Counties created a piece of history with their first joint Men's and Women's Championships. The athletes responded with top class performances and a number of championship records.

Pride of place on the first day went to Stewart Faulkner who shattered the former championship best by a massive 52cm with a leap of 7.84m.

Early success on day two went to Birchfield's Dave Humphreys, who was in a class of his own in winning the Junior Men's 110 hurdles in 14.73. Interestingly, the first championship best fell to a youngster named Denise Lewis, then of Wolverhampton & Bilston, who retained her Intermediate Ladies 100m hurdles title in convincing style by slicing nine hundredths off the championship record. Denise also won the shot putt contest.

Meanwhile the Stags looked to have unearthed a fine sprint prospect in Jason John. He completed a notable 100m and 200m double. His time in the 200m was faster than that of the under-twenty champion.

Whilst these youngsters could look to the long-term future, the club's senior international had more pressing matters. Judy Simpson's packed schedule was more fraught than ever as she fought to regain her place in world athletics following the injury problem. Judy had spent almost two months in Arizona in April and May. While the injury had held her back on her strong events, she was able to report some progress with her weaker events. 'I've done some good work. All that's happened is I've not been able to lift as heavy weights as I would like or high jump. I've not been able to get in as much sprinting either, but I've done lots of weights and exercises in the pool.'

Judy's domestic training sessions were taking place at Crystal Palace as her coach, John Anderson, had been based in London for the previous three years. So much of Judy's travelling involved meeting up with him away from Birmingham. The Commonwealth Champion readily acknowledged her luck in enjoying the full support of husband Robin, a pole-vaulter for Birchfield Harriers. 'Several years ago he said as far as he's concerned I'm a heptathlete. That's my profession and he doesn't expect me to miss a day's training unless there's a good reason. He treats it as my job and he supports his wife in her work.'

Whilst Judy was still battling away to get to Seoul, a persistent hip injury had destroyed Rob Harrison's Olympic dream. The 1985 European Indoor champion had struggled against the problem since the spring, and despite various forms of treatment, including acupuncture, had given up hope of reaching South Korea. He announced: 'I will definitely miss the AAA trial. It is heartbreaking because I was racing well during the winter on the road and indoors, and had my heart set on doing well at Birmingham – I felt really confident.'

So attention turned to the Alexander Stadium for the first weekend in August. In the 200m Michael Rosswess stormed through in the later stages of the race to overhaul Andrew Carrott for the third position. It was another impressive milestone for the local athlete. His personal best before the trials was 21.00 and Michael achieved the Olympic qualifying time when he lowered that to 20.77 in the final. This performance gave the Olympic qualifying mark.

Stewart Faulkner looked set to bring Britain's long jumping drought to an end. Putting behind him a frustrating fourth place in the World Juniors, the Birchfield boy unleashed a superb effort to increase his UK National Junior record to 7.98m – just a whisker away from eight metres. He said afterwards: 'If I could have combined the speed of my fifth jump with the height of my first, I would have shattered eight metres.'

Derek Redmond finished second in the 400m final to Kriss Akabusi, but what is also remembered about that day is that on winning his semi-final he heard: 'You haven't broken the world record Derek!' from the stadium announcer, as the clock, which showed thirty-seven seconds, was malfunctioning!

The trials were less uplifting for Judy Simpson. Hampered by injury she finished third. Within a week she was in Germany in competition with Shona Urquhart of Stoke. The latter had finished second in the trials but hadn't achieved the qualifying standard. Judy did achieve the qualifying standard this day and her performance gave encouragement for Seoul.

Sadly, although Judy started the Olympic heptathlon, her dreams were soon smashed when she had to withdraw after the high jump. So convinced was Judy that the original cyst problem was over that when the knee broke down she immediately thought it must be another injury. Early diagnosis put the pain down to torn fibres but further tests showed that another cyst had grown. Judy Simpson was to have the second cyst removed in October, in her second knee operation in the space of eleven months.

Drama and Derek Redmond were never far apart either. Leading up to the Olympics Derek suffered bouts of tendonitis and hamstring troubles. 'I was up and down and really cheesed off. It came to the day of my 400 metres heat and my tendon was killing me from the moment I woke up.' After waiting for medical attention and having two injections, which wore off too quickly, Redmond was facing a dilemma. 'I was in heat six, lane four. I did a couple of strides and was limping. I tried half a stride and it didn't work. I pulled out a minute before I was due to run.'

The withdrawal of Derek led to certain side issues within the 4 x 400m squad of which the major controversy centred on Phil Brown. At the conclusion of the Games Tony Hadley and Team Solent's Mike Smith wrote to the chairman of the BAAB to express their concern about the attitude of Frank Dick towards that squad. The letter included the following reference: 'With one member, Derek Redmond, injured, the rest of the squad only discovered who would be running in the heats late on the evening prior to the competition and this only by looking the event up on the computer. No one spoke to them until the morning of the heats at the warm-up track. It can only be a matter of conjecture as to whether the squad was used to the best advantage in heat and semi-final but what is certain is the callous lack of concern over the use of Phil Brown. Having run in heat and semi-final he was taken aside as the rest of the team began warming up for the final. Mr Dick informed him that he would make his decision on whether or not to use him only after the men's 4 x 100 final (timetabled only forty-five minutes before the 4 x 400). This was with a view to replacing Brown by John Regis on the anchor leg. For the record Brown is STILL awaiting confirmation that he will be running in the final!' The quartet eventually finished a disappointing fifth.

Happier times, fortunately, were in store for Michael Rosswess who reached the 200m final and finished seventh only a year after coming to notice when winning the considerably more modest Warwickshire Championship. His attitude upon arriving in South Korea was that this was not just a bonus. 'I was going to Seoul to compete. You don't train eighteen months to go out there and have a good time. Well I didn't anyway. I was in my bed by nine o'clock in Seoul, up early the next day training, sometimes twice a day.' Michael stuck to his tunnel vision and took it one race at a time. 'First I wanted to get through the heats. Then I wanted to get to the semi-finals. Then I just gave it all I had got in the final and ran down Bruno Marie-Rose.' This was no mean achievement as the Frenchman was former European Indoor champion at the distance.

Finally, from a Birchfield perspective, Stewart Faulkner finished sixth in the Group One qualifying pool with his furthest jump of 7.74m. However, team partner Michael Forsythe made the final. Later that year Stewart had the consolation of collecting the Joe Turner Memorial Trophy as the best junior at the AAA Championship and the Pepsi Cola award for the best performance by an athlete under the age of twenty-one. He was Britain's youngest team member at the Games.

Twenty-Two: A Merry Dance

The New Year opened to a combination of indoor and outdoor events. At the Omron Games at Cosford Michael Rosswess improved his 60m personal best from 6.77 through 6.66 to 6.60. It supplanted Elliott Bunney's 6.62 as an all-comers' record and was second of all time behind Linford Christie's 6.55. Left trailing in his wake were Barrington Williams, Ernest Obeng, Nigel Walker, Jamie Henderson and Ray Burke.

Michael's coach, Oluban, claimed of his charge that 'He can be as good as Carl Lewis in full flight' while the man himself displayed confidence: 'I can definitely go faster because the strongest part of my race is the latter part. So if I can do this for 60 metres – what about 100 or 200?' Michael had been working hard on his starts since the Olympics and had managed to regularly beat Barrington Williams out of the blocks in training.

Meanwhile, outdoors at the Midlands Cross Country Championships at Stoke former World Cup marathon runner Sally Ellis returned to competitive running with an emphatic victory on a stamina-sapping course. Sally had made a remarkable recovery following a 1988 season that was devastated by a knee operation. She had only resumed training the previous November.

The action was fast and furious from the outset as Elaine Foster, Di Scott, Maxine Newman, Heather Jennings and Ellis quickly detached themselves from the pack. Ellis allowed Foster and Scott to dictate the pace as they forged clear on the second small lap. With the first of the tough climbs completed on lap three, Sally made the decisive break to deservedly take the title in 21:37.

At the end of January attention turned to the Great Britain v. West Germany indoor international in Glasgow. Here, Michael Rosswess was to prove that his natural talent was awesome. For, in the 60m, after a stumble shortly after the start, which saw him way down on his rivals, he recovered to storm through for victory. The time was immaterial in view of the run – and he worked so hard that he tripped after the finish. The pressure on him was intense. One minute his coach was saying to the media: 'Don't rush him' and the next telling them that Rosswess would be trying the 400m that year, arguing that his potential was: '44 dead'.

A week later at the WAAA/AAA Indoor Championships at Cosford, sprint king Linford Christie put the young pretender in his place – whilst chalking up an AAA Indoor Championships sprint double. In the 60m Olympic silver medallist Christie progressed easily through his heats. Meanwhile, Michael had to overcome a very premature false start, without a starting shot being fired, before winning comfortably in his raw style – 'eyeballs shut' as opposed to 'eyeballs out'!

Bearing that in mind, pundits understood why he avoided what would logically be his best event, the 200m. Apparently he didn't like the tight bends! Running with his usual mole-like grimace it seemed likely to many that he wouldn't actually see the bends!

In the final the protagonists lined up side by side in lanes three and four. Christie was never headed, equalling his 6.55 national record. Michael once again came through the field to second place in the last few metres, narrowly ahead of Mike McFarlane. On the same day Phil Brown, remarkably, was winning his first AAA 400m title – indoors or out.

Away, in the warmer climate of Portugal, Birchfield Harriers were enjoying a weekend in the European Clubs Cross Country Championships, the ladies finishing second and the men's team first of the British clubs in fifth place. The first Birchfield woman home was Shireen Samy in fifth with John Hartigan the first Birchfield man home in eighteenth.

Later, in February, the Women's National was held in Birmingham and witnessed a real race between Angie Pain of Leeds AC and home star Sally Ellis. When Pain made her break only Sally Ellis went with her. Angie offered the following analysis: 'For about half a mile it was a battle between me and Sally but when I got in front I began to hope that everyone else was feeling as bad as I was over the mudbath.' In fact, Sally, a clear second, was also feeling the effects of a hard race the previous weekend. However, one of the main reasons the Stagbearer had competed was to try and help the home club defend their team title. 'Last week was for me. Today was for the team.' Birchfield eventually finished second to Parkside from London.

As March unfolded so too did the World Indoor Championships in Budapest, Hungary, which meant more of the rollercoaster ride with Michael Rosswess. In this competition he fell foul of his main problem, a bad pick-up from the start. The problem persisted in his semi-final of the 60m, almost costing him a place in the final. He did power through to finish second behind Cuban Andres Simon Gomez, who broke the Central American record in 6.54. In the final Gomez achieved victory and lowered his record by a further two hundredths of a second. Michael was left chasing backs early on but ran a good second half to record a time of 6.64, but could only scramble to fifth place.

Matters were back on the up the following weekend in Glasgow for a Great Britain v. USA v. USSR international. Here victory was achieved in the 60m flat. A good start for Michael was followed by a superb final twenty metres as he pulled clear of Americans Brian Cooper and Stanley Floyd. He was rewarded with 6.57, a new personal best.

While predictions about the future of Michael Rosswess were perhaps open to healthy debate, there was no divided opinion on Katharine Merry. The WAAA/AAA Under-Twenty Indoor Championship at Cosford in mid-March reinforced matters. She retained her Girls' 60m crown and broke the UK record three times en route! Georgina Oladapo's seven-year-old record of 7.55 was swiftly swept aside by Merry in the first round with a storming 7.46. Barely had the crowd got their breath back and the statisticians taken note, when Katharine was at it again with a semi-final 7.44. Even in the final with victory a formality, as none of her opponents had beaten eight seconds, Merry refused to compromise, reducing the record by a further 0.09 seconds to 7.35. A time bettered by only six women at the previous month's European Indoor Championships.

The modest Birchfield fourteen year old, who also took a comfortable 60m hurdles gold the next day, had not allowed her phenomenal success to go to her head. Katharine insisted that, despite her eyebrow-raising form, she did not consider herself a strong contender for the European Junior Championships. 'It was a surprise as my previous best was only 7.6. I've been working hard this winter with my coach, Dennis Baker, so I've got a better start now, and I hope there's more to come. I've got a chance to get to the European Juniors but there are obviously people older than me who'll get priority', she said.

That summer, Merry, who the previous year had topped the UK rankings at 100m, 200m, long jump and pentathlon, with second places at 75m hurdles and high jump, would concentrate on just the sprints and hurdles. Katharine was especially keen to break her legal personal best of 11.85, which she had set to win the 1988 Securicor National Sprint Challenge. It did not, however, spoil a fun Easter as part of the ESSA Young Athletes' Coaching Course over five days at Loughborough University where everyone was encouraged to swap specialities. Amazingly she won the hammer and cleared twenty metres for the javelin!

Around that time Sutton Coldfield was the location of the first of the Linx Five Mile Road Races. Birchfield's Ashworth Laukam took the honours. The race produced a keenly contested event with the additional interest that the club were using it for their final selection for the impending National Twelve-Stage Road Relays. Steeplechaser John Hartigan, who had moved to Tipton Harriers, was the first to show but his opening move was quickly covered by former club-mate Laukam. Ashworth edged into a five-yard lead, which he gradually extended to the finish to come home a very confident winner. With five finishers in the first eleven, Birchfield were shaping nicely for a renewed attack on the twelve-man title. However, on the following weekend it was Tipton who were victorious with Ashworth Laukam the first Stag home in ninth place.

Back at Sutton Coldfield, Shireen Samy continued her winning ways in the women's event to make it a Birchfield double. Her teammate Joanne Jones won an exciting tussle for third clinching the bronze medal from Tipton's Kath Hill.

For many club members their thoughts were now on the track and their prospects for 1989. Birchfield sprinter Geraldine McLeod was hoping to get her success rolling as a first year junior, after breaking through in a big way as an intermediate in previous years. During 1987 the seventeen year old had improved her personal best at 100m from 12.4 to a wind-assisted 11.84, while at 200m it had tumbled from 25.5 to 24.7. Geraldine had dominated the schools scene, winning both the English Schools Inter-Girls 100m title at Yeovil and the home international at Swindon. Despite an injury, which cost her several weeks of training during the winter, Geraldine was viewing the new track season with optimism. Being coached by Tony Hadley meant that Geraldine trained with an accomplished group of athletes including Derek Redmond and Phil Brown at the Alexander Stadium.

Also fired up for 1989 was Clova Court. Wanting to be Britain's best at the heptathlon was tough enough, but when you were nearly twenty-nine, ranked only ninth and working full-time it seemed a very tall order. However, Clova, the 1988 Midland Champion, and her husband/coach Howard were confident she could go all the way and set the Barcelona Olympics of 1992 as a target. Although her best was 5,184 at the time and well short of world class, Court, who had only been a serious athlete for a few years, believed that paradoxically her age could be to her advantage: 'As a late developer my body hasn't been through all that hard push and grind.' Ironically in 1987 – after her first heptathlon – Clova was very tempted to throw in the towel: 'It was a disaster and a killer. I finished with about 4,600. I vowed never to do one again!' Then at the 1988 Olympic trial she issued a warning of her potential. She scored 5,164 in wet and windy conditions for a brave fourth. 'It was a real bonus, especially as I was suffering with a cold.'

She had been outstanding in the Worcestershire Championships, collecting five titles at 100m, 200m, 100m hurdles, shot putt and javelin. The javelin was Clova's strongest event, her best of 50.60m ranking her ninth in Britain in 1988.

Clova's all-round ability and the general ability of the ladies' team saw them dominate the Midland Women's League Division One. Typical was a fixture at Northwood Stadium, Stoke in late May. Clova Court was inside the former stadium record with a win in the 'B' 100m, which was four tenths inside her 1988 best.

Fourteen-year-old sprint sensation Katharine Merry produced an awesome display on her way to a double. Her wind-assisted 100m 11.7 would have placed her equal first in the senior event with Phyllis Smith, while her 200m winning time of 23.8 was six tenths quicker than her senior counterpart.

Lorraine Hanson showed good form, stopping the clock at 59.7 in the 400m hurdles. Other notable Birchfield performances came from Cath Mijovic, who held off the challenge of Stoke's Kay Flannigan to take the 1,500m in 4:36 and Gill Dainty who was in a class of her own in clocking 9:24.5 for the 3,000m.

In the male domain, Stewart Faulkner was busy picking up the threads of his successful career development the previous season and at a high level of competition too. In the UK Championships at Jarrow he was one of three British jumpers who went over eight metres in one competition for the first time ever.

Champion Mark Forsythe, runner-up Ian Simpson and third-placed Stewart inspired each other to a new level, even if the wind was above the legal limit. The Stag, whose personal best stood at 8.04m, achieved 8.01m. Forsythe stole the show with a last round 8.05m. Simpson had been the first to go over the magic eight with 8.04m.

A week later Forsythe and Faulkner were in Portsmouth competing for Great Britain against Hungary and an International Select. They finished first and second respectively. The former reached 8.17m while Stewart almost repeated his eight metres with 7.98m. A few yards away there was a Birchfield – and GB – first and second in the women's 100m. With the wind changing to a following 1.6m/s Katharine Merry used this to her advantage to fly to an 11.69 time. Geraldine McCloud also ran very well to be second behind her swifter teammate.

Derek Redmond (back left), Katharine Merry
(back right) and Tim Ewynne (front left) enjoy a
coaching session.

The Stags were also performing consistently when it came to the Midland Counties Championships at the Alexander Stadium in June. Derek Redmond was back and in form. Having virtually strolled to a sub-forty-eight clocking in his heat, he turned on the pace in the final. His fluid style took him clear of the field and he scorched home in a season's best to remove Ainsley Bennett and training partner Phil Brown's 46.24 from the record books.

The Birchfield domination was also evident in the 200m. Lincoln Asquith ran a storming bend to enter the straight two metres up. Mark Thomas and Phil Brown powered after him but Asquith held on positively.

The indisputable star of the Women's Championship was emerging hepthathlete Clova Court. She claimed a marvellous sprints and hurdles hat-trick, with a javelin silver as a further bonus. Lorraine Hanson ran a season's best in the flat 400m.

By the time of this event Katharine Merry had returned from America. She was part of a small but elite squad of young British athletes who had travelled to the USA to compete in the Keebler International Meeting in Elmhurst, Illinois. Katharine continued with her form of the season with a time which would have given her a world record for under-fourteens had there not been an illegal following wind. Her time of 11.47 improved her previous best by two tenths of a second.

For a change Katharine didn't have everything her own way when she represented Great Britain in an international match against West Germany and Sweden at Ipswich in early July. Although often up against girls two or three years older, Katharine this time faced her German equivalent Katja Seidel, just one year older. Seidel improved her personal best by five hundredths of a second to finish clear in 11.66.

Miss Merry then found nothing to cheer herself up in Britain's disastrous 4 x 100m relay. Chief coach Richard Simmons was faced with last minute changes due to injuries. First leg runner Viv Francis had returned from France only the day before and had no baton-changing practice. It showed. The British team were disqualified as Francis and Merry were almost a quarter of the way up the back straight before successfully exchanging the baton!

The month of August provided many highlights at international, national and club level. In the Europa Cup at Gateshead twenty-year-old Stewart Faulkner proved a few people wrong who were concerned that he would find himself outclassed in a field that had consistently jumped well over eight metres. In the event the European Junior Silver Medallist, who led until the final round, gained several notable scalps by placing third. These included the 1984 Olympic and 1985 World Indoor Bronze Medallist Giovanni Evangelisti. Stewart jumped just below eight metres on a newly laid runway, which most of the competitors found difficult. His retort: 'People didn't even think I would finish in the top six today.'

The club's nine points victory in the British League Division One provided them with their ninth title, but the relegation of fellow Midlands club Wolverhampton & Bilston and the North's Sale Harriers left them isolated as the only non-London club in an amazing capital city dominance. The Stags were the first winners of the British Athletics League Division One title in 1969. Since then the fortunes of clubs from the South, North, Midlands, Scotland and Wales had ebbed and flowed, but there had not been a time when such Southern domination pervaded. Birchfield's team manager, Dave Lawrence, had seen the club slip back into Division Two in 1973, then bounce back straightaway, only to slip back and spend 1975 to 1978 in the Second Division. He was surprised the winning margin was so comfortable. 'I thought it would be a lot harder. The competition was a bit weak', he said, putting much of Birchfield's success down to their youth policy. 'We had between eight and twelve juniors in each match all the way through. It's nice to be able to develop young talent like that.'

Several local athletes tested their various levels of experience at the AAA/WAAA Championships at their home track. The event also to served as the Commonwealth Games trials.

Michael Rosswess, troubled by injury in the lead up to the Championship and race rusty, came in a disappointing seventh in the 100m final. He was then eighth in the 200m final.

In the long jump, defending AAA Champion Stewart Faulkner had been threatening a really big jump all season and then he did it! A new English record of 8.13m was unleashed. Stewart started off the final close to eight metres with an aggressive jump, which got the red flag. Two rounds later he had really made his mark. Fired up afterwards the young man was confident of continuing his progress onto the world scene: 'There's a few things I've got to change in my mental approach and I'll be jumping as far as them, if not further. It's mental strength. When I was a junior I was always worried – am I progressing to quickly? Will people remember me as a very good junior who never did anything as a senior? I've been a lot more relaxed now. My head is channelled into just running down the runway and jumping.'

In the 400m hurdles, Lorrane Hanson finished second and was rewarded with a best ever 56.70. In the women's younger age groups, the Merrys continued their dominance. Emma won the intermediate discus, while cousin Katharine was stunning in the girls 100m.

It was back to cup final action for the bulk of the club, with the Gold and Jubilee Cups at Stoke. In the former the men finished second to old rivals Haringey. The London club had a tally of 127 points to Birchfield's 106. Individual victories were gained by Lincoln Asquith (100m), Rob Harrison (1,500m), Stewart Faulkner (long jump) and Shane Peacock (hammer throw). The 4 x 400m relay was won by Birchfield.

There was a tantalising result in the Jubilee Cup. Birchfield beat Essex Ladies by 97 points to 96.5! Individual honours went to Lorraine Hanson in the 400m hurdles, Claire Summerfield in the high jump and Karen Pugh in the discus.

This exciting month finished with the European Junior Championships at Varazdin in Yugoslavia. Despite only being in her fifteenth year Katharine Merry ran a creditable 11.84 to finish seventh in the final of the 100m. She further confirmed her promise in the 200m, finishing fifth in 24.05. It had been a long season for the youngster but one that had been full of experience.

One of the most notable, but least publicised, success stories at these Championships was that of Birchfield's Paulette McLean. Prior to 1989 Paulette was a 200m specialist with a personal best of 24.9. Her meteoric rise in her new event, the 400m, started at the AAA Under-Twenty Championships at Stoke where she won the title with a new championship best performance of 54.52. A week later Paulette consolidated that performance with an emphatic victory in an international versus Italy and Hungary. Her time was 54.56.

All roads led to Varazdin where she took another chunk off her best time in being the fastest qualifier in the heats – a magnificent 53.73. Disappointment came in the semi-final when she was eliminated, even though it was her second fastest ever time – 54.14.

The climax of international action was to be the IAAF World Cup in Barcelona in mid-September. In action were a trio of Stags: Stewart Faulkner, Shane Peacock and the newsworthy Derek Redmond.

Stewart was to gain seven valuable points. His evening's best distance of 7.84m was achieved in very difficult conditions. 'The wind would be quite light and the there would be an almighty gust as you approached the board', he explained. As he was also suffering from a heavy cold he was very pleased with his performance: 'This gives me more satisfaction than anything. There's nothing that can match up to this but I'm not satisfied until I'm number one.'

Shane had an unspectacular competition. Whilst his throws were consistent, they were not outstanding, but his final effort of 67.68m elevated him one place to seventh.

The British team's gamble of putting Derek Redmond into the 400m as a late replacement for Brian Whittle, who had suffered a facial injury, was a brave one. His season had suffered disruption because of problems with his toe and at one point he had retreated to his Northampton flat and shut the world out. Derek was to explain: 'Then one day I thought that all this had to stop and I was going to get everything sorted out.'

Watching the Europa Cup on television left Derek with a desire to make it to Barcelona and the World Cup. The toe responded to treatment and allowed him to begin training towards his new goal. A relay leg in the Cup Final felt good at 46.8 and he competed in two meetings. So came the step back onto the world stage in Spain.

'Some people say I should not have gone. I did not know I was running the individual until the morning before. I came down from breakfast, got out of the lift and there were the team managers Frank Dick and Les Jones. As I got out they took me by either arm and my first thought was – what have I done?! They explained about Brian Whittle and his nose injury and asked if I would run the individual. As I was already running the relay I felt that I should also be good enough for the individual.'

Derek phoned home. 'My coach said I would either blast it or come plumb last. It was a risk. As soon as the gun went there was nothing in my legs and I was tying up with 250 metres to go. Everybody was going past.' Derek was to agree that it was a gamble that didn't pay off. His lack of competition and fitness was also revealed in the relay, where he replicated his individual race time. The only good news for Derek was that after those runs his toes did not play up.

Attention now turned to the selections being announced for the Commonwealth Games teams ready for New Zealand in January 1990.

From a club perspective there were stories about to emanate about two athletes at opposite ends of the scale of experience. They were the fledgling Katharine Merry and the veteran marathon runner John Graham.

One surprise omission from the England Women's Commonwealth Games team was to be Katharine. It had been anticipated that she would take a place in the 4 x 100m relay squad. However, her mother Jenny revealed that after discussions with the WAAA selectors it had been decided to withdraw her daughter: 'I do not wish to go too deeply into it but it had been decided a long time ago. She is only fifteen and that had a lot to do with it.' There were those who believed that the decision was probably a joint one between the WAAA and the Merry camp. The Association was aware of burning out another big talent as was presumed to have happened to Lindsey Macdonald, Margaret Cheetham and Rachel Hughes.

John Graham was one of Scotland's favourite athletes. A veteran of three Commonwealth Games, he had been hoping to make it a fourth in January. However, because of the expense of the trip down under, the small size of the Scottish team excluded him.

Graham's Commonwealth career had started at the 1978 Edmonton Games, where he competed as a steeplechaser. Suffering from a recurrence of malaria contracted on a visit to Morocco three years before, the Scot was eliminated in the heats. It was soon after that he made the decision to tackle the marathon.

The 1980 AAA Marathon Championships, which took place in Milton Keynes on the first Saturday in May, was to act as the Olympic trial. Along with Britain's best, John lined up in the quest for a place in the team for Moscow. It wasn't to be – he dropped out at the fifteen miles point. A foot injury also prevented Ian Stewart from completing his marathon debut.

Within six weeks John was to win the Laredo Marathon in Spain in 2:13.21. It was the first marathon that he had completed and, at the time, the fastest by a Briton.

Reduced to watching Dave Black, Ian Thompson and Bernie Ford all fail to complete the course in Moscow, John's sights were now set on a first shot at the New York Marathon. In the race, which he describes as the best performance of his life, he finished third in a personal best of 2:11.47. This was to be the first of four visits to the 'Big Apple' in five years – only missing out in 1982 when the Commonwealth Games took priority.

A 2:09.28 was achieved in Rotterdam on 23 May 1981. Operating at world record pace for three quarters of the distance, the Stag came close to erasing the world record figures of Australia's Derek Clayton. Eighteen months later at his second Commonwealth Games in Brisbane, his fourth place confirmed his status as a world-class marathon runner.

Rob De Castella as the Commonwealth Champion returned to defend his title in Edinburgh. During the week prior to the race De Castella stayed with the Graham family. The race itself witnessed a brave, but unsuccessful, bid for victory by John Graham. 'It was one of the worst tactical races of my life', he recalls.

De Castella led a field of twenty-one starters as they left the Meadowbank Stadium and was only headed on one brief occasion during the entire race. While the rest settled for battling it out for the silver medal, John set out to close the gap on his house guest. He succeeded in joining De Castella at the halfway point – but after a short period in the lead saw his challenge fade as the 1982 champion surged again at fifteen miles. Five miles short of the finish John was passed by the eventual silver and bronze medallists – Dave Edge of Canada and another Australian Steve Moneghetti.

The Birchfield Harrier's last completed marathon was the London in 1987, when he finished eleventh. Cortisone injections and operations to both Achilles tendons hindered a realistic attempt of making the Olympic team for Seoul. However, it is revealing to hear how his perspective differed from that of a track athlete: 'It's a shame that I haven't run in an Olympics. When you are a child the Games are the be all and end all. Things have changed, and there are now other high quality marathon events such as New York, Chicago and Boston.'

Despite his disappointment at not being selected to compete in Auckland, John was given Life Membership of Birchfield Harriers and made a family move to run a hotel in Berwick. However, John subsequently resumed his club involvement when he returned to live and work in the West Midlands.

Twenty-Three: Pain but no Glory

A recurrence of an Achilles injury ruled UK 400m record holder Derek Redmond out of the Commonwealth Games in January 1990. In a statement issued to the English team managers, Derek described how an injury to his Achilles tendon – the same injury that forced him to withdraw from the Olympic team in 1988 – had interrupted his training. On the advice of his doctors he withdrew, leaving his spot in the individual 400m and the 4 x 400m relay vacant. Auckland was to have been Derek's Commonwealth Games' debut, as injury had also ruled him out of Edinburgh four years earlier.

Soon, on the other side of the world, Derek's training partner Phil Brown also found himself in a painful situation. Phil, who had not looked sharp through the first two rounds of the 400m, went out in the most dramatic fashion in the second semi-final. After starting quickly in lane two, then slowing down after twenty metres, he tried to accelerate off the bend – only to tear a hamstring. According to reports, the Olympic relay silver medallist flew about a metre in the air, coming back down to earth on his head. This caused abrasions and concussion. Several minutes after the race actually finished Phil was carried off the track on a stretcher.

The women's heptathlon event also provided a lot of challenges for Judy Simpson. Jane Flemming, pipped in Edinburgh in 1986 by just four points, gained revenge on Judy by winning the gold medal. In addition she improved Simpson's Commonwealth record by 72 points and the Games record by over 400 points. Judy achieved her best score since her record in the 1986 European Championships but clearly was not at her best following all the injury problems which had prevented her reaching her full potential. So the twenty-eight-year-old Birchfield Harrier had to be content with bronze, which, with her 1982 silver, gave her a full set of Commonwealth medals.

In the 100m hurdles four years previously, Flemming had trailed 0.21 seconds behind Simpson. Therefore the signs were ominous when the Australian gained a comfortable victory. Her winning 13.21 gave her a 0.18 margin over Judy, which translated into a twenty-seven points advantage.

After the high jump, Sharon Jaklofsky-Smith of Australia moved into second place on the strength of her 1.76m, a height surprisingly beyond Judy who recorded 1.73m.

Judy was easily the best putter in the field and cut the gap between her and Flemming thanks to a useful 14.89m opener. This she matched with her final throw.

In the 200m Flemming gained her third win of the day, leaving the opposition trailing almost a second behind. Simpson's 25.29 lost her a lot of ground and she finished well down on her 1986 total of 3,855. It was clear, barring disasters from Flemming, that all her effort would be needed to hold off Jaklofsky-Smith for second.

End of first day standings were:

1. Flemming   3,892
2. Simpson   3,671
3. Jaklofsky-Smith   3,636

The second day started with the long jump where Flemming made it four out of five thanks to a personal best opening jump of 6.57m. Jaklofsky-Smith moved into second place, as, improving jump by jump, her third round 6.42m took 122 points out of Judy, who managed 6.03m.

The javelin round witnessed Iammo Launa inflict a narrow defeat on Flemming with a 49.30m throw which moved the Papua New Guinea athlete out of last place. However, the overall leader was more than pleased with her personal best which increased her lead by just over 200 points and gave her an excellent chance of the record. Judy's 39.42m lost a little ground on Jaklofsky-Smith's 39.94 and firmly set her up for a bronze medal.

Finally, in the 800m, Jane Flemming needed a time of 2.17 to break the record. She finished second in 2:12.54 to achieve her target. Judy was fifth in her pool in 2:14.59.

Final places were:

1. J. Flemming (Australia)   6,695
2. S. Jaklopsky-Smith (Australia) 6,115
3. J. Simpson (England)   6,085

Meanwhile, Stewart Faulkner had gone into third place after his second round 7.97m and held that position until the penultimate jump of the competition, when the eighteen-year-old Festus Igbinoghene of Nigeria cleared 8.18m. Stewart was regarded as not having done himself justice, fouling each of his last four jumps. As Sally Gunnell became the first British woman to win the 400m hurdles title, Lorraine Hanson finished a creditable sixth in 57.58.

Once back home the 'walking wounded' started to assess their physical ability to meet the demands of a new season.

Phil Brown hoped to return to training within five weeks after learning that the hamstring injury, which caused his demise at the Commonwealth Games, was not as bad as at first feared. When Brown was carried off the Auckland track the left hamstring was in a spasm and the fears were that the muscle had been ruptured. He reported: 'It's a tear in the belly of the hamstring, low down where the muscle fibre becomes softer tissue.' Brown revealed what the physios had told him: 'The damage is quite small and in two to five weeks I'll be three-quarters striding. I'm still getting treatment every day.'

The injury had come as a complete surprise: 'I'd had no previous stiffness or aches before the race. I can't remember much of what happened. I never lost consciousness but the worrying thing was that I was trying to move but nothing responded.'

Also in search of medical advice had been Derek Redmond. The result was surgery to remove pieces of bone from his foot and for a few weeks hopping around on crutches. Derek was determined to leave no stone unturned in his rehabilitation. In between weights and circuit sessions he was copying rival Roger Black in his path back to fitness. Black had missed several seasons with a foot injury. The Stags' copycat act had even gone as far as choosing the same surgeon as Black. Now, with the operation behind him, Derek was looking forward to racing the Team Solent star in the summer and putting the watching of major games on television into the past.

In her perspective on the new campaign Katharine Merry admitted that lessons had been learned from the Varazdin experience of 1989: 'My main target is the World Junior Championship in Bulgaria. I don't think Dennis will let me double up as I did in Varazdin. They were six hard races and it isn't going to be any easier in the Worlds.' Young Merry was guarded about which event she would tackle in Plovdiv. However, she did admit that Dennis Baker, her coach, had designs on the longer event: 'The 200 metres is going best in training and Dennis feels that it will be my best event next season.'

1990 would be Katharine's first in the intermediate age group, yet one in which no serious threat to her supremacy was expected. However, she was wary of turning to senior events in a quest for better competition: 'I will be doing senior races for my club but that won't be individual 100s and 200s. It will only be for the relay and then only once or twice where necessary.'

So we come to the indoor activities, initially with Mark Thomas recording an impressive 47.91 400m at a meeting in Sindelfingen, West Germany. Thomas was one of the athletes aiming for the European Indoor Championships, which were to take place in Glasgow in early March. Both he and Michael Rosswess, who also ran well in Sindelfingen, were looking to that event to prove a point, having missed out on Auckland selection.

The Birchfield pair were next on track at the Omron Games at Cosford in mid-February. Having won his heat, Michael was a little disappointing in the 60m final finishing equal fifth in only 6.77. As for Thomas, he had dedicated himself to an entire indoor season and until that weekend had enjoyed the position of Britain's number one over 400 metres. However, a lingering cold and Gary Cadogan put paid to any hopes that he would win in Cosford. Mark ran hard from the gun, grabbing the all-important pole position at the break, but round the last bend it was Cadogan who looked like he would overhaul him, and that's what he did. Subsequently, Rob Harrison won a slow 1,500m with a good turn of speed over the last metres.

A week later at the Great Britain v. East Germany match in Glasgow there were predictable clean sweeps in the sprints. The surprise was that in the field events the hosts won four of the five competitions – including the long jump by Stewart Faulkner with 7.93m.

The Kelvin Hall was busy again in early March for the European Championships and so was Faulkner. He did not match his previous position as 7.77m saw him in eighth place. He still performed well, however, and was only marginally over the board with a couple of his better efforts. Understandably, though, he saw the event as a missed opportunity for a medal, especially after an 8.05m jump in Spain in mid-week: 'After the Commonwealth Games the objective was to show everyone I could jump eight metres plus but I do feel a little jaded after all the travelling this week. I am not in the same condition as I was last week.'

It was the younger Stags who led the charge into the new outdoor season. In the Midland Premier Division of the Young Athletes League they beat off some tough opposition to take first place in the opening fixture. The Stags totalled 253 points to kill off the challenges from Cardiff on 176 and Leicester on 134.

It was another resounding victory in the second match at Stoke. The new generation came out on top by 46 points over runners-up Cheltenham on 242. Curtis Browne achieved a fine sprint double in the boys' section with 100m in 12.00 and the 200m in 24.9.

It was the turn of the senior athletes in June as they travelled to Jerez in Spain for the European Track and Field Clubs Championship.

Stewart Faulkner won the gold medal in the long jump with a leap of 7.90m. Jason John with a personal best of 10.46 in the 100m and Derek Redmond in the 200m received silver medals in the sprints. Club Captain Rob Harrison was placed third in a slow tactical 1,500m.

The club finished sixth in the men's final behind the hosts, Larios, who had imported athletes from five other countries – including Cuba!

The Birchfield ladies finished a commendable eighth out of twenty-two teams in the final at Vienna in an event dominated by the East Germans and Russians. The outstanding individual performance for the club was a silver medal won by twenty-five-year-old Lorraine Hanson in the 400m hurdles.

A fortnight later it was a very successful weekend for all sections. While the seniors were annexing no fewer than eight titles in the Midland Counties Championship at the Alexander Stadium, the junior men were keeping their unbeaten record at Sale.

On his home track Michael Rosswess recalled his Olympic season form by taking the MCAA sprint double with a 10.74 for the 100m and a 21.40 in the 200m. Sylvia Black retained her 3,000m walk title in 24:22.05, which improved the championship-best performance by twenty seconds. Lorraine Hanson switched from the hurdles to the 400m flat. The Commonwealth Games finalist found the lack of obstacles to her liking and won in a new club record of 52.78, from club-mate Suzanne Guize. Russell Payne arrived with a good throwing pedigree, as his parents Rosemary and Howard Payne were former Commonwealth Games champions. Russell followed in his father's footsteps by winning the hammer with a throw of 53.10m so retaining the championship record. Clova Court won the ladies javelin with 47.92m while her fellow international Kevin Brown retained his discus title with a winning effort of 53.53m. The eighth Stag to strike gold was Steve Thomas who sped around the 400 metres in a fine 47.47.

Birmingham Airport was a flurry of activity on the first Saturday in July when some of the country's top athletes flew in for the British League match at the Alexander Stadium. The third BAL match of the season came less than twenty-four hours after the IAC Grand Prix meeting in Edinburgh and many of those athletes taking part had to join up with their clubs in Birmingham. The home club was lying fourth in Division One and hoping to make up ground on leaders Haringey. To assist the cause Derek Redmond and Shane Peacock had caught the 7.00 am flight from the Scottish capital. Eventually Birchfield enjoyed nine victories in thirty-six events. This pushed them onto 335 points, 48 points behind keen rivals Haringey.

If the present performances were encouraging then the future continued to look bright too. Local schoolboy Curtis Browne was being hailed as 'the new Linford Christie' after becoming the English Schools 100m Junior Boys Champion. Curtis equalled the national record, which had stood since 1979, for the age group in the process. In winning the Blue Riband event he achieved a time of 11.1. In addition to this win, Curtis also picked up a second gold medal by being a member of the victorious West Midlands junior boys relay team.

The theme of emerging talent continued to the end of the month when, in front of their home crowd, the Young Athletes League title was clinched. The team had triumphed from five gruelling matches as the only undefeated one from the sixteen who had participated in the Midland Premier Division. In the final league table the Birchfield Harriers finished a mighty 92.5 match points clear of second-placed Cannock & Stafford.

On the final day itself the victory tasted particularly sweet as the Perry Barr youngsters, aged between eleven and sixteen, crushed their arch rivals Wolverhampton & Bilston by forty-six points. Birchfield rattled up forty-four victories including four out of five relay races. No fewer than eight AAA grade-one-standard performances and twenty-two personal bests were achieved in another outstanding team effort.

Two of the club's brightest prospects were to be involved in a junior international match against Australia and Italy in Horsham in early August. Noteworthy in itself but that day two teenage girls were to meet on track for the first time. The significance being that the last time they faced each other would be exactly a decade later in one of the most memorable finals in Olympic history! On this day in 1990 Katharine Merry would break the British age record by a fifteen year old for the 100m with a time of 11.60. The Birchfield girl claimed two useful scalps in defeating her keen rival Diane Smith with one Cathy Freeman of Australia in third place. The positions for Cathy and Katharine would be reversed at Sydney 2000 in a 400m final of much emotion. Little could they have realised their destiny at the time in that quiet corner of Sussex. All that Katharine registered was her delight with her performance having missed much of the season due to sciatica.

Jason John, then eighteen years old, recorded a personal best of 10.30 to finish just behind Jason Livingstone in a desperately tight finish to the 100m.

Back in the Midlands, Stewart Faulkner was the only local winner in the AAA/WAAA Championships at the Alexander Stadium. The 6 foot 5 inches Birchfielder propelled his body powerfully through the air with a second-round leap of 8.05m. Despite his tender years, Stewart was crowned AAA Champion for the third successive year. The last person to achieve that feat was the former Olympic Champion, Lynn Davies, in the late 1960s.

That October, buoyant Birchfield landed another prestigious crown in the Midland WAAA Road Relay Championships at Telford. It was a scintillating second-leg stage of 9:19 by Sally Ellis that was the turning point. Sally took over from Nicky Salisbury thirty-one seconds down but transformed this into a thirty-second lead. Cath Mijovic completed the final leg in 9:41 to lift the title in 29:39. Tipton were second.

More honours were gathered in November by Birchfield members – this time in the race walking arena. At the National Race Walking Association's Youth Championships at Aldershot, the Birchfield girls excelled themselves, especially in the under-fifteens 3,000 metres. Birchfield girls took the team title and were presented with the Australia Shield, which they had last won in 1983.

The Birchfield Harriers men veterans were not to be left behind either when they walked at Chigwell in Essex in the Veterans 20km Championships. Outstanding was George Mitchell, who won the over-seventy-five years group in 2:16. A club with talent emerging at both ends of the age scale!

Twenty-Four: Success Breeds Success

'Just brilliant Birchfield...' was the press verdict in mid-January of 1991 when the club took a string of honours, both indoors and outdoors, after a hectic weekend of athletics action.

Outdoors the club's youth squad stormed to another tremendous success in the Midland's Cross Country Championships at Nottingham, while inside at Cosford a strong Birchfield squad turned in some fine performances at the Omron Games.

At Nottingham the youth squad extended their impressive unbeaten record when taking the team title by ten points from long-time rivals Wolverhampton & Bilston. Individual honours went to Martin Dowling, who collected the silver medal.

Meanwhile, at Cosford, Michael Rosswess made an impressive return to form recovering from a slow start to finish second in the 60m final in 6.69. Geraldine McLeod came within 0.01 seconds of defeating Commonwealth champion Sally Gunnell in a thrilling 200m final.

A few weeks later talented heptathlete Clova Court produced one of her best displays in the Midlands Open Championships at Cosford. Clova ran to two excellent wins and threw for a personal best. She won the 60m hurdles in 8.7 and the 200m in 25.3. Clova was second in the shot putt with 13.8m.

Within seven days at the same venue Michael Rosswess was just edged out in a tremendous battle with Linford Christie at the end of the 60m final. The duo were both given the same time, a 1991 world best of 6.63. Michael was originally given the winner's bouquet immediately after the race, and a spot in the World Championship team. However, on studying the photo-finish of this cliffhanger sprint, the judges reversed their decision and Christie was awarded first place.

In March there was good news for the younger Stags as they retained their cross-country league title. In torrential rain at Wolverhampton, the under-seventeens ran away with it packing seven into the first ten places. Martin Dowling took the individual title. Adam Godwin finished second overall as the team ended the season 419 points clear of second-placed Solihull & Small Heath.

April meant the London Marathon and Sally Ellis was on her way to take on the world after running the race of her life in the capital. Millions of television viewers had watched as Sally was the first British woman home. This booked her berth in the Tokyo World Championships, at the end of a controversial and action packed season. Sally's fans and friends watched as she bravely held off former London Marathon winner Veronique Marot in the final few yards to finish in twentieth place in the women's race in a time of 2:34.42. It meant that both she and Marot could look forward to a trip to Japan in August. Many regarded this as a total vindication of a season that saw Sally have several brushes with the British selectors, as she pursued success.

Despite a third place finish in the British trials for the World Cross Country Championships, thirty-two-year-old Sally was controversially left out of the British squad after agreeing to run a marathon in Japan just three weeks before the Antwerp race. However, her magnificent season in the Grand Prix World Cross

Stewart Faulkner.

Country Challenge series gave her a last minute 'wild card'. The World Championship place came only weeks after Sally had been awarded the Amateur Sports Personality of the Year by Birmingham Sports Council.

Still unbeaten – that was the tag for the club's talented youngsters who marched to yet another win when the Midland Young Athlete's League kicked off at the Alexander Stadium. The boy's under-seventeen team, who had stormed to triumph in 1990 with an unbeaten record, made a magnificent start to 1991 with an amazing forty-two individual victories.

Meanwhile, the ladies started the Midland Counties League Division One in winning fashion with a six-point success over Coventry Godiva at Warwick University. Katharine Merry ran two intermediate sprints in times that took her to the European Junior Championships in Greece.

In June three Birchfield Harriers grabbed silver medals at the UK National Championships in Cardiff, with Michael Rosswess picking up a birthday brace of medals with some tremendous running. Michael picked up two marvellous presents for his impending twenty-sixth birthday with a second place finish behind European Champion John Regis in the 200m, and followed this up with a silver medal berth behind another European Champion, Linford Christie. The shorter sprint saw Rosswess return an impressive time behind Christie. In so doing he secured a spot in the 4 x 100m relay squad for the European Cup to be held in Frankfurt, Germany.

In the European Cup Final Lorraine Hanson joined Linda Keogh, Sally Gunnell and Jennifer Stoute to set a new UK 4 x 400m record. Lorraine's second-leg run of 52.00 sparked the team to a time of 3:24.25 and followed on the heels of a club record run in France two weeks before.

Back in Britain a young club member was performing superbly. Katharine Merry, just sixteen years old, ran faster than Britain's representative in Frankfurt to claim the 200m title at the UK Under-twenty Championship in Stoke, with a championship best of 23.74.

The AAA/WAAA Championships at the Alexander Stadium in late July were a major success for the organisers and provided the large crowd with some memorable performances. None more so than Derek Redmond's stirring fairytale win in the 400m, which was a triumph for his indomitable spirit over the previous eighteen months. The icing on the cake was the selection of five Birchfielders for the World Championships in Tokyo. These selections were announced immediately after the championships:

Sally Ellis (left).

Marathon: Sally Ellis
400m: Lorraine Hanson
Heptathlon: Judy Simpson
200m: Michael Rosswess
400m: Derek Redmond

A week later an outstanding performance in an event in Stoke earned Clova Court a place as replacement for the unlucky Judy Simpson, who was yet again forced out by injury.

Eventually, there was to be golden joy for one of those who travelled east. Derek Redmond completed his dream comeback to help power the Great Britain 4 x 400m relay team to a gold medal in those championships. In doing so he maintained the Stags' amazing tradition of happy returns in major relays.

Derek ran a 44.1 second leg as part of the squad's British, European and Commonwealth record time of 2:57.33. It was the fifth medal for a club member in the three World Championship relays held so far. In 1983 Ainsley Bennett and Phil Brown had taken home bronze medals from the relay, while in 1987 Phil and Derek were part of the silver-medal quartet.

At home the Birchfield Harriers Young Athletes Team put up their best display for five years as they improved three places from their fifth place in 1990 in the Young Athletes Final at the Alexander Stadium. The winners were Blackheath with Birchfield second on 387 points. The best individual performance came from Justin Barnett, who collected an impressive three gold medals. Justin won the Colts 100m in 12.9 and the 200m in 26.4 before leading the young Stags to victory in the 4 x 100m relay.

Another member receiving an accolade in September was Michael Rosswess – that of fastest British-born sprinter. Michael shook off the effects of a disappointing World Championship performance to record the fastest 100 metres ever run by a British-born athlete. His latest triumph came before a television audience of millions as well as 25,000 people at Sheffield's Don Valley Stadium. Michael smashed his personal best by 0.1 seconds to record 10.15 – a brand new UK native record.

Of great significance in club history at this time too was the acquisition of a new name for the pool of talent. Wolverhampton & Bilston's talented young heptathlete Denise Lewis had been recruited to the Birchfield cause. Denise, then aged nineteen, had finished fifth in the European Junior Championship heptathlon in Greece and was already a Great Britain international having recorded a promising 5,484 points in an international match in Germany in June.

Jubilant Birchfield ladies' team manager Kevin Reeve was delighted with the news of Denise's arrival at the Alexander Stadium: 'She already has a plethora of good events with a six-metre long jump, a forty-six-metre javelin throw and a sub-fourteen second 100 metres hurdles. With Denise, Clova Court and Judy Simpson available for selection next season, we will have some really prolific points scorers in the team.'

So thoughts were turning to 1992, but there was still much else happening in the autumn months and beyond. A jaunt halfway across the world to Malaysia certainly paid off for Andy Symonds. He ran one of the best races of his life for a second place finish in one of the top races in South East Asia. Andy, then twenty-six years old, had travelled the thousands of miles to run in the Penang Marathon where he was wearing a Great Britain vest for the first time. In an impressive performance Andy came home in 2:29.09, less than thirty seconds behind the winner His-Yi-Chung of China.

The race certainly had the desired effect of boosting Andy's experience of international conditions — and of the uncertain methods of stewarding to be found in less experienced athletics nations at the time. 'Parts of the course were like running against the traffic on the M25', he explained. 'Although some of the roads were closed as they would be in this country, others were not and you had to be very careful to dodge the traffic!'

Also busy at the same time was Sally Ellis. She enjoyed two triumphs in two days. Sally took her team to victory in the Midland Women's Relay at Sutton Park on a Saturday with a storming third leg. On Sunday she took individual glory in the Birchfield Ten Mile, finishing more than four minutes ahead of the field.

As colder times dawned so two of the up-and-coming female walkers were following up successes in the National Junior Championships at the Alexander Stadium with further progress in the Midland Winter League races. Joanne Pickett, aged eleven, who was the UK under-thirteen 2,500m Champion, had two minutes to spare in winning her competition. Also performing well that day was thirteen-year-old Joanne Orr, who was placed fourth in the National 3km event. Joanne had the satisfaction of defeating all three competitors who had won a National medal to win her race.

The walking section maintained some very useful performances in the final round of the Midlands Winter Handicap League at Worcester. There were triumphs at both ends of the age scale for the Stags who starred in both veteran and under-fifteen age groups. Star of the show was seventy-seven-year-old George Mitchell, who finished third overall on handicap for the three-leg series after leading home the club in the final 10km race.

The Birchfield junior girls finished the series in second place with Joanne Pickett, who won each of the three 2.5km races taking the overall individual title.

Twenty-Five: Shattered Dreams

In 1992 various Birchfield Harriers were to make the sporting headlines – especially during the Olympics. However, the New Year opened with Shane Peacock as the centre of attention.

The hammer thrower from Hull revealed that he was sharing training tips with one of the Soviet Union's best throwers. Ranked in the world's top ten in 1991, Igor Nikulin had accepted Shane's invitation to spend time in the Midlands. The pair, who had first struck up a friendship in 1990, were swapping ideas and were undergoing an intensive schedule together. Shane reported: 'We are training very hard, concentrating on technique. This has been a great opportunity for me. I am learning a lot from him and, equally, he is learning from me. I have spent three years changing my technique but now everything is looking good.'

Meanwhile, in the great outdoors, the club was enjoying double glory in the junior and youth cross-country team events at the Midland Counties Championships at Wollaton Park, Nottingham.

The junior team confirmed coach Ian Stewart's prediction that they would have four in the top fifteen and take the team title. Their total was 32 and that of second-placed Coventry Godiva was 51 points.

Howard Payne.

The youth race produced an exciting clash between Darius Burrows of Birchfield and Scott West of OWLS. The starting loop and a medium lap saw Burrows force the pace for much of the way. However, West matched all that was thrown at him to good effect. Having slipstreamed Burrows for much of the course, West struck at the perfect spot – the final demanding hill. Burrows held second place from a fast-finishing Billy Farquarson from Mansfield.

In a warmer environment that month, Katharine Merry, then seventeen, set a championship record of 23.90 in winning the 200m at the Scottish Indoor Championship in Glasgow. This was, incidentally, the sixth fastest all-time indoor performance by a senior woman in the United Kingdom. It was also 0.38 seconds inside Sally Gunnell's previous meeting best.

Katharine stated afterwards that this was merely a time trial, an assessment of how her winter training was going and whether she needed more or less hard work. She sped round almost a second clear of the 60m winner Marcia Richardson. 'I'm very pleased – my best outdoors is 23.5 and you're supposed to go a full second faster outdoors compared to indoors', Katharine said. 'This track is hard work. You lose your way when you come off the bend.'

Explaining her various aches and pains, none of which seemed to slow her up, Katharine continued: 'I've had a bad back for two years, my right hamstring is a lot tighter than the left and my right knee's got a niggling injury.'

Also on form at the same time – and no stranger to injury – was Derek Redmond. Running his first indoor 400m for ten years in the Belgium v. England v. Russia international in Ghent, Derek set a personal best of 47.32.

There was further good news for club and country at the beginning of February. Robert Weir, recognised as one of the greatest discus and hammer throwers Britain had produced, was back competing. This followed his adventures with the Miami Dolphins and, later, in Canada's American Football League. He returned to athletics in style, throwing the hammer 67m in only his third session.

Michael Rosswess was also planning to be competitive as he went into the AAA Indoor Championships at the National Indoor Arena in his home city. Michael did reach the 60m final, winning his heat in 6.68 and the second semi-final in 6.60.

Jon Drummond of the USA was amongst those in a strong field for the final itself. Michael left on-form Jason Livingstone at the start but Livingstone surged ahead at twenty metres before falling to the track with cramp. Jason John got the better of Michael, who took the bronze medal. Jon Drummond was the eventual winner.

In a more traditional context, the Birchfield ladies were third in the Women's National Cross Country Championships at Cheltenham. The winners were Parkside of Harrow on 103 points with Birchfield on 142. Shireen Barbour was the first club member home in seventh place.

Producing columns of copy at the end of the month was Judy Simpson, for she had decided to extend a period of recuperation in Australia. Judy was recovering from Achilles tendon surgery and was based at the Australian Institute of Sport in Canberra. Robin, her husband and coach, announced: 'The conditions are perfect for her recovery, so she has decided to stay there until May. She is getting stronger and stronger every day and is running faster and faster with each session.' Judy's major objective was, understandably, to make the Olympic team and she did not plan full competition back home until June. Sadly, Judy was to have her dreams unfulfilled – and time would show she would not be unique amongst the club's athletes.

As March dawned the club was in mourning for one of its greatest athletes. Howard Payne had been taken ill in the gymnasium at Birmingham University and died aged sixty-one.

Howard was certainly one of the most successful throwers in the history of Birchfield Harriers. Born in Rhodesia in 1931, he came to Cardiff in 1958 to represent the country of his birth at the Empire Games. Here he met his future wife and became a student at Birmingham University. He represented Great Britain in the hammer event in sixty-one internationals between 1960 and 1974, and competed at five Commonwealth Games. At those he won three gold medals and a silver medal. He was also selected for three Olympics and two European Championships.

In 1960 Howard had risen to the top of the British ranking list and stayed there for over ten years. He first threw over 200 feet in 1960 and improved to 208 feet in 1962. That remained his best distance until 1968, when at the age of thirty-seven he made a remarkable improvement – throwing a new British record of 223 feet 3 inches at the Mexico Olympics. He credited this improvement to a dance lecturer at Birmingham University who had helped to improve his balance and muscular co-ordination. Howard turned forty in April 1971, but continued to represent Britain in internationals, gaining his fiftieth vest in August 1972 in the match with France in Paris. From his fortieth birthday to the time he retired at the end of the 1974 season Howard actually appeared in sixteen internationals plus Olympic, European and Commonwealth Games. In his final year of serious competition, he was second in the Commonwealth Games in Christchurch, New Zealand. This ended a run of three successive victories. Howard returned to Britain to win the AAA Championship and then later in the year made his longest ever throw of 232 feet 6 inches in a match against Poland.

Howard obviously had a long and glorious career, but it was a comparatively new boy who would maintain the club's interest in the climax of the indoor season. At the European Indoor Championships in Genoa, Italy – while drama surrounded whether Jason Livingstone had qualified from his heat – Michael Rosswess and young Jason John were quietly progressing to the semi-finals. In the first, Livingstone finished well clear of John. Vitaly Savin of Russia, in front of Rosswess in the other, was equally impressive and ran 0.05 seconds faster.

In the final Rosswess was first away, but Livingston quickly levelled and powered up the track. At forty metres Savin showed on Livingstone's shoulder, but the Briton's reaction was to accelerate more. Michael Rosswess took third place while his club-mate Jason John, who had exceeded everyone's expectations by reaching the final, finished seventh.

A fortnight later the battles would continue back at base itself. Six months prior to the Vauxhall Indoor International at the NIA in Birmingham, Linford Christie had officially opened the venue. Now he attracted a capacity crowd to see him race. First he tested out the surface in an invitation 60m finishing well clear of Jason John. Then he took on Jason Livingstone and Michael Rosswess plus a group of top American sprinters. Local man Michael Rosswess added to the tense atmosphere by making a false start. It may have unsettled the rest of the field, but not the Birchfield Harrier. Running in lane seven, he again burst from his blocks, but was quickly headed by Livingstone. Ominously, the long legs and high knee lift of Christie were quickly closing the gap. Christie just got there first with Michael third to make it a British clean sweep.

On the very day that the top sprinters were 'strutting their stuff' in the West Midlands, Birchfield's junior men found that cheerleading helped them to a title in the east at Mansfield. In the English Cross Country

Relay Championships team coach Ian Stewart had his lads lined up around a tricky hill into the wind to encourage Karl Keska along. It worked as Karl stretched away to help the Stags to the 4 x 3km title.

So we come to a summer season dominated by thoughts of Barcelona. At the Olympic Trials there were inevitably mixed fortunes for club members. Katharine Merry carried the burden of local hopes on her teenage shoulders. She eased down to 23.48 in her 200m heat and improved that to 23.42 in the semi-final. These were both personal bests. Though she shaved another fraction off that in the final, Katharine never recovered from a sluggish start. The press comments at the time were that she was going to have work hard on that persistent weak spot.

In the 400 metres Lorraine Hanson was carrying an injury. She did reach the final where she started slower than she had done in her last three races. Although finishing seventh there was much press support for her selection on the team after her performances in Tokyo the previous year. Clova Court decided to enter the 100m hurdles where she reached the final and finished tenth.

Derek Redmond came into the Trials having struggled to clock 46.15 only seven days previously. He predicted that he would have to knock a second off that to make the Barcelona team. It was not a bad guess. An improvement of 1.01 made him the first Briton home behind Trinidad and Tobago's Alvin Daniel in the final. This gave Derek the automatic first slot.

Meanwhile, there was disappointment for Michael Rosswess. He was sixth in the semi-final of the 100m and third in his heat of the 200m.

There was plenty of action throughout the ranks that season before the main event, however. In the area under-twenty Championship Curtis Browne registered a good win in the 100m from Steve McHardy of Halesowen. Curtis also had the satisfaction of establishing a Championship best with his wind-assisted 10.68, while Sylvia Black continued the form which had won her the AAA bronze the previous week. She knocked almost fifty seconds off the championship best in the 5,000m walk.

At the European Under-twenty-three Cup at Gateshead, Katharine Merry and Geraldine McLeod combined with Marcia Richardson and Aileen McGillivary to finish second in the sprint relay behind the Germans. The manner in which Katharine closed down on Tina Schometzler on the last leg suggested that if Britain had got their baton changes right they would have come out on top.

The semi-finals of the GRE Gold and Jubilee Cups at Stoke provided some excitement too. Finalists of the previous year, Birchfield and Woodford Green qualified again in the former. The Stags, who were the day's winners by just three points from Woodford Green, went to their sixteenth final. In the latter competition Birchfield and Coventry led for most of the afternoon, and repeated their 1991 performance by qualifying for the final. By then Birchfield had two Olympic selections on view, Lorraine Hanson and Clova Court. Clova had a tremendous afternoon winning the 200m, 100m hurdles and the javelin. By way of an encore she anchored the 4 x 400m relay squad to victory. However, the hurdles win in 13.6, for the fastest recorded hand-time of the year, was the clincher in receiving the award of 'Athlete of the Match'.

Hanson had a very easy 53.5 400m win. Then she completely destroyed the field in the opening leg of the long relay to give Birchfield a lead they could not lose.

Injury and illness were to prove as much the talking point as qualifying times at the AAA Under-twenty Championships in Stoke. Katharine Merry competed in both sprints, despite a sore hamstring. Like twelve months previously, she found someone better in the 100m. This time it was the much-improved Donna Hoggarth of Preston who secured her ticket to Seoul for the Junior World Championships. As for Katharine, only her second-ever false start and the troublesome right hamstring made the difference. The race was lost from the blocks, Katharine explained: 'The hamstring is exceedingly bad, it's a hindrance. When you can see the other seven at forty metres – you know you've got a problem!' The gap was closing all the way to the line as a three metre lead closed to 0.04. With no 100m form that season, defeat for Miss Merry was far from disastrous. Of more concern was the sciatic nerve problem, which had blighted her championship preparations in the previous couple of seasons. Happily, a day later, Katharine returned to dominate the 200m in 23.90.

Katharine Merry was an Olympic prospect of the future – but the present was a hot and humid Spain as August unfolded. Only the toughest were likely to survive a women's marathon run on day two in temperatures of 29°C with seventy-three per cent humidity, and held on over a course notorious for its uphill finish over the last four kilometres.

Derek Redmond.

Sally Eastall was the first of the British contingent in fourteenth place, with Veronique Marot seventeenth and Birchfield's Sally Ellis twenty-eighth. They all deserved a medal for finishing!

Meanwhile, Clova Court's first day score of 3,535 equalled her corresponding mark in Tokyo in 1991, when she eventually finished sixteenth with 6,022 points. Again it was the high jump at 1.58m that held her back, but she performed well in the other events. She won her hurdles heat in 13.48, put the shot 13.85m and ran 200m in 23.95.

Derek Redmond, with a very quick 45.03, and Lorraine Hanson progressed to the next round of their respective 400m events.

On day three, as in Tokyo, Clova Court performed admirably. She improved her long jump from 5.99 to 6.10m, won the javelin round with 52.12m, and eventually finished nineteenth with 5,994 points. This was just short of her best.

It was day four – 3 August 1992 – that Derek Redmond was to hobble into Olympic history with a hamstring pull to finish his 400m semi-final, supported by his father for the last 100 metres.

The gathered throng rose to applaud him, as stubbornly trying to prevent his legs having the final say, Derek limped painfully on from the spot on the back straight where he had been stopped at full speed by that injury.

After falling to the track, swamped by an avalanche of pain, it had seemed probable that he would have to wait for medical aid. Instead, he got up, and, with a shuffling limp, carried on, staying in lane five. 'My first reaction was nothing was going to stop me finishing the race', he said.

As the crowd cheered Redmond's courage, one man leapt the barrier and ran on to the track to help. Few spectators would have known that it was his father, Jim. It was an extraordinarily emotional moment, as Derek realised who had grabbed his arm and broke down, a private moment – but on the world stage.

As we have read, Derek's medical history had prevented his appearance at several major games in recent years. This latest setback was understandably even more frustrating. When he had run that unexpectedly fast opening round it had seemed that, at last, the gods were smiling on him. Derek seemed set for the final when his right hamstring pulled after 150 metres. 'I was feeling good and it came out of the blue', he recalled. 'It was not a bad pull, but I heard a pop in my leg. It happened so fast, then it dawned on me that I was out of the final. But I wanted to just get up and finish the race, even if it was the world's slowest time!'

As for Jim Redmond: 'I just instinctively decided to get over the barrier to help Derek because the medical aid had been taking so long to arrive – but then he decided to continue the race!'

Derek takes up the story: 'It was about 100 metres to go when someone tried to put their arms around me, and at first I tried to shrug them off. Then I heard them call my name and realised it was my dad. He said: "You don't have to do this", but I said; "I've got to finish", and so he replied: "OK. We started your career together, so we're going to finish this race together." So we went round, and he was keeping away the people who were trying to be super-efficient and remove him. He was saying: "I'm his father!" and they were working out how he got on to the track without any accreditation. All the time I was trying to stay in lane five, where I started, as we were drifting a bit.'

The irony was – and still is – that, despite his injury, Derek Redmond is much better known to the British public than if he had reached the final. At the time the Birchfield Office at the Alexander Stadium in Birmingham was inundated with calls and mail offering sympathy and support.

Once the drama was over the club had to soon turn its attention to other challenges. In winning the GRE Jubilee Cup in Sheffield the ladies' squad had put Birchfield back into Europe. A powerful team cruised to victory in the final by twenty points and qualified for the 1993 European Clubs Championship in Cyprus. It was the first time in three years that they had captured the honour – but a dramatic improvement on the 1989 triumph, when they won by just half a point.

Olympic talents Lorraine Hanson and Clova Court plus young starlet Katharine Merry linked with the cream of the club to demolish the field, winning six of the fifteen events. It was team spirit that took them to glory with Lorraine Hanson running her final race of the season before going into hospital for an operation on the knee problem, which prevented much progress in Barcelona.

Clova Court competed in four events, while Katharine Merry claimed a prized scalp. Katharine, still seventeen, took on Olympic Hurdles Champion Sally Gunnell over 200m, and comprehensively beat the Essex Ladies' representative.

The Birchfield team won every event from 100m to 800m. Geraldine Mcleod took the short sprint in 11.62 seconds. Katharine Merry's 200m win was in a time of 23.64. Lorraine Hanson lifted the 400m in 58.63 and Suzanne Stanton grabbed further valuable points with an 800m in 2:10.57.

There was victory in both the 4 x 100m and 4 x 400m relays to add celebration to an event already won.

In the end Birchfield cracked the 100 points barrier by three points to comprehensively defeat Sale by twenty points, 103 to 83.

The men had a less successful day. They finished fourth behind winners Belgrave Harriers, Shaftesbury, Barnet and Haringey.

The league standings would also be settled soon. In the Men's British League Division One the ultimate positions were:

1. Belgrave	31 (1,493)	
2. Haringey	29 (1,364)	
3. Birchfield	20 (1,101)	

In the Women's UK Division Two they finished as follows:

1. Edinburgh	308
2. Birchfield	298
3. Croydon	270

International action was of interest in the Autumn. Great Britain's juniors warmed up for the World Championships in Seoul with emphatic victories for the young men and women versus France and Spain at Horsham.

In the 200m Katharine Merry flowed majestically down the straight to win in 23.48, some eight metres clear of her team partner Sophia Smith. Katharine had been denied the opportunity of a sprint double by losing to Donna Hoggarth, who held the edge throughout in a windy 11.55.

In the Home Countries Under-twenty-three International at Whitehaven, Geraldine McLeod was in fine form. She looked a class apart in the women's sprints, winning from Scotland's Sinead Dudgeon in the 100m and Wendy Young over 200m. Her club colleague Michelle Thomas was in both winning relay squads, and also set a stadium record in the 400m. Nick Pearson won the 800m.

Against all the odds the British Combined Events team won a match with Finland, Sweden and Estonia in Parkan, Finland. The home nation was fielding three athletes whose personal bests were over 6,000 points.

Unfortunately, the event got off to a bad start for Clova Court. In the hurdles she was running very fast, despite a head, wind but hit hurdle seven so hard that she broke it completely in half. Although, amazingly, she got back on her feet and struggled over the final hurdles the damage had been done and she recorded 14.39. Not having dropped out of a heptathlon before she was anxious to continue. However, her knee was so badly bruised that she found it difficult to walk, and sadly had to drop out.

Denise Lewis took up the mantle and produced a solid performance. Denise had a superb second day, starting off with a legal leap in the long jump at 6.15m, a sound javelin throw of 43.44 and she was not far from her best in the 800m with 2:19.05. Overall she improved her career best by 127 points to 5,812.

The final sojourn was to the IAAF World Junior Championships in South Korea. Nicole Mitchell of Jamaica had emerged as the favourite for the 100m title and confirmed that status in semi-final and final. Mitchell never looked like being headed, and after beating Katharine Merry 11.45 to 11.68 in their semi, ran away from the rest in the final itself. Katharine got away just too quickly at the first time of asking. Needing a fast start to get into full stride and perhaps inhibited by that false one, she was never in contention and placed fifth. Her 23.59 was slower than in her earlier two races. It seemed that she had paid the penalty for running hard in all her races and this was her seventh in four days.

This eventful year ended with an honour for an outstanding club member. In December Beryl Randle was awarded Life Membership of The Midland Race Walking Association. The citation on the commemorative plaque stated that it was for services as competitor, official, coach and administrator.

In her acceptance speech, Beryl made mention of her first race walk as a youngster in 1946 for Atalanta, who were based at Salford Park. She paid tribute to those people who had helped and guided her career, particularly the late Mrs Dorette Nelson-Neal. Beryl, a Birchfield Vice President, had joined the Perry Barr club in 1953.

Twenty-Six: Hammer Home

The first of two exciting weekends of international meetings took place at the NIA in February 1993. The Vauxhall International drew a healthy crowd plus ITV cameras for the Britain v. America challenge. There were many noteworthy performances, none better than by local favourite Katharine Merry, who continued to make her presence felt at the highest grade. She recorded a time of 23.53 to beat American Dyan Webber to the line in the 200m. Fellow Birchfield Harrier Geraldine McLeod crossed the line third. The Birchfield Ladies' Captain, Clova Court, equalled her own 60m hurdles time of 8.31 when second to Jackie Agyepong.

Overall the British women won nine events, with the Americans taking four, winning the match by 150 points to 120.

It was Clova Court who kept up the momentum the following weekend with her first ever AAA individual title in the 60m hurdles. In what was one of the most popular victories at the TSB AAA Indoor Championships, Clova improved her career best by eleven hundredths of a second to record a time of 8.20.

In March the senior men's team left it very late before snatching victory on the final stage of the Midlands Road Relay Championships. Later, there was another rewarding outing for the club with triumph at the Women's National Cross Country Championships. Old foes Sale Harriers were in second place.

There was plenty of emotion too at RAF Cosford that day, and none more so than for Birchfield veteran athlete Allan Meddings. Alan had won a sprint race at the venue as long ago as 1955. On this weekend he sprinted home to win the veterans 60m in 8.3 at one of the very last events to take place at Cosford.

There was even greater sadness for the club as the season reached June. The death was announced of Councillor Clare Fancote MBE, Honorary Vice-President of Birchfield Harriers. Clare had been one of the politicians instrumental in developing the new Alexander Stadium concept into reality and was responsible for the second grandstand being named after Mrs Nelson-Neale.

Spirits were lifted by various performances in the Pearl UK Championships at Crystal Palace. In the 200m final Katharine Merry won her first senior title, beating Sally Gunnell, and slicing 0.18 seconds off her personal best. After pre-event favourite Jennie Stoute withdrew, having tightened a hamstring in winning her heat, the Midland teenager had 100m champion Bev Kinch for company around the bend but stretched away to hold off the fast-finishing Gunnell and earn her place at the Europa Cup. The Olympic 400m hurdles champion commented: 'When Katharine matures over the next couple of years, she will be a mid-twenty-two runner for sure.'

Meanwhile born-again thrower Robert Weir believed he was set to make one of the greatest athletics comebacks of all time after winning the 1982 Commonwealth Games hammer title at the age of twenty-one. Robert, who competed in the 1984 Olympic discus and hammer finals before settling for a career in American Football, rediscovered his potential with a fine performance in those British Championships. He threw the discus 56.60m to take second spot. BAF Promotions Chief Andy Norman was to state: 'If Robert continues to improve over the next month as he has in the last month, Britain will have a world-class discus thrower. The younger competitors cannot remember the Robert Weir of ten years or so ago, but they give him the utmost respect – and he's earned it.'

Then thirty-two years old, Robert revealed that his comeback had been inspired by the memory of his old hammer-throwing mentor, Howard Payne, who had died in 1992. The Handsworth boy declared: 'Howard was the person who really started me off in athletics and we always kept in touch. I had considered throwing again before he died and left me heartbroken. I couldn't throw. I went back and played football again. But then I thought, "I told Howard I would start throwing again." I suppose in many ways this is for Howard.'

Robert had a reminder for those who were surprised that he had made his initial impact that summer with the discus rather than the hammer: 'When I was selected for the Olympics in 1984, it was because of the discus and it just so happened that I qualified for the hammer too.'

He also offered his perspective on the recent return and the prospective future: 'I was so nervous at Portsmouth. It was my first big competition for nine years. I went into the circle and tightened up so much I was surprised to throw the discus 58.56 metres. Now I'm going to start training properly and any honour that comes will be a bonus.'

Whilst the prodigal son was looking forward to action, the converse was true of the nation's favourite son. Derek Redmond, the limping hero of the 1992 Olympics, said he was not prepared to rush back into fitness after a recent Achilles operation. He revealed that he had decided in May to take the whole of the season off so that he could prepare properly for the 1994 Commonwealth Games: 'I kept it quiet because I did not want it blown out of all proportion. I thought that rather than fumble my way through the season hoping that everything holds out, I should take that decision. Over the years I had been having all sorts of little niggles and small investigative operations – and so I decided to have it all sorted out once and for all. The doctors have told me the operation was a success and I now have a nine-inch scar at the back of my leg.' One way of getting back was a plan to play basketball for the Birmingham Bullets in the winter season: 'Hopefully, I will get a couple of games or at least be on the bench for some game play', he said.

Rest and recuperation were certainly not on the agenda for the club's leading lights as June rolled into a busy July. Katharine Merry was in 200m action at the Europa Cup. In the race, Olympic 100m bronze medallist Irina Privalovagot of Russia beat France's Marie-Jose Perec with a last desperate stride. Katharine made a fine first appearance in the 'Big League'. 'I was fourth coming off the bend', she said, 'but sixth is where I should have come. This weekend has been a great experience. I've learned so much. I was lucky enough to warm up with Jenni Stoute.'

Michael Rosswess showed himself to be in top form taking the honours in the 100m and 200m in the Midland Championships at the Alexander Stadium. Michael achieved a championship best into the bargain.

It was a Friday evening blast for the 200m runners. Michael clocked 21.19 in victory. The triple European indoor bronze medallist added a second victory on the Saturday afternoon, recording a 10.64 win. His semi-final had produced that Midlands Championship record with a 10.54 wind-assisted time.

For the AAA Under-twenty Championship Katharine Merry was her usual ebullient self, clocking good times in her sprint double – not that onlookers would have believed so from her comments at the time: 'I wasn't pleased with the 100. I started like a snail. It was the first time I've been left in the blocks this year. I'm very annoyed with myself because I know I can run a fast time.' Yet, her victory was achieved with a championship best of 11.40.

The next day she added the 200m title, aided by a wind just over the limit. However, her perspective on the conditions was interesting: 'It was a terrible headwind around the bend. It was like a hurricane out there. I really think they need two wind gauges – one on the bend and one on the straight.'

At the Europa Cup heptathlon in Valladolid, Spain, Clova Court injured her back in the high jump but bravely battled through the pain to win the competition with 5,901 points. This was within ninety-three points of her best score the previous year. Clova led the British team to a victory that ensured their place in the highest level of the European multi-events competition for 1994.

Also successful abroad that weekend was Andy Symonds, who put up a great display of distance running when clocking 2:14.36 in the Bruges Marathon, Belgium, gaining second place, and beating his previous best by three minutes.

Back home at the Alexander Stadium, in the AAA Championships, Robert Weir scored a welcome local success. Until the fifth round, Fritz Potgeiter of South Africa had led with an opening throw of 56.48m. Then Robert reached out to 57.44m, followed by a 57.16m. The next three positions were occupied by overseas opposition.

However, major disappointment for local fans in the 200m heats was the last-minute absence of Katharine Merry. The British Champion, accustomed to protecting her dodgy back, which was why she did not risk an appearance in the 100m, was advised by her physio to withdraw after tweaking a hamstring during her warm-up. It was only a precautionary move but proved, in time, to be sensible, for at the European Junior Championships in San Sebastian, Spain, there were no such problems this time around. The only trouble she had was her slow start, which cost her the gold in the short dash. She couldn't quite haul back the deficit and had to be content with a silver medal. In the 200m, however, Katharine was not to be denied. Her gold medal run was all the sweeter for beating the very Czech girl who had beaten her in the shorter sprint. Only 0.02 of a second had denied Katharine, Hana Benesova winning that race by the width of an envelope. Katharine's winning time over 200m was 0.18 seconds faster than Benesova. The Birchfield starlet then capped a memorable weekend when stepping up a distance to join Britain's victorious 4 x 400m relay squad.

So it was 'gold at last' at a major level for a young athlete who for many seasons had gone to championships and not come back with the title she was favoured to win. Her reaction was understandable: 'It was a great relief more than anything', she said. 'It is a great weight off my shoulders. Obviously I was over the moon at winning. The main thing is that I believed in myself much more this time. I knew I had the ability and had done the training. Winning the silver in the 100 metres was a bit of surprise and I was not quite sure if I was doubling up because of the hamstring.'

Other teenage athletes in a mood of celebration were the Birchfield Harriers young athletes squad. They had lifted their ninth successive Midlands Premier League title. Confirmation of the Stags success came at Cardiff when they registered their biggest win of the entire season. Birchfield won a remarkable forty-four events, including fourteen double wins in 'A' and 'B' events plus four of the five relays.

Birchfield's senior men finished their British League Division One programme in August with third place behind London clubs Haringey and Belgrave. In the final meeting at Edinburgh, Michael Rosswess again won the 100m and 200m double.

Four club members were selected for the World Championships in Stuttgart. Katharine Merry was in the 200m and 4 x 100m relay squad, along with Geraldine McLeod. Rob Weir was competing in the discus while Clova Court was involved in the heptathlon and the 100m hurdles.

The early highlight of the autumn campaign was the renaissance of the club as a top-flight force in road relays. At Sutton Coldfield during the Midland Counties Championships this was very much in evidence. The women collected bronze medals, the men silver and there were also medals for the young Stags Under-fifteen team.

Twenty-Seven: The Great Breakthrough

The 1994 indoor athletics season opened with the Birmingham Games at the NIA. Here, Michael Rosswess forced himself into contention as a medal contender for the European Indoor Championships in March.

Michael had lost only one of six British League sprints the previous summer – a 100m to Linford Christie. Having shifted his training emphasis from weights to speed since he had switched coaches at Birchfield, he shrugged off the irritations of two false starts in the 60m final to blast out a time of 6.63, within 0.06 of his indoor personal best.

Later, Clova Court won the 60m hurdles from UK number one Lesley-Ann Skeete in 8.33, a mere 0.1 seconds outside the games record for the competition.

In the great outdoors, meanwhile, for the Midlands Cross Country season, the men carried off the trophy for the club with the best aggregate over the four winter races.

It was a lady, however, who was even more in the limelight after the Midlands Championships at Wollaton Park, for Shireen Barbour earned a place in the World Trials at Alnwick alongside Bev Hartigan and Elaine Foster in most interesting circumstances. Shireen was hailed as the inspiration for all young mothers for gaining a bronze medal, watched by her family – except her three-month-old daughter who slept throughout the 6,050 metres! Shireen herself played down the 'Super Mum' tag: 'I only do forty or fifty miles a week now', she said. 'I used to do a lot of training before I had the children, up to eighty miles a week.' Then contemplating her medal she added: 'Makes you wonder why, doesn't it?'

Shireen got back to the serious business of training in October 1993 on a stair climber, having carried on running for twenty minutes three times a week until some ten days before Naomi arrived as a sister for Tom.

'When I had Tom I couldn't decide whether I wanted to run again or not. I didn't get going until ten months later. But this time I started running three times a week after Naomi came along. I actually shuffled around for twenty minutes in the Midland Road Relay. After a month I moved up to training five days a week. I found it horrible running uphill, and it was even more difficult while I was breast feeding.'

Another distance runner on form was nineteen-year-old Darius Burrows who raced within eight seconds of Rob Denmark's under-twenty course record at the National Cross Country Relays in Mansfield to prove that he was ready to perform well at the World Trials.

Darius transformed a twenty-nine-second deficit into a fourteen-second lead for the Stags, who were then swept to the most decisive victory of the day by Scott West. West, the under-seventeen winner when the 1993 trials were incorporated in the Inter-Counties Championships, was only four seconds slower around Mansfield than Burrows – an awesome double act for the club.

The official result of the 4 x 3km Under-twenty Men went to Birchfield in 36:30. Competing were: Martin Dowling 9:28, Rob Foster 9:14, Darius Burrows 8:52 and Scott West 8:56.

At the World Cross Country Trials, Darius Burrows and Scott West were to prove the prominent juniors early in their eight-kilometre race. Having helped Birchfield to that National title the previous week, it came as no surprise when they pulled away on the second lap.

Burrows, fourth in the 1993 European Junior Championships 5,000m, began as favourite. However, a spike went through his shoe as the gun went off and he admitted: 'It hurt for the first 100 metres, but you don't think about it, do you?'

AAA Junior 1,500m Champion, Neil Caddy of Newquay, worked his way back to the Birchfield pair at the end of the second lap with a positive display. Twice National Under-seventeen Champion Scott West had looked dangerous on the inclines, but when Burrows went ahead he did so decisively. Stretching his lead with every stride, he eventually won by fourteen seconds. He then received medical attention for his bleeding foot. Darius reported: 'It's a bit painful now, but it didn't bother me during the race. Scott West is very fast, and I knew I had to go with two laps left. I put a burst in around the small loop, and knew once

I'd shaken him off that I was going to get away. I knew I had the strength to get away, but conditions weren't easy. It was a bit frosty. It was thawing out, but it was very hard underfoot and a bit bumpy.'

Meanwhile, Caddy had moved well clear of West but the young Stag said philosophically: 'That was the heat. The final is in Budapest. Neil ran very well, he's very strong.'

Suffering challenges of a different kind outdoors was Andy Symonds. A freak accident had interrupted his build-up to the London Marathon. Andy had fractured three ribs during a rugby match – and he wasn't even playing!

The Stag, a PTI with West Midlands Police, was refereeing the match when he was hit from the side, landing on his elbow. He said: 'Before the injury I was in the form of my life, probably in 2:12 shape.' Andy was hoping to recover quickly to complete his marathon preparations.

There was better news for his wife: as being called up as travelling reserve for the Chiba Ekiden Relay in Japan gave Joanne Symonds all the motivation she needed. Her call-up the previous November was followed by a pleasing run in the National Women's Road Relays. Joanne reflected: 'It was a really good trip and a good experience. It really gave me the motivation.' She hit top form in the Alsager 5, taking sixty-five seconds off her previous best to win by fifty-nine seconds in 27:18. She was quick to praise coach Alan Harding: 'I met him on a trip to France and I've never looked back.'

So we now return to more confined spaces and the AAA Indoor Championships. There, Linford Christie found that he could not add the title of AAA Indoor Champion to his ever-growing portfolio, losing to a Briton for the first time in six years. It was Michael Rosswess who finally deposed Britain's number one, although there was little to choose between the two. They both crossed the line in a time of 6.56.

In a competition riddled by false starts, many onlookers thought that Christie fell out of the blocks. 'I did – but it's history now', he pronounced. Michael, in his first year back from injury, could not believe it, exclaiming: 'I'm not hot – I'm boiling!' Not a bad performance for someone who had his international career 'frozen' because of a long line of hamstring, back and foot injuries.

Michael emphasised: 'My injuries were caused by doing the wrong training. I am now trying to learn from the Americans. They get a fast start whereas we try to try and make up the speed at the end.' To get that start Michael had enrolled Katharine Merry's new coach Keith Antoine to help him, while long-time coach Michael Oluban was now responsible for conditioning. In fact it was his starting which had convinced him that he could defeat Christie. Two days earlier they had been practising together and Michael saw his chance: 'I was beating him' he recalls. Interestingly, the last time Christie was pipped to the line indoors it was by another Birchfield Harrier – Lincoln Asquith – at the 1988 National Indoors.

Meanwhile, in the 60m final, Clova Court looked strong in third place. She was only one metre down on her much younger rivals Bev Kinch and Marcia Richardson.

Also to provide excitement on the boards was Katharine Merry during the Great Britain v. USA match at the Kelvin Hall, Glasgow in early February. Katharine was agonisingly close to becoming the first British woman to crack the twenty-three seconds barrier for the 200m indoors. Her victory in 23.00, over the impressive 60m winner Holli Hyche, nevertheless propelled her to the top of the British all-time list, which had been headed by Joan Baptiste since 1985. Katharine revealed afterwards that she had been considering withdrawal because of a hamstring strain.

In the fresh air in Hungary in March at the World Cross Country Championships, Darius Burrows was the first Briton home in 27th place, while Scott West finished 118th. Darius commented: 'I feel I had a good run, but I'm disappointed by my position. I think the standard was higher than last year. I'm going back to training in Cyprus and will come home for the last of the Northumberland Castles Challenge. I don't know about the twelve-stage yet.'

At the Midland Twelve-Stage in early April at Sutton Park, Coventry Godiva turned the tables on defending champions Birchfield Harriers, winning by fifty-five seconds after a closely fought tussle. Team manager Maurice Millington commented: 'I'm pleased with our performance, although it's always nice to win. We'll have Darius Burrows and Scott West back for the National, although we'll have to see how those who do the London Marathon are. We were also without Darren Pemberton, who's got a stomach injury, but it was a good race.'

With that London Marathon on the agenda, Sally Ellis was the latest to join the 'Super Mum' club! She led home the Britons and stated: 'I'm pleasantly surprised.' Sally had started training only a fortnight after giving birth to her daughter Lucy.

While she began to make a move after going through ten miles at almost six-minute mile pace, she reasoned: 'I started racing at eighteen miles. For me that's the half-way point in terms of effort as far as a marathon is concerned.' Sally Eastall was in her sights from fourteen miles but not until the finishing straight did she believe she was beginning to catch her. 'It's not my best', said the Birchfield lady, who had run 2:34.49, 'but I was positive. I was focussed and the preparations had been good.' Sally was also the first veteran over thirty-five to cross the line in 2:37.06.

As many thoughts turned to the track and field season, there was an important preview from team manager Dave Lawrence. He believed that the homegrown talent would improve their 'B' performances and take them closer to the title. Dave himself had competed when the club had won the first BAL title in 1969. 'I'm against big-name recruits', he said. 'I think it's going against what the British League was set up to do. If you bring in people from all over the place then you run the risk of losing your club basis.'

Therefore there was much satisfaction when Birchfield won the first fixture of the season at Wigan. With wins from Michael Rosswess in the 100 metres, Tim Gwynn in the 'B' 110m hurdles and the 400m hurdles, and Martin Nicholson in the 'A' 110m hurdles – they edged home from Newham & Essex Beagles.

In May, Michael Rosswess continued to build on the platform of an excellent indoor season with a 10.4 heat over 100m in the Warwickshire Championships. His club colleague Katharine Merry won the Warwickshire 400m title in 54.0 but coach Keith Antoine emphasised it was only a training run for his 100m/200m golden girl. 'She will run more 400s this year, but only as part of her training', he said.

All eyes now turned to the AAA Championship at Sheffield in June. In the 100m Michael Rosswess picked up the bronze medal, then went to hospital with a suspected dislocated shoulder after falling over the line. Michael had actually led winner Linford Christie and was also caught on the line by Toby Box.

In the women's equivalent, Katharine Merry produced a lifetime – and windy – best of 11.27, despite a dreadful start. The European Junior 100m silver medallist was actually left at the start, but such was her talent that she powered through in the final fifteen metres to win her first National senior title at the distance. From the heats it was obvious she meant business, clocking a legal 11.49.

Five races in two days took its toll on Katharine in the 200m, but left enough in her legs to record the fastest 200m so far that season by a British woman.

The Birchfield flyer was going from strength to strength, although she stated that she had not stopped growing and therefore had not begun any kind of weight training. 'Maybe later this year I will begin some kind of weight training programme, but not until I stop growing, it would be too dangerous', she confirmed. 'We were all very sore out there today with aches and pains. But that is all part and parcel of having five races in two days.'

As with the 100m, Katharine produced the fastest qualifier with 23.10, with the other contenders very much the same. It was Stephanie Douglas who led Merry into the home straight, but once into her flowing stride, Katharine was untouchable.

As for the other Birchfield ladies, Clova Court provided a major upset winning the 100m hurdles from Sally Gunnell and Jacqui Agyepong. Clova stormed to a lifetime best of 13.06 and a Commonwealth Games place, beating defending champion Gunnell into the bargain.

In the long jump Denise Lewis set three personal bests on her way to winning the silver medal, while Yinka Idowu won the title with her fifth-round effort of 6.58. Albeit windy, she was only two centimetres further than Denise. Fascinatingly, in light of impending events in Denise's career, she was pondering whether to choose the long jump or the heptathlon for the Commonwealth Games – having gained qualifying standards in both events.

A more immediate drama was being played out in the men's discus circle. Two days after flying in from the USA, hot favourite Robert Weir watched his Birchfield Harriers club-mate Kevin Brown snatch the title in the last round. Brown, a fitness instructor who had been photographed pulling a bus a few days previously, paced his effort superbly to bid for a ticket to the Commonwealths. Never out of the first three after his 54.68m opener, twenty-nine-year-old Brown saw first Weir, the title-holder, and then Glen Smith, overhaul him. However, he edged two centimetres ahead of Smith in the fifth round at 56.08m and then struck gold in the sixth.

Much of the same Birchfield cast list assembled later that month at their home stadium to represent Great Britain in the Europa Cup. Robert Weir was in a somewhat happier mood on day one when he produced a season's best of 58.92m just when it counted and kept British hopes alive with his three points.

The same day Katharine Merry knew she had to perform well in the 100m on her home track and she did not disappoint. Two weeks previously we have noted that she produced one of her worst starts, which had left her an awful lot of work to do if she was to win. This time she settled into her blocks echoing the advice of Linford Christie: 'Move on the B of the Bang!' Katharine recalls: 'Knowing my starting had not been good, I had been hovering around Linford in the hope that he would offer some advice, and he did. He told me to put my head down, pump my arms and move on the B of the bang. I got my best start of the season.'

The nineteen year old ran brilliantly to record a lifetime best of 11.43 for second place, gaining more team points than expected.

So we come to the 4 x 100m for women. If practice makes perfect then the proof of the pudding was in the running! Britain's relay squad had been in Birmingham practising on the final few days leading up to the Cup, ultimately proving that phrase correct with a commendable second, and seven valuable points.

Stephanie Douglas got them off to a great start with some solid bend running, handing over to Katharine Merry marginally in the lead. Once the long legs of Katharine got moving there weren't many who could pass her, and this race was no exception. She increased the lead, giving Simmone Jacobs a handsome buffer. It was no discredit to Paula Thomas that the Ukranian Zhanna Tarnopolskaya, the final leg runner, was faster with a personal best of 11.08.

What is remembered is that the British women looked well drilled and allowed their team to finish the day in an unfamiliar position as leaders. This was the first time ever for British women in the history of the competition.

The second day dawned and in the long jump Denise Lewis could not quite reach her personal best of 6.56m but jumped well for fifth place in 6.42m, to gain four vital points.

Competing in her more favoured 200m event, Katharine Merry was a little disappointed to find out that the wind had moved to a headwind. Even so the sprint sensation stormed from the blocks and charged around the turn to enter the home straight ahead. Then Silke Knoll of Germany, who had taken the European Indoor silver medal that year, drew on all her strength and experience to run Katharine down and finish in first place.

In the final analysis Germany were match winners by a single point, 98 points to 97 over Great Britain. This was the best ever result for the British women in the Europa Cup. The men also finished second to Germany in their match, scoring 106.5 points to the victors' 121 points.

Afterwards, Denise Lewis declared that she intended keeping busy prior to her Commonwealth Games debut in August. Following the Europa Cup and Combined Events Competitions on consecutive weekends the twenty-one-year-old heptathlete hoped to take in the Under Twenty-three Europa Cup and several club matches. 'It is a busy schedule, but I don't intend to wear myself out. I am sensible and know my limitations', she said.

Her close ally Clova Court, meanwhile, was a very relieved woman as she strove to prove her fitness after suffering an adductor strain that she suffered in winning the AAA championship. It was a make or break time for the international heptathlete, who needed to convince herself that she was back on course with major games looming. She contested the Midland Championships at Stoke in July, competing in the 100 flat and hurdles. Clova powered to victory in the sprint with a wide margin of victory, clocking an impressive 11.77.

She held back in the hurdles heats, recording a victorious 13.65, but knew what she would be up against in the final when former European and World Junior medallist Keri Maddox eclipsed her championship mark of 13.28 by taking her heat in 13.24. In the same heat Denise Lewis improved her personal best to 13.49.

Maddox pushed Court all the way to the line in the final. Clova demonstrated her competitiveness by taking the tape in 13.46. Maddox took silver, 0.06 behind the winner.

After the race, the Birchfield Captain declared: 'I can't tell you how nervous I've been today. I desperately needed to do well to convince myself about my fitness. My arms were literally shaking in the set position. I needed the four races to improve my sharpness as I've not competed since the AAA. My 100 victory convinced me that my speed is still there, although I ran more off strength than speed today. My hurdles were not fluent and Keri put me under a lot of pressure, but that has done my confidence a power of good.'

Before the Commonwealth Games there were, however, other major events in which club members were competing.

In the World Junior Championships in Lisbon, future Birchfield stars tasted action. In the 5,000m, Darius Burrows was unable to stay with the blistering pace and, after qualifying as fastest loser for the final, finished thirteenth. In the shot putt American Adam Nelson's gold medal was never really in doubt after his opening throw. The sixth competitor to enter the circle, he looked daringly to the 18m marker and launched his 18.34m effort. Competition over!

In the European championships in Helsinki, Katharine Merry, worried by tendonitis, was unable to get anywhere near in the semi-finals, and finished in eighth place. So, sadly, she was about to face missing her second consecutive Commonwealths.

Those friendly games were to start in Victoria, Canada within weeks and club athletes enjoyed mixed fortunes including a remarkable career breakthrough.

In the women's 200m, Geraldine McLeod may have finished last in the final but she ran faster and faster as the competition progressed.

Robert Weir, twelve years after winning the Commonwealth hammer title, took the discus bronze. He talked of his future ambitions in the sport: 'If I get through a complete winter's training, I will say now that the British record will go next year.'

However, top of the bill, and with a birthday surprise which was rather extravagant, was Denise Lewis. The gift arrived four days early, was bright gold, and was helped in its delivery by a javelin in full flight. It left Denise on cloud nine, and the defending champion, Australian Jane Flemming, in tears.

Denise Lewis's two-day performance was a great and unexpected triumph that lit up the whole meeting. Starting as Birchfield Harrier's second string behind the experienced Clova Court, Denise lay fourth after a relatively poor 100m hurdles and high jump. Then she was lifted by a shot personal best of 25.11m and ended the first day third after a reasonable 200m. She was 245 points behind Flemming and 148 adrift of Bond-Mills, who enjoyed massive support from her home crowd.

Day two began without Clova Court, who had hurt her arm and back in the high jump and withdrew after the 200m. First, Denise returned a 6.44m leap from her main event, the long jump. So on to the javelin runway. Her first throw soared and soared past her previous personal best of 48m, over the 50m line, all the way to 53.68m. 'That was the turning point', recalls Denise.

Suddenly a 197 points deficit was a 72 point lead over Flemming with just the 800m to go. 'My coach, Darrell Bunn, told me to run my heart out. So I ran my heart out, then I ran my legs off, then everything else dropped off!'

Denise Lewis wobbled over the line for a personal best by two seconds and she had beaten the previous champion by just eight points. This was the smallest margin of triumph yet, to finish on 6,325 points. The foundation of a glorious career was in place.

Robert Weir and Geraldine McLeod carried their international endeavours forward to the World Cup at Crystal Palace in September. In the men's discus one legal throw was enough for Robert to win the two points Britain expected in a competition won by European Champion Vladimir Dubrovshchik of Russia. The team finished second on 96 points to that of Africa on 101.

As Geraldine took the baton in the 4 x 100m she felt a twinge in her left leg, and this cost Britain dearly. Throughout the event the host nation had managed to stay around third or fourth, but the last run pulled them down to fifth in the relay. The Africans won again, with Great Britain in fourth position.

While the senior athletes were busy in the World Cup in London, potential future team members were enjoying their own cup competition in Birmingham.

At the start of the season a record number of 296 clubs had set their boys out on the road to a place in the McDonald's Young Athletes' Final, with just eight making it through as regional champions. It was Blackheath Harriers who lifted the overall trophy for a record sixth successive year. They led from start to finish amassing 484 points – just seven points short of the record. That accolade remained with Birchfield with 491 points.

The home club made their tenth appearance in the finals, having won in 1978, 1980 and 1986 – but this time they could only finish fifth.

It was the ladies who brought the track and field season to a happy conclusion, for, with Shaftesbury, they deservedly won promotion to the First Division by finishing in pole position in the final league match at Wigan. Birchfield were dominant on the track, winning twelve of eighteen places to add to half a dozen of the forty in the field.

So we move into the autumn and winter, with a special performance in the Birmingham & District League at Longbridge in November. The day's individual star was Darius Burrows, who recorded his first league victory with twenty-nine seconds to spare from Godiva's Ciaran McGuire. At the end of the second lap Darius had opened a gap from Alan Jackson of Stourbridge and McGuire. He continued to dominate. Birchfield finished second in the team places, but were third in the league at that stage, behind Coventry and Tipton.

As the year rolled to a conclusion the excitement was unabated – and not just on the courses! There were fierce rows over Britain's teams for the European Cross Country Championships. Shireen Barbour thought she had done well enough to get into the original team after members of the British Athletic Federation Cross Country Commission hinted she should run at the Women's National Road Relay and the Mike Sully cross-country races. This prompted Gill Dainty, the club's new road and cross-country manager, to pen a letter for publication which included the following:

'The selectors have clearly not picked a team of in-form athletes, particularly women, for the European Cross Country Championships. Instead the team seems to have been picked on the basis of history. If athletes are not running well now, they will not run well at Alnwick.

Two omissions from the team illustrate my point – Shireen Barbour and Heather Heasman. Barbour is the current 5,000m champion, was second fastest at the National Road Relays and was second in the Mike Sully cross-country race. The latter two had been heavily hinted as the races to do... Perhaps the selectors see the Euro as a grooming ground for the World Cross?

This argument is flawed on two fronts. 1. We have a genuine chance of becoming champions of Europe, so why send a team below par? 2. The people selected for the Euro Cross are unlikely to make the World Cross team because selection of the Worlds is largely on a trial race elsewhere – a system that selects in-form athletes. I'm sure Barbour and Heasman would welcome the chance of a fair trial!'

One Birchfield Harrier who did make it to Alnwick in December was Bev Hartigan. She finished thirty-seventh and commented; 'It was exceedingly hard. You prepare mentally. You prepare physically. And it's still very hard! The pace is furious from the start. But it can't do you any harm. I'm going to do a full cross-country season again.'

Further good news for the club's distance running was that Sally Ellis had resumed training following a foot operation. She had been out of action for six weeks after having a ganglion removed, but kept herself fit with gym work, swimming and an exercise bike. Sally reported: 'I had the problem for a year. I had to miss the National Women's 10km at Liverpool because of it, so I decided to have it done after the Commonwealth Games.' There, Sally had finished eighth in 2:37.14.

The last meaningful activity of a busy year in the club's history was the Warwickshire Championship at Princethorpe College. James McCook was a most impressive winner of the under-seventeen race, winning by more than thirty seconds from the 1993 Under-fifteen Inter-counties champion Paul Moreby. McCook certainly displayed good strength and determination as he led his team to a three points win. Birchfield trading places with Solihull & Small Heath.

Twenty-Eight: New Year Resolution

One local athlete who was reinforcing a New Year message was Michael Rosswess, who chose the last day of 1994 and the Birmingham Games at the NIA to demonstrate that he could be the man to beat over 60m in 1995.

Michael cruised through heat one in 6.86, with Jason Fergus of Belgrave strongly improving his chances with 6.75 in heat five. Michael won the first semi-final from Fergus, while Haroun Korjie of Belgrave edged ahead of Solomon Wariso of Haringey in semi-final two to record 6.78. The final was all about Michael Rosswess with a fine 6.67 to win from a happy Josephus Thomas of Woodford Green, who had recorded a best ever 6.71. Wariso was placed third.

The women's sprints provided a great deal of interest too, with Stephanie Douglas of Sale retaining her title in 7.40 from Clova Court and Samantha Farquarson of Cardiff. There was general pleasure to see Clova back in action following her bad fall in the Commonwealth Games in Canada, and she was encouraged by her 7.55 in second place.

Commonwealth bronze medallist Farquharson had no trouble winning the 60m hurdles in 8.42, Clova having had to scratch from the event following a slight injury from the previous day's sprint.

Michael and Clova were among club athletes who competed successfully in the AAA Indoor Championship at the NIA a month later. Michael won the 60m title yet again in 6.63, while Clova pipped Commonwealth bronze medallist Samantha Farquharson to the 60m hurdles title in 8.22. Denise Lewis was third in 8.49. Denise went on to take the long jump title with 6.28m.

She was again on form during the Great Britain v. France International in Glasgow's Kelvin Hall in mid-February. She won her favourite event, this time with a personal best of 6.35m. It was then announced that Denise had been selected in the 60m hurdles as well as the long jump for the England team to take part in an indoor match against Austria, Hungary and the Czech Republic in Vienna. The additional good news was that club-mates Sarah Oxley in the 200m and Michelle Thomas in the 400m were also selected. Despite being taken ill in Vienna, Denise jumped a creditable 6.38m from the only two leaps she could muster.

February was to close in sadness and March open in controversy. The death was announced at the age of seventy-nine of Godfrey Brown, who had anchored Britain's 4 x 400m relay team to victory in front of Adolf Hitler at the 1936 Olympic Games in Berlin.

March exploded in dissent for Michael Rosswess, who appeared to have been cruelly robbed of his chance of reaching the World Indoor Cup in Barcelona. An administrative oversight when he stayed at his home, rather than the athlete's city centre hotel, meant Michael was not informed of a change to the race schedule at the KP Invitation meeting at the NIA.

The argument that followed completely overshadowed the meeting, with Darren Braithwaite defeating Linford Christie in a stunning 60m final. The next twist came a week later, when an exhausted Christie withdrew, allowing Michael to take his place in Barcelona. However, the drama was by no means over.

Dr Primo Nebiolo, President of the IAAF, was keen to have Linford Christie in Barcelona, incredibly suggesting Britain consider withdrawing Michael Rosswess to find him a place – and that after the Birchfield man had been called up to replace Christie!

'Surely the young man would consider it an honour to stand aside to allow a man who will soon be thirty-five to challenge for the one major title he has not won', said Istuan Gyulai, General Secretary of the IAAF.

Obviously Michael saw it differently. Indeed, after the way he was ejected from the final it was unlikely that IAAF members would feature on his Christmas card list!

Initially he was listed as having made the last eight but the start lists were updated when Michael lost the toss of a coin. He had the same time as Germany's Marc Blume – 6.619 – to the thousandth, so the decision for a coin toss to decide the final qualifier. Blume ran, Rosswess didn't, Braithwaite won silver for Britain – and Christie watched from the stands.

Enjoying a more fruitful return for his sprinting efforts was Birchfield veteran Alan Meddings, who retained his three indoor titles at the NIA, although just outside his British indoor records.

The club were arguably the best sprint club in the 1950s when, with the likes of Mike Rawson, Johnny Salisbury and later Peter Radford, they regularly won the AAA 4 x 110 and 4 x 440 relay titles. Among their number, for a time, was Allan Meddings. He was a member of the club's sprint squad until he retired from the sport in 1958 at the age of twenty-nine. It took him thirty-four years to return to sprinting, but when he came back in 1992 he performed better, relatively, than he ever had as a senior.

Allan got back on track after meeting an old athletics contact, Colin Simpson, and was talked into running a race: 'I ran in a charity event over 100 metres', he explained. 'I was surprised at how well I ran after all that time away from sprinting. I wasn't sure I could even finish 100 metres!' Finish he did, and went on to run for Birchfield in veteran league meetings, win double sprint gold in the BVAF Championships and take the World Vet's 100m title in 12.71, at Myasaki, Japan, in 1993.

In 1994 Allan won the three British sprint titles, following that up with a pair of silver medals at the European Championships in Athens, Greece.

At the time of his 1995 triumphs, Allan was training three nights a week with the Birchfield squad. He accepted it was difficult for veterans to train and race. He respected those who: 'Train and don't get any reward for that training. I've been lucky', he added. 'I've had the rewards and it is a big motivating point for me. Those people who persist with training and don't ever make the first three – some don't even make the finals – they are the real cream of athletics.'

The month also brought the World Cross Country Championships in Durham. Britain's second scorer behind young Paula Radcliffe in eighteenth, Bev Hartigan, was having a storming run. Competing in her first World Championships, Bev moved up four places in the final lap, finishing a creditable twenty-fourth. 'I couldn't believe it. I kept passing people and thinking: "I'm going to blow", but I didn't. This was my first World Cross and it wasn't as hard as I thought it was going to be. I felt good all the way round', she said. This gave Bev a confident platform to contest the 'Belfast Telegraph', Laganside 10km in Belfast event a few weeks later. She took the women's title after coming through a mixed field to finish thirty-fourth overall in 33:02.

As the track and field diary developed, so several leading club athletes were making a variety of statements about the season ahead.

Derek Redmond was considering a racing comeback towards the end of the campaign, with the possibility of competing in the 1996 Olympics. The former British 400m record holder announced; 'I've never officially retired, though I probably hinted as much. I had another operation on my Achilles last November and there's a small chance I'll make a comeback. I'll just see what happens. I'll perhaps do two or three races at the end of this season. If it doesn't work out I can say at least I gave it my all. I don't want to look back in a few years and wonder what could have been. If I get some races in between now and March I'll seriously consider going for the Olympics. I'm not training hard. I haven't had the time or inclination, but it doesn't take me long to get fit. There's life in the old legs yet.'

Meanwhile, Katharine Merry was visiting the British Olympic Medical Centre in a bid to find the cause of her knee problems. Britain's number one woman sprinter, still only twenty, feared a return of the problems that wrecked all of her European and Commonwealth ambitions in 1994. After finishing eighth in her 200m semi-final in Helsinki, she did not travel to Victoria for the Commonwealth Games.

However, Katharine wintered without pain, trained well, grew an inch in height – and went top of the UK rankings with an 11.47 seconds 100m clocked in Granada, Spain in late May. The bad news was that she returned to her Birchfield base feeling discomfort in the knee again: 'I just have to monitor the situation and play it by ear', she said.

For the foreseeable future, Katharine had ruled out doubling-up over 100m and 200m – and was debating which to concentrate on: 'Last year everything went downhill in two weeks. I don't want that to happen again. I really wish somebody could tell me what it is. I put it down to being waif-like, but I have worked a lot on that over the winter.'

She emerged from the examination hoping that a diagnosis would put her firmly back on course for the Europa Cup Final. However, she stated; 'I'm afraid they weren't able to tell me anything I didn't know already.'

It was the National Championships in Birmingham in mid-July that was the opportunity for other leading lights at the club to gauge their competitiveness.

In the men's discus event, Robert Weir had a valid reason to be three metres below his season's best. A strength and throws coach at Stanford University in California, Robert had only landed at Birmingham Airport on the Thursday before the competition – and claimed that had that been on the Friday he would have been okay: 'If I fly in the day before, jet lag isn't so bad', he said. 'But coming in two days before meant I couldn't get to sleep until 8 am on the morning of the competition.' At least that throw earned him a place in Gothenburg for the World Championships, giving him a chance of improving on his season's best 63.56m, set earlier that year in America.

After the heats of the women's 100m hurdles, where Clova Court and Keri Maddox of Cannock both clocked 13.48 and Denise Lewis stopped the clock at 13.51, all eyes were on the centre lanes in the final.

Court was the quickest away and in contention right up to the final flight, which she hit badly. This made her stumble and hobble across the line in eighth place. The race was won by outsider Melanie Wilkins of Aldershot, with Denise Lewis in fifth place.

In the women's 400m, Scottish multi-record holder Melanie Neef of Glasgow defended her title in style. Behind her Lorraine Hanson and Georgina Oladapo of Hounslow were having their own private battle for second and third places. It was Lorraine who just managed to edge in front in the final few strides.

Denise Lewis had difficulty in finding her best form in the long jump. She still managed 6.42m with her last jump, pushing defending champion Yinka Idowu of Essex Ladies into third place; Nicole Boegman of Hounslow was first. Denise commented: 'The conditions didn't help any of the girls today, but the crowd were very supportive.'

Michael Rosswess withdrew from the 100m final after winning his heat and having been second in his semi-final.

At Gothenburg in August, Robert Weir, Lorraine Hanson and Denise Lewis all produced high quality performances but failed to come back with a medal. Denise Lewis took pride of place, finishing seventh in the heptathlon after setting several personal bests.

At home there was some consolation as three young Birchfield athletes claimed prized AAA national titles. Triple jumper Jonathan Walker aged sixteen, 5km race walker Sarah Bennett, fifteen, and sprinter Ben Lewis, fourteen, all showed good form.

The focus of club attention now fell on the ladies. In the UK Women's League match at the Alexander Stadium, Birchfield needed to finish at least second on the day to retain their First Division status. They tried very hard, but in the end had to settle for third place behind Edinburgh by a single point.

With so many senior internationals supporting their club sides there were bound to be some fine performances and so it proved. The 400m was a superb race. Lorraine Hanson – improving steadily as she returned to top fitness – blasted away at the start. Phyllis Smith of Sale closed Lorraine down in the final few metres. Lorraine finished in 52.6, her season's best.

Melanie Neef of Glasgow was in great form in the 200m, winning in 23.9 after being given a tremendous race by Clova Court. Clova demonstrated top form in winning the 100m hurdles in 13.4, beating the AAA silver medallist Michelle Campbell of Essex Ladies.

Denise Lewis was limited to three events by league rules, winning the high jump with 1.80m and the 'B' 100m hurdles in 13.6. The club must have wished for her availability in the long jump, as her presence might have ensured a Division One slot for the 1996 season. Sale won the UK league title for the 1995 season, from City of Glasgow and Edinburgh Woollen Mills. The Stags finished fifth in the BAL Division One table.

The under-twenty junior team were the toast of the club after winning the National Junior League title. They grasped the championship from the grip of Kent side Blackheath, who had held the title for the previous four years. This was achieved in front of their home crowd.

More celebration – and some consolation for the disappointment of relegation – came with an outstanding victory for the ladies in the Jubilee Cup Final at Stoke in September. They were made to battle hard in the closing stages by Windsor, Slough & Eton, who clearly relished the prospect of their first appearance in the Cup Final. The newcomers threatened to cause a major upset going into the final event when they came within four points of Birchfield. The Birchfield nerve held, however, and the Stagbearers' experienced campaigners led them home by 104 points to 98 points.

As the weather turned chillier, so the distance runners began to create the headlines. Sally Ellis had had a knee operation in a bid to save her running career. In plaster from the top of her thigh to her ankle, Sally was encouraged by the surgery and still hoped to get back to international standard: 'I'm still highly motivated. My mind is willing but the body has packed up on me, although my physio is more confident I can get back from the operation. Before he said it was 50–50 whether I'd run again. I haven't run a step since the beginning of June, but they've reconstructed my tendon and I think I'm on the right side of getting better. An operation is always the last resort but it had got to the stage where I was running with a limp. I think it might have had something to do with compensating when I had a ganglion on my foot last year.'

That October, a day in the park for the family had a golden lining for Shireen Barbour in her first race for nine months. She spearheaded Birchfield Harrier's second successive Women's Four-Stage victory, in the

Midlands Road Relays at Sutton Park, to crown her comeback after damaging her left foot at the County Durham International Cross Country the previous December.

Although a veteran and pained by her injured foot, the mother of two contributed to some anguish for the officials, for her time of 14:39 was equalled by her club-mate Cath Mijovic, in sprightly form a week after leading the British home in the World Half-Marathon, plus Rhona Makepeace, the surprise leader of Charnwood's quartet. Makepeace went home with the individual gold medal, Shireen and Cath had to have theirs sent on subsequently!

Women's AAA 10km champion Cath Mijovic had plenty in common with her male counterpart Paul Taylor. Both had been bitten by dogs in the past year and suffered after-effects from the resulting tetanus injection. Both had been forced to change race plans that year by illness, but the pair were delighted to win their first AAA titles in the PGE Redditch 10km races.

Cath commented: 'I was really pleased to win at Redditch. I've won team medals with my club but this was my first individual title. I was hoping to run the World Half-Marathon and I was tempted to run in either Liverpool or Glasgow that weekend, but I felt I'd be better off doing a fast 10km.'

Her attempts at the marathon distance itself were problematic as she explained: 'I was looking to run sub 2:35 in London this year because I felt in shape to make the team for Gothenburg. I'd run a personal best for the 10km in February and ran 73.43 in the Portsmouth Half-Marathon, which really pleased me. But then I got a stinking cold just a week before London, and I had to drop out halfway.'

One week later Cath was bitten by a dog, but she still had marathon plans and entered for Rotterdam. She continued: 'I had a good nine miles and was on for the time when a man tripped me. He landed on top of me and squashed me. I carried on and finished covered in blood in 2:44.'

Cath was coached by Joe Lewis – who also advised teammate Bev Hartigan. She felt that she benefited from training with Keith Holt's group at Birchfield: 'There are some very good vets and young lads in the group. I'm very lucky to be able to train with such a good group.'

A week after the Sutton Park success, Shireen Barbour would step into the Midland Women's Cross Country League at Northampton with almost as much trepidation as when she first began running twenty-two years previously. Shireen stated: 'I know it will hurt for the first mile. It's just a question of seeing whether I can get past each race.' The fact that she was on the way back owed much to treatment from Simon Costain, the podiatrician who looked after all the top British cross-country women. Also Shireen's determination was undiminished. She would leave a company car in the garage so that she could run to and from work as part of her training. It had helped to increase her weekly mileage to forty-five miles and so she was able to contemplate trying to reach the European Championships in December, after her disappointment the previous winter.

As the year came to a conclusion the club was still producing headlines and good copy for publications, but it was the summer participants who were to the fore this time. Michael Oluban had been appointed National Sprints Coach for Japan on a one-year contract. Oluban made his mark from 1988 when his protégé, Michael Rosswess, sprang to prominence. He announced: 'I leave Britain next week and will live full-time in Japan. I am really excited and thrilled by the appointment. All my British squad have been taken care of by other coaches, which makes me very happy.'

After helping Newham & Essex Beagles win the Guardian Insurance Cup that season, Jason John resigned and rejoined Birchfield Harriers. The twenty-three-year-old 100m sprinter first joined the club as a thirteen year old and stayed until 1989, when he left to join Newham & Essex. He provided a perspective: 'I enjoyed competing for the Beagles and it was satisfying to finish on a high note. However, I was educated in North Birmingham and have always lived there. In my heart I always knew at some point I would come home to Birchfield Harriers where it all began in 1985 when I won the Aston Schools title at the Alexander Stadium.'

The World Indoor 60m finalist, who was ranked third on the 1995 100m lists, had operations on both his Achilles tendons in 1994 and had rehabilitated by training with Tony Hadley's sprint squad at the Alexander Stadium.

Team manager Dave Lawrence was obviously looking forward to 1996: 'This is an important part of the jigsaw and I'm absolutely delighted that Jason sees his future at Birchfield.'

Lastly, Denise Lewis was all set to fly into action at the next two Olympic Games flanked by her own 'Magnificent Seven'.

They were a group of West Midlands businessmen who had agreed to sponsor her up to the 2000 Olympics. The deal stemmed from a chance meeting in 1994 at the *Birmingham Post and Mail* Sports Personality of the Year Dinner.

'Denise was sitting at our table and absolutely captivated us', said Mark Bevan, spokesman for the businessmen when the arrangement was publicised. 'We decided we should help her prepare for the Atlanta Olympics, and, hopefully, will continue to support her on to the next Olympics. We agreed we would put £1,000 into each of the seven disciplines. Not only is she a magnificent athlete, but she's a credit to British sport.'

Denise would be able to spend the greatly appreciated funds on her nutrition, equipment, physiotherapy and training at home and abroad.

Twenty-Nine: Ladies' Day? Ladies' Year!

The indoor season would soon occupy the attention and the column inches – but certain younger members of the club who created interest too in the early part of 1996. A search was on for a coach to look after Darius Burrows, the highly regarded twenty-one year old, who had been guided so far by Ian Stewart.

With his work as the British Athletics Federation Events Manager taking an increasing amount of his time, Ian was seeking someone who could give more attention to developing Burrow's obvious talent. The Birchfield youngster had been in the Great Britain junior team for the World Cross Country Championships of 1993 and 1994 and was beginning to make his mark as a senior track runner, both indoors and out.

So Ian Stewart – who uniquely won the World Cross Country Championship and the European Indoor 3,000m gold medal in successive weekends – was seeking: 'a coach who knows his stuff and lives close enough to Darius in the Birmingham area to meet up with him four or five times a week.'

Ian added: 'I would be happy to advise the pair of them, but I would be more than willing to pass him on to a good coach who Darius and I would be happy with.' Harry Wilson, who had guided Steve Ovett to Olympic success, eventually answered the call.

Meanwhile, UK Indoor 200m record holder Katharine Merry had undergone surgery in a bid to rid herself of the recurrent leg problem, which had dogged her career in recent seasons. Katharine had been unable to live up to her potential because of her injuries. Even so, she was reluctant to agree, but after careful thought had the operation and expected to be back on track that summer.

'Before I had the operation at the back of my leg I had an arthroscopy on my knee which showed my cartilage was pristine. But behind the knee, fibres had grown so tight they were rubbing and producing problems', she explained.

Winter training had been going well for Katharine but she was plagued by a constant niggling pain. 'We decided to have the op over Christmas and I should be back in training in six weeks, so it hasn't been that bad', she said.

Back in Birmingham, 500 competitors had travelled through snow and ice to support the first meeting of the season at the NIA – the Midlands Open. Clova Court was seeking the 8.25 selection time for the 60m hurdles in order to qualify for the European Indoors Championship. She started her winter season in great form with a good win against Diane Allahgreen, the 1993 European Junior Champion, and Keri Maddox. Clova, then thirty-five years old, won in 8.47, a solid season opener which also broke the World W35 best.

At the Birmingham New Year Games the veteran was again in record-breaking mood, winning this time in 8.27, again with Diane Allahgreen of Liverpool in second place.

This momentum carried into the Great Britain v. Russia match later that month at the NIA. Clova won the international 60m hurdles, clocked this time at 8.35. Also victorious were Denise Lewis in the long jump at 6.45m and Geraldine McLeod in the 'Development' 200m in 23.82.

The same day at the Midland Cross Country Championships at Sutton Park the under-seventeen/under-twenty race saw a victory in her category for Birchfield's Josie Grey. She reported: 'The race felt quite easy. The cold didn't affect me during the race but I can't feel my hands now.'

Welsh International Viv Corneely gave coach Keith Holt a one-two and he was further delighted when fifteen-year-old Rebecca Everett came fifth to take the under-seventeen title. Rebecca commented: 'I didn't set off too hard as I was with under-twenties, and I tried to stay with them as long as possible.'

February once again brought the AAA Indoor Championship to the NIA and a third title for Michael Rosswess over 60m timed at 6.68. As ever, there was a lot happening around him.

Linford Christie, then reigning Olympic Champion, had asked to be included as a late entrant, just a few days before on his return from some very fast races in Australia. He coasted to an impressive 6.59 in his semi-final to reinforce the point. However, after starting quicker than anybody else in the final, an adductor strain spectacularly forced Christie off the gas, allowing Michael to victory. 'I was vaguely aware something was up. I was trying to latch on to his stride length and then he was gone', Michael recalled. Jason John also pulled up, perhaps, was the speculation, because Christie's start was suspiciously quick. 'Experience tells you do not pull up', Michael emphasised. 'I didn't see if it was a flyer or not', he added.

The indoor season continued to be busy and competitive for some of the club's leading lights in late February and early March.

At the MacDonald's Indoor International in Glasgow, Clova Court may only have been third in the 60m hurdles on this occasion, but her time of 8.20 bettered her own World over-thirty-five record. She had actually set a record at the same meeting in 1995 when few people, if any, acknowledged the achievement. The statisticians could, perhaps, be excused at that time as the run came just twenty-four hours after Clova had joined the veteran ranks. Despite these fine efforts France eventually clinched the women's team contest by a single point.

Jason John put himself into European Championship contention with a blistering run in the 60m invitation event in a personal best 6.59, which was also the fourth fastest by a European so far that year. To emphasise his claims for selection he won the match 60m in 6.62 just forty minutes later. Michael Rosswess followed him in second place in 6.70 to complete a club double. In this match Great Britain beat France eventually by 72 points to 68. The aggregate result was Great Britain 142 and France 138.

So we come to Stockholm, and those European Championships. Jason John was in the Swedish capital to move up from a plateau that had earned him relay medals at the majors, a spot in the final at the European Championships in 1994, but no more than that in the individual glory stakes. Jason even had a much greater plan than competing in Atlanta: 'My career has flattened out', he confirmed, 'and I need to get it back on the road.' This statement was after narrowly missing out on the 60m gold.

Jason led for 40 metres of the race, but found lane six, the outside berth, to be too isolated. 'They were racing each other and I was racing myself', he explained, 'but I'm pleased with the silver.'

In equally crisp climes, Birchfield's Darren Daniels was moving into form and hoping to book a visit to Scandinavia too. For Darren, it was a birthday trip to Denmark for the European Police Cross Country Championships. The twenty-five year old had recently won the Police v. RAF v. Fire Service match and then the Midland seven miles race some four days later. Now the Police Championships in April were uppermost in his mind in a bid to clinch European selection for 2 September – his birthday.

Darren's perspective was: 'I didn't feel brilliant in the match in Humberside but I felt great in the Midland seven and I wouldn't mind doing the UK trial now, if I can get a run. It's going well at the moment, which is about time, although I'm getting a few niggles with my knee. It comes and goes but I haven't had too many injury problems in my career so I can't complain. The biggest problem is getting time off work, as I've only been in the police force for seven months. I have to try and plan my races well ahead.'

Also looking to stretch her legs was former Midlands Cross Country Champion Bev Hartigan. She was on the comeback trail just six weeks after giving birth to Georgie. 'I started waddling around – I wouldn't call it training – in early April', said the thirty-five year old. 'I'd had a Caesarean and so it was a case of walking and jogging. I've not raced since last June and I miss it.' Having got back into action in the open 3km at the BUPA International Road Races in Portsmouth, and finishing ninth in 10:37, Bev said: 'It was a bit of fun. I just want to get fit by the Autumn.'

Also progressing was Karl Keska from Wolverhampton. He clocked 13:56.05 for the 5,000m in Eugene, Oregon. Karl was studying at Oregon State University.

While all this was happening – the track and field athletes were obviously active too. In May the ladies travelled to Milan to contest the European Champion Clubs event. They finished fifth. Individual victories were enjoyed by Katharine Merry in the 200m and Lorraine Hanson in the 400m hurdles. The 4 x 400 also saw a Birchfield victory thanks to Sarah Stevenson, Vicky Sterne, Denise Lewis and Lorraine Hanson.

In June the men secured a Division One victory at Copthall for the first time for some years. In the 'A' 100m Jason John earned maximum points as he headed home Allyn Condon of Sale. A contender for 'Man of the Match' was Paul Hibbert, winner of the Midland title for the fourth time the previous week, who clocked a best-ever time in the 400m hurdles. The thirty-one year old easily defeated Southern Champion Lawrence Lynch in the process. At the conclusion of a successful afternoon, team manager Dave Lawrence commented: 'This is a young team. Five-sixths of our squad are less than twenty-five years old and we have more promising youngsters coming along.'

All returned to watch the AAA Championships at the Alexander Stadium with interest.

Birmingham's favourite trans-Atlantic commuter, Robert Weir, was far from happy after booking a 'home meeting' in the Olympics, a dozen years after his Olympic debut in Los Angeles. The thirty-five year old was pleased enough at his selection to compete in Atlanta, it was the absence of class in his discus throwing that annoyed him. That said, Robert was still two-and-a-half metres up on Simon Williams who had not got near enough to the Olympic standard of 62m.

In the women's 200m, Simmone Jacobs inflicted a surprise defeat on Katharine Merry, who was simply delighted to be pain-free after missing nearly all of the previous season. Katharine had looked the favourite after cruising through the semi-finals.

In the women's long jump, Denise Lewis won the competition with her first leap – precisely matching the Olympic qualifying distance of 6.55m. Denise subsequently declined the invitation to compete in the long jump in Atlanta, this so that she could concentrate on the heptathlon, in which she was regarded as having a strong medal chance.

However, there was no choice for Clova Court after she was controversially refused a lane for the BUPA Games at Gateshead. 'I have no intention of quitting', she said defiantly after losing her last chance to get to the Olympics. It was the latest in a long line of knocks for the Birchfield stalwart, but she vowed to fight on and be: 'A thorn in the side of British athletics if that's what it takes.'

Clova was particularly incensed that she was refused an opportunity to run at Gateshead and that a BAF spokesman publicly stated that: 'Every athlete in the country knew they had to be at the trials.' Clova argued: 'If that's the case, that means there's one rule for one and another for others. Steve Backley, Jackie Agyepong and Jonathan Edwards did not compete at the trials and were all given the opportunity to compete at Gateshead.'

'I wrote to Malcolm Arnold and followed it up with a telephone call explaining my injury situation', said Court. 'I was led to believe I was in.' She watched helplessly from home on her television as Agyepong ran and made the team.

There were glum faces too when Birchfield Harriers made a mess of the home advantage in the BAL fixture in July – after winning the second match in June. Sale Harriers prevailed for the second time in three matches. They would go on to the final match at Kingston one point up on reigning champions Belgrave Harriers.

Birchfield's 'A' sprinter Michael Rosswess withdrew with a hamstring twinge suffered in one of three false starts. The club then had so many of these twists and turns of fortune that manager Dave Lawrence was reported as thinking he was already on the spit being used at the after-match barbecue!

The long jump encapsulated the range of Birchfield emotions. Former National Champion Stewart Faulkner withdrew after injuring a hamstring in the warm-up – before Steve Phillips deputised and won for the Stags.

Other high points for the home squad were Paul Hibbert's third successive 400m hurdles win with Paul Thompson winning the 'B' race. Robert Weir registered another discus win less than twenty-four hours after flying in from his USA base. New Zealander Richard Potts ran away with the 5,000m so comprehensively – after making a break with one kilometre to go – that he was considering searching for a race to give him an Olympic qualifying time.

From left to right: Judy Thomas (with daughter), Geraldine McLeod, Clova Court and Denise Lewis chat to Steve Ovett.

The men may have had their heads on their chest at the end of the day – but the ladies had their heads held high. They dominated their host UK Women's League Division Two fixture, winning by a fifty-six points margin from near rivals Coventry Godiva.

This followed up their fifty-three points first victory at Watford and meant the Birchfield ladies led the table with a maximum sixteen points, from Windsor, Slough & Eton who had thirteen points.

The meeting produced a league record in the pole vault with both Birchfield competitors, Paula Wilson and Emma Hornby, equalling Linda Stanton's best height of 3.40m set in May at Cardiff.

Former Commonwealth 1,500m bronze medallist Bev Hartigan cruised to a win over 3,000m. Birchfield continued their success in the middle distance events where Rachael Jordan won her 800m, and the 1,500m saw an exciting race for Sarah Bentley. She chased for the finish after opening a gap on the third lap for a two-second win from Sarah Bull of Derby.

Denise Lewis was in great form, achieving three individual events plus a leg in a relay. She was a winner in the shot and javelin. There was a bigger challenge in the high jump when a jump-off with club-mate Rachael Forrest and Wigan's Susan Jones was needed before victory.

This was Denise's platform for the Olympic hepthathlon later that month in Atlanta. Here she was to snatch the bronze medal from the deepest pit of despair. The twenty-three-year-old Commonwealth Champion almost withdrew in tears after a terrible first day was followed by a disastrous long jump by her standards. However, coach Darrell Bunn and physio Kevin Ludlow perked and patched her up, and, as in the Commonwealth Games, a javelin personal best earned her glory. Denise recalls: 'I was in despair out there. I didn't really think I could save anything but, lo and behold, the javelin was my saviour again.'

While the event was eventually won by World Champion Garda Shouaa of Syria with the 1992 World Junior Champion Natalya Salanovich second, Denise found herself in a fascinating battle with the 1991 World Student Games silver medallist Urszula Wlodarczyk, for bronze.

In the 100m hurdles heat Denise clipped the last barrier but hung on to clock 13.45, placing her fifth. She then found herself tenth, sixty points outside the medal positions, after clearing the high jump with 1.77m, seven centimetres below her best.

Denise moved up to seventh with the shot putt, even though her furthest effort was forty-four centimetres below her best.

In the 200m the only faster sprinter than Garda Shouaa, Natasha Sazanovich, clocked 23.72 to move to within twenty-four points of second-placed Wloarczyk. Second to Sazanovich was Lewis, whose 24.44 clocking gave her a first-day total of 3,727 – 265 behind Shouaa.

Day two began with the long jump. It also marked the Birchfield Harrier's near exit. Looking for something over 6.50m from her strongest event, she fouled twice, managed only 6.32m, some thirty-five centimetres below her career best – and departed in tears. However, like the champion she is, the battle was still on.

The tears dried by the breaking sun, Denise Lewis relived one of her greatest moments so far in her athletics career, when a javelin soared 53.68m in Victoria, Canada to help win her the 1994 Commonwealth heptathlon title. Except this time it was better. Her third and final effort flew for 54.82m. The 954 points lifted her from eighth place to third. Denise now had a sixty-three points advantage over Wlodarczyk, whose 42.64m effort was almost eight metres down on her best.

So we come to the showdown. Denise, with a personal best of 2:16.84, had to stay within thirty-five metres of Wlodarczyk, whose personal best was 2:10.92 and counted the 800m among her favoured disciplines. Shades of those Commonwealth Games again!

She found it a struggle to keep her rival in sight with the Pole out in front from the bell and Lewis alongside Shouaa. 'It was not my most confident race', she said. 'I could see the Polish girl moving away…' Not far enough. Not by just a few tenths.

The statisticians, with their calculators working overtime, worked out that Denise had clinched the bronze medal with a score of 6,489 – just five points ahead of her rival.

As for her club-mates elsewhere in action, the Britons went out in the second round of the women's 200m. Katharine Merry had two close-up views of the power of eventual silver medallist Merlene Ottey as part of her learning curve.

Now with her status as an Olympic medallist, Denise Lewis returned to this country ready to express her general views on the state of British athletics. 'We had the athletes, had the ability to be in the top ten or even top six in the medal table. We should have brought home a lot more medals. It really will get worse unless we pull our fingers out and get more financial backing. In Holland, or Italy, or Sweden, any of these countries in Europe – not that I want to live there – but I would be treated like a queen. Sponsorship is extremely important, there's been a big hoo-hah about the lack of funding for sport. It is not enough. The money is always circulating to the top few, the Linfords, but we need to put the money back into the sport in order for people to come through.'

Denise also had some harsh words to say about the organisation in Atlanta, which had come in for severe criticism. 'It was horrific, the food was terrible, the transport was a joke. I felt really isolated because the transport was so difficult. I felt reluctant to travel out shopping and see the sights, to get out of the intensive atmosphere of the village. It didn't feel like the Olympic Games. There was no rest area for the multi-events, and it was very difficult to find somewhere you could relax and take the weight off your feet – and your mind.'

She conceded that the organisation paled into insignificance after she grasped the bronze – the only British female athlete to claim a medal – and realised all her potential.

There would be quite a few more happy days for Denise at club level before the season finished. The Birchfield ladies' team completed the formality of adding the UK National League Division Two title to their Midland League victory. They scored 253.5 points at Derby to win the league by 28.5 points, ahead of second-placed Windsor, Slough & Eton.

Of course, Denise scored heavily, with a hat-trick of individual wins in the long jump, shot and high jump. Club Captain Clova Court won the 100m hurdles in 13.7 and clocked 23.8 for third in the 200. Lorraine Hanson won the 400m in a time of 53.3. Geraldine McLeod clocked 11.8 for a close third in the 100m, before anchoring the team to victory in the sprint relay. Marina Semenova improved her own Division Two hammer

Coach Darrell Bunn and Denise Lewis
show off the spoils of Atlanta.

record to 48.2m, while Julie Kirkpatrick with 46.24m helped secure maximum points. Pauline Richards made the long journey from Edinburgh to achieve a 'B' event double – long jump and 100m hurdles.

The field events continued to produce rich pickings. Emma Hornby and Paula Wilson both had impressive pole vault clearances of 3.40m. Kate Evans won the triple jump with a 12.9m distance, while Sarah Henton threw the discus 46.60m.

There was less celebration for the men at Kingston. They finished fifth in the match with 293 match points and fourth in the league with 23 points. Sale Harriers' second place put them level overall with Belgrave on 27 points but the Manchester club won Division One for the first time on total match points.

Robert Weir won the discus with a league record – 61.52m – and he was awarded the 'Man of the Match'. This may have helped compensate for the disappointment of not making the Olympic Discus Final. Paul Hibbert kept up his remarkable sequence by winning the 400m hurdles. Birchfield took the 'A' and 'B' string long jump with Steve Phillips on 7.59m and Julian Flynn on 7.48m.

August was to climax with Cup action for both teams at Copthall in North London. The men finished seventh on 74 points with Belgrave Harriers the winners on 112. The field events created interest with Robert Weir going to the top of the UK rankings with a Cup record throw of 62.40m – again winning the 'Man of the Match' award to achieve a double within two weeks of the league performance.

As for the ladies, they defended their title in style, amassing a record number of points in the process. With heptathletes Denise Lewis and Clova Court leading the way, the team went into the lead from the first event and then on to take eight of the seventeen events on the programme.

After an initial no-throw in the early hours of the programme, Marina Semenova hurled the hammer 47.02m to put Birchfield into a lead they were never to relinquish.

In leading from the front, club captain Court set the tone for Birchfield's team spirit as she took the 100m hurdles on a photo finish ahead of her great rival Jacqui Agyepong of the host club Shaftesbury Barnet. Both crossed the line in a windy 13.30. Clova then went on to place second to Catherine Murphy of Shaftesbury in the 200m, with her injured teammate Katharine Merry watching from the sidelines.

Denise Lewis was also totting up the points as the Olympic bronze medallist toured the arena in covering four events. Probably her best performance was the long jump, for which she headed the season's rankings. This time she had to give way, however, to a 'Woman of the Match' winning effort by Jo Wise of Coventry Godiva, with 6.47m. Denise achieved 6.23m.

With Birchfield winning in style by taking both relays, it was an ecstatic Clova Court who received the Jubilee Trophy for the second consecutive year. This was the club's fourth success.

October proved an uplifting time for the club too – and, again, especially for the Ladies' Section. The venue was Sutton Park.

First up were the men for the AAA of England Six Stage Road Relay. Whilst Bingley Harriers, the most successful team in the history of the event, won for the fifth time, Birchfield picked up their first ever National Six Stage medals in third place.

Matt Clarkson showed his liking for the opening stage as he gave Birchfield a lead of four seconds over Shaftesbury's Dominic Bannister. Matt, a mainstay of the Stags British League team over 5,000m, had been second on the first stage of the Midland Relays two weeks earlier but this time ran twenty seconds quicker in windier conditions.

On stage two, Mick Hawkins, a reserve for Britain's World Relay Championship team, gave Bingley a 100-metre lead over Birchfield.

However, on stage three Ian Gillespie produced a superb run to pull Birchfield level with the defending champions. The twenty-six year old was delighted to run within nine seconds of Bingley's Richard Nerurkar in the final analysis. He said: 'I just hope I've done enough to get into the Ekiden Relay team. I've only raced twice, but I was just twenty-two seconds faster today than I ran in the Midland Relays. People were shouting out the time difference and it was going down from eighteen seconds to fifteen to twelve and I knew I had a good chance of catching Steve Green.' Ian – fourth fastest on the day – was only second fastest on the stage as Paul Taylor scorched around in 16:19. Right from the start of stage four Richard Nerurkar moved ahead of Toby Gosnall and his 16:15 put the title out of reach.

On the fifth stage Darius Burrows produced a fine run for Birchfield to become their third athlete among the day's fastest eight times. However, the World Cross Country Championships performer could do nothing about Bingley's lead. Colin Moore handed a sixty-two seconds lead to Steve Brookes, but Burrow's effort had given the Stags a twenty seconds cushion over old rivals Salford.

Steve Brooks went on to secure the title for Bingley. Jimmy Newns overhauled Mike Shevyn to repeat Salford's silver medal of a year earlier. However, Birchfield without Darren Daniels, who was working, were happy to collect their first ever medals in this event.

The next day was even brighter for the club as the National Women's Road Relays were staged. A glorious weekend was completed with the capture of a fourth national road-race title.

It was obvious right from the gun that the quartet meant business, with lead-off runner Bev Hartigan bringing the team within one second of pole position behind Havant's Zara Hyde. No one was going to better these two performances throughout the day as the blustery wind kept the times down.

Zara Hyde had built up a commanding lead on Bev Hartigan only to have her training partner dramatically cut it back on the closing stages of the last, stiff climb into an increasingly biting wind. Bev, who was no stranger to Sutton Park and the National Road Relays, was happy with her run: 'After training with Zara on Tuesday I knew she was in good shape but I was surprised she took it on so early as the wind felt very strong all the way around. After the break I began to move away from Liz Talbot and from then on I was on my own. Then I could see Zara and realised she was struggling a little so I just stuck my head down and went for it.'

So to stage two and Rachael Jordan, who was born in Sutton Coldfield, chased Havant's Jane Harrop hard and by the time they reached the monument she was only twenty yards adrift. Then the 800m specialist began to show why she had a personal best of 2:07.5 as she edged ahead.

'It was hard all the way around. The wind was very strong and I had to keep pushing al the way', she uttered. 'Jane was about twenty yards ahead and seemed to be pulling away, but by the Jamboree Stone

I knew that there were only 600 metres left and that's when I really began to push it hard. I think being primarily an 800 metres runner helped me today.'

Sarah Bentley, running her first ever National Road Relay, consolidated Birchfield's lead on stage three. The European Cross Country representative stated: 'As I've never actually raced in Sutton Park before, I've run here but usually the wrong way around cheering the team on, I came here yesterday to watch the men and ran the course to familiarise myself. I've only been back training for about five weeks after the summer so I'm not as fit as I could be. I was a little worried about having Angie Hulley of Leeds behind me, but I managed to stay in front and give Sally a good lead.'

With a lead of about 200 metres Sally Ellis looked sure of the gold medal, but with the very much in-form Lucy Wright of Leeds chasing she knew she could not sit back and relax. 'It was nice to have such a big lead but then also quite nerve-racking to have so much pressure as well', she said. 'When I set off I could not see which team it was behind but I was told I had about thirty-three seconds. At first everyone was shouting for me to relax as Lucy was nowhere in sight. Then as the race progressed their shouts became more urgent and I knew she was closing. I'm quite fit really so I never panicked and just kept concentrating. This time last year I was on crutches having had a knee operation and not knowing whether I'd really get back to this level of running again. It's been a long time since Birchfield won this title and so it's very pleasing especially as the men did so well yesterday.'

Of those men, Ian Gillespie and Darius Burrows got their heartfelt wish and competed in the Ekiden Relay in Japan in November. Great Britain repeated their second place of the previous year. Darius Burrows closed the gap on the second stage with the second fastest on that leg with 13:49 for the five kilometres. Ian Gillespie clocked the swiftest stage four with 14:09 to give Martin Jones a twenty-seven seconds lead going into the final stage. There, Shadrack Hoff ran the fastest leg of 23:20 to give South Africa a twenty-five-second victory.

Afterwards, Ian Gillespie commented: 'The Ekiden Relay is one of those things you've just got to go to. The way you're treated and the way the event is organised is great. Also it was live on television for three and a half hours.'

Looking to the summer of 1997 he felt: 'I've only done six 5,000-metre races, of which five were last year. I believe I can get the qualifying time for the World Championships in Athens.'

Ian was delighted with the news that Birchfield would end an excellent year by being strengthened by the arrivals of Carl Udall, Rob Birchall and Andy Hussey from disbanded Omega. 'Birchfield are one of the only clubs looking forward and we should do well.'

Thirty: Stag Party

The influx of new talent into the club, blended with the existing experienced distance runners, was to ensure that the endurance running section was to have a major profile and a major impact in 1997.

Bev Hartigan was pondering how to get to the World trials through the red tape of regional qualification. Recent rule changes meant Bev could run for the North of England, where she was born, or the South, where she lived. The problem obviously was that the Birchfield Harrier was running in the Midland Championships – of which she was a former winner. Bev, who lived in Hampshire because her husband John, a former steeplechaser, worked there, was probably the highest-profile victim of the decision to tighten rules in an attempt to persuade athletes to remain loyal to their local clubs. This was a frustrating situation for an athlete who had come back so well from the birth of baby Georgie in 1996 that she was selected for the Great Britain team at the European Cross Country Championships. However, a bad cold prevented Bev from competing for her country, which made her desperate to make a bid for the Worlds.

Meanwhile, Carl Warren, equal third in the 1996 UK 10km rankings, was the latest international to join the club. He left Cannock & Stafford to link with training partner Carl Udall in the hope of finding better competition as he sought to prove himself in the steeplechase. With a ban ruling him out of team competition for the winter season, Carl would sharpen up on the roads.

Also on the schedule was the AAA Half-Marathon Championship at Reading. This would be only his second attempt at the distance, having clocked 66:00 on his debut at Derby. Carl commented: 'It's about time I had a serious attempt at the half-marathon. I would love to go under twenty-three minutes at Alsager but it might come two or three weeks too early because illness wiped out the end of November and all of December. Carl Udall is running Alsager and we've been trying to psyche each other out in training, saying, "that was easy".'

Warren had joined Birchfield on 2 January and hoped to qualify to compete in the track season. He said: 'I've written to the Hardship Committee asking to be available for the track season. The reason for my move isn't pot hunting, it's competition hunting.'

As Carl spoke, new teammate Darius Burrows was setting out to copy his mentor's route to track success. The twenty-one year old had been reared in the 'tough of the track' tradition of Ian Stewart. Even though Darius was now coached by Harry Wilson, he aimed to take in the 3,000m at the World Indoor Championships in Paris in early March on his way to the World Cross Country Championships in Turin. Ian Stewart had uniquely won the European Indoor 3,000m title and the Cross Country Championships in Morocco on successive weekends in 1975.

Darius had already begun to mix the surfaces. Having run for Britain in calf-deep mud at the European Cross Country Championships, he stepped onto the boards at the Birmingham New Year Games to win the 3,000m in 8:03.11 and clock 3:48.83 for fourth in the 1,500m.

It was a move that found favour with Stewart. The past master stated: 'You've got to be able to run at indoor 3,000 pace these days if you want to live with the best at the World Cross.'

While Darius was sorting his strategy out, Carl Udall certainly seemed to favour the five-mile distance. He staked a claim for the year's fastest time with his 23:05 personal best at Alsager. The former Omega athlete was equal top of the previous year's UK five-mile lists with his 23:14 in the Portsmouth Victory Five, tying with Mark Flint's course record at Alsager. After a disappointing fourteenth place in the Midland Cross Country Championships, Carl bounced back by eclipsing Flint's Alsager record by nine seconds. Now he would seek two more fast fives in Welwyn Garden City and Portsmouth, although his main target of the year was the World Championships 10,000 metres trial.

Carl offered the following analysis: 'I was fairly happy with Alsager and I'm hoping to go back there next year to try to go under twenty-three minutes. I was there in 1993 but until this year hadn't been back. I'm disappointed it's taken so long because I always wanted to do it again but I've either been ill, injured or it's just not been convenient because of other plans. It's a good race and gets a good field and I must admit I did find the pace a bit tough – it was relentless, not least because Noel Berkeley did most of the running and refused to relinquish the lead. I was so tired with fifty metres to go and I couldn't have given any more. I'd love to have broken twenty-three minutes, but everything went into that race.'

It was announced that Rob Birchall was staying loyal to Omega Racing Club founder Dominic Keily, despite the collapse of the Midlands 'Super Club'. Although Rob was now able to represent Birchfield, he would still be coached by Keily. 'Dominic has not got the credit he deserved', pronounced the England international. 'He has put a lot of time and effort into this sport.' Rob added: 'I'm excited about starting over with Birchfield. It's like when I first joined Omega.' 'There are a number of runners better than me and it's good motivation to get up there with them and be in a winning team.' Having had his winter ruined by an Achilles injury, he was giving the trials a miss and concentrating on the English National.

As the warmer weather began, Ian Gillespie planned to return to the United States in May after a successful road debut there in March. Ian, who ran the third fastest short stage at the Midland Twelve-Stage Relay despite suffering from jet-lag, would go back to the States for a couple of track races. He had met his girlfriend, American 10,000m runner Nicole Woodward, at the Chiba Ekiden Relays in Japan and planned to make America his winter base in future.

Before then Ian hoped to help Birchfield to the National Twelve-Stage title and there was little doubting they were everyone's favourites after the number of quality runners they had signed. Ian emphasised: 'We've got a good team and everyone gets on well. Sometimes when a lot of people come in it causes resentment but there's nothing like that at Birchfield. I'll run a short stage again in the National Twelve-Stage and will be looking to get back down to around 13:41, which was the time I had in mind for the Midlands after running that last year. But I was jet-lagged, we were out in front and it was difficult to motivate myself.' Nevertheless, he clocked 14:04 for the fastest on the stage and third fastest of the day.

The plan was to transfer his road and indoor form onto the track with a 5,000m slot at the World Championships his goal. He stated: 'My personal best is 13.40 but I've only been running the 5,000 metres for a year, so I'll take a couple of years to get used to the event. I ran five 5000-metre races last year but I want to get more races abroad and go under 13:30. I was upset not to get picked for the World Indoor Championships but if I can transfer that form outdoors I can get close to the qualifying time for Athens.'

That disappointment with the indoor season saw him beaten in the closing stages by Ian Grime at the BAF Indoor Trials and John Mayock at the BUPA Grand Prix.

Those Birchfield athletes who were selected were Katharine Merry (200m), Clova Court (60m hurdles) Michelle Thomas (4 x 400m) and rising star Richard Knowles (4 x 400m). Richard ran well in the heats; Katharine qualified for her final but had to pull out through injury; Clova came fourth in her heat whilst Michelle was a member of the squad that set a new British time of 3:32.25.

So to the great outdoors and in the first men's BAL Division One match in May, Belgrave Harriers finished seventy-seven points clear of a fabulous five-way battle for second.

Going into the relays, only five points covered Thames Valley Harriers, Sale, Newham & Essex 'Beagles', and Birchfield. The Stags were without more of the heavy points scorers than most because, it was reported, they felt it was too early in the season and, partly, with the Alexander Stadium track being re-laid, they didn't have a home to train in.

Immune to such domestic problems, Belgrave received an instant return for flying AAA bronze medallist Michael Edwards in from America when he finished second on countback to Birchfield's Midlands Champion Michael Barber in a dramatic pole vault. The club also enjoyed victory with Julian Flynn in the long jump with 7.66m. Overall the club finished fifth on the day with 271 points.

The future of the club was on display that month in the Area Junior Championship at Solihull.

In the under-seventeen section, AAA Champion Ben Lewis was in great form. He won both the 100m and 200m from Birchfield teammate Myrone Levy in 10.82 and a championship best of 21.43 for the longer sprint. Fellow Birchfielder and English School's Champion Brian Robinson was also in double form – winning the long jump in a championship best of 7.04m and following with triple jump success in 14.61m.

When it came to the under-fifteen age group it was interesting to note that one Mark Lewis-Francis was reported to be: 'another fine Birchfield prospect' as the fourteen year old posted a warning to others in his age group. Mark recorded one of the fastest 100 metres for his age in missing the championship record by just one hundredth of a second. Mark recorded 11.19.

Away from these young men it was to be the senior women who were about to take centre stage. They battled for every point in the European Clubs Cup Final in Valencia, and their fighting spirit paid off. They won the final event, the 4 x 400m relay, to finish second to Sporting Club Lisbon and ensure that the British Cup winners would compete in the 1998 European Clubs 'A' Final.

Birchfield overcame the absence of five internationals, including Denise Lewis and fellow heptathlete Clova Court, giving several young athletes their first taste of international competition.

In the opening event, the javelin, Lynne Miles threw 37.04m for fourth place as Jette Jephson from the Danish club Aarhus 1900 won with 55.46m.

Aarhus also won the second event, the long jump, with 6.23m. The wind was against the jumpers and played havoc with the run-ups. Deborah Rowe finished fifth for Birchfield with 5.24m. Aarhus kept the pressure on by winning the high jump, but Birchfield's Rachael Forrest picked up valuable points finishing equal second with 1.75m.

Aarhus still had maximum points after four events with victory in the triple jump. Katie Evans reached 12.42m in fifth position, leaving Birchfield in third.

The discus throw was the next victory for Aarhus. Sarah Henton was fourth for Birchfield with 45.20m.

The first track event, the 400m hurdles, saw Stephanie Jeanson first for Amiens of France in 62.53. Birchfield junior Eleanor Chamberlain ran courageously to take second place with a new personal best of 63.27.

Katharine Merry was down for both sprints and the relay. Unfortunately she was suffering a bad migraine. Katharine pluckily took second in the 100m in 11.75 behind Lucrecia Jardim from the pre-meeting favourites Sporting Lisbon.

Rachael Jordan became Birchfield's first winner when she won a tactical 800m in 2:09.4, beating Susana Cabral from Lisbon by 0.66 seconds after running a second lap in 60.2.

Birchfield were left without a specialist 100m hurdler in the absence of their heptathletes, and triple jumper Katie Evans stepped into the breach for the point.

It was hot and humid and the 5,000m runners were suffering, with the 'A' and 'B' combined. Sarah Bentley was third in 16:29.44.

Another brave run by Katharine Merry earned her second in the 200m timed at 23.69.

Rachael Jordan returned to the arena after a short rest to contest the combined 1,500m. After a steady start she worked her way through the field and, having made sure of victory in the 'B' race, attacked the 'A' runners ahead of her. Rachael finished fourth overall with a new personal best of 4:26.66, an improvement of over eight seconds.

The meeting doctor would not allow Katharine Merry to run in the sprint relay, forcing Birchfield to make a late change. The quartet of Judy Thomas, Michelle Thomas, Zoe Wilson and Sarah Oxley ran brilliantly and snatched second in 46.80 as Lisbon won with 46.10.

With just the 4 x 400m left, Birchfield were third – two-and-a-half points behind Aarhus. To earn promotion for Great Britain, Birchfield had to win.

Suzanne Holyfield made her debut for the senior team on the opening leg with a new personal best. Sarah Damm kept Birchfield in second place but Lisbon opened up a forty-metre lead. The experienced Lorraine Hanson chased hard on the penultimate lap and slowly but sensibly reduced the deficit to hand over side by side with the Lisbon athlete. As they hit the home straight Michelle Thomas was just fast enough to hold on to give Birchfield victory and promotion. The gallant girls were timed at 3:44.01.

Sporting Club Lisbon won the title with 78 points and Birchfield achieved their aim with 69.5 points.

Meanwhile the absent Denise Lewis was also impressive in Austria. She had neither the quality training behind her nor the general standard of opposition around her to expect to take the UK heptathlon record in the prestigious Gotzis meeting for the second successive year. However, a dream second day enabled her to total 6,736 points. This was ninety-one points more than she had amassed twelve months previously when finally eclipsing the ten-year-old UK record of former club-mate Judy Simpson, by then plying trade as Gladiator 'Nightshade' on television.

Denise also became the Commonwealth record holder, overtaking the 6,695 points with which Australia's Jane Flemming won the Commonwealth Games in 1990.

There were shades of the way in which Denise had pipped Jane Flemming for the 1994 Commonwealth title on that 'Super Sunday' in Gotzis. Except this time it was not so much a javelin personal best but her entire attitude which grabbed the attention.

In the absence of the injured Olympic Champion Garda Shouaa, the Syrian who had dominated the world stage for the previous two years, Lewis' first day was not up to the 1996 standard.

She started day one by hitting the ninth hurdle so badly that she had to climb over the last but still clocked 13.32.

Her high jump went so smoothly she had first-time clearances all the way to 1.82m and was unlucky not to make 1.85m.

In the shot putt Denise went to within fourteen centimetres of her personal best after touching 14.50m in the warm-up.

The day ended with a comfortable lead over Sazanovich, who had taken the silver medal in Atlanta, and her fastest legal 200m at 24.10.

Not even that prepared anyone for her second day. 'Denise suddenly sparked', reported her nutritionist Brian Welsby. 'Everyone realised she was going to do something great and the crowd warmed to her. I have never felt such an electric atmosphere as she generated.'

It started with a windy long jump of 6.77m – the furthest by a Briton so far that year and ten centimetres further than her legal best.

Then came a javelin throw of 52.30m, modest by the 56.50m of Victoria in 1994, but still over 4.50 metres further than in Gotzis in 1996.

Saving the best until last, she ran the 800m in a personal best of 2:17.70, astonishing even her coach, Darrell Bunn. 'It was beyond our expectations – a nice, steady, strong performance', said Darrell of not just the 800m but the whole event.

'We made a decision that this would be a stabilisation year and next year we'd be back for the Europeans and the Commonwealths. We didn't specifically prepare for Gotzis this year. We did last year – she was in red-hot shape then. But she is about four or five weeks away from the point she was at in her training last year. She has hardly done any real running work and we still have to fine-tune some of the technical elements. That 800 personal best came from pure strength. If we had finished on 6,500 and had not done a personal best we would have been well pleased.'

It was the fifth-highest total recorded at that point in the 1990s and hoisted Denise from eighteenth to twelfth on the world all-time list. It also confirmed her future potential.

With their successful Continental exertions complete everybody returned to the only slightly less glamorous Enfield the following weekend – to keep that momentum rolling in the opening match of the UK Women's League. The team produced six winners and won the 4 x 400m to cap a fine day.

Denise Lewis won the long jump and sprint hurdles and also picked up points in the shot before taking part in the 4 x 100m relay. She confirmed: 'I've done nothing since Gotzis, not even a little jog, but it was important to compete for the club as it may be the only one I do this year. I've had a busy week, but I enjoyed it today.'

Meanwhile, Birchfield stormed to both 400m races. Lorraine Hanson was well clear as she took the 'B' string in 53.2 – quicker than Michelle Thomas' 'A' string victory. Indeed Lorraine's personal best broke the twelve-year-old ground record for the Queen Elizabeth Stadium. At this stage five events were completed with Birchfield and Shaftesbury equal on 57 points.

Then Birchfield achieved another double in the field. Denise Lewis and Clova Court – who had also missed the previous weekend's European event to take the AAA of England Heptathlon title – both won their long jump events. Denise produced jumps of 6.10m, 5.08m and 6.14m before opting not to take her remaining three jumps as the 100m hurdles were looming.

Those sprint hurdles – delayed when a brief but heavy shower left a pool of water on the track – couldn't have been much closer, Denise holding off Jacqui Agyepong of Shaftesbury with both athletes given the same time. Denise's two victories had given Birchfield a six-point cushion over Shaftesbury.

Eventually a quartet of Michelle Thomas, Tanya Taylor, Lorraine Hanson and Helen Frost made no mistake in the 4 x 400m, leading from start to finish, and wrapping the match up for Birchfield.

In the men's BAL Division One at Copthall Barnet, Birchfield finished eighth on 208 points with Sale the victors on 339 points. Many regarded the next fixture at Solihull as a relegation battle for the club with the previously promoted clubs Woodford Green and Blackheath. The match could not be staged at the Alexander Stadium as the track was still being resurfaced.

Before that, several Stags would enjoy the rigours of international competition. In an under-twenty-three match at Hexham between Great Britain, France and Germany there was an exciting 400m race. Jared Deacon pipped Birchfield's Richard Knowles to give Britain a one-two. The multi-lingual Richard was at home in the international sphere, but struggled in the cold, blustery conditions to get near his season's best of 45.84, a one-second improvement from the previous season.

In the 4 x 400m relay, hamstring victim Deacon supported from the sidelines as Richard Knowles ran a storming leg to put Britain in the lead. Nick Budden lost a big margin on the final lap only to kick again with 80m left to grimly hang on.

The final result was:

1. France	137
2. Germany	121
3. Great Britain	114

June also brought the European Cup in Munich. In the men's discus, Robert Weir's second place behind Olympic Champion Lars Riedel was the inspirational field result which Britain needed, entering the nail-biting final stages of the two-day competition.

'I was worried about the rain early on', said Robert, newly-arrived from California, 'but then I realised it's the same for everybody. My experience in the 1996 World Cup taught me that. It poured with rain then – and I finished last.'

Helen Frost.

This time he was disappointed not to improve on his second round of 61.62m: 'I went for it on my last throw but pulled off at the last minute.' His seven points left Britain nine points ahead with just three events to go. The final result was:

1. Great Britain	118
2. Germany	105
3. Russia	104

In the women's long jump competition it was full credit to Denise Lewis who narrowly missed out on a placing with a best of 6.56m in the final round. That performance opened up a fairly respectable gap of four points ahead of the Ukraine and hopes of a first-three placing were quickly sounding realistic. The final result was:

1. Russia	127
2. Germany	112
3. Great Britain	86

It was subsequently announced that Denise Lewis had dropped out of Great Britain's team for the following weekend's European Combined Events Cup – but emphasised it was nothing to do with a disappointment over an application for lottery funding. Although the only British woman to win an athletics medal at the 1996 Olympics was asking how she was expected to subsist on £6,000 a year, she cited the need to train for the World Championships as the reason for opting out of the two-day event.

Coach Darrell Bunn further explained: 'We sat down and talked about it long and hard and came to the reluctant decision that if she competed in Tallin, she would have to rest for a week afterwards and would then have, in effect, only two weeks in which to prepare for Athens. It was a very difficult decision for a patriot like Denise to take but she wants to go to Athens in shape to win a medal.'

The immediate focus, however, was on the British League at Solihull in early July. While Belgrave Harriers were clear, Sale were involved in a six-way battle for second place – which Birchfield eventually secured with an inspired team effort.

As the third of the early field events, the pole vault was won by Birchfield's Michael Barber with 5.20m. The twenty-three year old despatched a strong Sale pairing of Duncan Pearce and Andy Ashurst.

The Stags had finished last in the previous match but brought in their 'big guns' this time. They came no bigger than Robert Weir – fresh from a British discus record in the States, if 'fresh' was the right choice of words. For Robert, who had broken Bill Tancred's twenty-three-year-old record in California a few days earlier, entered the Norman Green Stadium in the nick of time after more than twenty-two hours of travel.

Landing at Gatwick just four hours before his event began, Robert drove himself to the venue. He arrived three minutes before the first round and with no warm-up, brushed aside jet lag to set a British League record of 61.90m – improving his own 1996 mark of 61.52.

The Birchfield rollercoaster continued as the track events started. Paul Thompson, recently back from Idaho University, was close to his personal best of 50.45 in the 400m hurdles. Coach Tony Hadley had implemented a new training programme with more emphasis on speed. It seemed to be working.

In the 800m, back in fifth, nineteen-year-old James McCook took four seconds off his best with 1:51.1.

Mark Mandy complained of being 'rusty' after recent prolonged rain had affected his high jump training. However, the Irishman did not look it as he cleared 2.24m to beat UK number one Brendan Reilly of Belgrave.

Fourth in the steeplechase was Darius Burrows making a surprise appearance. A surprise to no-one more than Darius himself! He had completed a one-hour training run at lunchtime and turned up at the stadium in jeans and T-shirt intending to spectate, only to be pressed into service at the last minute.

In the 1,500m, Matt Yates of Belgrave just held off Ian Gillespie in a fraction over 3: 40. Ian's second place for Birchfield was converted to full points by Karl Keska in the 'B' race. Karl led from gun to tape.

Richard Knowles took three tenths of a second off his 200m personal best to solidify the Stags' second place. He was Europe's fastest 400m runner entered for the European Under-twenty-threes. The twenty-one year old described his Solihull run as a 'confidence booster' but said it was a shame that the under-twenty-threes and the trials clashed.

The meeting finished with an exciting 4 x 400m relay. Belgrave took an early lead, but Puma TVH went ahead on leg two. Then Belgrave regained the lead on leg three and it looked good for them as they entered the final leg. Birchfield were third with Richard Knowles around fifteen metres behind.

In-form Richard clawed back Belgrave and Puma Thames Valley Harriers over the first 300 metres and then was stronger than Phil Goedluck of Belgrave over the dying metres.

Although Richard's performance caught the eye with his 46.1 split, also gaining plaudits was Birchfield's first leg runner Daniel Price. Daniel had run 49.99 for 400m at the AAA Junior Championships at Bedford in the morning, before being transported the sixty miles to Solihull to run that vital relay leg.

Overall, the club received much media praise for proving that, in the British League, matters could be turned around.

On the same day the UK Women's League Division One teams paid their first visit to the upgraded Grangemouth track. This was an exciting match thanks to the in-depth quality on display.

Lorraine Hanson was the only Birchfield 'A' string winner as she took the 400m race, with Helen Frost winning the 'B' event. This laid the foundation of victory in the 4 x 400m relay. Match result:

1. Windsor, Slough & Eton	187
2. Shaftesbury Barnet	178.5
3. Birchfield	146.5

The positions after two matches saw Shaftesbury and Birchfield in equal first place with fourteen points each.

Leading up to the British Championships, which included the World Trials, Katharine Merry went public in praise of the British Athletics Federation. This was because of not being condemned for rejecting a relay place at the European Cup and going instead to Cork.

Katharine, who sped to the top of the UK rankings for the year by winning the 100m in 11.43 and the 200m in 22.47, stated: 'I'm very glad the BAF respected that I didn't want to go to Munich just for the relay. I was disappointed with my 100 in Cork because it didn't go well technically as I wanted it to. So I was surprised by the 200.'

She was determined not to get carried away, explaining: 'I missed so much training at the end of the winter. I took some good advice and decided not to try and race myself back to fitness. I'm still getting a lot of treatment on my lower back, and racing sparingly is working quite nicely.'

At the trials at the Alexander stadium, her perfect preparations for the year paid full dividend in the 200m when Katharine held off the respective 100m champion and 400m champion Simmone Jacobs and Donna Fraser. With a following wind of 1.10m/s she entered the home straight with a narrow advantage over her London rivals. When Jacobs applied pressure with fifty metres remaining it seemed it would be a fight to the bitter end. Katharine, urged on by a partisan crowd, responded incisively. Her long legs extended more rapidly, widening the gap between her and the short sprint champion.

Afterwards she commented: 'It meant a lot to me to win today as I feel there has been a lot of pressure on me to win. I have been struggling recently, I've been getting very lazy for a reason I don't know after about fifty metres. I have been working on that, I saw them come back at me but I knew that I was strong, as I have done some good training. So I knew I could come through. Donna and Simmone have been running well so I had to perform well today and I'm really pleased.'

Robert Weir also treated his home crowd to a fine display with a series of throws all over 60m. Every one of them was good enough to win the competition.

The downside was that none of the posse of possibles behind Robert managed to reach the World Championship qualifying mark of 62m.

Finally, the bulk of the crowd made Sylvia Black feel anything but at home as she completed the 5km race walk. They deserted the stand and went to tea while the Birchfield Harrier put on a golden display. Sylvia made all the pace to leave her rivals in her wake. Her kilometre splits read 4:36.60, 9:14.51, 14:10.97 and 19:05.19.

Whilst these athletes had cause for celebration, Ian Gillespie had been left fuming after being overlooked for the third time in 1997. The Birchfield Harrier smashed his 5,000m personal best in Hechtel in mid-July but was left out by Great Britain selectors for the World Championships in Athens.

His year began with the disappointment of non-selection for the World Indoor Championships 3,000 metres, despite having the fastest time of 7:49, which he had set in the USA after paying his own way to race over there. Then Ian was overlooked for the European Cup 3,000m, despite having run ten seconds faster than anyone else in the country.

It was understandable that he had found the latest blow hard to take as Keith Cullen and Adrian Passey were selected to join Rob Denmark in the team: 'I am very, very annoyed and feel totally let down. If I ran for any other country in the world, apart from Kenya or Morocco, I would be going to Athens now. I just feel that I have been banging my head against a brick wall.'

Ian's anger was shared by his coach, Mike Down, who complained bitterly about the British selectors: 'Once again they have not applied the selection policy consistently. In the British trials, Ian, Paul Walker in the 800 metres and Matt Yates in the 1,500 metres all finished third and all subsequently achieved the qualifying time in Hechtel. Walker and Yates have been picked while Ian wasn't. Where is the consistency in that? He deserves better treatment than this.'

At the other end of the spectrum of emotion when the dust eventually settled on Athens was Denise Lewis. She came through the toughest two days of her athletics life so far and smiled: 'That's the first time I've really enjoyed a major competition.' Showing strength of mind and body, she survived two eighteen-hour days against more experienced opponents – and put Britain on the medals table. Moreover, the Olympic medallist did it at a time when the team needed an inspirational act. 'I have been very professional and come away with a silver medal. I have shown mental toughness over the past two days.'

Denise did not clutter her mind with doubts after hitting hurdle eight so hard in the first event that she almost fell. She lost as many as forty or more points at that moment. Also, with that stumble went all realistic chance of pressuring Germany's Sabine Braun into a mistake.

Such was Denise's determination that she clung to her golden aim until the end of event six before acknowledging: 'Sabine has experience on her side.' However, Denise added: 'I wouldn't underestimate myself at all. I'm really strong. It's all about putting the jigsaw together and making it perfect. I had a shaky start in the hurdles. Once I had hit that one, I had to stay on my feet. Anything else would have been a disaster.' She was fifth in 13.43 with Braun first in 13.16.

'High jump? In the last couple of championships, I've let myself down. After three attempts at 1.81, I thought – not again! I just didn't want to go out like that because I'm in great shape. So 1.84 was OK.' Braun went to 1.90m. 'I expected PBs in the shot because I've been working really hard on my throws.' Her 14.55m did not make an impression on Braun with 15.05m. 'The 200 metres wasn't quite a PB. I did 24.10 in Gotzis. But after such a long day, everybody's times were down.' Sazanovich clocked 23.92. Braun's 24.46 still allowed her a comfortable overnight lead.

'The long jump at ten past eight the next morning was all about preparation – getting up at 4.30 am and being alert for such a ridiculous start time. I just aimed to be competitive and make the best of a bad situation.' Her 6.47m was sixteen points better than Braun's 6.42m. Poland's Urszula Wlodarczyk pushed for bronze with 6.63m.

'Before the javelin, Darrell and I agreed that I would have to go four metres ahead of Sabine. Once I'd finished only 1.22 metres in front of her, I knew realistically gold had gone.' No top contender topped Lewis's 52.70m. Sazanovich's hopes dissolved with 43.70m.

'In the 800 I just had to be steady. We knew the Lithuanian and the Pole would go out hard because there was so little between them for the bronze. Darrell and myself went through the best and worst case scenarios. I just had to be sensible and, for a change after an 800 metres – I was still standing!'

Her 2:17.54 brought her in just behind Braun. Denise had cause for happiness and optimism as she mounted the podium at a major games, yet again.

Meanwhile, in the women's 200m, both Katharine Merry and Simmone Jacobs went out at the second round. Katharine complained that she didn't hear the command 'set'. Realising that the other athletes were actually in the set position, she was just following suit when the gun went off and she was left with a massive challenge.

Britain did reach the 4 x 400m women's final with Michelle Thomas on board as they achieved sixth in 3:26.27.

In the men's discus competition, German giant Lars Riedel extended his domination to a fourth world title. All four of his legal efforts flying beyond anything his rivals in the final could manage. Robert Weir, fourth after the first round with 63.06m, could not improve on this distance and finished eighth.

The month of August also provided opportunities for the club's emerging talent to enjoy competitive outings. Richard Knowles looked impressive when he ran away with his first Midland 400m title in a time of 45.90. He felt he had something to prove after his sixth place in the European Under-twenty-three Championships: 'I was disappointed. I did not do myself justice in Finland, which may have been due to nerves', said Richard. 'I ran 46.2 seconds in Zurich and was delighted to get close to my PB today.' His club-mate Adrian Bryan was runner-up with a personal best of 47.42.

Jason John, returning after a season of playing rugby with Moseley, recorded a sprint double in championship best performances of 10.47 and 21.60. He commented; 'I am three-quarters of a stone overweight and had no idea what times I would run but it is good to be back.'

His Birchfield club colleague Sarah Oxley also recorded a sprint double. She and Richard Knowles would miss the AAA Championships and the Cup Finals as they would be at the World Student Games in Sicily.

The following weekend, again at a busy Alexander Stadium, the AAA Under-fifteens and Under-seventeens Championships were held.

The much-anticipated clash between British under-fifteen 100m record holder Mark Lewis-Francis and English Schools' Junior Boys 200m Champion Tristan Anthony was everything they had promised. Both had high hopes of a sprint double, but neither succeeded as each took the other's title.

The 200m was first on the Saturday, with each being drawn in separate heats. Anthony clocked marginally faster times, which put in the foundation for an exciting final. Then, after only a few strides, Anthony pulled up leaving Lewis-Francis to win as he pleased in 23.02.

The next day Anthony was on the start line of the 100m looking very confident and progressing through to the final with ease. Mark and Tristan were out of the blocks on equal terms but at around seventy metres it was the Verlea athlete who began to edge ahead of the record-holder. Mark explained afterwards: 'I would really liked to have won the 100 metres but after the 200 metres I felt very tired. I did not think I could do it over 200 metres, but I did.'

Denise clears the events' first hurdle.

There was to be a feast of athletics over the August Bank Holiday period with a Women's League match on the Saturday and the AAA Championships on the Sunday and Monday.

In the League, Shaftesbury Barnet brushed aside the challenge of Birchfield Harriers to win their first Division One title. The two clubs went into the third and final match tied on fourteen points but Shaftesbury's quest was made easier by the lengthy list of Birchfield absentees. For a variety of reasons they lost the services of Denise Lewis, Clova Court, Katharine Merry, Michelle Thomas and Sarah Oxley. Match result:

| Shaftesbury Barnet | 227 – first |
| Birchfield Harriers | 148 – sixth |

League result:

1. Shaftesbury Barnet	22 (596)
2. Windsor, Slough & Eton	18 (499)
3. Birchfield	17 (511)

At the AAA Championships, Mark Mandy, having beaten Brendan Reilly at Solihull in a British League match at the start of July, did it again with 2.20m to Reilly's 2.15m.

Robert Weir set himself high standards and was disappointed with his discus performance in that he was not nearer to throwing his usual 64m. He returned 61.60m in victory, having once again barely stepped off a plane after competing in Germany.

Lorraine Hanson, the unpublicised squad member of Britain's endeavours at the 1996 Olympics and that summer's World Championships, came up with a storming finish to score a 'home' win. Lorraine powered past Stephanie Llewellyn in the last fifty metres.

124

Finally, Roy Tilling also became a 'winner' over this weekend. Roy, who had arranged the rapid succession of events at the Alexander Stadium in August, was presented with an inscribed tankard by AAA President Sir Arthur Gold on behalf of grateful colleagues.

So we move on to early September and Cup competition. In the men's final at Bedford, Belgrave Harriers continued their stranglehold on the 1997 season as they retained the Gold Cup to book a place in Europe for 1998.

Dave Smith got the 'Bels' off to a good start as he won the hammer with 72.04m. Birchfield played their trump card early with new signing, Igor Nikulin, a bronze medallist in the 1992 Barcelona Olympics. However, the thirty-seven-year-old Russian could only manage 70.54m for second place.

Former British discus record-holder Robert Weir must have enjoyed flying. After winning the AAA title in Birmingham the previous weekend, he had flown back to his American base on the Monday and then, clubman that he was, flew back to Britain on the Saturday to earn Birchfield valuable points.

It all very nearly went wrong as his flight was delayed. Never one to panic, he contacted the club. Team manager Dave Lawrence declared him, and as the penultimate thrower was about to make his second-round effort – Robert arrived at the Bedford arena.

He promptly went about his business with his first attempt of 60.92m, setting a ground record. He wound up the competition with 64.12m and maximum points.

Other Birchfield victors – again in field events – were Mark Mandy in the high jump with 2.20m and Michael Barber in the pole vault with 5.00m. Result:

| Belgrave Harriers | 125 – first |
| Birchfield Harriers | 92 – fifth |

The Jubilee Cup at the same venue was won by Shaftesbury Barnet with 121 points to complete the league and cup double. Birchfield were sixth with 63 points. They had no individual winners who scored but in a non-scoring pole vault a one-two was achieved by Paula Wilson and Emma Hornby. They achieved heights of 3.40m and 3.20m respectively.

The same weekend Ian Gillespie was among those crowned British Mile Club Champion in the final meeting of the hugely popular BMC Grand Prix series at Bristol. These races had dominated the national rankings that summer.

In the men's mile Ian was up against Kipkirui Misoi, who had broken the World Junior record for the steeplechase earlier that year, and also Frenchman Samir Benfares, who had run 3:38 for 1,500m the previous weekend. The pace was spot on sixty seconds at 400 metres, 2:00.3 at 800 metres, and 3:00.7 at 1,200 metres with Benfares leading Gillespie and Justin Swift-Smith. Misoi was just behind and so was Steve Green.

With 300 metres to go, Gillespie and Swift-Smith were about to make their move on Benfares when Swift-Smith appeared to trip. As he fell he brought down Gillespie as well, leaving Benfares with a ten-metre lead over Misoi. Ian managed to roll over, turn around and begin to chase – having lost over twenty-five metres on Benfares and dropped down to fifth place.

The crowd gasped as Ian Gillespie put in a 'Chariots of Fire' burst and came through to take Misoi for second place. His final time was 4:01.37 and his last 300 metres must have been about forty-two seconds.

Ian was crowned champion as the highest placed BMC member and would be merit ranked as number one in the BMC/Nike races that year. This was little consolation to Ian on the day as he thought he was going to run about 3:57 based on how good he had felt at the bell.

The following weekend the Alexander Stadium was the venue for the Young Athletes' final. There were no league records in the boys' section, but sprinter Ben Lewis notched up a couple of meeting records. The English Schools' Champion came first in his main event, the 200m, where he was an easy victor over Blackheath's Daniel Plummer. Ben's best came in the 100m where he registered 10.66 for the second fastest time ever by a Briton at this level.

'The 100 went well', admitted Ben. 'I knew that if I was to beat Daniel I had to get a good start and go out hard. I was quite happy with the 200 but would liked to have beaten the league record though.' Had he done it would have broken one of the league's oldest records of 21.5 set by Birchfield's Jamie Nixon in 1985.

Teammate Mark Lewis-Francis had a mixed day. The British under-fifteen record holder was denied victory in the 200m by Liverpool's in-form Ben Inatimi. His rival beat Mark by four one hundredths of a second, but it took a personal best by Inatimi to get ahead of him.

Later Mark came back to win the 100m in a meeting record of 11.13, a little short of his own league record of 11.00 set earlier in the year. Match result:

Blackheath Harriers	475.5 – first	
Birchfield Harriers	321.5 – fifth	

Within seven days the SMC National Junior Games were to be staged in Birmingham. Blackheath Harriers and Birchfield Harriers under-twenty women ran out convincing winners and earned themselves a place in Europe for the following season.

In the men's under-twenty match Ben Lewis continued his unbeaten run over 200 metres and this time took the scalp of European Junior bronze medallist Mark Findlay.

Ben commented: ' I'm absolutely thrilled to bits to win and to beat Mark was something else. Coming off the bend I looked over and realised that I was still in contact with him, so I just decided to really go for it. I'm really pleased. Match results:

Under-twenty women:

1. Birchfield Harriers	306
2. Wigan & District	278

Under-twenty men:

Blackheath Harriers	372 – first
Birchfield Harriers	250 – fourth

October proved to be a month of much celebration as the club's talented distance runners came to the fore again.

In the Midland Six-Stage at Sutton Park, the team survived a first-stage fright to lead a repeat of the medals distribution at the Area Twelve-Stage race in April.

On a sunny and chilly afternoon and under the gaze of a sizeable crowd, Birchfield overcame the absences of Darius Burrows and Ian Gillespie. They relegated reigning champions Tipton to second place ahead of Westbury Harriers.

Birchfield Harriers	1:42.49 – first.
Julian Moorhouse (8)	17:34
Carl Warren (2)	17:04
Matt Clarkson (1)	17:05
Paul O'Callaghan (1)	17:13
Carl Udall (1)	17:09
Rob Birchall (1)	16:44

This was the taster for the main dish of the National Six-Stage event. The Midland Champions made up for their disappointment earlier that year with victory over the shorter version. Main rivals Bingley had absences – but so too did the Stags. Ian Gillespie was in America and Paul O'Callaghan was injured. They were also without Midland Cross Country Champion Justin Pugsley as team manager Maurice Millington opted for only one change from the team who had won the area title at the same venue earlier that month. This entailed Darius Burrows moving in to the line-up.

Maurice Millington commented: 'Telling Justin he wasn't in the team on Monday was one of the hardest things I've had to do.' O'Callaghan's calf injury earned a reprieve for Julian Moorhouse and it was the former Leeds City athlete who gave Birchfield the lead on the second stage before they eventually went on to win by seventy-one seconds from London Irish, who held off Bingley by three seconds.

Richard Nerurkar of Bingley edged in front briefly on stage three on his way to the day's fastest stage, but Matt Clarkson regained the lead and Birchfield were never headed from then on. Clarkson's was described by Millington as the performance of the day: 'He was only the fifth fastest in the team but to hold Richard the way he did and have the confidence against that quality made the difference between leading or having to chase.'

With the hard work done, Carl Udall was left to savour the moment as Birchfield clinched their first National Six-Stage title. This was the glory leg or as Carl put it: 'I had the easy leg because Rob Birchall had given me a good lead.' However, Carl was anxious to put his name in the frame for an Ekiden Relay shot. So he was in no mood to coast around as he clocked the fastest of the stage to extend the lead beyond a minute. Team result:

1. Birchfield Harriers	1:40.36
2. London Irish	1:41.47
3. Bingley Harriers	1:41.50

Carl Warren (8)	16:52
Julian Moorhouse (1)	16:48
Matt Clarkson (1)	16:51
Darius Burrows (1)	16:38
Rob Birchall (1)	16:39
Carl Udall (1)	16:48

With history being made for the club – a Stag party was guaranteed!

Thirty-One: Glory, Glory, Hallelujah!

Although 1998 was likely to see the club's established names make their impact in a year in which two major games were to be staged, it was the fountain of youth that first claimed attention.

The Dunford brothers, Edward and James, were being hailed as two of the brightest all-round talents to appear on the British scene for many years. Edward was the oldest by fourteen months and judging by the way that he had dominated the under-thirteen boys' rankings, it appeared his only problem was going to be which event to concentrate upon.

1997 had seen the Dunford family travel the length and breadth of the country to seek competition in open meetings. Eventually, Edward laid claim to two UK all-time bests with a long jump of 5.74m and a pentathlon total of 2,560. Added to this, his 75m hurdles of 11.8, triple jump of 11.78m and javelin of 42.92m were all good enough to place him second on the all-time lists. Admitting that Daley Thompson was his favourite athlete, Edward's declared aim was to compete in the decathlon.

James would still be eligible to compete as an under-thirteen for the 1998 season and at that stage of his improvement was likely to challenge many of his brother's marks. James declared: 'I like the 400 metres and 800 metres best of all.'

Both were pupils at Alcester High School, and they maintained a gentle training regime – attending the Alexander Stadium only twice a week under the watchful eye of coach Steve Platt. To break the monotony of the winter months they competed in the Sportshall competitions.

Waiting in the wings was another Dunsford brother, William, who had already cleared two metres in the pole vault. Younger still was sister Jennifer, who not to be overshadowed, had already gained a silver medal in an under-eleven pentathlon.

Also creating attention in the New Year was Katharine Merry, who had left her long-time Birmingham base to move to South Wales. There was also the appointment of a new coach whose name was instantly linked with success – the 1992 Olympic 100m Champion Linford Christie.

Victors and a happy team manager. Back, left to right: J. Pugsley, J. Moorhouse, P. O'Callaghan, C. Warren, M. Clarkson, R. Birchill. Front: M. Millington.

After being guided by Keith Antoine for the previous six years, this was not an easy decision. Especially when she emphasised: 'Keith got me to run faster than I have ever done.' Her 22.77 for 200m in June 1997 was a personal best, while her 11.43 for 100m also topped the UK rankings.

Frustrated by injuries in recent years, Katharine was adamant that she would not give up until she fulfilled her potential as a senior. She was based in Cardiff and training with Jamie Baulch, Darren Campbell and partner Andrew Walcott under the guidance of Christie. She was approaching the new season with a fresh start and full of hope.

'It wasn't a case of being stale with Keith', Katharine explained, 'but if you feel you need to make a change then I feel you have to make one. No one could believe how quickly myself and Andrew left Birmingham. We were gone in the space of four to five weeks. Linford heard I'd decided to leave Keith and came forward with the offer of coaching myself and Andrew. I spoke to Keith about my reasons for wanting to leave and the need to have a change after a period of time. I kept starting off every season by running a personal best and then always got injured at the wrong time. It wasn't that I didn't get on with Keith – we were good friends. But being in Wales our paths don't cross any more. It's not as if I stayed in Birmingham and began to train with someone else in Birmingham.'

Katharine analysed the difference in training regime: 'With Keith we trained hard and now we're still training hard but it's a different kind of training. It's not as intense. With Keith we'd do a lot of fast running. Linford likes to do a lot of tempo running. He doesn't like to be running fast all of the time. Basically we never go down to the track and run six 100s all fast. But I find it harder to run slower and evenly paced. I do more reps now and am out on the track longer. We're not lying flat on our backs at the end of the session throwing up all over the place but it is still very, very hard. We never sit around or rest indoors once we've stepped on the track. We're always moving. The difference is that there's a mixture – nice up-tempo stuff with a bit of fast stuff in there as well. It's 50-50 instead of being fast all the time. And this definitely helps my legs. All sessions are faxed or spoken over the phone by Linford. There's a lot of communication. Even though he sets all the training, he's still living in London and he's got a group down there, John Regis, Tony Jarrett, Darren Braithwaite and a couple of others. He's got two squads basically.'

Katharine admitted that, at first, she found the surprise element of Christie's training difficult to handle. Under Antoine she always had a rough idea of what to expect. Under Christie she had no idea of what she would be doing next week. 'I got told off during the first few weeks, not for questioning him, but for trying to understand the training, and why we were doing it. If I do something I want to know why I'm doing it. I got told off by Darren and the guys. I think I was analysing too much. It's strange as all the training we've been doing since October is geared towards us going away to Lanzarote. About fifteen of us are going and then we come back for eight days and then go onto Australia for nine weeks. All training is geared to when we're together – those in Wales plus those in London. It's hard but you know it's going to be ten times worse when we go away.'

Not that Katharine had regrets back: 'I haven't looked back at all. You have to look forward.' However, she pointed out: 'Everyone thinks if you're coached by Linford then you're laughing, but it may not happen this year. You have to give it a bit of time. Things don't happen overnight.'

Meanwhile, Denise Lewis was going for gold in a unique multi-event challenge during the BUPA Indoor Grand Prix.

Denise would compete against herself in the 60m hurdles, high jump and long jump at Britain's top indoor meeting. To attain the gold standard, she would have to improve on her personal bests; silver would be set at ninety per cent of her best; bronze would be eighty per cent.

Denise accepted this public test of her fitness, knowing that the sport was cash-strapped at the time and needed novelties to attract crowds back into the stands. It was an experiment and the multi-medallist passed the test with flying colours. However, her performances were somewhat lost in the proceedings. The crowd loved competition and her battle against herself was always going to be a losing one in that context. One idea floated was to pit Denise against a top junior or two in each event. In reality, Sabine Braun was the opponent everyone wanted to see Denise take on.

60m hurdles:	8.38
High Jump:	1.75m
Long Jump:	6.09m

In February Birchfield Harriers ladies retained the English Cross Country Relays title at Mansfield. This was with such breathtaking ease that it was easy to sympathise with Bev Hartigan. When she took over in second place from Sarah Bentley, who had clocked an opening stage in 10:22, Bev completed the second leg sixty-seven seconds clear of her nearest challenger and stated: 'I wait all this time for a race – and then there's nobody to run with.' Rachel Jordan completed the formality of victory with a final leg in 11:07. Bedford & County eventually finished in second place overall, Birchfield Harriers having closed in at 31:54

Sarah Bentley travelled to Morocco as a stand-by for Paula Radcliffe in the Great Britain 4km team at the IAAF World Cross Country Championships in Marrakesh. Sarah accepted the role after Bev Hartigan turned down the invitation to travel in case Radcliffe decided not to run both the 8km and 4km races over that weekend. Happily, Sarah did get to compete, finishing sixty-ninth in 13:54.

For the senior men Julian Moorhouse finished fifty-fifth in 11:43 and Ian Gillespie fifty-ninth in 11:49. Not surprisingly, British entrants found the going far tougher as they attempted to come to terms with their African rivals, who between them packed sixteen runners in the first twenty finishers. Ian Gillespie confirmed that it was really tough: 'My legs just left me', he said. 'Julian Moorhouse went by and my lights went out!'

In April, Birchfield recorded the biggest winning margin for twenty years in the Midland Twelve-Stage Road Relay at Sutton Park, despite not hitting the front until the ninth stage. Tipton had taken the lead on the fourth stage through Nick Jones with the fastest long stage of the day. At one point they were almost two minutes clear of the Stags. Julian Moorhouse began the fightback on stage five and there was no looking back from the moment; Justin Pugsley swept them into the lead on stage nine.

After that Birchfield got stronger while Tipton faltered and the eventual winning margin was more than four minutes. Westbury were third for the third successive year.

Birchfield Harriers	3:46.54
Steve Edmonds	27:17
Mike Shevyn	14:35
Mark Hirsch	14:54
Carl Warren	27:31
Neil Lawrence	15:41
Julian Moorhouse	14:16
Paul O'Callaghan	26:50
Andy Symonds	15:17
Justin Pugsley	14:14
Matt Clarkson	26:56
Mike Bouldstridge	15:01
Rob Birchall	14:22

The National Twelve-Stage Road Relays were at the same venue. On this occasion Birchfield overcame the considerable handicap of missing five key members to win the title for the first time for fifteen years. The Stags exceeded themselves to beat defending champions Salford by almost two minutes, with Tipton taking the bronze medal.

Birchfield took the lead on the fifth stage through Carl Warren and held it, apart from a short spell on stage seven when Salford led.

Virtually the whole team ran quicker than in the Midland Relays two weeks earlier, with committee member Steve Edmonds entrusted with the glory leg. 'It was the most stressful fifteen minutes of my life', he announced after steering the Stags to a comfortable victory.

It was achieved despite the loss of Justin Pugsley and Julian Moorhouse, who were both on international duty; Ian Gillespie, who hadn't recovered from the travelling and racing involved for the World Cross Country Championships; Karl Keska who had problems with travel from the USA and Carl Udall who was struggling to train because of work commitments. To win without such an array of talent spoke volumes for the dozen who were on duty with Mark Hirsch, in particular, having a storming run.

Team manager Maurice Millington commented: 'Everyone performed to the best of their ability and that is what it's all about. We needed a good start and Matt Clarkson gave us it and everyone ran out of their skins from then on. Rob Birchall was again a star performer but if you had to single anyone out today it would be Mark Hirsch!'

Despite their victory, the club remained angry at the race calendar, which forced them to be without their two fastest runners from the Midland Relays. A letter was dispatched to UK Athletics Chief Executive Dave Moorcroft making their feelings known.

Matt Clarkson	26:06
Andy Symonds	14:53
Darren Daniels	26:38
Mark Hirsh	14:34
Carl Warren	26:39
Neil Lawrence	15:21
Paul O'Callaghan	26:31
Darius Burrows	13:56
Rob Birchall	25:57
Mike Shevyn	14:48
Mike Bouldstridge	26:44
Steve Edmonds	14:59

The opening British League Division One match at Watford in May was won by reigning champions Belgrave Harriers. The 'Bels' seemed more immune than their rivals to the counter attractions of a throws international in Germany and the AAA match at Loughborough. In total, Birchfield found itself with no less than twenty-seven athletes absent because of other fixtures or injuries.

Jason John finished second to Darren Campbell of Sale in the 100m in a time of 10.56. By doing so he confirmed that his appetite had returned after a winter of Rugby Union, in which it was said that he had more calls from coach Tony Hadley than tackles from opponents in his temporary new sport. Jason went on to win the 200m in 21.48, faster than anything that he had managed the previous year. This proved the only 'A' victory for his club on the day.

Denise Lewis' early season plans, designed to lead to autumn glory, were rudely interrupted when she damaged the lateral ligaments in her left ankle at the Staffordshire Championships, where she contested the high jump, long jump and hurdles. This was to prove a significant problem for Denise in the months ahead.

More immediately, the injury cost her a week's training and, on the advice of physio Kevin Lidlow, Denise missed the representative match at Loughborough. There she was scheduled to high jump, race the 200m and put the shot.

'It would have meant that Denise had completed the set because she never runs an 800 outside of a heptathlon' explained her coach Darrell Bunn. 'That's the way we've done it in the past, and it's unfortunate her routine's been interrupted this time – especially as she was looking forward to Loughborough. Kevin advised us that if she had competed there, it might have cost her another week's training. We simply couldn't afford to take that risk.'

Denise was available in June to take part in an historic day at the Alexander Stadium. The first ever joint British Men's League and UK Women's League meeting, an event that was met with nods of approval from almost all quarters.

In the men's fixtures a lot of interest was generated by the long jump, for Birchfield's nineteen-year-old Nathan Morgan with 7.86m (wind assisted) and forty-two-year-old Barrington Williams with 7.48m won the 'A' and 'B' events respectively.

While possibly still the nation's favourite event, the middle-distance races fell a little flat – bar Ian Gillespie's effort in the 'B'-string 1,500m. The American-based Stag advised the club to play safe and make him the 'B' runner as he had only arrived in Britain on the previous Wednesday. A stomach problem picked up at the World Cross Country Championships in Morocco back in March was also on his mind. It had caused him to drop out of a 5,000m race in Eugene recently but didn't bother him at Birmingham. With splits of 58.2 (400m); 1:58.6 (800m) and 2:44.7 (bell) Ian front ran 3:46.11 – four seconds quicker than 'A' race winner Ian Grime.

Carefully nurtured by coach Steve Platt, fifteen-year-old Mark Lewis-Francis had been 'blooded' in the 4 x 100m relay, running the final leg. Mark's rivals included senior internationals Darren Campbell and Damien Greaves but Mark hung on for third. Match:

1. Shaftesbury Barnet   330
2. Birchfield Harriers   297

Denise Lewis continued to be troubled by injury – having missed Loughborough, she missed Gotzis too.

She showed a good return to form with a 14.45m win in the shot. Afterwards she warned: 'I'm getting there and my tanks are revving.' Denise was desperate to get back into full competition, but argued that she often performed better in the heptathlon than when she was concentrating on a single event. However, her contribution helped Birchfield to a thirty-two-point win over Sale in second place on a good day for the host club.

Lorraine Hanson featured in an exciting 400m race, beating Stephanie Llewellyn of Shaftesbury Barnet by eleven hundredths of a second.

The Stagbearers' strength in depth was illustrated by Katharine Merry being part of the 4 x 100m relay team only, while recent AAA heptathlon champion Clova Court was absent suffering from food poisoning. The club romped to victory in both relays – winning the 4 x 400m by over eight seconds.

Later that month in a National Junior League fixture at the Alexander Stadium, another local teenager was beginning to make an impact after troubled times. Sprinter Samantha Davies certainly understood the

National Champions! Back row, from left to right: Edmonds, Hirsch, Birchall, Clarkson, Millington, Warren, Lawerence, O'Callaghan, Burrows, Shevyn, Bouldstridge. Front row, left to right: Daniels, Symonds.

importance of mental strength only too well, for the eighteen year old had spent much of the previous three years hobbling from one injury to the next. First, it was tendonitis in the knee. Then it was stress fractures in the shin. However, Sam was positive that matters had cleared up and she was looking forward to the future. 'I'm well and truly tuned in. It's all down to mental attitude. I go into training with the same kind of mental attitude as I do when I compete. Positive. I really believe in myself and my ability and I know I can show people out there I'm up with the rest and I have the ability to succeed.'

Samantha then let her feet do the talking as she comfortably took the sprint double and rounded off a record-breaking day with a stunning display of relay running. In the 100m the GB junior international flew out of the blocks and was never headed from as far as eighty metres from the line as she registered 11.8 to reduce the three-year-old UK Women's League record by 0.2 seconds. 'It was a bit of a surprise', she reported. 'I wasn't expecting to run so fast as I've been out injured for most of the winter and to run so fast with very little background is pleasing. I also wanted to show one or two people out there that I can run that fast. I've always been in the frame but never quite made it to an individual performance.'

Later Samantha easily won the 200m in 24.6, only two tenths short of the 24.4 league record, but she was disappointed with the time. 'I was aiming for around 24.0, and after the first 100 metres I thought it was on, but it was quite windy around the bend which held me back a bit, but I'm very pleased with how today has gone for me.'

In the men's match, pole-vaulter Paul Miles collected the 'Athlete of the Match' award. Clearing a height of 4.25m, a personal best by five centimetres, the Birchfield athlete did enough to collect maximum points for his club. It was quite a comeback for the young man considering that he had been diagnosed with a career-threatening lung condition three years previously after winning a bronze medal in the English Schools' at Nottingham. He was told that he would not be able to compete again, but surgeons at the Children's Hospital in Birmingham decided to operate. It proved a success and now the seventeen year old was able to enjoy his athletics once more. 'I began as a cross-country runner and then I tried the javelin, but now I'm happy doing the pole vault', he confirmed.

Less happy, to a degree, was Julian Moorhouse. His bid to win the Northern 5,000m crown failed at the final hurdle – in more ways than one – in a classic duel with Borders' Paul Taylor in Liverpool. The pair recorded two minutes two seconds for the final 800 metres as Taylor kicked for home.

Julian responded, and coming off the final bend looked well placed for victory until he encountered the hurdles, which ground staff had set out for the 110m final. These reduced the track to two lanes, an error of judgement by officials even had there not been lapped runners to contend with. Julian pushed one lapped runner out of his way then found his final effort blocked by the hurdles as Taylor won by less than a second.

The Leeds-based Stag was sporting in defeat: 'I'm not saying I would have won it but if I hadn't been blocked we would have both dipped for the line together and it would have been anybody's race.'

The same weekend the ladies were in action in a Midland Women's League Division One match at Derby. Here, Emma Hornby went to fourth on the UK all-time pole vault list with a 3.81m clearance – a ten-centimetre improvement on her personal best.

Her club-mate Paula Wilson also joined the candidates for the Commonwealth Games by winning the 'B' event with 3.70m.

To complete a busy final weekend of June for Birchfield athletes – the European Cup was being staged in St Petersburg.

The long jump was shrouded in controversy. Nathan Morgan rose from sixth to third after insisting on an extra jump, and stayed there even after an appeal ruled out his best effort. While rival officials lodged an official protest, the European Junior Champion explained his first leap had been measured at 7.54m. 'No way!' he protested to the judges, 'I jumped closer to eight metres.'

He seemed justified, when, at the end of the round, there was one unattributed mark of 7.85m. 'That's mine', insisted Nathan, totally unfazed by the fact that on season's personal bests he should have settled for eighth place. The judges could not give him that measurement but they agreed he could have a fifth attempt, and after fouling at around 8.10m with his fourth effort, he kept his nerve magnificently to record a legal personal best of 7.93m with his bonus jump.

The appeal remained unresolved until after all of Saturday's events had been completed. Then the meeting's technical director explained that a transmission breakdown had led to Nathan's first round distance being incorrectly recorded. He was given 7.85m but had his personal best taken away from him. He was placed third on the countback system.

In the discus, Robert Weir, making his eighth European Cup appearance, took fourth place with 59.75m in the last round.

On track, Karl Keska in the 5,000m scored three points, which was one more than the pundits anticipated and kept British hopes of victory alive. There was a frantic finish as the heat topped 90°. Karl's valiant run had a cruel twist when Russian Vyachlslav Shabunin, ten metres adrift at the bell, caught him in a battle that was much more for team points than fifth place.

All's well that ends well, however, as in the final standing Great Britain were again Champions of Europe with 111 points.

So to the ladies' battle. In the 200m, Katharine Merry, in contention for third after running a superb bend, had to settle for fifth. Crucial was her defeat of the nations most likely to push Britain towards the relegation zone. It was only the second 200m outing of the season for Katharine, who had been bedevilled by injuries. Michelle Thomas was in the 4 x 400m quartet, which finished third. Final standings:

1. Russia	124
5(of 8). Great Britain	81

It was back to league action in early July. At Meadowbank Stadium, Edinburgh, the Stags looked fairly safe in sixth. Robert Weir and Glen Smith finished within thirty centimetres of Nick Sweeney of Belgrave in one of the best discus competitions of that year.

It was welcome back to second placers Richard Knowles in the 400m, after twelve months out of the country, and Michael Barber in the pole vault, after injury. Match:

1. Belgrave Harriers	377
6. Birchfield Harriers	227

Not that far from the Scottish capital the UK Women's League match was taking place at Grangemouth. Birchfield was one of the clubs suffering from clashes with the European Cup of Combined Events, AAA Under-twenty Championship and the Budapest GP.

Claire Wilson clocked an excellent 800m personal best in seventh while Nikkie Talbot took a third in the discus – despite wearing the 'B' vest.

Denise Lewis made her competitive comeback for the club. She was second in the 'B' 200m in 24.9, third in the 'A' shot with 13.66m and contributed lively legs of each relay. Match:

1. Windsor, Slough & Eton   194
6. Birchfield Harriers   129

As news of the major games loomed it was announced that Ian Gillespie in the 5,000m and Pauline Richards in the heptathlon had been named in the Scottish Commonwealth Games squad. However, not such good news for Ian was a back scare. He would not be opening any bedroom drawers in a hurry again after putting his back out on the eve of his first serious 5,000m race in Lisbon. The twenty-eight year old put a facet joint in his spine out while cleaning at his home and found that he could not walk, never mind run. A physiotherapist friend came to his rescue within hours of the accident and manipulated the damaged joint back into place. However, the trauma left him very stiff and this was compounded by his flight from Bristol to Lisbon.

Determined to take his place in the race, having already got his ticket, he had more sessions on a physio's couch in Lisbon. Then, although unable to stride out properly when attempting to warm up, Ian took his place on the start line.

Wary of doing any further damage and with the temperature at 28°, he set off cautiously and finished in 13:44.08.

'It's been a real nightmare as I had been hoping to get the European Championship qualifying time of 13:29', confirmed Ian, who only forty-eight hours earlier had shown his form by running the fastest ever mile in the West Country at 3:57.6. 'But I felt I had to give it a go as these opportunities are few and far between these days. If it had not been for my physio, it would have been impossible to run at all. And I was still unable to relax at full stride as it felt so stiff, but at least I do not seem to have done any further damage. Unfortunately my problem now is that I need to try and get another good 5,000m to try and get the qualifying time before the European and Commonwealth trials.'

July ended with the AAA Championships and Trials being held at the Alexander Stadium. Karl Keska was 'ecstatic' to have won a 5,000m race that raised more questions than answers for the selectors. By defeating fellow trans-Atlantic traveller Jon Brown in a sprint finish, Karl proved the GB selectors had been right to choose him for the European Cup task in St Petersburg. He also lodged legitimate claims to places in both the European Championships and Commonwealth Games.

Ian Gillespie was in sixth place, hoping for European selection as several ahead of him had not yet achieved the qualifying time.

The pace played into the hands of Brown and Keska, the latter back home in the Midlands after spending six years at Oregon University. Through the first three kilometres in 2:51.05, 5:40.29 and 8:28.62, the fact that twenty-five metres covered the twenty-four starters screamed that none of them was going fast enough to guarantee automatic selection. A 29.47 last 200 metres enabled Karl to hold off Jon Brown by eleven hundredths of a second for the title.

In the men's long jump – and wearing a Birchfield club vest borrowed after officials objected to his clearing 7.74m in the first round in a sponsor's garment – Nathan Morgan went to 8.04m in round two. This equalled the personal best set seven days earlier. Nathan then had two marginal fouls beyond eight metres, passed in round five, and produced a glorious finale of 8.11m to go fourth on the UK all-time list.

At the other end of the age scale, Robert Weir won his fifth AAA title with a second-round 62.82m. New Birchfield club-mate Glen Smith took second place with a second-round 60.56m.

Meanwhile, Denise Lewis had worried selectors by turning up with her left ankle strapped, but the put their minds at rest when she beat Britain's best women long jumpers with a 6.44m leap. The World heptathlon silver medallist had a busy day – also taking part in the javelin and sprint hurdles finals. She was

Karl Keska, first European home, 10,000 metres, Sydney 2000.

fifth in both. 'I'm a little disappointed with my hurdles', she reported, 'but the javelin and long jump went very well. I've learned a lot from this weekend', she added, 'but the main thing is my lack of speed, which I shall now work on for the next few weeks.'

Denise then commented on the ankle injury that had troubled her since May: 'It's a precautionary measure only', she stated, referring to the strapping. 'I don't want to take any risks before Budapest.'

Katharine Merry just pipped the surprise packet of the championships – Joyce Maduaka – in a thrilling 200m race. The only woman member of 'Team Linford' to raid the championships, Katharine won with 23.46 in only her fourth 200m race of the season. Maduaka, the 100m champion from the day before, looked the winner until running out of gas in the final desperate few yards. Katharine's advantage at the tape was two hundredths of a second.

The victor was quick to credit her mentor: 'Linford's probably been the most successful coach here this weekend. But the main idea was not to set the world alight at the trials. We have to run well in Budapest. I've got 100 per cent faith in his technique.'

'Joyce was really quick – which is what I expected', she continued. 'I knew that it would be neck and neck all the way.'

The club looked forward to a quiet weekend at home for these championships – after members had competed at eight venues on the previous weekend. They had provided many of the Midlands team at an inter-regional match at the Alexander Stadium. Notably, Nathan Morgan, who jumped 8.04m to qualify for the European Championships.

Katharine Merry, Lorraine Hanson, Denise Lewis and Clova Court were among the Stagbearers at the BUPA Games at Gateshead.

Birchfield women finished second in the Jubilee Cup semi-final at Liverpool. Among the major points scorers, Michelle Thomas won both sprints. The men qualified for the Gold Cup final. Nathan Morgan was second in the 200m as they took second place to Shaftesbury Barnet in the semi-final at Derby.

Six of the club's under-seventeens contested the British School's International at Ayr. Mark Lewis-Francis and Donna Maylor won over 100m; Daniel Plank was second in the high jump with a personal best of 2.05m; Shaunette Richards was second in the shot; Helen Thieme third in the 300m hurdles; and Andrew Ball was third in the 3km walk.

Stoke, 250 miles south, was the venue twenty-four hours later for the three female athletes. Shaunette Richards was 'Field Athlete of the Match' in the McDonalds' Young Athletes Girls' Premier League match.

The boys won their match at Swindon by ninety-one points. 'Athlete of the Match' awards went to debutants Geoff Djan, who ran 400m in 50.00, and Calvin Hall, a 1.85m under-fifteen high jumper discovered via the Nike Schools Project.

To complete the sequence, Samantha Davies was second in the under-twenty women's 100 metres at a junior international match in Alicante.

At the next British League Division One match at Barnet Copthall in early August, Birchfield were best in the distances. AAA 5,000m champion Karl Keska, preparing for faster challenges to come in Budapest, won the 'A' 1,500m, going five metres clear at the bell and doubling it by the line before Julian Moorhouse won the 'B' event. The 5,000m itself was just as rewarding. Front-running Matt Clarkson knocked sixteen seconds off his winning time in the match at Birmingham despite the competition falling away with more than two kilometres left. Carl Warren moved through for second place.

That crowned an afternoon of revitalisation for Birchfield, who were also boosted by victories from twenty-year-old Michael Tietz in the 100m in 10.60, and twenty-three-year-old Tayo Erogbogbo in the triple jump of 15.79m. Match:

1. Belgrave Harriers	398
2. Newham & Essex Beagles	309
3. Birchfield	292

Final league positions:

1. Belgrave Harriers	31 points
6. Birchfield Harriers	16 points

The Welsh Games in Cardiff provided a useful indication of form for impending major events in the international arena.

South Wales based Katharine Merry was impressive with a stadium record of 52.76 on a rare appearance over 400m. She smashed the seven-year-old record of 53.55 to stake a claim for European Championship 4 x 400m selection.

Katharine commented: 'If they want me I'll run. The selectors didn't say I had to run another 400 to get in the relay team but I decided to run one after a run at Sheffield. I had planned to run the 200 but I was pleased with how I ran in Sheffield with a season's best of 22.93, so I decided to switch to the 400 tonight. I ran my first 200 way too slow because I was worried about the wind, but I felt quite strong and didn't feel too bad after the race.'

Katharine, who lay third on the UK 400m list that year with a 51.7 in Barry, added: 'I plan to run a lot more 400s next year, combining it with 200s and then maybe move up to concentrate on the 400 the following year. But Linford wants me to wait until after the Sydney Olympics before moving up so we'll see how it goes. I fear the training more than the racing!'

Denise Lewis was looking forward to the European Championships after ending her trio of events on a high. She received a massive confidence boost following her ankle injuries of that season. Denise clocked a season's best for second in the sprint hurdles, finished equal second in the high jump, but saved the best until last by setting a personal best of 14.72m in the final round of the shot for another second place.

Denise was missing from the UK Women's League match at Watford, but the performances of Clova Court and Pauline Richards kept the club in the points. There was a track double with Helen Frost in the 400m and Vicky Sterne in the 800m. Sarah Bentley ran a personal best of 4:22.2 in the 1,500m, two seconds behind Kerry Smithson of Sale.

Birchfield won the 4 x 400m with legs from Lorraine Hansen, Sarah Damm, Vicky Sterne and Helen Frost. Match:

1. Windsor, Slough & Eton   191
2. Shaftesbury Barnet   179
3. Birchfield Harriers   175

League:

1. Windsor, Slough & Eton   22 points
2. Birchfield Harriers   17 points

The end of that month also saw the start of the European Championships in Hungary. British hearts – full of three successive gold medals in sprint events immediately before the 5,000m – started beating fast again with the sight of Karl Keska puffing along in third place. It didn't last but at least he was able to state after finishing ninth: 'I gave it a go. Training in America has given me a different perspective. The guys over there believe attacking is better than running defensively.'

For the long jump final, Nathan Morgan sat in the stands. He was resting his bad back as well as he could in an orange plank of a seat, and watching twenty-two-year-old Russian Kiril Sosunov win his first major senior title. The twenty-year-old Stag had inflamed a disc in qualifying and announced: 'I've had a problem before – the disc and muscles lock in my back. On the second jump of the qualifiers, I came back to the board and heard a crunch in my back. I knew that I didn't have much else to offer.'

An effort of 7.62m was his best in the qualifiers, though he added: 'In the third round I attacked as hard as I could but I just wasn't good enough on the day.' He flew home for a scan to determine the extent of the problems, no doubt musing where he might have finished in what proved to be a low-key final.

Robert Weir was to be Britain's sole finalist in the discus competition. It was not a happy return to Budapest, where he had thrown his personal best of 64.60m the previous year. He couldn't improve on his second effort of 61.92m and finished eighth, as in the 1997 World Championships.

The giant Birchfield Harrier also had problems in the qualifying round, which took place in driving rain. After a modest 58.92m in round one Robert confirmed: 'The circle was very, very slippery.' Also the judges started the clock for his second attempt while he was still waiting for his preferred red discus to return from the infield. 'I only had ten seconds left on the clock', he said, after keeping his nerve to reach 61.36m.

Fellow Stag Glen Smith went out in the qualifying round, seventh in his group with 58.97m, 3.47m down on his personal best.

Meanwhile, while Katharine Merry was bitterly disappointed to go out in her semi-final after finishing second in her 200m heat in 23.23, Denise Lewis produced the only gold medal of the championships by a British woman in the event she labelled: 'The survival of the unfittest.'

As is well chronicled, Denise had been struggling with an ankle injury since May. Thanks to physiotherapist Sarah Connor, whom she called the 'Terminator Woman' and her coach of fifteen years, Darrell Bunn – not to mention her body's remarkable knack of healing itself after injuries – Denise Lewis was ready just in time to give the British women something to cheer about.

Day One:
110m Hurdles: Denise's ankle injury meant that she was unable to do much speed work. This, and the 200m, would be her weakest events. However, as long as she was 'strong right across the board' then she never doubted her ability to pull it off.

A 13.59 clocking put her just behind Sabine Braun's 13.52. It soon became apparent that, as Denise expected, Urszula Wlodarczyk (13.42) and Natasha Sazanovich (13.40) would prove greater threats. 'Very disappointing', Denise said of her opener.

High Jump: A 1.83m leap was another solid performance by the Birchfielder. It was one centimetre more than the 1.82m she had jumped at the AAA Championships – the meeting which convinced her that she was over the injury and on the road to glory. All her main rivals managed 1.80m.

Shot Putt: A personal best of 15.27m put Denise in pole position. She was now thirty-four points ahead of her own British and Commonwealth record going into the 200m. 'Denise would not have come here unless she was in a position to do well', commented Darrell Bunn.

200m: 'I missed a lot of speed work and it showed in the hurdles and 200', she offered. 'I felt a bit dead after 150 metres and this was well below what I am capable of. But I always said I didn't have to be 100 per cent for these championships.'

Denise struggled with 24.75. Sazanovich ran a swift 23.62 to maintain the pressure on the Briton.

Day Two:

Long Jump: A long jump of 6.59m confirmed her superiority over the field. It was close to her best and better than all her rivals.

Javelin: A 50.16m throw left the final event a formality. Those final days prior to the Championships spent tuning her technique in the South of France paid off in the Nepstadion. 'If the competition is as intensive at the Commonwealth Games', she stated later, 'then that will allow me to perform even better.'

800m: Denise could afford to finish 8.6 seconds behind Sazanovich, her Belarussian threat. She finished two seconds ahead of her in 2:20.38.

The cushion of victory was ninety-nine points. 'It's the first time she's not had to work hard in an 800', commented Darrell Bunn, 'as she had a buffer.'

There was further club interest in the 4 x 400m relay where winning the bronze medal proved easier than picking the team! Donna Fraser to Vicki Jamison to Katharine Merry to Alison Curbishley was the final choice.

Commented Katharine: 'I had to run third, it was the only one I could be trusted with as I have no experience of this at all.' No one spectating would have guessed it as Katharine 'wound it up and wound it up' to hand over to Alison Curbishley with a staggering 50.4 leg.

It was the second medal by the women's team, who were keen to stress that a squad of six – as another Stagbearer Michelle Thomas and Natasha Danvers had played their part in the heats – deserved credit too.

Domestic fare now took the centre stage with the British League Gold Cup final at Bedford. The press reports stated that the biggest surprise was American Adam Nelson winning the shot with his only legal effort, 19.45m. It was only one of two Stags wins, the other coming from Tayo Erogbogbo in the triple jump. Match:

1. Belgrave Harriers	141
4. Birchfield Harriers	91

In the Jubilee Cup Final at the same venue, Birchfield had a rollercoaster ride to fourth place with Sale as the winners on the day. Emma Hornby won the pole vault with 3.60m, whilst Clova Court and Lorraine Hansen gave their all over several events as usual.

In the McDonald's National Young Athletes Final at the Alexander Stadium, Mark Lewis-Francis was thrilled with being voted 'Track Athlete of the Match' registering 10.80 into a 0.9m/s wind and commenting: 'I'm happy with the time because of the wind. To run 10.80 into a wind, you have to be happy with that.' Mark collected four gold medals on a busy September afternoon. He began with a resounding win over 200m – only his second over the distance that year. He anchored the 4 x 100m to victory and the league record, beating the nineteen-year-old standard set previously by Haringey. He also helped his club to victory in the 4 x 400m relay.

'The 400 hurt', he complained. 'My hamstrings are really tight and sore now. I only did it to help out and get some points. I'm hurting now though!' Match:

1. Sale Harriers	414
2. Birchfield Harriers	361.5

A week later in the National Junior League Finals at Cannock, the women successfully defended their title in a tense end-of-term fixture. It was a much tighter affair than the result suggested a ding-dong battle

Denise's leap of faith.

between Northern Premier Division runners-up Birchfield and Southern Premier Champions Shaftesbury kept everyone enthralled.

Club joint managers Suzanne Guise and Brian Holyfield had nothing but praise for the set-up at their Alexander Stadium headquarters. 'We can't thank enough all the coaches for the work they have put into the team as a whole. They have got the girls in top condition this season. It is only our third year in the League Final and we've won it twice', reported Brian. 'The girls excelled themselves today. Whatever we have asked of them they have done and some have surpassed that expectation. We were quietly confident we would do well. We know what the girls are like. They will always lift themselves for this one.'

Under-twenty Women's Final:

1. Birchfield Harriers	309
2. Shaftesbury Barnet	274

The under-twenty men's team was also in action. Match:

1. Blackheath Harriers	344
2. Birchfield Harriers	244

Rather further away, the globe-trotting Robert Weir was throwing a season's best 64.39m to finish fifth in the discus event at the IAAF World Cup in Johannesburg. His efforts were consistent as three throws into the wind were over 64m. His scoring effort was just twenty-one centimetres short of his lifetime best. Final standings:

1. Africa	110
6. Great Britain	89

Robert then flew on to Malaysia for the Commonwealth Games. Sixteen years after first striking gold in the men's hammer, Robert became one of the true greats in the history of the sport when he won the discus with a championship record. The thirty-seven-year-old's 64.42m beat South Africa's Frantz Kruger into silver by forty-nine centimetres and broke a Games record, which was set when Robert was a hammer thrower in 1982.

To quote *Athletics Weekly*: 'The gentle giant epitomises everything good about British athletics – humble in victory, gracious in defeat, always a gentleman and like one or two Britons in 1998 – a champion.'

'It was very competitive out there', admitted Robert. 'To think I won the hammer sixteen years ago in Brisbane is something very special and I appreciate it a lot more now than then.'

'I was not favourite going into the competition. Three other people were ahead of me. It was quite an occasion for me and especially at my age.' As with all great champions who mature with age, everyone wanted to know what his secret was. 'I just keep at it', he pronounced, adding that he didn't analyse competitors too closely. 'I don't think, oh I'm ranked third or so. I look on every contest as an opportunity.'

When asked by the media present if he would be back in four years to take, say, the shot or javelin title, Robert replied: 'It's my third Commonwealths and I'm just so pleased to have a medal in all three.' Glen Smith was fourth with 60.49m. His season's best would have snatched a medal.

In the men's 5,000m, Karl Keska finished as first 'Non-Kenyan' in fourth place in a hot and humid atmosphere. If conditions had been favourable, he might even have won a medal.

'If the conditions had been "normal" then I think I would have caught the third Kenyan', said Karl after finishing in 13:40.24. 'I'm in 13:15 shape at the moment, no question. But that's the difference the heat made.'

Karl, who only qualified for the final as a fast loser, collapsed at the finish. He recovered by the time the stretcher arrived. An asthmatic, his 'breathing had gone' in the intense heat.

The Stag echoed the demands of the 800m men who claimed that they were not getting the chance to compete in fast races. 'I haven't got in one fast race this year', he pronounced, pointing out that in his recent personal best of 13:26.37 he led for the last five laps. 'It's a catch twenty-two. You've got to be given the opportunities to progress.'

In his schooldays, Karl had attended Regis High in Wolverhampton. He became head boy and his long-time classmate, friend and fellow athlete, was one Denise Lewis. Karl stood proudly by as he witnessed Denise defend her title to make it a double celebration for the club. The European Champion followed on from Robert Weir's discus victory by confirming the gold medal many had predicted.

She then revealed that she still led Robert in a personal wager: 'We always have a personal bet that my heptathlon score will be higher than Robert's discus distance. I scored 6,513 points tonight so Robert would have to throw over 65.13 to beat me.'

In 1998 it would have been a major surprise if the 'Golden Girl' of British athletics had failed to retain the title she won in Victoria four years previously. However, the circumstances were so different, as she recalled: 'Then I was an unknown athlete who'd done all the work for years and then got very nervous before the 800 metres having been thrust into first position. Now everybody knows me and I came here to win. That was all that mattered.'

Just as before that 800m in 1994, Denise had worries on her mind going into the seventh and final event. She explained: 'After the javelin I felt a slight tightness in my adductor, a sort of spasm, and it's your biggest fear. You know all you have to do is get round the 800, but you start worrying.'

Until then everything had been under control, as Denise produced the best shot, long jump and javelin of the competition, also the equal-best high jump, having failed when attempting a personal best of 1.85m. In the sprint hurdles and the 200m she was the second fastest, bettered only by club-mate Clova Court.

Denise took nothing for granted as she confirmed: 'I never underestimate anyone and Jane Jamieson kept me on my toes. It wasn't as easy as some expected, I couldn't afford to make any mistakes.'

With the gold medal secured and with an English flag draped around her waist, she buzzed: 'I feel great, if I could run an 800 metres like that every time I'd be very happy'... 'Scoring more than 6,500 points for the second time in four weeks puts me in very good stead for the next two years. This year is a year of consolidation. The long-term aim is to win Olympic gold in Sydney. To score 6,513 points after doing only eighty per cent of the work and to still come out on top makes me feel really good.'

During the competition Denise became friends with eighteen-year-old Belize schoolgirl Candace Blades. 'Bless her, she's so sweet. She was a bag of nerves from start to finish but she had a great time and hopefully just got something from here that will stay with her for the rest of her career.'

'She was in awe of me, but I'm just a human being. During the javelin she gave me her address and we're going to stay in touch. The first thing I'm going to do is make sure she gets a decent pair of spikes.'

Denise finally announced that she was taking a break: 'I'm tired and looking forward to getting away in the sun. Usually at this time of the year I'm on a beach, not competing, but I've enjoyed it.'

Club companion Clova Court was troubled by a back spasm on the second day and after completing the final event admitted: 'I got round, I finished and that was my main aim.'

In the 4 x 400m relay England earned a silver medal. On the first leg, Michelle Thomas overcame the handicap of being drawn in lane eight to clock 53.4.

There were younger club members also enjoying the cut and thrust of international competition abroad in September. Six days after her nineteenth birthday, Samantha Davis was named: 'Track Athlete' of the European Women's Under-twenty Champions Cup Final in the Turkish capital, Istanbul. Samantha took home a brace of gold and silver medals in the relays. She began by clocking 24.9 for the 200m. She followed this with the anchor leg of the 4 x 100m relay in a championship best performance of 46.8. The other members of the quartet were Kemisha Robinson, Donna Maylor and Alexi Walker. Samantha rounded off the day with the first leg in the 4 x 400m relay. She handed over to Chantelle Cox. The two other runners were Karlene Trommans and Svreeta Williams, who were runners-up in a time of 3:55.21. The Stagbearers also received an award for the best club performances in the two relays.

The AAA Under-seventeen and English Schools Champion Donna Maylor took home a hat-trick of gold medals and provided evidence of her potential as a heptathlete. Donna won her speciality, the 100m, in 11.96 and the 110m hurdles in 14.71. In the 4 x 100m Donna ran an impressive second leg.

The fifth of the titles secured went to Denise Andrews with a best of 5.81m in the long jump.

October meant less exotic locations and the autumn and winter racing calendar. Rob Birchall eased back from a year of sciatic problems to retain the Midland Six-Stage Relay title for Birchfield. Twelve months and two lengthy lay-off periods after clocking the fastest time in the previous year's relay, the twenty-eight-year-old quantity surveyor did it again. The difference was, rather than setting off with a forty-seven second cushion, he had a twelve-second deficit to make up, a legacy of the club not having a second-leg runner until ten minutes before the start of the race.

Neil Appleby had not overcome the foot injuries which had kept him out of action for two years. His prospective stand-in Paul O'Callaghan went down with a heavy cold overnight. So nineteen-year-old Danny Everett, a 'C' team runner with a 19:26 clocking in 1997, was hastily promoted to fill the gap.

The ever-reliable Matt Clarkson ran the first leg as positively as he attacked his British League 5,000m races on the track and built an eight-second lead.

Weighed down by nerves, Danny Everett slipped back to eighth, one-and-a-half minutes off the pace. He commented later: 'I froze. I went round faster on my warm-down.' The fact that he was an impressive twenty-seven seconds faster than the previous year seemed scant consolation to him.

Carl Warren began the fightback on stage three. He clocked 17:08 – joint second fastest of the entire race – and hauled Birchfield to fourth within fifty-eight seconds of the new leaders, Tipton. Justin Pugsley's 17.09 on stage four further shrank the 'Stags' deficit to twenty-nine seconds. On the fifth leg, Matt Smith kept Tipton twelve ahead of Birchfield. The 'Stags' were up to second place thanks to Julian Moorhouse defying a streaming cold to snaffle the second-fastest time of the stage in 17:20.

So we come to the crunch. Aaron Keene hung on defiantly for Tipton. Rob Birchall confessed: 'Until halfway, I didn't think I would be fast enough to catch him. But once I could see him, I felt more comfortable and managed to get in front on the way back from the Jamboree Stone.'

Rob's time of 16:55 was eleven seconds slower than the previous year but considerably quicker than he expected after the problems he had overcome.

As the autumn rolled into winter, Julian Moorhouse was pontificating. Having cut his teeth on road relays and cross-country races Julian commented that he wanted more 3,000m indoor races, not just for himself but for the good of Britain's distance runners.

'We only get two chances to run a qualifying time for the major championships. That's because there are only two 3km races at the NIA each winter and without a fast time, we'll struggle to get into fields on the Continent.'

'Peter Elliot asked at the AAA Indoor Championships last year – "Why don't you go for it? You were only two-and-a half seconds off the qualifying time." It was only our second race of the winter indoors. We need more to get us used to the tactics that are necessary to succeed at a higher level. And there's definitely enough interest. There were about twenty guys in each of the 3K's last winter. They've got to have more like this.' Even so, his coach Harry Wilson was taking no chances. 'He's pestering to get me some races abroad', added Julian, who had run sub-eight minutes the previous winter.

For a club that had enjoyed so much success that year, there was an interesting news climax in December, as Commonwealth 800m finalist Bradley Donkin had decided that if he wanted to fulfil his ambition to become one of the world's top half-milers, the best thing to do was to join one of Britain's biggest clubs.

Bradley had come from nowhere to place sixth in the Kuala Lumpur men's two-lap final with a personal best of 1:46.86. Following his decision to sign first-claim forms for the Stags, his appearances in the gold and blue striped vest of his club Barton & District would be restricted to the odd open meeting.

Bradley had been disheartened to turn up to Barton's training sessions and find no one there. However, he was adamant he would retain links with the Humberside club.

'Joining Birchfield opens up so many doors for me, more races and increased chance of sponsorship. I'll be able to link up with Julian Moorhouse, who's a good friend of mine. I've also got family just outside Birmingham whom I can visit.'

Thirty-Two: Silver Lining

A new year witnessed the usual assortment of distance races and indoor meetings with coverage of the various athletes involved.

Sarah Bentley was back on yet another comeback trail – following a blood-curdling scare. After finishing third in the Barnsley 10km in November 1998 but pulling out of the Birmingham Challenge the following weekend, she went to her doctor for a check-up. They discovered that Sarah had virtually no white blood cells! The thirty-two-year-old athlete, who had finished sixth for England in the 10,000m in Kuala Lumpur confirmed: 'My white blood cells count was 2.8 when it should be between 4 and 11. I suppose it was to do with over-training. I had taken time off after the games and was hoping I might be able to do something towards the Europeans. But I wasn't doing more than I would normally.'

Sarah had returned to racing action by finishing second to Hayley Parry in the 4km at Cardiff. She added: 'I'm still on half training and I think I will be for some time. The count is up to 3.9 – but I'm still not in the proper range yet.'

In a better state of health was Rob Birchall, fresh from three weeks of warm weather training in Australia. Rob ran away with the men's 12km title in the Midland Championships at Bristol in late January.

Carl Warren, with a successful record in the event in recent seasons, was Rob's closest ally in a much-depleted Birchfield Harriers team.

Rob Whalley of Stoke was side by side with Birchall after the first of four 3km laps. By halfway, Rob Birchall's lead was forty metres and the procession in the quagmire extended the gaps within the field until he was able to cruise the last lap to come home in 39:37.

'That's the one I really wanted', announced Rob, whose previous Midland's best was seventh. Carl Warren finished eighth. Team:

1. Tipton Harriers	62
2. Bristol AC	119
3. Birchfield Harriers	178

Birchall's golden run in Bristol turned into a welcome double, for a couple of days later the performance earned him a sponsor. Asics came up with a kit deal, leaving the twenty-eight-year-old chartered surveyor stating: 'It's really topped off a good week... all I want now is a job. I've two sponsors so far – my dad, Ted, and my club. At the moment I'll consider any job – preferably in civil engineering – that enables me to continue training.'

His enjoyment of cross-country running had never been in question: 'It's the surface I love best.' His appetite was increased by the fact that injury had prevented him racing for most of the preceding winter. Now his confidence was beginning to match his preference. Previously, despite running the sixth-fastest leg in the National Six-Stage in autumn 1998 – while living in a caravan on the building site on which he was working in the London area – he had said: 'I originally thought I was lucky to get to the Chiba Ekiden Relay.' The modest Stag could not have raced more confidently to win his first Midland title in the Bristol mud. 'If you're running well, you can run on any surface. But I always like it muddy.'

Parallel to the outdoor activities, the diary was getting busy at the National Indoor Arena. The AAA Championships saw a 1,500m victory for Rachel Jordan, in a modest time of 4:25.88. However, Rachel used her fifty-six-second 400m speed to kick to victory under the watchful eye of coach Mike Rawson, the 1958 European 800m Champion. Daniel Caines was second to Allyn Condon of Sale in the race for the 400m title.

In the BUPA Indoor Grand Prix, Katharine Merry opened the night in spectacular style with a UK indoor record in the 200m. Katharine ran 22.83 to erase by thirteen hundredths the best of the season. As well as beating the clock, she left former Olympic silver medallist Juliet Cuthbert of Jamaica half a second behind.

'I don't think I've ever been number one in the world before on rankings', commented Katharine, after learning that her time had leapt over that of German Esther Moller's 22.86. 'But I'm still not going to the World Indoor Championships. I have a plan and that is to go to Australia and train.'

Fascinatingly, Katharine added that she did plan to move up to 400 metres that summer: 'I'm dying to, if the truth be known', she admitted. But Linford and Ron think it's a bit too early to have me dealing with rounds at championships and all that.'

Michelle Thomas won the 400 'B' event in 53.62 and announced: 'I was pleased to run a PB. I was getting a little worried because I hadn't run one for such a long time. My last PB was in '97, so I was pleased to come out with a PB. I have just started training with Linford Christie's group, and I won't have the opportunity to run any more meetings. If I am picked for the World Championships I will probably get a call and be flown back from Australia. I just want to wait and see.'

The major events at the NIA wound up with the AAA Under-twenty Championships towards the end of February. Mark Lewis-Francis equalled his indoor UK under-seventeen record and beat the championship record in the 60m. Mark blasted to a 6.77 clocking to beat Verlea's Tristan Anthony by some distance.

March brought an outstanding milestone for the club. At the English National Cross Country Championships at Newark, Justin Pugsley became Birchfield Harriers' first winner of the Men's National title since Eddie Webster won in a snowstorm at Leamington Spa seventy years before.

The twenty-seven year old won the 12km race by ten seconds in 38:32 and then declared: 'I hate running, I really do. It's the bane of my life… my nemesis. I would much rather be singing in a West End musical.'

'My coach, Mike Moffatt told me I'd win two weeks ago. He can't be here today because his son's ill. But he told me he'd be thinking of me at three o'clock. I told him he was mad, as I'm not superstitious at all. But now, well, this one goes to him.'

It was some performance by Justin, whose previous best results came when he placed third in 1998 and fourth as a junior. Earlier that winter he had come sixteenth – 'a nightmare run' – in the Inter-Counties.

In third place was Justin's great friend Spencer Newport. Justin had been the best man at the Blackheath athlete's recent wedding to women's winner Angela Newport (née Davies). After staying at their Loughborough house the night before, it proved to be something of a lucky household!

Then on one of the busiest days of the year for high standard domestic half-marathons in late March, Carl Warren went to the top of the 1999 UK rankings to complete a good financial week. Carl clocked 65.58 for second in Reading to run quicker than the first Briton home in Hastings and Portsmouth. He also set a personal best as he prepared for his marathon debut in London.

Earlier that week Carl had won an industrial tribunal case against his former employers, having been sacked upon his return from running in November's Chiba Ekiden Relay. 'It was a bit unsettling over Christmas, but now I've got a great office job and I finish at 4.45 pm which gives me plenty of time to train.'

Carl was anticipating another training partner soon as newly crowned National Cross Country Champion Justin Pugsley was about to take up a teaching post at Lichfield's Cathedral School.

Rob Birchall hoped to be back to bolster Birchfield's defence of the National Twelve-Stage Relay. The former Inter-Counties 10km silver medallist had been troubled by an abdominal injury for six weeks and missed the Midland twelve-stage relay in late March. In this, Tipton Harriers had ended Birchfield's hopes of a hat-trick by leading every step of the way. Rob had also been named as second reserve for the IAAF World Cross Country Championships but had to relinquish his place as well as dropping out of the European 10,000m challenge team.

He confirmed: 'I felt the injury the day after the World Cross Country Trial, although it hadn't affected me during the race. I've been able to run twenty minutes a day gently but I hope to be able to run in the National Twelve-Stage.'

Carl Warren was back in focus in May when he was delighted to have been given a chance to redeem himself as he looked forward to a second GB vest in June. The twenty-nine year old had been named for the Enchede half-marathon in Holland.

Carl commented: 'I had a nightmare when I made my GB debut in the Chiba Ekiden Relay last year and was ready to jump in front of the nearest train. I drank too much water and after flying for five kilometres I had the stitch from hell.'

Rob Birchall.

Richard Knowles.

Carl had used the track to hone his speed for Enchede, having finished third in the steeplechase at the British League opener. In that match there were two event victors for Birchfield. Glen Smith – who had thrown a season's best of 60.56 in Halle earlier – was just below the 60m barrier on this occasion. The 400m was currently Britain's top event and in a close race Richard Knowles gave Birchfield a rare track success in 47.28. Match:

1. Belgrave Harriers	395
8. Birchfield Harriers	207

In the UK Women's League Division One match at Wigan in early June, Helen Frost took the 400m in an encouraging 53.5. She then anchored the 'Stagbearers' to victory in the 4 x 400m relay. Match:

1. Shaftesbury Barnet	189
2. Birchfield Harriers	175

On the same day the men were in action back at home. They were altogether better organised and more focused than at Haringey in May. These qualities were exemplified by 400m winner Richard Knowles. He sat a German examination at Sheffield University for three hours in the morning before dashing down the motorway and easing home in 46.59.

The hosts had more to cheer when Julian Moorhouse won the 1,500m, gliding past Belgrave's Mark Miles in the last sixty metres to clock 3:48.23. The Stags overtook their first match points total after only twelve of the thirty-six events. Match:

1. Belgrave Harriers	360
2. Birchfield Harriers	323

Subsequently, Nathan Morgan withdrew from the European Cup in Paris and was keeping his fingers crossed that he did not have to endure a repetition of the previous summer's injury problem.

Nathan had tweaked a hamstring while training in the USA at the end of April and did not want his season to disintegrate in pain and disappointment again. He had jumped 7.81m at the British League meeting at Birmingham, a centimetre behind Chris Davidson, whom he defeated by 40cm at the 1998 AAA Championship.

The selectors kept faith with him and initially named him in the team for Paris. Then Nathan suffered a heavy cold in the intervening period and could muster no better than third at the Bedfordshire Games.

His coach, Darrell Bunn, confirmed: 'So far we've had only one run-up session and only one jumping session. He was in red-hot form last summer and then a huge frustration of being injured in Budapest and not being able to go to the Commonwealths. Now we do not want to rush things.'

Another of Darrell's charges also had a furrowed brow. Denise Lewis had withdrawn from the British team for the European Cup of Combined Events. Announcing her decision Denise stated: 'I really thought I was ready, and given how special this event is, I was hoping to compete. However, the last few days have proved that I am not quite ready. It is important that my first competition is a good one.'

Happier times for Mark Lewis-Francis as he led a junior men's 100m final at the AAA Under-twenty Championships and European Trial at Bedford in early July. It was a quality line-up and Mark's winning time of 10.38 was a UK under-seventeen age best. He edged Belgrave's Chris Lambert by two hundredths of a second.

His performance was made more remarkable by the fact he had been carrying a hamstring injury since an indoor junior international in France in February. 'I twinged my hamstring in the winter', he explained. 'It's why I've only had six races this year and it was very tight after the semi-final here. It was 50-50 whether I'd run or not. As for my start, it's always been my weak point.'

Ben Lewis ran 21.58 to finish second to Chris Lambert in the 200m.

A week later the English Schools' Championships were held at Bury St Edmunds. Here, matters caught up with Birchfield's rising star. Initially, Mark comfortably eased his way through rounds one and two of the intermediate boys' 100m with 10.92 and 10.95 respectively. Then disaster struck when he pulled up clutching his hamstring in the heats of the 4 x 100m relay – ending his championship on the spot.

'I'm gutted'; he reported. 'It felt a bit stiff in the heats of the 100 metres and afterwards I went to do some stretching and a few strides before the semis. It felt okay after the semi, but this morning when I got up it was really stiff. I tried to stretch and jog a bit before the relay, it was still a bit sore but I decided to run. I wish I hadn't now.'

In the junior boys' events, Edward Dunford won his first English Schools' title. The multi-talented athlete opted for the 80m hurdles. His 11.10 winning effort – into a 3.2 wind – was the second fastest time by a Briton.

Finally, in the senior girls' section, Helen Thieme won the 400m in 54.59. Helen was third in 1997 and second in 1998. 'So you can say I've moved up gradually', she said. Her personal best improved dramatically however, as she had a best of 56.2 and then ran 54.32.

The same weekend, the senior club members were in league action. At Barnet in the British League, Robert Weir, in only his second competition of the season, showed that he was well on the road to full fitness when his first effort of 60.34m in the discus proved to be the winner with only Kevin Brown of Belgrave close on 60.19m. Match:

1. Belgrave Harriers	340
7. Birchfield Harriers	246

In the UK Women's League match at Eton, Sarah Bentley won the 3,000m in 9:38. Match:

1. Shaftesbury Barnet	215.4
6. Birchfield Harriers	134

There were mixed fortunes at their home venue for the club's leading athletes at the AAA Championships and World Trials later that month.

A bizarre injury prevented Nathan Morgan from defending his title. With the final due to begin at 1 pm, Nathan was on the AstroTurf outside the stadium and just finishing his warm-up routine when the injury happened.

'Darrell it's me neck!' shouted Nathan to his coach, Darrell Bunn, who thought that his athlete was joking. In fact, Morgan had pulled the facet joint on his neck. A freak occurrence that can, Bunn claimed, be triggered by a simple cough. 'It was in spasm and he was in great pain', recalled Darrell, 'and as soon as he took his hand away you could see it swelling.' Nathan was taken to a local hospital, despite World Championship selection looming.

The men's discus was underway and while fans were trying to tot up how many AAA titles Colin Jackson had won, the winner of that field event made an interesting observation: 'How many have I won? I don't know but I do remember winning a couple in the eighties.'

It was, in fact, Robert Weir's eighth title, but the thirty-eight year old admitted that runners got noticed more: 'Because people can relate to running', he explained. Nevertheless, Robert was one of the most popular winners of the weekend. His 61.35m second-round effort beat Glen Smith's 59.25m.

Across on the track and dealing with the hardship of lane six in the 400m as if she had been born and bred to the toughest sprint of all, Katharine Merry swept to fifth in the 1999 world rankings for the one-lap distance, also to third on the UK all-time list behind the legendary Kathy Cook and Phylis Smith. The fact that she entered this Midlands Hall of Fame at the head of a Birchfield 1-2-3 made it quite an occasion!

Katharine crossed the line in the only Women's Championship best of the weekend at 50.62. To the attentive media pack who caught up with her as she recovered, Katharine reported: 'I've seen Linford at the finish, and he seems happy, so that's okay.' It certainly was. Christie, her manager and mentor, proclaimed: 'The thing is, it's not about times here, it's about winning. And it's not about my success. I just try and help them to believe what they can do and make certain that they can do it.'

Teamwork made sure Katharine did it. She revealed: 'When I first heard I was in lane six I thought it was terrible. But all the guys told me it was a massive advantage because I could run my own race without having anybody else pull me around. So lane six was a blessing. Going through 200 I glanced at the clock and saw it was twenty-four-ish, which was great. I knew I would come home strong.'

By halfway, she was two metres up on her anticipated greatest rival, Donna Fraser. Katharine opened up a five-metre lead as the last bend unwound and never looked in distress as she became the first woman since Kathy Cook to complete a set of AAA gold medals at 100m, 200m and 400m.

Christie's expert assessment of the race oozed approval; 'Kath ran it really well. The only danger with her is running the first 200 quite fast. But she was confident that she could win. She told me she thought she'd run fifty points and that's great.'

Of her new ranking Katharine mused: 'Now I hope it gives me respect within world sprinting. I still believe I'm lacking strength because I've had a winter of 100 and 200-metre training. I'm already looking forward to a winter of 400 training.'

Completing the Birchfield joy, twenty-five-year-old Helen Frost snatched the silver medal in 52.43, the second time that weekend she had taken half a second off her personal best. Michelle Thomas powered past Donna Fraser for third in 52.59.

There was more cause for celebration when news filtered back that Mark Lewis-Francis had won a gold medal in the inaugural World Youth Games in Poland. Mark took the 100m title in 10.40, despite suffering from that hamstring problem which denied him the opportunity of winning his second English Schools' title. His winning time was fractionally slower than the British age-group record he had set in June.

A personal best was of 11.76 was achieved in Poland by Donna Maylor in the 100m.

Also on his travels the next weekend was Nathan Morgan. He made it to the European Under-twenty-three Championships in Gothenburg following a remarkable recovery from his neck injury. In the final event of the championships, Nathan won Britain's eighth medal when he leapt 7.99m for long-jump bronze. Yago Lamela of Spain, the world indoor silver medallist, easily won with 8.36m. It was the first time that Lamela had managed to beat Nathan in international competition. With his date in Sweden, Nathan would obviously miss the final British League match at the Alexander Stadium.

Here, Belgrave Harriers maintained their unbeaten season to clinch their third successive title. Robert Weir and Glen Smith gave the host club full points in the discus. The pair were first and second in the previous week's AAA Championships but neither had the 63.50m qualifying mark for Seville. Robert had thrown 61.88m in Bergen on the Tuesday and reached 61.31m this time.

Paul O'Callaghan ran his first track race for seven years, then joked: 'That was twenty-five miles too short for me.' Having made his marathon debut in London earlier that year with 2:22.58, the Irish international considered that to be his distance. So a 1,500m was a bit short and sharp for the thirty-five-year-old teacher. He finished eighth in 4:00.93 and was looking forward to getting himself fit for the Dublin Marathon in October. 'I was planning to make my marathon debut there last year but then I got injured. My training has been going well, I've just been neglecting the races so I'll try to do a few more now.' Match:

| 1. Belgrave Harriers | 363 |
| 2. Birchfield Harriers | 299 |

Final league positions:

| 1. Belgrave Harriers | 32 |
| 2. Birchfield Harriers | 17 |

In the UK Women's League match, a hat-trick of victories were accomplished in a home joint fixture. Joining Michelle Thomas, the 400m victor, were triple-jump winner Debbie Rowe and Sarah Oxley in the 200m.

Sarah, sixth in the AAA Championships, was a comprehensive winner as she ended the hopes of Marcia Richardson of Windsor to achieve a sprint double. Sarah was backed by Zoe Wilson, who took the 'B' string for the Stagbearers to help them place equal third on the day. Match:

1. Shaftesbury Barnet   194
Equal third: Birchfield Harriers 167 with Aldershot, Farnham & District

Final positions:

1. Shaftesbury Barnet   24
2. Birchfield Harriers   14.5

At the beginning of August, in the British Grand Prix at Crystal Palace, Katharine Merry lowered her 400m personal best to 50.58 behind current world leaders Cathy Freeman of Australia and Falilat Ogunkoya of Nigeria. 'It was only twenty minutes before the race I decided to compete', she revealed. 'I had a slight problem in my left knee and on any other weekend in any country but my own, I would not have run.'

The same weekend Mark Lewis-Francis was in action at the European Junior Championships in Riga, Latvia. In the 100m final Mark couldn't keep up with Frenchman Fabrice Calligny. It was generally recognised that Mark was not fully fit and different circumstances might have seen him become the youngest-ever winner of the title at sixteen years old.

In the women's 100m Donna Maylor finished a fine sixth but was disappointed after not running as quickly as her heat time. She had finished in the same position at the recent World Under-eighteen Championships and in Riga ran 11.80. Donna was suffering with shin splints and a sore hamstring. 'I tried to block it out, but I tensed up towards the end of the race. I'm not happy with that.'

Less than two months after the death of his brother, top British hurdler Ross Baillie, from an allergy to nuts, eighteen-year-old Chris Baillie won the European 110m hurdles title. The Scottish teenager, who had made his Birchfield debut in June, stopped the clock in a wind-assisted 13.92. This also gave him the Scottish junior record previously held by his brother, as well as a junior club record.

However, the photo-finish judges were (unusually) unable to separate the Stag from the Spaniard Felipe Vivancos. This meant that both athletes were awarded gold medals.

Chris was delighted with his medal but felt if he had run a clean race he would have had the honour to himself: 'I didn't get out of the blocks right. I hit the second hard and made it difficult for myself. I thought that if I could get out well and run a clean race then I'd win easily. I'm angry with myself really. But I won, which is the main thing.'

Back home the Jubilee Cup Final was staged in mid-August. Shaftesbury Barnet completed their second women's league and cup double in three seasons. The Stagbearers were able to cheer another fine 400m by Helen Frost, who powered past Michelle Pierre of Shaftesbury before the halfway point and went on to clock 52.76. This was within reach of her personal best of 52.43. There was also a triple-jump win by twenty-six-year-old Debbie Rowe, the only competitor to exceed twelve metres. Match:

Shaftesbury Barnet   103
Birchfield Harriers   73.5

The month reached a climax with the event of the year – the IAAF World Championships in Seville, Spain. In the men's discus event, Robert Weir and Glen Smith didn't make the cut in the qualifying rounds, the former by one place and eight centimetres at 62.71m. Robert, who had made a late start to the 1999 season due to injury, produced the unlucky thirteenth longest throw of qualification. He pronounced: 'I should have stood closer to the front of the circle! That must be one of the longest throws never to make a final.'

Glen Smith, the twenty-seven-year-old teacher, who had thrown 65.11m earlier that season, managed 58.27m. His first effort, however, which was judged a foul, was at least 61m, but his foot apparently touched the back of the circle.

So, the smiles were to be reserved for the Birchfield ladies on duty. The precocious talent twenty-five-year-old Katharine Merry, first revealed half a lifetime ago, finally shone through on the big stage when she finished her first-ever four-round test by taking fifth place in the 400m final, narrowly won by defending champion Cathy Freeman.

Katharine, in lane one, knowing she would have to break fifty seconds for the first time to get on the podium, made up the stagger on Russia's reigning World Junior Champion Natalya Nazarove before halfway but never quite got to Lorraine Graham in lane three.

Katharine, with 50.52, took the scalps of Nazarova, reigning World Indoor Champion Grit Breuer and the European bronze medallist Olga Kotlyarova. 'My aim was not to come last', said the AAA Champion. 'To finish fifth from the inside lane isn't easy. I'm over the moon. But everything aches!'

The usual painful experience was also unfolding for Denise Lewis in the heptathlon. However, Denise was to give Britain a silver lining that long, hot weekend. Yet, despite all the injury setbacks she had to overcome on the road to Seville, she was disappointed. The Birchfield battler was beaten by an electrifying personal best of 6,861 points from France's new import from Sierra Leone, Eunice Barber. Eunice had never previously gone over 6,416 and was instantly dubbed: 'The Barber of Seville'!

After totalling 6,724, within a dozen points of the Commonwealth record she had achieved at Gotzis in 1997, Denise conceded: 'I would have to be exceptional to beat Eunice.'

Behind the top two, reigning Olympic Champion Garda Shuaa snatched the bronze medal with 6,500, just three ahead of the previous World champion Sabine Braun.

Day One:

100m Hurdles: 'I heard the gun and there was Eunice at hurdle two!' said Denise. The Briton finished fourth in 13.61. This was 0.12 slower than in her trial race a week earlier.

High Jump: Two personal bests kept Barber at the head of the pack. 'I thought I was going to be blown away after just the first two events', admitted Denise. Her response was to clear a personal best of 1.87m at the second attempt and go agonisingly close to 1.90m, twice dislodging the bar with her left heel after her body had sailed over. The effort put Denise firmly in second place.

Shot Putt: This time it was Denise who came up with the big personal best – 16.12m – just as her coaches predicted she would. The outstanding effort came with her third and final attempt on a hot and humid Saturday evening. Her previous best was 15.27m. 'You'd improve like that if you'd spent ten weeks injured and only able to practise the shot', she uttered. For Eunice Barber, it was her weakest event. She reached 12.37m. Suddenly, Denise had a lead of sixty-five points.

200 m: It became a one-point lead for Barber by the end of the first day. That was much better than Denise could have wished for during the afternoon break. Eunice clocked 23.57 in her heat. Denise was in the next heat and pushed hard around lane eight in 24.26. Well short of her personal best of 24.10 but as well as could be expected after her truncated competitive preparation for Spain.

Day Two:

Long Jump: Dreams of golden glory turned into an acrimonious nightmare in the first event of the second day. After a foul and a modest 6.20m, Denise finally found her fluency on the runway – only to discover the judge holding out his red flag to indicate a foul. As Denise questioned the decision, the television replay showed that her foot placement could not have been more perfect on the take-off board. After a prolonged argument the officials measured the effort at 6.64m. Even so, the judge's decision stood with Denise credited with the 6.20m. 'I didn't make a mark on that board', she stated. 'There were millimetres in it but it was valid. I would never try and get something I could not justify.' With an extra 141 points at stake, the team management filed a protest. The intervening period was a distraction to Denise: 'I didn't hear the result of the appeal until I was on the warm-up track getting ready for the javelin.' The good news was that she had her 214 points for second place in the competition. The bad news was that she was beaten by Barber, who went to 6.86m in the second round to score 1,125 points to Denise's 1,053.

Javelin: All hopes of a gold medal were brought to an end by Denise's dodgy shoulder. She managed 47.44m in the first round. This was a personal best with the new implement introduced but not enough to trouble the inspired leader. Barber opened with a personal best of 49.88m, which meant having to beat the newly recruited French lady by a full seven seconds in the last event.

800 m: There were only five metres in at the line – but Eunice Barber clinched the gold medal in the best manner by winning the race in 2:15.65 with Denise sixth in 2:16.87.

High-flying Denise Lewis.

The European and Commonwealth Champion had been defeated in six out of seven events by Eunice Barber for the world title. However, she knew that she could have done better in the 100m hurdles, javelin and 800m with another month's training. Denise was also convinced that her Commonwealth mark of 6,736 would have been eclipsed if she had obeyed her new Dutch coach Charles van Commenee in the 800 metres and pushed herself to her limit. 'I went through 600 thinking – "I'm not tired enough." I should have given it more.' She missed the record by twelve points.

'But the two positive things to come out are that my mental strength is very good and physically I was as good as I have been, despite not being able to train properly for ten crucial weeks this year.'

Considerable optimism in reality for Denise and for the club management as the track and field season reached the last lap of the diary.

In September the women's under-twenty team had been confirmed as the best in the UK for the third year in succession. They defended their National Junior League title at Derby by twenty-seven points from Sale with Liverpool Harriers in third place.

Helen Thieme, aged seventeen, was named 'Track Athlete of the Meeting' for her 400m hurdles victory in 62.6. Helen was also second in the 100m hurdles. Birchfield came out on top in both relays, and maximum points were achieved in the 400m with Svreeta Williams winning the 'A' race in 56.7. Denise Andrews, aged nineteen, recorded a fine double, taking the honours in both the long and triple-jump competitions.

At the same venue, the Stags, despite the absence of three of their internationals, were runners-up to Shaftesbury Barnet in the junior men's competition.

The Birchfield women ended the season on a high note with an epoch-making performance at the European Champions Clubs Relays meeting in Rennes, France. It was the first time in the club's long and illustrious history that they had captured a European team title – and they took two: the 4 x 100m and the 4 x 400m!

Two members of the winning teams were also the two youngest members of the eight-strong Birchfield squad, making their debuts for the Stagbearers.

The baby of the team, sixteen-year-old Lindsey Singer, winner of the Home Counties 300m, and who ran in the 4 x 200m relay, had joined Birchfield from Royal Sutton Coldfield. She helped establish a club 4 x 200m record. It was also an encouraging end to the summer for hurdler and multi-eventer, Sharon Davidge, eighteen, who had missed most of the season through injury.

'It was a big thrill being there and a wonderful finale to the season. It was the proudest moment of my life in athletics', said team manager Lyn Orbell, who had not witnessed much success for the ladies in 1999.

In an unusual move, the organisers did not issue medals but commemorative batons to the teams. 'There's no way they're going to be used for relay practice. They are the prize possessions of the athletes who took part', added Lyn.

Forty-eight hours before they were due to set out, Katharine Merry dropped out with a chest infection. Michelle Thomas and Sam Davies were also injured and unavailable. Lyn hunted around and found the two youngsters who were thrilled to go and make memorable debuts for their club.

Thirty-Three: The Race of All their Lives

This was a year when the attention would gravitate towards those chosen for the Olympic Games in Sydney.

Back home in late January, the NIA staged the AAA Indoor Championships and Indoor Trials. The final event of the weekend – the men's 400m – produced the winner most pundits had been commenting on for several weeks. Iwan Thomas had mentioned his name as 'one to watch' at a press conference the day before the championships began. Jamie Baulch had been ringing him up to offer words of encouragement and advice. By the end of the meeting that new star had been unleashed: Daniel Caines.

His parents had enjoyed some profile in their time too. His mother, Blondelle, was a UK record-holder over 100m hurdles in the 1970s. His father, Joseph, was a forty-six-second 400m runner.

Daniel had placed third in these championships in 1998 and second in 1999 behind Allyn Condon. After missing the previous summer with a stress fracture in his back – an injury that returned briefly to haunt him at the beginning of 2000 – he had an outdoor best of 47.1. His victory, allied to equally impressive outings at recent indoor meetings, meant that Daniel was among the thirteen early selections for the European Indoors.

The Birchfielder had a simple tactic – hit the front and stay there. This day he held off Paul Slythe, Adrian Patrick and Mark Hylton to win in 46.89. He then conceded: 'Today I was petrified before the start, so going to Ghent will do me the world of good.'

Before that was the CGU Indoor Grand Prix at the NIA in February and a further learning curve for young Daniel. A press report described him as blasting away 'like a man possessed'. He led the world number one Alesandro Cardenas of Mexico until the final straight. Cardenas, the world outdoor bronze medallist, cruised past to win in 46.54, with an exhausted Caines being caught on the line by fellow Briton Mark Hylton. Both men had a dead heat with 46.85. Daniel trudged off the track, but had won nothing but admiration for the gallant way he took the race to the Mexican.

The European Indoor Championships were held in Belgium. There, hampered by 'duff lane draws' Daniel finished a fighting sixth in the final. The twenty year old could not have run a gutsier race as he blasted away from lane one, and, remarkably took the lead going through 200m in 21.77. Three races in three days, in his first major championships, took its toll however, and he inevitably faded to a 48.36 time. His best was 46.79. 'I did my best', proclaimed a disappointed Daniel, 'and there will be a day when I don't die.' He added that Sebastian Coe went out in front in his earlier races. 'Then one day he was good enough to hang on and win', continued Daniel.

The next major championship involving a Stag was the IAAF World Cross Country Championships at Vilamoura, Portugal in mid-March.

Karl Keska was languishing in the fifties after the first half mile but picked off runners one by one to finish a magnificent thirteenth. This was his first World Cross and 'only about my fourth cross-country race in the past

Daniel in the lion's den.

four years', stated Karl. The twenty-seven year old had been part of the British team that won gold medals at the European Championships in Slovenia the previous December. On that occasion he was ninth.

Karl had prepared for this race in Boulder, Colorado, training at high altitude with British teammate Jon Brown. He missed the UK Inter-Counties and Trial at Nottingham, instead using races at Amorebieth and Haro to sharpen his body. His mind, on the other hand, was sharpened by Brown, who gave him 'valuable insight' on how to succeed in one of the world's toughest races.

'As I ran I just kept looking at the next person and thought "just run at them", then the next, and the next, and the next…'

Indeed, there was nothing fancy about his tactics: 'Ian Stewart told me to run hard. With a lap to go I thought someone shouted: "You're fortieth" and I thought: "I'm higher than that aren't I?" but it made me go harder.'

Karl was coached by Alan Storey, advised by Ian Stewart and trained with Jon Brown – but not all of the time. 'Bear in mind Jon's marathon training. In Boulder I've been doing my own sessions, set by Alan. But Jon's insight gave me confidence. I've never enjoyed cross-country in the past, but I've come away from here with a positive experience.'

This positive attitude impacted on Karl's participation in the European 10,000m Challenge in Lisbon on 1 April. He put the atrocious conditions at the back of his mind as he pushed forward his claim for a flight ticket to the Sydney Olympics.

A superb run on his first real attempt at the distance put the Stag into pole position for Olympic selection. His silver medal saw him become the first British man to achieve a top three placing in what was the fourth staging of the Challenge.

Despite the high wind and rain, television schedules dictated that the programme would go ahead. Karl got on with the job in a very positive manner, which brought him home a couple of strides behind the highly experienced Spaniard Enrique Molina.

Debutant he may have been, yet Karl ran his race in a professional and authoritative manner. After a steady start he settled in the pack behind teammate Julian Cullen. Lap-by-lap the Midlander gradually moved forward into the top ten, then leading half dozen at half distance. An injection of pace at that stage saw Karl's tall frame at the front after six kilometres. Afterwards he remained constantly with the medal contenders. At nine kilometres he went to the front. At the bell Molina and fellow Spaniard Alberto Garcia were on his shoulder – all having pulled clear of the rest of the field.

With 250 metres remaining the two Spaniards made their moves. Karl did not give up and, with a battling sprint up the home straight, narrowly failed to catch Molina, but edged ahead of Garcia with virtually the last step of the race to finish with 28:00.56.

The tired but contented Birchfield athlete confirmed: 'I came here to run a good race and obviously a lot of pressure is off me as I also got the qualifying time. The conditions didn't help at all. They were terrible. I knew I could do it. But finishing in a good position was more important than getting the time. I just wanted to run well.'

The very same day the club were dominating the Midland Twelve-Stage Relay at Sutton Park. They achieved their third win in four years. The 1999 winners, Tipton, finished a distant second. Such was Birchfield's dominance, they were never headed from the moment Carl Warren handed over in front at the end of the opening stage.

At stage twelve, Dave Miles was still in the Birchfield tent when Mike Shevyn completed his stage. Such was the lead he was able casually to remove his T-shirt, push through the spectators and set off for the glory leg. Dave was still able to run the fastest of that stage – the fifth Birchfield athlete to achieve that feat – as he brought them home in 3:44.08.

Team Manager Maurice Millington felt that the solid runs by those athletes on long stages were the key to success.

Carl Warren	26:08
Richard Burman	14:58
Steve Edmonds	15:08
Mark Flint	26:27
James McCook	15:06
Julian Moorhouse	14:00
Paul O'Callaghan	26:36
Mark Hirsch	15:26
Darius Burrows	14:16
Mike Bouldstridge	26:18
Mike Shevyn	14:46
Dave Miles	14:59

Early May saw both the men's and women's teams in league action at Eton. Birchfield were sixth in the men's event, despite providing the youngest winner of the day. Seventeen-year-old Leigh Smith enjoyed a long jump of 7.29m – a personal best by a massive 44cm – to take the scalps of 1994 Commonwealth triple-jump champion Julian Golley and reigning BUSA title-holder Chris Davidson. Match:

1. Belgrave Harriers	366
6. Birchfield Harriers	228

For the ladies it was a puzzle to many that Birchfield had five 'A' wins yet finished the match down in sixth place. Great Britain Junior Captain Helen Thieme looked strong in her first 400m of that summer, clocking 54.98. Lizzie Patrick triple jumped 12.70m to win by more than a metre. Twenty-three-year-old Zoe Wilson was the sprinter of the meeting, following her swift 100m with 200m in 24.66 into a strong headwind. She then joined forces with Donna Maylor, Syreena Pinel and Katharine Merry to help win the 4 x 100m relay.

Katharine also ran the glory leg of the 4 x 400m for the Stagbearers, having just returned from training in Australia and 'wanting to do something for the club'.

1. Sale, Manchester	201
6. Birchfield Harriers	141

Not taking part that day was Denise Lewis. Since finishing second to Eunice Barber in the 1999 World Championships heptathlon, Denise had been bedevilled by so many injuries that she had not high jumped since that day.

Following an operation on her right calf in December 1999, she had what Charles van Commenee described as 'a relay of injuries in her body' including the continuation of a long-standing shoulder problem. 'It was only in March that we were able to do any athletics', he reported. 'At the moment her body doesn't seem to want it and we've had to do a lot of improvising and rehabilitation. Her body has not been co-operating, but we will never use that as an excuse. With the Olympics three months away there is no escape any longer.'

Whilst Denise aspired to the highest level of international competition, one young club-mate was determined not to get involved with the exploits of the Great Britain juniors that summer. Jonathan Moore and his advisers preferred to concentrate on his repeating his victories of the summer of 1999 in the AAA and English Schools' triple jump. The under-seventeen had recorded a UK age best of 15.33m at a McDonald's Young Athletes' meeting at Cheltenham. This was just an hour after recording a league record long jump of 7.45m. Jonathan and his father, former British international Aston Moore, were insistent that Jonathan would not step up the age groups prematurely.

Another former international, Du'aine Ladejo, had joined the club that season and in the Midland Championships at Stoke had a superb tussle with Brendan Ghent of Rugby in the 100m. Ghent held the upper hand throughout, relegating Du'aine to runner-up in both the heats and final. The heats produced the better time with Ghent stopping the clock on 10.85 to Ladejo's 10.92. In the final Ghent's victory was more comprehensive. He recorded 10.88 against a head wind of minus 3.9.

However, he was unable to repeat his winning exploits in the 200m. Brendan encountered the in-form Richard Knowles. Richard clocked 21.56, with Ghent 0.08 seconds adrift in second place.

In the 400m hurdles, Paul Hibbert was in decisive form to defeat club-mate Bradley Yiend. Paul produced a winning 53.26, with Bradley having to settle for runner-up spot in 55.10. Bradley gained consolation by winning the 400m flat. He covered the one-lap race in 48.14.

The field events produced some of the women's best performances. In the pole vault, winner Irene Hill of Windsor and Emma Horby of Birchfield both cleared 3.70m. Emma had failed in her first attempt at 3.50m, allowing Hill to claim the senior crown. Birchfield's Nicola Talbot peppered the forty-four and forty-five metre lines in the senior women's discus event. Having two throws over forty-five metres and her best of 45.36m was good enough for gold.

June was also a successful time for Katharine Merry. She captured several notable scalps in a great start to her 400m campaign with victory in the Helsinki Grand Prix. She stopped the clock in 50.72, despite blustery conditions, and reported: 'I'm extremely pleased with the time particularly as the wind was so strong on the back straight and final bend. After all the training that I have put in, I believe that I can go under fifty seconds this summer.'

Within ten days Katharine was in Nuremberg delivering a blow to the confidence of Germany's top two 400m runners, Grit Breuer and Anja Rucker. She ran a tremendous race, winning in 50.28, the second fastest time of her career. Deliberately placed outside of Breuer and Rucker so the Germans could track her, she treated them with disdain as she won comfortably. Katharine commented: 'That has to be my best 400 ever. I think out there I proved I am one of the best in the world.'

This she went on to reinforce in a Great Britain v. USA match at Glasgow in early July. Katharine looked in control throughout the 400m, and especially over the last 70m, as she had done in all her unbeaten one-lappers so far.

'I was glad Jamie Baulch ran before me', she reported. 'I asked him about the conditions and he basically said it was tough all the way.'

Katharine took it easy over the first part of the race, with American Makel Malone making up the stagger on her. She could see that she was gaining on the in-form American Michelle Collins and passed her at the halfway mark. Collins tried to come back as they entered the home straight but to no avail and Katharine added another sub-fifty-one race to her year's tally.

'I know I'm strong, especially over the final part of the race', she proffered. 'It's important psychologically at this time of the season to be ticking people off and I'm glad the way things are going. I'm missing Lausanne – I want to race Cathy Freeman when I'm ready – so the next race is in Nice. It's good to race. I think people are silly not to race early on.'

Also having cause for celebration that weekend was Birchfield's own American, twenty-five-year-old Adam Nelson, when he achieved a shot putt of 21.70m at Stanford University in California. It took Adam to second spot in the rankings behind C.J. Hunter and established a new club record. This had been held by the top class British international, and former 'World's Strongest Man', Geoff Capes for over two decades.

Adam's coach, Robert Weir, then flew the Atlantic to compete for Britain. The Commonwealth Champion threw the discus 59.14m for third place. Glen Smith was fourth with 57.84m.

While fans of Denise Lewis were worried that a winter spent on the physio's couch would undermine her chances at the Sydney Olympics – the athlete herself was joking and jigging with Maurice Greene on the infield before her first event, the high jump.

Then, after a solid 1.78m clearance, she threw the shot 15.50m and dashed across to the 100m hurdles start. Breathless before the gun even blew, she ran a slightly disappointing 14.14 from lane one, or, as Denise called it: 'The Outer Hebrides!'

Overall, the multi-medallist was happy to get through her first competitive outing since 1999 and set out on the road to Australia.

It was subsequently revealed that Denise had been brushing up on her hurdles technique under the eagle eye of Colin Jackson's coach, Malcolm Arnold. Amsterdam-based Lewis had been travelling to Bath for hurdles sessions every Tuesday, 'and she's driving Malcolm mad', reported Colin. 'He says to Denise: "Every time I tell you to do something you do! It makes my job too easy".'

Both Denise Lewis and Robert Weir were to keep themselves sharp with further competition in mid-July.

At the European Cup in Gateshead, as British Men's Captain, Robert led by example. He finished a creditable fourth in a contest won by the reigning Olympic and European Champion Lars Reidel of Germany. On season's performances Robert should have finished last. However, he demonstrated his vast experience, in his ninth European Cup appearance, to throw 60.78m to Riedel's 63.30m. Reidel was eight metres short of his best, Robert four below his. 'But the conditions were awful', stated the team captain, who added that he was disappointed with his performance.

Interestingly, the night before, Robert had been woken by a telephone call in his room from Adam Nelson. Adam had just won the US Olympic trial shot putt with one of the longest throws in history. Together, with the subsequent team triumph in the competition, Robert had quite a weekend!

Final standings:

1. Great Britain	101.5
2. Germany	101
3. France	97

On the same weekend at the Netherlands National Championships in Amsterdam, Denise Lewis won one gold in the high jump, one silver in the long jump, and two bronze medals in the shot putt and 200m. She also had a fourth place in the javelin.

Despite all this, Denise wasn't too happy with her performance: 'I just wasn't there this weekend. I just wasn't really focussed. I get that sometimes in single-event meetings. But I more often have an off-weekend in the run up to a major competition. From here on, it is supposed to go up until the Talence heptathlon.

Denise won her gold with a modest result, a 1.70m high jump with a 1.73m jump-off. 'The long jump didn't feel bad', she added. 'The run up was good, but the sharpness and acceleration in the last few strides just weren't there.'

So, within a fortnight, and in her first heptathlon since Seville, Denise broke her own Commonwealth record with an outstanding performance in Talence. Racing to a new mark in the Decastar 2000 meeting of 6,831 points, an improvement of ninety-five points on the score she achieved at Gotzis in June 1997, Denise dominated the competition from start to finish. Runner-up was Poland's Urszula Wlodarczyk, who scored 6,351. Nathalie Teape of France was third on 6,214.

The European Champion turned up the heat in the very first event by winning the 100m hurdles in a lifetime best of 13.13, striking 0.05 seconds off her four-year-old fastest. The victory earned Denise 1,105 points and the lead from the three 100m hurdles races. She continued in a positive vein when clearing a season's best 1.84m high jump to retain the overall lead. Looking very relaxed the multi-medallist increased her score to 2,134.

Although Wlodarczyck produced the best throw of the day with 15.48m in the shot, Denise managed a fine effort of 15.07m to maintain a sixty-four-point buffer ahead of her Polish rival and 128 in front of Muriel Crozet of France.

With only the 200m remaining, Denise looked well on course to record her best first day if she could run quicker than 25.22. This she duly did with a wind-assisted 24.01 time behind South Africa's Maralize Visser Fouche. That final performance, aided by a 3.6m/s wind, allowed her to close the first day on 3,980 – 113 ahead of her Commonwealth record. Told she was on target for that record, Denise retorted: 'Am I really ahead of the record? I'd never thought about it.'

Summarising her Saturday efforts, she added: 'I've been working really hard on my hurdling technique and I almost got it right. I nicked the sixth and eighth ones but I kept my discipline, particularly in the closing stages. I feel fantastic. It's so great to be competing again after so many injuries. Many people don't realise what I have gone through.'

Denise had a dream start on the Sunday morning producing a lifetime long jump legal best of 6.69m to win the competition. Despite throwing 49.42m with the new javelin, Denise scored only 849 points, which meant she knew the final target would entail running the 800m faster than 2:18.19.

The double Commonwealth Champion rose to the occasion. After tracking the leader on a first lap of 64.85, she powered away from Marie Collonville of France in the final fifty metres to produce another dream time of 2:12.20.

A delighted winner announced: 'I never thought at any stage about breaking records. What was important was giving it everything I had and performing to the best of my ability. I think I did that, particularly in the 800. Overall I think I showed I'm pedalling in the right direction towards the Olympics.'

Whilst the senior stars were working hard towards their ambitions, there were younger club athletes making their impact too. The British Grand Prix at Crystal Palace in early August witnessed Mark Lewis-Francis produce arguably the performance of the day. He won the 'B'-race 100m in 10.10. The run, which originally flashed up on the board as 10.09, was wind-assisted at 1.9m/s.

Mark had run faster than the world silver and bronze medallists Bruny Surin and Dwain Chambers, faster than Ato Boldon, and faster than Darren Campbell, who was the favourite for the trials. Mark's 10.10 was the sixth fastest ever by an under-twenty athlete. It improved his previous best of 10.25, set at Loughborough in May.

Afterwards Mark repeatedly insisted that he would not be going for Olympic medals that year: 'I've got loads of Olympics ahead of me and this is my first and only World Juniors. I'm still doing speed endurance at the moment. I haven't started speed work properly.'

Ato Boldon agreed with the younger athlete's decision to target Santiago instead of Sydney: 'It's more of a confidence booster to be World Junior Champion than to go to Sydney to go out in the heats.'

The same weekend in the UK Women's League Division One match at Solihull, Helen Frost confidently outstripped her 400m opponents. She felt that she had two points to prove. One was that she was fit from a quad injury, and the other was that she was justified in feeling robbed of a relay place at the European Cup. Despite, at that point of the season, being ranked third by times, she wasn't selected and admitted feeling hard done by: 'Gateshead really knocked my confidence. Something like that can be a real blow.'

Three runners now had the individual qualifying time for Sydney. Helen's confidence was helped by the fact that she went into the league race aiming to reach 200m in a target time. A recent trip to Spain for training seemed to have paid off – she achieved her target time and pointed out: 'Anything after that was a bonus.' She clocked 52.62. Match:

1. Shaftesbury Barnet	205
6. Birchfield Harriers	135

Overall league standings:

1. Sale, Manchester	23
6. Birchfield Harriers	10

In the BAL Division One match at Hendon the same day, three-times European 400m Champion Du'aine Ladejo continued his progress in his new event. Returning to the track where he made his 400m hurdles debut a month earlier, Du'aine posted another personal best of 50.09 in his third race over the distance.

Running fluently with thirteen strides over the first five flights, Du'aine looked to be going well. Then he dropped to fourteen and hit the eighth, ninth and tenth hurdles. 'I really thought I was going over this time', stated Du'aine. 'Conditions were difficult. It was windy and although I did a PB I wasn't happy with it. I just misjudged bringing my leg up and caught the hurdle with my heel.' Match:

1. Belgrave Harriers	398
6. Birchfield Harriers	233

Final league positions:

1. Belgrave Harriers (holders)	29.5
6. Birchfield Harriers	13

Mark Lewis-Francis' presence in the AAA Championships and Olympic Trials at the Alexander Stadium was greatly anticipated. At that time Mark had warned that he might not be strong enough to handle heats and a final. The only time he showed his inexperience, however, was when he slept on his blocks in his semi-final. Mark was last after twenty metres, yet stormed through to almost catch winner Dwain Chambers on the line.

Before the final Mark stated: 'Whatever happens, I won't be upset, even if I finish last in the final.' Instead he finished third behind Dwain Chambers and Darren Campbell and edged out Jason Gardner. He clocked 10.24.

Afterwards, Mark was under pressure to reconsider an Olympic place. 'We'd like him there in the relay team!' exclaimed Darren Campbell. 'There's plenty of time yet for people to be brought into the team.'

A man with a clear direction was Robert Weir. With victory in these Olympic Trials and an Olympic qualifying mark under his belt, Robert Weir planned to head for Australia earlier than he first intended to make sure he was fully acclimatised before the games began. Robert beat Glen Smith with a throw of 62.13m. Glen, who was still chasing the qualifier of 63.50m, threw 60.84m.

'It's all coming together', said Robert, 'I just keep fingers crossed and hope my pre-season plan comes good and works by the time I get to Sydney.' He would base himself in Brisbane but first there was some cup action to enjoy that month.

The Gold Cup Final was held at Bedford. With five of the first six results going their way, Birchfield quickly built up a solid platform to go on and deprive Belgrave of their fourth consecutive league and cup double.

It was appropriate that, as one of the pillars of the club, Robert supplied the meeting performance. His first discus attempt went out to a personal best of 65.08m to obliterate his own cup record of 64.12m and grab top spot in that year's ranking list. Ever the perfectionist, Robert announced: 'I need to improve on my technique.'

Adding to the Birchfield tally, Mark Lewis-Francis pulled away from Jonathan Barbour of Blackheath over the final twenty-five metres for a clear 100m victory.

Rob Birchall dominated the 10,000m to show that the stress fracture gained soon after his third in the National Cross Country was now a distant memory.

Dave Lawrence summed it all up: 'I was confident this could be our day. What confirmed it to me was Nigel Bevan dragging himself away from a holiday in St Tropez just to compete for us in the javelin. I knew then we could do it.' Match:

1. Birchfield Harriers   136
2. Newham & Essex Beagles   125

In the Jubilee Cup Final at the same venue that day, Shaftesbury Barnet fought hard to keep their crown but Sale Harriers were not to be denied. Birchfield finished third.

Denise Lewis also regarded the event as a preparation for Sydney. She went out to a personal best javelin throw of 51.13 for third place. Third was also the placing for Denise with 15.47m in the shot, just three centimetres off her season's best.

Match:

1. Sale, Manchester   123
2. Shaftesbury Barnet   112
3. Birchfield Harriers   86

It was soon announced that Robert Weir and Paula Radcliffe would captain the British teams at the Olympic Games. Robert had proved a popular captain at the European Cup at Gateshead in July. He lifted the men's trophy after a thrilling half-point victory, but modestly reacted by saying the honour in Sydney should have gone to a more famous athlete such as Colin Jackson or Jonathan Edwards. There was still plenty to enjoy on the domestic scene for the club before the biggest event of the year dawned.

At the AAA Under-twenty Championships at Bedford in late August, Chris Baillie produced the performance of the weekend. He sped to a stunning 110m hurdles championship with a legal 13.84 for a Scottish under-twenty record. An elated Baillie confirmed: 'I got a good start and apart from sighting Rob Newton mid-race, I felt at ease. For the last month I've had hamstring problems which meant missing out on Birchfield's Cup win here last weekend but there were no problems today.'

Another flying Stag was Mark Lewis-Francis as he took the 100m in 10.46 into a headwind. In his fourth major race in as many weeks, Mark admitted: 'That's enough races for me now. The legs are a little sore and apart from National Junior League Finals in a couple of weeks, it's down to serious training.'

Those finals were to take place at his home stadium. In the men's event, after a three-horse race which involved Birchfield, Belgrave took the team title. Mark had a comfortable win in the 100m, clocking 10.47. In the absence of Jonathan Moore, Paul Ferdinand took on that role in both triple and long jumps. He won both with 14.49m and 6.79m respectively.

As a teammate of Jonathan he conceded it would be good if they could compete on occasions: 'I don't get to jump against him much, so we don't have the opportunity to work together. It is nice to have someone doing so well at the club in the event', he confided. Match:

1. Belgrave Harriers   295
2. Enfield & Haringey   270
3. Birchfield Harriers   253

The battle for the women's title raged between reigning champions Birchfield and Sale. For Birchfield, despite their domination of the 'A' races, it was not enough following a series of 'B'-string wins for the eventual victors. Sale's success was the club's first in this competition.

However, earning valuable points for second-placed Birchfield was Helen Thieme. At the end of the competition she was honoured for her performances with the women's 'Track Athlete of the Match' award.

Early on in the day, Helen took her first title in the 400m hurdles. 'It was an easy run, but I'm saving myself for the 400 flat', she explained. She went on to comprehensively win that race in 55.32, as well as the 200m 'A' race.

In both relays Helen played a crucial last leg role. In the 4 x 100m she brought her club home to victory after a close battle with Sale. The Manchester squad were strong in the 4 x 400m and Helen, after a great leg, crossed the line in third after a hard day's competition.

She was not the only multi-talented star for Birchfield. Donna Maylor extended her normal sprint talents to the field events with a win in the 'B' shot putt, an equal second in the high jump, and a victory in her speciality – the 100m. Match:

1. Sale   311.5
2. Birchfield Harriers   254

So we come to late September, and Sydney. The *Athletics Weekly* of 27 September 2000 described the women's 400m final as 'the race of all their lives'. It was the moment Cathy Freeman, the Aboriginal icon, and Australia, had waited for so long.

Two Britons were among the seven rivals for the title. Katharine Merry was on top form and charged away determinedly in lane three. Donna Fraser was in lane two. Cathy Freeman was in lane six. Into the home straight, Freeman, Lorraine Graham of Jamaica and Katharine were almost stride for stride. Then the 110,000 capacity stadium roared as Cathy Freeman began to pull away towards her destiny. Lorraine Graham just edged Katharine who held on to bronze, ahead of the fast-finishing Donna Fraser. Katharine's 49.72 was a lifetime best.

On her lap of honour, Cathy Freeman carried, as promised, the Australian and Aboriginal flags. The crowd stood choked with emotion. For Katharine that race in Horsham when they were just fifteen years old must have seemed a million years and a million miles away. This day they had played their part in one of the most memorable Olympic finals of all time.

'It was awesome!' reported the Birchfielder. 'I remember the race very clearly. Coming into the straight it seemed the last sixty metres went in slow motion. I was just digging in. I am extremely proud of myself. The atmosphere was incredible, even the moths went into hiding it was so loud.' Katharine then admitted that despite all she had achieved in the one-lap distance in such a short time, she would still prefer to be competing in the shorter sprint races: 'Before the Olympics, I said to the technical directors of Team GB that I did not like this event anymore. It is too long and too scary, but they said unfortunately the event liked me so I am lumbered with it! I cannot believe the enormity of being in an Olympic final – it is the most awesome experience I have ever had. I just wanted to get on that podium so badly, it is what I have dreamt of for so many years.'

The race of one's lifetime was also about to be relevant to another athlete who was about to pull on the heartstrings back home – and especially in Perry Barr, for the Olympic dream was about to unfold for Denise Lewis.

Her thrilling victory, achieved in the final nail-biting 800m, ensured her place in the sport's history, being only the sixth British woman to achieve Olympic gold in track and field. Again, she had to push her body through the pain barrier. When asked to talk about her injury, she replied: 'Which one?'

Day One:
100m Hurdles: Denise got off to a solid start as she stayed in touch with World Champion Eunice Barber. Denise ran well with 13.23, compared to the 13.13 she ran when she notched a Commonwealth record in Talence. In the months prior to the games, Denise and Charles van Commenee had worked on this event, probably more than any other.
High Jump: 'I prepared my mind for a couple of events not to go well and the high jump was one', she admitted. 'As a result I got rid of my emotional baggage very quickly and just got on with the next event.' While Barber was flying high at 1.87m, Denise cleared only 1.75m. Valuable points were lost, and the battle was on to lift herself mentally for the next event.
Shot Putt: Denise bounced back by throwing further than any of the thirty-three other competitors. The Birchfielder improved with each of her three throws, from 14.83m to 15.27m to 15.55m. Eunice Barber managed only 11.27m.

200m: Denise put increased pressure on Eunice Barber by beating the adopted Frenchwoman 24.34 to 24.47. Yelena Prokhorova of Russia was now beginning to show and achieved 23.72.

Day Two:

Long Jump: Denise leapt 6.48m in round two but later reported: 'Something happened to my foot and it was a mystery to the physios.' Meanwhile, Eunice Barber jumped only 5.93m – and withdrew. Prokhorova and Natalie Sazanovich of Belarussia were also jumping well with 6.59m and 6.50m, respectively.

Javelin: 'Going into the javelin I couldn't walk properly', admitted Denise. 'But this is the Olympic Games. You try everything you can and dig right down into your soul. There was fear in my mind that I would have to pull out, but things went better than I thought and I was fine. I could throw pain-free.' Her 50.19m was a good mark too, and ahead of Sazanovich and Prokhorova.

800m: However, behind the scenes there was still doubt about her fitness for the 800m. Buttons were being pressed overtime to work out what Denise had to do to hang on. She led the competition with 5,717 from Sazanovich's 5,654 and Prokhorova's 5,571 and needed to remain no more than 4.3 seconds behind Sazanovich and finish no more than eight seconds behind Prokhorova.

Prokhorova burst into the lead immediately and led through the bell in 62.38. Denise was about three seconds behind in fifth, and, crucially, ahead of Sazanovich. Prokhorova extended her lead and won the race in 2:10.32. Denise pushed herself through an agonising final 100 metres to finish in 2:16.83.

Soon the overall result was confirmed on the public address system. Birchfield Harrier's greatest athlete set off on the victory lap she so thoroughly deserved. Britain's 'Golden Girl' indeed!

1. Denise Lewis	6,584
2. Yelena Prokhorova	6,531
3. Natalie Sazanovich	6,527

Denise's school pal did himself and his nation proud too. In a 10,000m race, which witnessed Haile Gebrselaisse pip Paul Tergat in a sprint finish, Karl Keska finished as first European home in eighth. As such, he completed an excellent Olympics with his second successive personal best as he ran 27:44.09, having achieved a previous personal best of 27:48.29 in the heats.

The Stags won their first-ever transatlantic medal as American Adam Nelson claimed silver in the shot putt. The twenty-five year old was trained by Robert Weir and had taken up the invitation to join the club three years previously on his coach's advice. 'I definitely consider myself a Birchfield club member', said Adam. 'My commitments, along with injuries, prevented me from turning out for them this summer but it is very much in my plans for 2001.'

Robert Weir and Glen Smith both failed to proceed to the final. The elimination of Robert with a best of 60.01m on the day was a surprise given that the AAA Champion was in good form. He was distraught at the press briefing afterwards.

He had the consolation of a long and worthwhile career to look back on. Come October, Mark Lewis-Francis would be looking forward to his burgeoning career and the immediate challenge of the World Junior Championships in Chile.

The 'Darlaston Dart' met the pressure of being favourite for the 100m, and succeeded Christian Malcolm as the Junior World Champion. His winning time of 10.12 equalled the championship best.

Mark produced his best start of four rounds when it mattered, with a reaction time of 0.141 seconds in the final.

'I'm overwhelmed, this is what I've wanted all year. I went into winter training wanting to be a World Junior Champion because coming second at the European Juniors left me disappointed', reported a very happy young man. 'I was feeling good. I know I could have run a lot faster today but it's all about winning a race and getting the gold medal, it's not about times... coming here, winning the world title and showing everyone what I'm capable of means a lot.'

Mark then joined Tyrone Edgar, Dwayne Grant and Tim Benjamin to run an outstanding 4 x 100m in 39.05 to claim the gold medal for Britain.

In the heats the team broke the British, European and Championship record with a 39.14 performance. In the final, Edgar, Grant and Benjamin ran well to hand the baton over to Mark. He overtook the French anchorman down the home straight to claim victory. The winning time of 39.05 was the second-best ever, behind only an American altitude-assisted world record of 39.00 dating from 1983.

'This is a medal I am much more excited about than my own individual one in the 100 metres', exclaimed the Walsall wonder. 'I wanted this one badly after disqualification at the World Juniors in 1998 and the fourth place in the Europeans last year.'

In the women's 4 x 400m Helen Thieme drew inspiration from her club-mate to join Kim Wall, Jenny Meadows and Lisa Miller to win the gold with another British record in 3:33.82. During the third, leg Helen Thieme (53.2) went past Aneisha McLaughlin of Jamaica on the third leg and handed the lead to Lisa Miller.

There was more to celebrate in Sydney that month. At the Paralympics Deborah Brennan added to her 100m bronze medal with a world record of 33.87 to take the T34 200m gold. In the inside lane, she pulled clear in the straight, admitting: 'I couldn't believe it when I looked up at the scoreboard. I just collapsed when I saw world record against my name.'

There was a downside too. Deborah had even conducted her winner's post-race interviews when she learned she had been disqualified from the T34 400m for going out of her lane.

This tumultuous year in the club's history ended with a blend of past, present and future. First, the death was announced of the 1958 European 800m champion, Mike Rawson. He died aged sixty-six, after suffering a heart attack after reaction to treatment for leukaemia. Secondly, at the National Six-Stage Road Relays in Sutton Park, Birchfield took the bronze medal. The fact that the anchor leg Mark Flint wasn't among the runners entered caused comment in some corners.

He wasn't listed as he was due to fly out to Kuwait with the RAF on the day of the race, but that trip was delayed by a week. Team manager Maurice Millington got permission for Mark to take his place in the team and he ran solidly on the final stage to bring the Stags home in third.

1. Morpeth	1:44.14
2. Tipton Harriers	1:44.21
3. Birchfield Harriers	1:46.35

Thirdly, the under-fifteen rankings saw Edward Dunford making a mark in ten events. Edward achieved eight top-twenty marks in the high jump, hammer, long jump, triple jump, shot putt and discus throw, two of which he topped in the 100m hurdles and the octathlon, where he scored 5,420 points.

There was also an interesting profile in the end of season awards. Olympic gold medallists Denise Lewis and Jonathan Edwards were named as: 'Athletes of the Year' by the British Athletics Writers Association.

Denise received the award for: 'Best British Female Athlete' for the fourth time, having previously won in 1996, 1997 and 1998.

The 'Male Junior Athlete of the Year' award went to Mark Lewis-Francis for his World age-seventeen best for 100m before going on to win gold medals in the 100m and 4 x 100m at the World Junior Championships in Santiago.

There was a surprise when the 'Women's Junior Athlete of the Year' was announced. The winner, or rather winners, were the 4 x 400m squad at Santiago – which included Helen Thieme.

After the ceremony Denise Lewis announced that she planned to resume training on 1 January 2001 in Stellenbosch, South Africa with the Dutch national squad and the coach who had guided her to Olympic gold, Charles van Commenee.

The Olympic Heptathlon Champion had experienced a hectic post-games period with media, sponsor and social commitments. She had also been attempting to find out more about the foot injury, which occurred in the middle of competition in Sydney and very nearly spoilt her chances of winning the ultimate prize. Denise emphasised that she wanted to defend her crown in Athens in 2004.

Above left: Adam Nelson.

Above right: Deborah Brennan.

Thirty-Four: Daniel Canes the Opposition

2001 was to be a year with a very busy diary at all levels of age and experience, but there were happy memories of 2000.

Golden girl Denise Lewis had been awarded an OBE to cap a remarkable year in her athletics career. The twenty-eight year old had also been given 'The Freedom of Wolverhampton', honoured at a civic reception in Birmingham and awarded Birchfield's prestigious Leah Wright Trophy.

The club was also delighted that the National Coaching Foundation chose Steve Platt as the 'Coach of the Year'. This well-deserved accolade was all the more worthy because the award could have been given to a coach from any sport. In common with all the club's coaches, Steve held a full-time job away from his athletics commitments.

The NIA was the venue for several indoor meetings, starting with the AAA Combined Events in January. Athletes competing knew that placing first would gain them selection for an international match in Prague, later in the month.

However, after Birchfield Harrier Kelly Sotherton won the women's pentathlon, she declined the opportunity to gain a first senior Great Britain vest. 'I was disappointed not to go as it would have been my first senior GB', stated Kelly. 'But I'd have only been going to get the kit. Trevor Marsay had discussed it before the indoors and Prague wasn't on my agenda.'

The newly crowned AAA Champion improved her personal best by 200 points, taking her pentathlon score up to 4,116. Clocking a best in the hurdles, Kelly continued: 'I don't need to improve on my pentathlon now, and I don't want to do two pentathlons one weekend after the other. I have a AAA title to my name, which, to me is more important than not doing so well while wearing a Great Britain vest.'

The Birmingham-based athlete had last represented Great Britain in 1997, but had a bone spur in a knee and took 1998 and 1999 out of competition to recover from an operation on the problem. Returning to the track in 2000, Kelly had stepped up her training from three sessions a week that year, to six times a week as 2001 unfolded. Having made the decision to compete at the AAA Championship, Kelly explained: 'I need to improve in the long jump and hurdles, and I would like to make a name for myself in individual events.'

The venue soon staged the Indoor trials and AAA Championship. Here, Daniel Caines brought the house down in the final event of the weekend. He became the fourth-fastest British 400m runner in history behind Jamie Baulch, Todd Bennett and Solomon Wariso.

Daniel, who was Britain's number one male 400m runner in Sydney, hit the bell in front and held off a strong challenge from Mark Hylton down the back straight before clocking a spectacular 45.75 to Hylton's 46.24.

'I was hoping he'd run slower and go to the Worlds as an unknown', said Daniel's father and coach, Joseph. 'But now the secret has been taken away.'

Mark Lewis-Francis's bid to run at the World Indoor Championship 60m qualifying time of 6.65 was hindered when his moped broke down on the way to the NIA. He was left stranded by the side of the road for an hour when the clutch on the bike broke and he almost missed the race. When he eventually made it to the venue for the Midland Open meeting, Mark had only thirty minutes to prepare and ran a sluggish 6.69 ahead of Curtis Browne and Nathan Morgan.

In February, Katharine Merry set a British indoor 400m record in Cardiff for her first race since the Olympic Games. Running her first-ever indoor 400m, Katharine covered the first 200 metres in 24.84 to stop the clock at 51.54. This was a time only bettered by Russian Olga Kotlyarova so far that year.

A week later Katharine was competing in the 400m at the Norwich Union Indoor Grand Prix in Birmingham. She had a slow start from lane five and then got into her stride. Katharine passed Deon Hemmings and was chased by Catharine Murphy. The pace was fast – faster than her record run in Cardiff. Catharine Murphy was in determined pursuit. Over the last 100 metres Katharine pulled further away from the Welsh athlete and clocked 50.53, a full second ahead of her time seven days previously. Her run, the second-fastest in the world that year, placed Katherine ninth on the world all-time list.

At the press conference Katharine was tired but upbeat: 'It's fantastic to set two records in two places that I love – Cardiff and Birmingham. But that's it, I'm not prepared to run rounds and there would be too much pressure. I'm only here because I went to the AAA and thought "I'd like some of that." This run has given me the confidence to know that I can produce quality when I want to... but if I'd run 48.5 I still wouldn't go to Lisbon... I surprised myself in Cardiff but this was my first big race since Sydney and it was great to compete in front of my home crowd... I took time off to November but I've had a really solid winter's training. I've had to because I know that Catharine and Donna Fraser are training hard too, and that's great for us and it's great for Britain.'

The men's race was the finale of the meeting. At the gun, Daniel Caines went out fast from lane five and by 150 metres had caught Mark Hylton. They were locked together until the bell was passed in the amazing time of 21.1. Daniel was in pole position and now commanded the race, pulling away over the final 100 metres to win in 45.61, his fastest ever time. Hylton chased him home in 46.42.

Daniel provided an honest assessment at the press conference: 'This is my first full year in the sport and I'm still learning. The opening 200 was too fast, it was stupid but Mark made me go that fast. I'll go round by round in Lisbon and see how it goes.'

Later in February, the AAA Under-twenty Championship was staged at the NIA. Mark Lewis-Francis was odds-on favourite for the 60m. His victory over Tim Benjamin was as exciting as it was expected. While on top of the podium, Mark received several other accolades for performances in 2000 and left fully laden with silverware!

There was further cause for celebration that weekend. The English National Cross Country Championships were being run in Durham. Mike Openshaw was making his National debut but soon found himself in an epic duel with Sam Haughian of Hounslow for the gold medal. This contest continued all the way to the finish. Mike won by just a second, the shortest winning margin since 1966.

Due reward for Katharine.

He then revealed that his victory in this 12km race could be interpreted as remarkable: 'Birchfield rang me on Thursday to say I'd been entered as a non-scorer but I had no plans to and hadn't even thought about it. It was only when my coach, Gordon Surtees, rang me this morning that he even mentioned it to me for the first time. The plan was to do an eight miles steady-to-fast run and we talked about me coming here to run instead. I've never watched a National before, never mind run one.' Openshaw, twenty-eight, lived at nearby Chester-le-Street. He followed in the footsteps of Justin Pugsley who won the event in 1999 – seventy years after the Stags' previous champion Eddie Webster.

In March came the IAAF World Indoor Championships in Lisbon. Daniel Caines became Birchfield Harrier's first World Champion for more than a quarter of a century when he took gold. The twenty-one-year-old law graduate achieved something no Stag had been able to do since Ian Stewart won the World Cross Country title in March 1975.

Daniel, in lane five, controlled the 400m final from the beginning. Away first time, he was out fast and by 100 metres had caught back the stagger on Danny McFarlane of Jamaica. American James Davis had already dropped out injured after just fifty metres. Daniel now had the race under control. He flew down the bend into the back straight for the first time, reaching the bell in 21.41. Now the danger-man was Milton Campbell of the USA as McFarlane faded. Ahead, Daniel was not to be denied and, although Campbell pressed hard down the long home straight, the young Stag won convincingly in 46.40.

'This is all very surreal', uttered Daniel afterwards. 'I can't believe that this is happening. I'm living in a fantasy world. There were quality guys out there, including Danny McFarlane, and I beat them. Last year at the European Indoor I was running and learning at the same time and it was crazy. But the Olympics has given me real confidence. Last year I was just a twenty-one-year-old lad.'

On another successful weekend for the club, Adam Nelson took a silver medal in the shot for the USA, as he had done at the Olympics in Sydney. He reached 20.72m with his only legal throw.

Mark Lewis-Francis was a revelation in the 60m. His opening heat was full of determination and style and he set a personal best of 6.61. He went even better in the semi-final, running second to Nigerian Deji Aliu's 6.55 with 6.56. It was extraordinary to realise that Mark had struggled to make the qualifying time back in Britain.

Mike Openshaw.

The start of the final was a tense affair. Deji Aliu was disqualified for two false starts. A further false start was incurred – by Mark himself. They finally got away at the fourth attempt, with Mark steady. However, he came through behind the Americans, Tim Harden on 6.44 and Tim Montgomery on 6.46, to take the bronze medal with 6.51. This time broke the twelve-year-old junior World record of former GDR sprinter Sven Matthes by two-hundredths of a second.

'I can't believe this', Mark exclaimed. 'I guess it's because I have learnt to start. Last year when I ran 10.09 I really couldn't start. It's made all the difference. I stood on my blocks, looked up and thought: "I'm here now and I'm gonna give it everything!"'

The indoor highlights wound up with the Norwich Union International in Glasgow that month. Greg Saddler of the USA won the 60m in 6.60 from Mark Lewis-Francis and Christian Malcolm – but only after the latter two had false starts against their name. 'The season has been great', Mark reported. 'Now I'm off to the USA for warm weather training to prepare for the outdoors.'

In the 400m Daniel Caine's undefeated season came under pressure. Troy McIntosh of the Bahamas ran a strong first 200 metres and led the World Champion. Down the back straight Daniel took control and ran in the winner in 46.21 (?). Andrey Semenov of Russia pipped McIntosh for second.

'I wasn't going to push it to the bell', Daniel stated afterwards. 'I thought that I'd get to second for a change because it just takes it out of you. It was a case of: "Don't panic", just reel them in, like on a fishing line. I had to work hard down the back straight but I did it in the end.'

April brought the Midland Road Relays at Sutton Park. This time Tipton had a day to remember with Birchfield as runners-up for both senior men and senior women.

Daniel Caines: Top of the world!

Men:

1. Tipton Harriers	3:49.40
2. Birchfield Harriers	3:52.23

Women:

1. Tipton Harriers	1:47.36
2. Birchfield Harriers	1:48.05

Amanda Allen injured her hamstring on stage two but still went on to break club-mate Sarah Bentley's course record by sixteen seconds.

At the end of the month, Bev Hartigan exceeded even her own expectations by being the second British woman to cross the line in the London Marathon. In a very impressive debut at the distance, the thirty-three year old came seventeenth overall in a time of 2:37.45.

Deborah Brennan also had a busy weekend. The Paralympic 200m Champion took part in no less than four track races in Nottingham on the Saturday. Deborah was then off to London where she was runner-up to Tanni Grey-Thompson in the wheelchair marathon. Deborah stopped the clock at 2:35.50 hours.

Tipton men were again on good form in the National twelve-stage at Sutton Park in May.

1. Tipton Harriers	1:47.36
4. Birchfield Harriers	4:12.48

This was the month in which the first BAL Division One match was held at Barnet Copthall in London.

1. Belgrave Harriers	345
5. Birchfield Harriers	271

In the 100m 'B' event, Nathan Morgan with a time of 10.38 (1.5m/s) ran faster than Daniel Money of Sale, the winner of the 'A'-string event. Rob Birchall was the only man under 14:30 in winning the 5,000m.

The second BAL match of the season was at the Alexander Stadium in early June.

1. Belgrave Harriers	377
2. Birchfield Harriers	321

Mark Lewis-Francis lived up to his new star billing. He cruised to a comfortable win in 10.28 in the 100m from his teammate in the Great Britain junior squad, Dwyane Grant of Blackheath. Mark was having his first race in Britain that summer. He had clocked 10.12 and 10.13 for the 100m during his time in America.

The Birchfield ladies were also on parade at home that day in the UK Women's League Division One. One week after Eunice Barber had confirmed her return to form with a 6,736 tally in Gotzis, Denise Lewis 'blew away the cobwebs' with a 13.41 clocking in the 100m hurdles and a 15.45m throw in the shot. It was her first performance since the Olympic Final. Denise described her performances as: 'reasonable to good' and added that: 'it was really good to be back competing on home soil.'

Katharine Merry decided to make her first outdoor race of the year a 4x 400m relay leg for Birchfield. She took the baton on the final leg with an eight-metre lead from Allison Curbishley of Edinburgh Woolen Mill. At the finish Katharine had almost doubled her lead. Despite the presence of Denise and Katharine, the match went to Sale.

1. Sale, Manchester	212.5
3. Birchfield Harriers	175

The Midland Counties Championship was held at the Alexander Stadium in mid-month. Honours were even in the men's sprint races. Rugby's Brendan Ghent successfully defended his 100m title in 10.52, but was chased hard by Birchfield Harrier Ben Lewis. Ben clocked a personal best of 10.58. Richard Knowles narrowly edged out his training partner Curtis Browne for the bronze medal.

The Rugby athlete led with forty metres remaining in the 200m but was narrowly overtaken by the in-form Lewis. This was Ben's seventh consecutive Midlands 200m title.

In the 400m hurdles, thirty-six-year-old Paul Hibbert just held off a late surge by his club-mate, twenty-year-old Brad Yiend. Paul had won this title on six occasions since 1992.

Edward Dunford improved his score by a massive 321 points to 5,741, establishing a UK under-seventeen best performance for the octathlon. Edward recorded a brace of personal bests, with 15.98m for the shot and 47.71m for the discus. Mark Mandy won the high jump with 2.00m.

The European Cup was staged in Bremen, Germany later in June. A nineteen year old making his senior international debut outshone the established stars in the Great Britain squad, not to mention the Olympic 200m Champion Kostas Kederis, who finished two hundredths of a second behind Mark Lewis-Francis in the 100m. Mark clocked 10.13.

The World Junior Champion had not even been first choice for the event. He had been scheduled to spend his weekend training with the British junior 4 x 100m squad in Birmingham. Then Dwain Chambers, Darren Campbell and Jason Gardner all suffered injury problems, so in stepped fourth choice Mark.

Appearing to start well, Mark picked up impressively and powered down lane eight to victory. From the head-on angle it appeared as if he had lost. Kederis certainly looked confused, waiting for the replay. Mark had no doubt at all and immediately started his lap of honour.

Later, Mark admitted to not knowing that an Olympic Champion was in his race until a few hours before: 'I wasn't nervous on Friday', he stated, 'but then I heard the Greek guy was running.'

British men's team captain Robert Weir was not smiling as broadly as he was in 2000, when he lifted the cup for Britain. A record-equalling tenth appearance in the European Cup should have been the subject of celebration. But Robert managed to throw 58.23m for seventh behind the winner, Lars Riedel of Germany. Men's match:

1. Russia	126.5
4. Great Britain	82

The same weekend an under-twenty-three international with Spain was organised in Liverpool. Instrumental in the women's 94 to 65 win was an outstanding 400m from World Junior gold medallist Helen

Thieme, who not only smashed her personal best by nine tenths of a second but with 53.25 went inside the time required for the European Championship in Amsterdam.

At the gun Helen powered around the first bend and it seemed unlikely that she would last the pace. Indeed it seemed with about fifty metres to go as though she was about to tie-up. However, she managed an extra spurt, which saw her grab the time. A couple of hours later the Birchfield Harrier anchored home the 4 x 400m team to a clear victory.

Ben Lewis won a silver medal in the 4 x 100m relay whilst Chris Baillie won a bronze from the 110m hurdles. Overall result (men and women combined):

1. Great Britain   177
2. Spain   150

There were other talented Birchfield youngsters showing their mettle as June rolled into July. At the AAA Under-twenty Championship at Bedford, seventeen-year-old Jonathan Moore was on top form on the first day of competition in the long jump. He leapt 7.98m on his second attempt, with a 3.1m/s wind at his back.

Having already qualified in the triple jump for both the World Youth Championship and the European Under-twenties, he decided to not take part in the event.

According to his coach Ted King: 'He decides what he does. He is a super athlete and always gives everything but he obviously wants to avoid any stresses or strains now.'

At the English Schools' Championship in Exeter a week later, much was now expected of Jonathan. If there was pressure, he did not feel it. Jonathan broke the championship record of 7.65m with a jump of 7.68m.

However, Jonathan had expected to jump further: 'Why am I not smiling? If I jump over eight metres then people will see a big smile on my face. A 16.80 metre triple jump would make me smile too.'

Pundits did not think there would be much to choose between Julian Thomas, Jamahl Alert-Khan and Marimba Odundo-Mendez in the 200m. In the event Julian ran out a clear winner breaking the championship best of 22.2 with a time of 22.03, with the help of a wind of 2.9m/s.

There was a BAL Division One match at Eton in early July. A new league shot putt record of 20.76m came from Olympic silver medallist Adam Nelson, who was back competing for match winners Birchfield. This overtook Geoff Capes' record of 19.74m, which had stood since 1975. Another import, Egveni Koziov, ensured a club double when he won the 'B'-string with 16.67m.

A tight discus competition was won by Robert Weir with 59.81m. Glen Smith ensured maximum points for Birchfield with a final heave of 59.11m. In the long jump, Nathan Morgan leapt 7.44m for victory.

On track, another Birchfield import, Kenyan Eilud Kirui, came from behind in both the steeplechase and 5,000m to score a useful double in 8:49.95 and 14:14.34.

Before rain descended Du'aine Ladejo impressed with a narrow victory over Matt Douglas of Belgrave in the 400m hurdles, as both went sub-fifty, Du'aine in 49.77.

With Frenchman Olivier Theodore taking the 'B' event for Birchfield, Du'aine observed: 'It's a shame we were not in the same race.' He added: 'I trained really hard and am a bit tired.' Match:

1. Birchfield Harriers   340

The women's team was also on league duty at the same venue that day. Match:

1. Sale   212
2. Birchfield Harriers   141

The next major event in a full calendar was the European Under-twenty-three Championship in Amsterdam.

400m silver medallist Helen Thieme had seen her season go from strength to strength with personal bests repeatedly achieved. Starting with an outdoor personal best of 54.30, Helen reduced it to 53.25 at Liverpool in June before further improvements to 52.88 and 52.75 through the course of the championship.

'I knew because of the work I was doing that I was due an improvement at some point, but it is doing it which is the hard part! Now I've done this I've got the relays to think of', she announced. In the 4 x 400m, Helen's home-straight power pushed the Polish quartet back into second place. Sharing in that gold medal triumph with Helen were Tracey Duncan, Jenny Meadows and Karen Gear.

Mid-month brought the AAA Championships and World Trials to Birmingham. In the 100m, Dwain Chambers clocked a record 10.01 with Mark Lewis-Francis second in 10.12. Mark was just short of his 10.10 lifetime best, which had been recorded at Crystal Palace the previous year. 'I came here for experience and knew I had an outside chance of qualifying', stated the World Junior Champion. 'And I confirm what I said earlier that the first three past the post should be selected for the World Championships.' Christian Malcolm finished third.

Glen Smith won the discus title at the eleventh attempt. Glen, twenty-nine, unleashed a throw of 59.99m in the final round to leapfrog Robert Weir's round two effort of 58.72m. 'I can't believe it, I am over the moon', said Glen, who still needed 62.40m if he was to go to Edmonton. 'This is my eleventh AAA Championships, I've never won it and have come second for the past four years.'

Forty-year-old Weir commented: 'There is no better way to win than on your last throw and I had every opportunity to respond but I didn't. It was a fantastic job by Glen.'

Denise Lewis used the championships to have a run out in several events, including the javelin and the 100m hurdles.

Nathan Morgan cleared 7.80m to take the long jump title, while Sarah Reilly won the 200m to record the club's third victory of the championships.

Du'aine Ladejo finished runner-up in his new discipline of the 400m hurdles in 49.44. Triple jumper Debbie Rowe recorded a distance of 12.96m to win the silver medal behind World Indoor Champion Ashia Hansen.

The same weekend in Hungary, the World Youth Championships were mounted. In the triple jump, Jonathan Moore was struggling with his run-up and lying second, but on witnessing the medal ceremony for high jumper Aileen Wilson, Jonathan seemed to draw inspiration. His reaction was to leap into the lead with a jump of 16.36m on his fourth attempt.

The young Stag still had a tantalising wait, however, as his nearest rival, Cuban David Giras, pulled out a huge last leap. Jonathan and the British team held their breath as that jump was measured at 16.33m. Celebrations ensued as Britain won its second gold medal.

Seven days later, Grosseto in Italy was the stage of the European Under-twenty Championship. The 100m final was not short of drama with two false starts, the first to Mark Lewis-Francis, and the second to the Frenchman in the lane next to him. When it did get started Mark seemed slow to rise, but countered that by driving hard through to seventy metres before Germany's Tim Goebel appeared to catch the favourite.

As they crossed the line together, Mark looked muted and left the track. The German athlete began celebrating what he knew was a precious silver medal for his country. For the spectators not in full view of the finish, it looked as though the German was celebrating victory, and that Mark was conceding defeat.

With 10.19, albeit wind-assisted to 10.18, it wasn't that close a race after all between the first two, but as Mark explained later: 'I am glad I came here. It's a title I didn't have and more importantly it is championship experience, whatever the level. I felt sluggish after last weekend. I was slow out of the blocks and my legs didn't feel that great but I've got the title and the time was good.'

Tim Benjamin, Tyrone Edgar and Dwayne Grant combined with the new European Junior Champion for an expected but impressive gold in the 4 x 100m relay. Their 39.24 was a championship record.

Jonathan Moore, the youngest competitor in the triple jump final, took silver with a personal and age-group best of 16.43m. The sixteen year old only jumped twice. However, the performance did not satisfy Jonathan: 'I didn't feel right, it wasn't good enough', he commented. 'I felt tired after last weekend and the jumps take it out of me.'

Back home that weekend, the Gold Cup Final was underway at Bedford. An exciting day's action saw a battle to the end with the result coming down to the last event – the 4 x 400m relay. With just six points separating Birchfield and Belgrave, the Stags managed to dominate the relays taking full points. The final result saw the reigning holders take the cup back to Birmingham with the Belgrave team just ten points behind in second place.

In the long jump, Nathan Morgan had dominated throughout with the main fight being for what was left of the points. Nathan finished with a jump of 7.71m.

In the discus, Robert Weir stepped aside for the AAA Champion Glen Smith to take the scoring role. Robert took part as a guest in a bid to chase the qualifier for the World Championships, so making the competition even hotter. Robert's eventual throw of 63.03m was not only the furthest by a British athlete that year, but ensured him the 'B'-standard qualifier for Edmonton. Glen Smith finished third with 58.69m.

James Hillier won the 400m hurdles in 52.00, before teaming up with Brad Yiend, Bradley Donkin and Geoff Djan to win the vital 4 x 400m relay in 3:13.7. As Birchfield team-manager Dave Lawrence prepared for the traditional soak in the water jump, he observed: 'We had all-round top performances, it's a thoroughly good team.'

In the Jubilee Cup Final at the same venue that day, the women were unable to emulate their male counterparts but finished second to Sale.

Helen Thieme made an appearance in the 200 after her 400m performances at the recent European Under-twenty-three Championships. Helen showed no sign of weakness when winning the race in 24.53, with Kelly Thomas of Sale hot on her heels. 'I didn't think it would be an easy race as I've been a bit worn out from the whole European experience', she admitted.

In the first competition for the Jo Smith Trophy – presented to the best combined score by a club men's and women's team, Birchfield eventually emerged victorious but only after eagle-eyed Kelly Sotherton had subsequently spotted an error which had seen Sale announced as winners and take the trophy away. It was not until bank clerk Kelly checked the scores on the way back to Birmingham that she realised that nine points had been missed off the total. That was enough to ensure victory and the trophy was sent down the M6 to take up residence in the Alexander Stadium trophy cabinet.

The World Championships arrived with August and there was controversy for Mark Lewis-Francis. Mark ran 9.97 to shatter Dwain Chambers' World junior record of 10.06 in the second round of the 100m, but his time would not stand because the wind gauge broke down. The eighteen year old improved his lifetime best by thirteen hundredths of a second to beat Obadele Thompson of Barbados and Bruny Surin of Canada in heat three.

Most statisticians agreed that the races had probably been helped by a slightly illegal wind on a still night. However, Emmanuel Hudson, manager of Maurice Greene commented: 'They won't give Mark that record but, you know what, every junior in the world knows who owns it!.'

Matters then took another downward twist. Within twenty-four hours Mark was sitting in the athletes' tent at the back of the stadium, trying to come to terms with a clocking of 10.26 in the first semi-final of the 100m. A dejected Lewis-Francis said: 'I didn't get a good start and then thought about it too much.' Steve Platt, his coach, commented: 'It's all part of the learning curve.'

When it came to the heptathlon – at 9 am on the Saturday, the athletes lined up for the first of seven events, the sprint hurdles. In the third race, lane six was empty and on the scoreboard a 'DNS' appeared next to the name of the Olympic Champion.

Denise Lewis had withdrawn the day before citing a stomach problem. Denise stated that she was very disappointed not to be competing and that it was a bitter blow to come so far and not be able to compete. It was a double blow for the British cause as Katharine Merry had already withdrawn from the championships because of an Achilles injury.

In action was Robert Weir but he bowed out during the qualifying round, finishing eighth in his group with 61.05m. He had competed in the first World Championships in Helsinki in 1983.

Adam Nelson, for the third championships in a year, won silver in the shot putt. Helen Frost was drafted into the quarter final of the 4 x 400m relay, where she ran well on the second leg to record the fastest time by any member of the makeshift quartet.

Later that month the final BAL Division One match of the season was held at Jarrow. Belgrave clinched their fifth successive title with Birchfield runners-up, despite a fifth place in the match.

Glen Smith enjoyed an easy win in the discus with a throw of 58.16m. Richard Knowles and Jared Deacon fought out the finish of the 'B' race with Richard first in 21.26. Match:

The high-performance centre.

1. Shaftesbury Barnet	341
2. Belgrave Harriers	332
3. Birchfield Harriers	281

Final league positions:

| 1. Belgrave Harriers | 29 |
| 2. Birchfield Harriers | 24 |

In September the Birchfield girls' team would sweep the McDonalds' Young Athletes Auxiliary Final on their home track. Led by twelve-year-old Jade Surman, who won the 70m hurdles and recorded 5.12m in the long jump, Birchfield beat their nearest challenger, Bromley, by seventy-one points. Taking an amazing forty-eight of the available sixty-three medals, the girls tallied a record score of 381.

In total the host club won twenty-five gold medals, eleven silver medals and a dozen bronze medals. In the under-thirteen age group alone, Birchfield won ten of the fifteen available gold medals.

There was a happy ending to the month for those Stags who took part in the Midland Relays. From the very start the men's race turned into a battle between the two dominating but depleted West Midlands sides, Tipton and Birchfield. Despite a cushion of thirty-one seconds as stage six started, it was not enough for fifty-one-year-old veteran Mike Hager to bring the title home to Tipton, especially when Rob Birchall was down to run the final stage for Birchfield.

By the first passing of the Jamboree Stone, the gap was twenty metres. By the second passing it was still twenty metres, only this time the positions of the first two had reversed. The thirty-one year old brought the title back to Birchfield for the fifth year in succession.

| 1. Birchfield Harriers | 1:49.32 |
| 2. Tipton Harriers | 1:49.36 |

The year ended with much positive anticipation following the autumn announcement that Sport England had made a £2.5 million lottery award for the development of a high-performance indoor athletics training centre at the Alexander Stadium. This would be as part of the English Institute of Sport network.

The facility would include a 132-metre sprint straight, two long-jump pits and run-ups, practice areas for high jump and throws plus a weights room.

Steve Cram MBE, Chairman of the English Institute of Sport stated: 'Birmingham is home to a lot of top international athletes and the EIS is delighted that these new facilities, combined with our support services in sports science and sports medicine, will provide an excellent foundation for success on the world stage.'

Ashia Hansen, the World Indoor Triple Jump Champion, who had joined Birchfield Harriers, confirmed: 'The indoor centre will be a real boost for athletics both locally and nationally. Having top-class training facilities is vital for today's modern athlete, particularly if we are to compete and win competitions at home and abroad.'

Thirty-Five: Leap to Glory

Darius Burrows won the Staffordshire Senior Cross Country title in early January 2002 at Sandwell Valley – to record his first victory in eighteen months, after battling back from cancer. Darius had been forced to undergo intensive treatment to remove a tumour from his chest, but he fought back bravely and covered the 9.5km course in 31:03.

'On 15 January last year, it was discovered that I had a tumour in my chest, which was obviously a terrible shock. I have been through all the treatment and there was a period of about three months when I felt too ill to even think about going out to exercise. For the last nine months I have been able to do some gentle running just to maintain a very basic level of fitness. I am now in remission and I feel a lot more positive about things. I am told that the chances of recovery are very high. It is hard to describe how happy I felt today, a year after wondering whether I would live. It is just amazing.'

The Wolverhampton-based athlete confessed that he was still only seventy-five per cent fit and had only recently started running sessions as part of his training schedule.

The same weekend Mark Lewis-Francis was the star performer on show in the Birmingham Games at the NIA. Citing a slight tightness in his hamstring, Mark chose not to run in the final. The nineteen year old looked sharp in his heat (6.69) and semi-final (6.67) as he eased down well before the finish line.

One of the most exciting races of the weekend was the women's 200m. Lane six seemed to give Sarah Reilly the slight advantage that was crucial in a competitive one-lapper in which Catherine Murphy, in lane five, was never more than a metre off the lead. Both women had clearly benefited from training together, and were pleased with their early season times. For Sarah, with 23.30, it was a new Irish record to go with the outdoor mark of 23.02 she had recorded the previous season.

Later that month Rob Birchall recorded his third victory in four years in the Midland Cross Country Championship at Newbold Comyn, near Leamington.

Rob sprinted out at the start, eager to avoid the mid-pack mash, but once clear of the danger allowed himself to sit in as defending champion Billy Farquharson of Mansfield and Darius Burrows took on the early pace.

By the time the men returned from their first run alongside the steep rise – a black vest appeared ten seconds clear from the next runner, also wearing a Birchfield strip. Rob began to pull away, and the recently rejuvenated Burrows was initially the only athlete with enough pace to stay with his teammate. Eventually Nick Talbot of Notts AC would overtake Darius.

After trotting in thirty-six seconds ahead of Talbot, Rob reported: 'It feels good to come here after all the training and win… it still means a lot to me to win this title and have my name on the trophy.'

There was a strong line-up for the women's race. From the gun it was a tale of Charnwood versus Birchfield. In the same way that her club counterpart sprinted out at the start of his race, Amanda Allen made a similar dart before moving alongside Tara Krzywicki. The field of more than 160 was strung out from the off as Tara and Amanda pushed on with a pace that consolidated their position to the extent that neither was seriously challenged by the rest of the field.

Krzywicki's lead was thirty seconds by the time she entered the final straight, with Amanda Allen enjoying a forty-seconds cushion over Sam Gray of Bristol.

Meanwhile, indoors at the NIA for the Midlands Open, Mark Lewis-Francis continued to improve with a time of 6.56 in the 60m. Mark 'did not expect to run so quick' being used to three rounds or more and 'taking time to get going'. He added: 'I did not get a good start and felt stiff.'

Kelly Sotherton claimed indoor personal bests in three events during the championships – 24.11 (200m), 6.09m (long jump) and 11.98m (shot). She followed this up by claiming a personal best of 4,188 in the pentathlon in the Combined Events International in Zaragoza, Spain. 'I've got my motivation and drive back, and realise there is a Commonwealth Games place to go for.'

Kelly was amongst a number of Birchfield athletes who travelled to Cardiff in early February for the AAA Indoor Championships and Trials. Here she maintained her promising indoor campaign by breaking her personal best to win the long jump with a fifth-round leap of 6.22m. A happy Kelly reported: 'I'm over the moon. I had a couple of very big no-jumps, put my run-up back and nailed one.' She also revealed that she was working on weights for the first time in her career and had guidance from a very interesting source: 'Charles van Commenee', who had coached Denise Lewis to the Olympic gold medal, 'gave me some advice the week before on how to prepare mentally for the big effort in competition. I put this into effect before my penultimate jump, and the result was that I won by two centimetres, which is great.'

Ashia Hansen was below her best as she won a fourth AAA indoor title with a modest leap of 13.53m. This was a fourth-round effort and she didn't compete any further, confident that she had secured gold. Ashia explained: 'I don't really get up for the AAA Championships. I perhaps need more of a challenge.'

It was possible that the edge was taken off her performance following a rare outing over 60m earlier in the day. Ashia was nine-hundredths short of her personal best in the heats with 7.61m before being eliminated at the semi-final stage.

In the men's 60m final, Jason Gardener pipped Mark Lewis-Francis by a mere two-thousandths of a second in a thrilling final. Mark was controversially judged to have committed a false start, handing his rival a crucial advantage. Gardener, a very slick starter, made the most of the situation by getting out of the blocks much quicker than the Birchfield man. Mark protested that he didn't think he had false-started and added: 'That's so frustrating, but the way I came back from the start I suppose has got to be a good sign of the form I'm really in. I must be pleased because this is my first indoor season.'

Within a fortnight the star-studded Norwich Union Grand Prix was being staged back at the NIA. This time Mark was runner-up to South Africa's Mornie Nagel in a time of 6.53. The nineteen year old had been troubled by a hamstring injury in the days leading up to the event and explained: 'It's an old war wound. It's a trapped nerve and affects my left hamstring.'

Daniel Caines produced one of the most emphatic victories of the afternoon in the 400m and would have been a hot favourite to lift the European title in Vienna in March – but the twenty-two year old did not wish to compete in that event. Leading through 200 metres in only 20.83, Daniel looked a clear winner with one lap remaining. He retained pole position from Jim Laursen of Sweden and then powered away into the straight to win in 46.06 – the fastest time in the world that year.

It took the Olympic Champion to beat World indoor record-holder Ashia Hansen, but the Stagbearer was disappointed with her 14.36m jump. Ashia, who opened her season promisingly in January with 14.44m, had three jumps over fourteen metres as Bulgaria's Tereza Marinova recorded 14.59m to win. 'I was hoping to go further', stated Ashia, who had jumped her world record 15.16m in 1998 to win the European Indoor title.

March meant another European title was there to challenge for in Austria. Ashia produced her best jump since winning the IAAF Grand Prix Final in 1999, to win a silver medal.

According to Ashia, her first-round leap was well over fifteen metres, but it was ruled a foul as her toe was over the board by just one centimetre. Her second-best effort in a consistent series was 14.71m in the third round, leaving her a frustrated runner-up to Olympic Champion Tereza Marinova, who jumped 14.81m. 'The first one got away', said Ashia. 'I absolutely went for it, gung ho. It was a big one, but unfortunately a no-jump.'

In the men's 60m final, Jason Gardener lived up to his nickname of the 'Bath Bullet' as he shot out of the blocks. After crossing the line he and runner-up Mark Lewis-Francis embraced and then embarked on a lap of honour carrying a Union Jack flag.

'The opposition was great with Mark', confessed Gardener, 'so I couldn't afford any mistakes.' Mark commented: 'I was determined to win a medal.' Mark clocked 6.55, six hundredths behind his fellow Briton.

After winning his 200m heat, Daniel Caines improved his lifetime best to 20.62 in the semi-final before finishing fourth in the final.

As the month progressed, Amanda Allen finished second in the National Cross Country Championships and third in the Short Course Trial. These performances qualified Amanda to make her World Cross Country Championships debut in Dublin. She was pleased to be the third Briton home in sixtieth and said she enjoyed the camaraderie of a cross-country championship as opposed to the road scene: 'Road running is so different, as everybody does their own thing. This was more of a team competition and I've enjoyed it.' The 2:40 marathon runner added: 'I came here with a niggle as I slightly dislocated my sacro-iliac joint at the trial. But I finished in one piece and didn't let myself down.'

In early April Denise Lewis's manager had cast doubts on her competing in that summer's major championships following the birth of her daughter. The Olympic Heptathlon Champion had enjoyed a trouble-free birth at a North London hospital, and baby Lauren weighed 7lb 4oz. Her agent, Jonathan Marks, said she was unlikely to return to competition as quickly as Sonia O'Sullivan. The Irish distance runner had given birth on 23 December 2001 and was in training by New Years Day. Then Sonia came seventh in the World Cross Country Championships in March.

'There are no plans for Denise's competitive return as yet', said Jonathan Marks. 'Multi-event is so different from the distance or sprinting disciplines, as there is the technical side of things to cope with and so we are unlikely to see Denise springing straight back into competition mode. Denise won't know how much fitness ground she has lost until she can get back into full training and seek the advice of Charles van Commenee, her coach. She has been in light training throughout the pregnancy so she should have a good base level of fitness.'

At the MCAA Road relays in Sutton Park, there was a silver medal for the Stags in the twelve-stage.

1. Tipton Harriers   3:50.55
2. Birchfield Harriers   3:53.00

In the women's six-stage, Bristol beat defending champions Tipton. Like Birchfield, Tipton had never been outside the first three in the event.

1. Bristol 1:43:55
3. Birchfield Harriers   1:46.13

The same month, Paul Hunt was a creditable thirteenth in the wheelchair race at the London Marathon in a time of 2:3.27, which was an improvement of ten-and-a-half minutes.

Ian Stewart, the club's most successful runner, at the age of fifty-three made his London Marathon debut to raise money for Cystic Fibrosis. Ian completed London in fifty-eight seconds over three hours after slowing down for the last nine miles with a painful calf injury. He said that he would train more thoroughly next time!

In May, Glen Smith achieved the qualifying distance for the European Championships with a 63.10m discus throw in California.

Back home at Loughborough, and despite damp and unhelpful conditions for sprinting, Mark Lewis-Francis won the 100m at the Aqua International in 10.10. This time equalled his legitimate best performance and shaved 0.07 off Dwaine Chambers' stadium record.

Seventeen-year-old Jonathan Moore achieved 8.03m in the long jump to create a new UK under-twenty record. This performance was followed in early June by Nathan Morgan achieving a personal best of 8.17m for the long jump in Riga.

At the same time club members were winning a series of titles at the Midland Counties Championships. Emma Hornby was first in the pole vault with a clearance of 3.75m, which was a championship best performance in the event. Nicky Talbot and Glen Smith took their respective discus titles. Michael Tarran was victorious in the javelin by more than four metres. Debbie Rowe succeeded in the triple jump. Brendon Ghent won his third successive 100m title – but his first one in a Birchfield vest. Brendon completed an impressive double, winning the 200m. Lindsey Singer was triumphant in the 400 metres. Edward Dunford came out on top in the junior decathlon, whilst thirteen-year-old Jade Surman was 200 points ahead of her nearest rival in the under-fifteen pentathlon.

The English Commonwealth Trials took place in Manchester in mid-June. Mark Lewis-Francis felt it was a travesty that the track at the City of Manchester Stadium was going to be ripped up after the impending games. The young Stag followed Dwain Chambers home in a lifetime best of 10.07, which was good considering that he was carrying a hamstring injury.

Mark commented: 'The track is seriously fast. When the sun is shining and the wind is behind us, then who knows what will happen.' Mark's hamstring injury was a cause for concern. It was a long-term problem that worsened when he tweaked it when running at the Loughborough International in May.

Daniel Caines ran a lifetime best of 45.30 in the 400m heat, and was disappointed to run 'only' 45.32 to win the final by a quarter of a second from Jared Deacon.

Ashia Hansen admitted that she was in her best shape for years but could be a year away from finding her very best form. The Birchfield Harrier scored a routine triple jump triumph, leaping 14.03m to win by over a metre from Michelle Griffiths in her first full competition of the outdoor season. A bruised heel had delayed her debut but she believed victory with a fourteen-metre-plus jump was a solid base from which to work with the twin goals of Commonwealth Games and European Championships on the horizon.

'It seems years since I've been injury-free but because I've had so many problems it won't be until next season when I'll be jumping consistently at 14.70m and beyond fifteen metres.'

Helen Karagounis sliced more than half a second from her personal best and came within half a stride of defeating Olympic 800m Champion Maria Mutola. The Mozambique athlete was making a rare outing over one lap and predictably claimed victory in 52.03. However, she was forced to scrap hard down the home straight to defeat Karagounis, aged twenty, who led for the majority of the race.

The European under-twenty-three silver medallist went into the championships with a best of 52.75. She lowered that mark in the heats with 52.49, before stopping the clock at 52.17 in the final.

Within seven days several leading club athletes were in action for the European Cup in Annecy, France. Daniel Caines took the 400m in 45.14 from World outdoor silver medallist Ingo Schultz of Germany. The Stag appeared to go off like a rocket, but later stated that he had actually paced himself very well and his first 200 metres only looked impetuous because the runners on his outside were so slow. In addition to Schultz, Daniel disposed of Marek Plawgo, the European Indoor Champion, and Marc Raquil, the Frenchman who had won the 400m at this event the previous year.

Daniel observed: 'This event has the novelty factor. Athletics is usually an individual sport, but here the team element is all-important.' Men's final result:

1. Great Britain   111

Meanwhile, Ashia Hansen had questioned the performance of the winning triple jumper after an unknown Russian, Anna Pyatyich, snatched a shock win by five centimetres from the Birchfield Harrier. Ashia produced her furthest leap outdoors for three seasons with 14.62m in round three. It was still not enough to overhaul the twenty-one year old, who had jumped 14.67m in the preceding round.

The leading British athlete pondered: 'It was a bit worrying, I must admit. People don't just come from nowhere and jump 14.60. I know she jumped 14.48 metres last month, but it does make you wonder.' However, Ashia was delighted with her own individual efforts after jumping her furthest outdoor mark since the 1999 Grand Prix Final in Athens, when she won with 14.96m. 'It's the fittest I've been for years. It's quite exciting because so many people were saying: "she's getting old and losing her form" but I knew it was just injuries which held me up in the past.'

By the time of the women's 4 x 400m, Britain were fifth and had to finish in front of Poland and the Ukraine to ensure survival at that level of competition. Catherine Murphy ran a solid 52.5 opening relay leg and by the time the athletes broke from their lanes at the beginning of the back straight, Birchfield's Helen Frost was third. She was a long way behind the leaders, Russia, but significantly ahead of Poland and the Ukraine. Helen Frost (52.5) handed the baton to Helen Kargounis. She made British hearts flutter when she got away slowly and dropped to sixth – behind the Poles – at the beginning of the back straight. However, the European under-twenty-three silver medallist moved up a gear down the final 100 metres to put Britain third with a 52.6 leg before handing to Lee McConnell. The Scottish athlete unleashed a brilliant kick down the final straight to lead Britain to second in the race and safety. Women's final result:

1. Russia	122.5
5. Great Britain	84.5

With the European Championships to follow, the AAA Championships at the Alexander Stadium incorporated the Trials.

Ashia Hansen flew into Birmingham from Rome both jaded and unhappy with her performance in the Golden League meeting the night before. The Commonwealth Champion expected to go through the motions as usual to defend her domestic title but instead she found Yamile Aldama, a twenty-nine-year-old London-based Cuban, who had jumped 14.77m in 1999. It certainly perked Ashia up. She set a championship record of 14.29m in the third round, only to see Aldama take the lead with 14.40m in the fourth. Ashia responded in the final round with a leap of 14.50m. 'I'm really delighted to have this domestic challenge', she pronounced afterwards. 'It makes a big difference to be pushed and not have to go through the motions.'

In the women's 400m, Helen Karagounis finished third in 52.45 to Lee McConnell and second-placed Catherine Murphy. Helen Frost was fifth with 53.27.

Mark Lewis-Francis won a close-run final in 10.06, with Darren Campbell streaking through for silver ahead of European Indoor 60m Champion Jason Gardener. His post-race celebrations were muted as he instead gave priority to applying ice to his troublesome hamstring.

One of British athletics' finest servants, Robert Weir, took his ninth AAA discus title with a throw of 58.22m.

The Commonwealth Games in Manchester were the climax of a busy July. There was a major surprise in the much-anticipated 100m when both Mark Lewis-Francis and Dwain Chambers pulled up injured. The unheralded Kim Collins took gold for St Kitts and Nevis.

In the medical examination that followed the race it was discovered that Mark had suffered a micro-tear in a hamstring. He explained: 'I'm disappointed. I had cramp in my hamstring going into the event and I was not 100 per cent fit. I've suffered from a problem in my hamstring for a long time – in my left hamstring but not my right hamstring.'

At the age of forty-one, Robert Weir completed his twenty-year involvement with the Commonwealth games by bagging a bronze medal in the discus. Ranked eighth coming into the event, Robert raised his game with a second-round throw of 59.24m to finish behind South Africa's Frantz Kruger and Jason Tunks of Canada.

Standing on the podium at his fourth Commonwealth Games meant that Robert had equalled the record for the longest span over which any competitor had won medals, starting with gold in the hammer in 1982 through discus bronze in 1994, gold in 1998 and now bronze again.

After the competition, a tearful Robert admitted that he had been tempted to give up the sport in 1998. However, when hearing the 2002 Commonwealth Games were to be held in Manchester, Robert decided to press on until that year's competition.

Gold medallist Frantz Kruger paid tribute to Robert: 'I met Robert at my first international meeting in 1993 in Bedford and he's been a very good friend. It'll be a sad day when he stops throwing, as competing with him is always a pleasure, actually more of an honour.'

Nathan Morgan had forecast victory in the long jump competition, despite the scepticism that surrounded the statement following a foot injury at the Commonwealth Games Trial. On the day of the final Nathan backed up his promise by winning gold with a best of 8.02 – the only jumper to go over eight metres.

Nathan provided an insight into the challenge he had faced: 'At the Commonwealth Trials I tore my plantar fascia and I've not competed until now. In qualifying I injured my heel and had to "local" the heel area for the final.'

In the women's triple jump, spectators witnessed Francoise Mbango celebrating prematurely, after taking the lead with a sixth-round leap of 14.82. Meanwhile, Ashia Hansen still had to make her final attempt, the last of the event.

Needing to produce not only her best jump of the year but of recent years, Ashia summoned every ounce of her competitive spirit. 'When she jumped 14.82, she thought she had won and started celebrating. I thought: "Hey, I'm on the runway and I've got another jump here" It kind of wound me up a bit.'

The defending champion had led throughout with a 14.49m opening jump – a Commonwealth Games record. She improved to 14.66m in the second round. Like all true champions she responded in style, leaping to 14.86m for victory, the only 1998 champion to retain their title.

England's Helen Frost ran 52.4 for the first leg of the women's 4 x 400m relay. Then Helen Karagounis, a 400m semi-finalist, enjoyed the run of a lifetime to sweep past Olympic Champion Cathy Freeman of Australia with an inspired leg of 51.00 to hand the baton to Melanie Purkiss in the lead. Tamsyn Lewis of Australia did manage to pass the English woman down the home straight and set up a duel between Jana Pittman and Lisa Miller of England. Jana Pittman's greater strength took Australia to the gold. The English team, missing both Katharine Merry and Donna Fraser through injury, had performed wonders to win silver. Helen Karagounis, who ran such a famous leg against Cathy Freeman uttered: 'You've got to make the most of your opportunity... I'm just really happy to win my first senior medal.'

1. Australia	3:25.63
2. England	3:26.73

In the final event of the games, a spirited Welsh team took on the home nation in a magnificent battle, which had to be settled with a photo-finish. Daniel Caines, the unlucky fourth man in the individual 400m, appeared to have taken England into a winning lead with fifty metres to go. Wales' 400m hurdles silver medallist Matt Elias was not ready to settle for second and attacked Daniel with great vigour. Elias squeezed into a gap on the inside and dipped furiously at the line. The Welshman celebrated but Daniel had done enough and the result went to England. Just one hundredth of a second separated the two nations.

1. England	3:00.40
2. Wales	3:00.41

It was a brilliant and entertaining ending for the capacity crowd.

It wasn't long for athletics fans to wait for the next major feast of track and field action. The European Championships were in Munich in the second week of August.

In the men's 400m, home hero Ingo Schultz broke Britain's sixteen-year hold on the event by holding off the challenge of Daniel Caines and running to gold. The giant German dwarfed the diminutive Daniel and set off the quicker of the two athletes. By the home straight, however, the Stag had reduced the gap and was only a metre and a half down. Yet every time Daniel made inroads into the lead, the German responded and clung on to claim a narrow win from the fast-finishing Spaniard David Canal, as the Briton was relegated to bronze in 45.24.

For Daniel it was mixed emotions as he claimed his first outdoor medal, and this went some way towards making up for the disappointment of finishing fourth at the Commonwealth Games.

Daniel declared: 'It's not time to make excuses, Ingo ran an exceptional race and I say well done to him. I'm disappointed but I can hold my head up high that I've given my best shot. I'm not as gutted as I was at the Commonwealths.'

In the 4 x 400m, however, Daniel held off the challenge of Russian Yuriy Borzakoskiy to maintain Britain's success in this event. This was the fifth successive British victory. Daniel (44.7) completed the victory by a mere nine-hundredths of a second. The team finished on 3:01.25.

Karl Keska also ran well in torrential rain to finish fifth in the 10,000m with 28:01.72, despite almost a year out of competition through injury.

In the twilight of an illustrious career, Robert Weir bowed out of his last European Championships with a 58.37m discus throw.

In the women's triple jump, Ashia Hansen produced an inspired leap of 15m in the sixth and final round to overtake Finland's Heli Koivula. Ashia began the contest with solid 14.54m and 14.60m efforts but the

Robert Weir guides young Natalie Kerr.

Above left: Nathan Morgan.

Above right: Helen Karagounis (née Thieme)

Ashia Hansen.

Finn was slightly luckier with the weather, producing a couple of wind-assisted efforts of 14.83m and 14.67m.

'I was tired from rounds three to five, but then produced a 15m jump in the fifth round that was a foul. Aston told me to take my marker back a foot – and it worked!' Aston Moore, former British international jumper and father of Jonathan, was Ashia's knowledgeable coach.

Helen Frost and Helen Karagounis once again teamed up in the British 4 x 400m quartet, who placed fourth.

The end of the month saw the climax of the BAL Division One campaign at Wigan. There was a surprise as Woodford Green claimed their first-ever Division One match in a closely fought battle with Birchfield. Belgrave, although finishing third in the match, collected a record-breaking sixth successive British League title.

After a long, hard and continuous international season all eight clubs were forced to file severely depleted teams. The race of the day came in the penultimate event, the 3,000m steeplechase. Woodford Green's American, Adam Batliner, denied Birchfield's Eliud Kirui an historic double whitewash of British League distance events.

Earlier in the day, Kirui had held off a late charge from Batliner to win the 5,000m in 14:33.2 to make it four wins out of four that summer. He was a red-hot favourite to win the steeplechase. Indeed, the East African looked set for victory as he cleared the barrier in front and was expected to produce his trademark kick finish to ease to another routine win. However, on the run-in Kirui had to give way to the American. Final league standings:

1. Belgrave Harriers	30
2. Woodford Green	26
3. Birchfield Harriers	24

The UK women's title had been decided early in the month. Birchfield retained their status in sixth with Sale as the champions.

September saw Edward Dunford cruise to an eighth English Schools' Championship title. In the process he broke through the 7,000 points barrier by fifty points. 'The ESSA have presented me with a commemorative plaque to recognise my achievements, which will be something to treasure', Edward remarked.

There was also further international competition with the World Cup in Madrid. It took the Olympic and World silver medallist, Adam Nelson for the USA, all the four allotted rounds to get going in his shot putt event. It was only in the fourth round that Adam, with 20.80m, asserted himself. Robert Weir, in his third and last World Cup, threw 59.91m for seventh. Final points:

1. Africa	134
2. USA	119
7. Great Britain	86

In the women's triple jump, only two athletes – including Ashia Hansen of Europe – had taken their first-round jumps before a thunderstorm hit the stadium. This meant a mass dash for cover and delayed events by forty minutes.

On resumption and at the end of the first round, Francoise Mbango of Africa had posted what turned out to be the winning jump of 14.37m with Ashia in second place on 14.15m. A distance she managed to improve to 14.32m in the third round. 'I have had some sort of virus for the last couple of weeks and a sore back', reported Ashia after the event. 'I felt okay to start with but the rain interruption cooled me down and I just could not get back into it.' Final points:

1. Russia	126
2. Europe	123

The month had a happy ending with a successful defence of the Midland Six-Stage Road Relay title at Sutton Park. The 2001 race had been a nail-biting affair in which Rob Birchall snatched victory from old

Club stalwarts. From left to right: the late Roy Tilling, Ken Etheridge, Mrs Jean Etheridge, Tom McCook.

rivals Tipton by the slender margin of four seconds. This time, Birchfield established a new course record of 1:48.21 – seventy-one seconds quicker than the previous year. The margin of victory was extended to two minutes and six seconds.

In October over 300 Birchfield Harriers from many generations assembled at the Botanical Gardens in Birmingham for a celebration of the 125th anniversary of the first club AGM. This special evening also celebrated the 80th birthday of the Ladies' Section.

The current generation of such international stars as Daniel Caines, Helen Frost, Katharine Merry, Jonathan Moore and Kelly Sotherton mingled with great champions from the past, including Gill Dainty, Mike Farrell, John Graham, Diane Leather, Aston Moore, Peter Radford, Beryl Randle, Sue Reeve, John Salisbury, Peter and Mary Stewart, and Blondel Thompson.

The oldest member to attend was ninety-one-year-old Winnie Hayward, who made the journey from her home in Diss, Norfolk.

Seventy years after they had won the Women's National Cross Country Championships at Coventry, two members of the winning quartet met up to reminisce about their pre-war successes. Mary French, who won the individual bronze medal in a race won by Gladys Lunn, was joined by Ethel Wiltshire, who had emigrated to South Africa in 1947.

Later that month Darius Burrows answered an SOS call from team manager Maurice Millington the night before the National Six-Stage at Sutton Park. Darius was sitting at home enjoying a beer and a curry when Maurice asked him to run the final leg after Mike Bouldstridge went down with flu.

Darius, who had only been back in training three weeks after knee and hamstring problems, took up the challenge and produced a brave run to grimly hang on to the bronze position by nine seconds.

1. Belgrave Harriers	1:44.24
2. Morpeth	1:46.24
3. Birchfield Harriers	1:46.52

The year ended on a further up beat note when Rob Birchall produced one of the very best performances of his career to win the Puma Cell Cup in the Danish town of Ejby. The three-times Midland Cross Country Champion covered the 6km course in 17:17 to record his first overseas cross-country victory by a margin of nine seconds. In the process, the thirty-two-year-old Stag defeated a useful field, including the entire Danish squad from the recent Chiba Ekiden Road Relay in Japan.

Thirty-Six: High Performance

2003 was destined to be yet another significant year with Birmingham hosting the ninth World Indoor Championships.

One Birchfield athlete who could look back positively, as well as forward to the New Year, was Kelly Sotherton. She followed in the footsteps of Mark Lewis-Francis by scooping a top prize from the club sponsors. For the previous two years Aga had awarded a cooker to an athlete who had made an outstanding contribution to club success. Kelly, the AAA Indoor Champion at long jump and pentathlon, received an Aga six-four series cooker at a ceremony.

Lyn Orbell, the senior women's team manager, stated: 'Kelly is a most worthy recipient for this wonderful and unique prize. She has shown an exemplary attitude in supporting the team in both league and cup competitions. Her question is invariably: "What points do you need me to score for the club?" Kelly always turns out for the club and won the 400 metres in the UK cup final.'

William McGrath, the Chief Executive of Aga added: 'Kelly Sotherton has worked incredibly hard and always wears the Birchfield colours with pride. Her performances last year were outstanding.'

The endurance runners also began January with the prospect of their 2002 form continuing. Julian Moorhouse captured several illustrious scalps when he finished runner-up in the Great North Cross Country 4km race. Julian maintained his impressive form when he was the first home in the Midland Cross Country Championship at Alton Towers. Mark Dalkins received the individual bronze medal. Mark had placed first in the Staffordshire Championship with club-mate Martin Whitehouse second. A week later, Mark placed runner-up in the Birmingham Division One Cross Country League match at Rugby with teammate Phil Hinch third.

In early February, Mark Lewis-Francis broke the British indoor 100m record at the opening of the new £3.3 million High Performance Centre at the Alexander Stadium. He crossed the line in 10.34 to beat the previous record of 10.40, which Darren Braithwaite had held since 1996.

Funded by Birmingham City Council and Sport England, the state-of the-art facilities were available for athletes of all ages and abilities – from Olympic medallists to local schoolchildren. The facilities included an eight-lane 110m sprint track, triple-jump and long-jump pits, a throws practice area and facilities for the high jump and pole vault.

The Centre would prove a further incentive to better performances by a group of young Birchfield athletes who were in good form during that month. Edward Dunford improved by more than 500 points when he scored 5,260 points to finish third in the under-twenty pentathlon competition against the best teenage multi-event athletes from France, Spain and the UK in Cardiff. Julian Thomas advanced seven places to second on the UK under-seventeen all-time rankings, when he won the AAA 200m title at the NIA in 21.77. Andrew Thomas, the AAA under-seventeen Champion, had two metres to spare when he won the under-twenty shot title with a 15.43m putt.

Thirteen-year-old Jade Surman won the AAA under-fifteen Indoor long-jump title with a leap of 5.37m. Amy Harris won the AAA Indoor under-sventeen long-jump title to add to the under-fifteen title that she won in the summer of 2002. Sarah Patterson ran a finely judged race to win a thrilling under-seventeen Women's 800m final by 0.09 of a second in 2:17.16.

At a more experienced level, Rob Birchall finally gained selection for his World Cross Country debut in Lausanne after placing third in the Inter-Counties at Nottingham. Eventually, he was the second Briton to finish in uncustomary heat – when he placed sixty-ninth.

Daniel Caines delighted the 8,000 capacity crowd at the NIA when he ran away with the Norwich Union GP 400m title. The Stag had a real scrap with the 1999 World Indoor Champion Jamie Baulch to get to the bell first, but then led decisively to a victory in the year's fastest time of 45.75.

Daniel then slammed the decision to stage the All England Badminton Tournament at the Arena earlier that month. This had prevented British athletes from using the track at a critical time in their preparation for the impending World Indoor Championships.

Ashia Hansen recovered from a troublesome heel injury to defeat a strong international field in her first competitive outing of the year. She opened at 14.59m, which would have been sufficient for victory even if she had not improved. Her 14.71m effort in the third round thrust her to the top of the 2003 rankings in a most encouraging start to her season.

Birmingham welcomed the World Indoor Championships for three days in March. A quartet of Birchfield Harriers represented Great Britain. Cedric van Brantegham represented Belgium in the 400m.

Ashia Hansen produced yet another dramatic performance to win gold. She overcame that heel injury to add another title to her collection. The Stagbearer took an early lead in the final with a season's best of 14.77m. The Commonwealth Games silver medallist Francoise Mbango immediately responded with an African record of 14.88m. Ashia, however, was not to be beaten and hit back in the fifth round with a breathtaking leap of 15.01m. Afterwards she praised the crowd for her win: 'I knew the crowd were going to be loud but I just did not realise how loud they would be!'

'I had a lot of problems with my foot and had to have an anaesthetic to allow me to compete. It has been a long hard road to get here and I really did not think that I would make it. I want to thank my coach Aston Moore for putting up with me and pay tribute to my medical team for their work.'

Daniel Caines narrowly failed to become the first Briton to defend his title successfully, in these championships, in the 400m final. However, he added a relay bronze to his individual silver.

Mark Lewis-Francis just failed to repeat his World bronze medal of two years previously in Portugal when he placed fourth in a time of 6.57 after he had won his semi-final in 6.55.

Kelly Sotherton did not get a chance to race in the relays, because they were straight finals. She was, however, able to defend her AAA pentathlon title successfully in Cardiff with a career-best score of 4,226 points. The twenty-six year old achieved a hat-trick of personal bests to retain her title by 367 points. Edward Dunford made it a Birchfield double when he struck gold in the junior heptathlon in a UK best-ever score of 5,343.

In April a young Birchfield Harrier – born with seven vertebrae missing and no spinal chord – displayed qualities of courage and determination as he was first past the post in his race at the London Marathon. Mickey Bushell, aged twelve, returned home from London bearing his medal and prestigious winner's trophy. He had been victorious in the three-mile under-thirteen race.

Mickey completed the course in a time of 15:29 to convincingly win by a margin of twenty-five seconds. In an impressive performance, Mickey defeated several older competitors en route. His time was fast enough to have given him a seventh place in the under-seventeen event.

Another Birchfield youngster, Jade Surman, won the Girls' Under-fifteen All Rounder title by six points in the UK Sports Hall Finals at the NIA.

The club was never out of a medal position throughout more than four hours of competition at the National Men's Twelve-Stage Road Relay Championships. After leading for the first three stages, and being in the silver medal placing at the end of stage nine, the team eventually took home hard-earned bronze medals from a tough race in Sutton Park.

As an indication of her level of commitment to succeed, Kelly Sotherton spent all her savings to pay for a visit to Irvine University in Southern California that month. 'I scored 5,794 points in the last European event in Poland, which was eighty-six points short of lottery funding', she explained.

'I couldn't obtain financial support from anywhere but I managed to scrape together £2,000 to fund the trip myself. There was constant sunshine, which enabled me to train for four or five hours a day. I received invaluable technical advice from Greg Richards, who was a training partner of Daley Thompson and who now coaches Dean Macey. I even met Daley for the first time when he paid a visit to his old training base.'

In May, Sam Herrington smashed the Prince of Wales Stadium record when he threw the discus 56.70m at Gloucester. It also added four metres to the teenager's career-best throw. Sam had won the 2002 English and British Schools' title and was the son of long jumper Sue Reeve. His mother had won the 1978 Commonwealth Games title in her event.

Young athletes were also to the fore in June. On the day that Mark Lewis-Francis was winning twice in Bedford, his cousin, Ben Newman, went one better in the Midland Premier Young Athletes' match at the Yate track in Bristol.

The twelve year old, who had joined the Birchfield Academy earlier that year, won the under-thirteen sprints in times of thirteen seconds and twenty-seven seconds respectively. He then took the long jump victory with 4.70m. Ben also crossed the line first in the 4 x 100m relay after clawing back a thirty-metre deficit. Unfortunately the squad had been disqualified for a faulty changeover earlier in the race.

Eleven months after suffering a career-threatening patella tendon injury, Jonathan Moore successfully returned to competition at Loughborough, sporting a five-inch scar on his left kneecap. A day after his nineteenth birthday, Jonathan exceeded the European Junior long jump qualifying standard of 7.50m by one centimetre. Helen Karagounis took the honours in the women's 400m. Scott Rider won the shot putt by 1.7m with 17.66m.

Anything but a veteran himself, Mark Lewis-Francis recorded the first Grand Prix victory of his career in the Golden Spike meeting in Ostrava. The twenty year old stopped the clock in a meeting record time of 10.07 on a hot, windless evening. The time placed Mark just 0.01 of a second in front of Commonwealth Champion Kim Collins, and half-a-stride clear of European Champion Dwain Chambers. To top that, Mark scored eight points for Britain in the European Cup Final. He ran away with the 100m sprint title.

The young Stag stopped the clock in a time of 10.22 to win by a margin of 0.14 seconds in a 1m/s head wind. The victory repeated his win in Bremen two years previously. The temperature that day had reached 35°C. 'I've never run in this kind of heat before and I nearly passed out in the warm-up', Mark reported, 'but I got maximum points, which is a good achievement. The weather gets you focussed for what you are going to expect in Athens at next year's Olympics.'

Helen Karagounis and Katharine Merry constituted half of the 4 x 400m relay quartet, which achieved the highest position by a British squad in the thirty-seven-year history of the European Cup competition. Helen was away first with a 52.7 leg. In her first appearance in a British vest for two years, Katharine surged through from fourth to first place with a 51.4 clocking. Catherine Murphy and Lee McConnell were assisted by that leg to come home in an excellent second place. The British women were within half a second of the victorious Russian team and nearly two seconds clear of France.

After missing the European Cup a week before through illness, Daniel Caines was the 400m runner-up in the match against the USA and Russia in Glasgow. He recorded a time of 45.44, which was 0.12 of a second behind the American Derek Brew. Kelly Sotherton produced one of the surprises of the match when she went over 6.50m for the long jump on three occasions, for the first time in her career.

To cap an incredible month for him, Mark Lewis-Francis helped bring down the curtain on one of the sport's most famous arenas. He was the final winner of the 100m sprint at the Bislett Stadium in the Norwegian capital, Oslo. In seventy-nine years, the stadium had seen no less than sixty-two world records but like Wembley was to be rebuilt.

July opened with Helen Karagounis on top of a high quality 400m at Bedford to win the AAA under-twenty-three title in a championship best performance of 52.47. The twenty-one-year-old Birchfield Harrier beat defending champion Jenny Meadows by 0.2 of a second.

Helen went to Poland later in the month to be crowned European Under-twenty-three Champion. She improved 0.19 of a second in a new career-best time of 51.78. Helen, winner of the silver medal at these championships in 2001, dedicated her victory to her late father who had died the previous winter.

Denise Lewis made an impressive return to competitive action as she booked her place at the World Championships in Paris. The Olympic gold medallist scored 6,282 in the Estonian capital of Tallinn as she completed her first heptathlon since that glorious night in Sydney in 2000.

Club-mate Kelly Sotherton also did well, scoring a personal best of 6,059 to finish fourth as the Great Britain team won the women's division of the European Cup of Combined Events.

While Denise's return understandably hogged the headlines, Great Britain team leader Charles van Commenee believed it was Kelly Sotherton who produced 'the performance of the day'. 'It was her first time over 6,000 points with several personal-best performances, including long jump and javelin', van Commenee remarked.

Kelly Sotherton.

'The Olympics are within reach all of a sudden. She would have moved to 400 metre hurdles now if she had not scored 5,990, which qualifies her for lottery funding. Why would she move to an event that she would have to learn basically? As far as I am concerned, she has got no choice.'

Potential internationals of the future were doing well too. Amy Harris became English Schools' Champion at long jump. The fifteen year old demoralised the opposition when she leapt 6.03m in the first round. Aimee Palmer won the bronze medal with a 5.58m leap. Jade Surman won the junior competition to complete a club long-jump double.

Julian Thomas achieved his third English Schools' 200m title in 21.54. The sixteen year old successfully defended the intermediate boys' title, despite the handicap of tearing a hamstring in May.

Sam Herrington and Andrew Thomas gained valuable experience of international competition at the World Youth Championships in Canada. Andrew threw close to his career best with 53.11m to miss out on a final spot by two places. Sam, who is four months younger, threw 52.00m.

Back in Birmingham, Daniel Caines and Helen Karagounis each recorded their first outdoor AAA title on their home track. Daniel returned from a debilitating virus to record his first victory of the summer in a time of 45.56. Du'aine Ladejo dipped under the forty-six seconds barrier by 0.07 to make it a memorable 1-2 for the Stags.

Mark Lewis-Francis was obviously disappointed with third place in his defence of the AAA 100m title.

Kelly Sotherton was one of the club members to win AAA silver medals. In a frustrating afternoon in which she was given five 'no-jumps', Kelly achieved a distance of 6.38m in her only legal leap. She had performed well to finish second to Jade Johnson by eleven centimetres.

Other silver medals came from the men's throwing events. In his first season as a Stag, Scott Rider put the shot 17.79m to finish second to Carl Myerscough. Glen Smith occupied the same position in the discus.

Nine Birchfield Harriers were named in the first thirty-seven selections for the Great Britain team at the World Championships in Paris. This was double the representation by any other club, even though injury and illness eventually prevented Ashia Hansen and Katharine Merry from taking part.

It proved a week of occasional highs and personal lows for the contingent once they reached the French capital.

American Adam Nelson maintained his remarkable record in global events when he won the silver medal in the shot putt. He threw 21.26m to advance six positions late in the competition. Adam had previously won silver medals at the Sydney Olympics and both the World Indoors in Lisbon and the World Championships in Edmonton in 2001.

Denise Lewis recovered to finish fifth in the heptathlon with 6,254 points. Sweden's Carolina Kluft became only the third woman in history to exceed 7,000 points in the event. Denise ended the opening day's four events in seventh place after languishing in a lowly seventeenth spot after a poor high jump.

Karl Keska produced a season's best time of 27:47.89 while finishing a creditable ninth in the 10,000m. Karl was the second European to cross the finishing line behind an array of African long-distance runners.

Three other Stags suffered problems. A leg injury restricted Nathan Morgan's participation to two long jumps in the qualifying pool. Daniel Caines and Mark Lewis-Francis both failed to qualify for their respective finals in the 400m and 100m events.

Daniel ran a season's best of 45.38 just behind the World Indoor Champion, Tyree Washington, to qualify from his 400m heat. In a fiercely contested semi-final he placed third. With the two fastest losers emerging from the first of three semi-finals, the only consolation that Daniel had was recording a further improvement of 45.29.

He ran the anchor leg in both the semi-final and the final of the 4 x 400m relays. The quartet qualified for the final in second place and finished fifth eventually.

Mark had come into the championships on top form, so his disappointment was acute. In the first-round heats, he clocked 10.17, which was faster than either Dwain Chambers or Darren Campbell. After clocking a similar time in the quarter-final, matters went wrong the next day when Mark tailed off to finish his semi-final in 10.44. There was some consolation also in his case with a silver medal from the 4 x 100m relay, having run the final leg in the semi-final.

Also checking his passport that month was Brad Yiend. He won a 4 x 400m relay bronze medal at the World Student Games in Korea. The twenty-two year old, who advanced fourteen places on the UK rankings to fifth, also qualified for the semi-finals of the 400m hurdles where he placed third.

One of the most outstanding performances of the month had been that of Deborah Brennan on her home track at the British Open Athletics Championships. The Birchfield Harrier, who was born with cerebral palsy, scored an impressive hat-trick of victories. She came out on top in the 100m, 400m and 800m races on the first day of competition. Deborah returned to the fray the next day to complete the sprint double with victory over 200m. The question was how quickly she could go in her fifth and final discipline – the 1,500m for which she already held the T34 world record of 4:25.

The fact that she would win the classification seemed a foregone conclusion but all eyes were on the clock. Deborah once again smashed her record by nine seconds and finished twenty seconds ahead of Canadian Chelsea Clark. Amazingly, in the previous six years, Deborah had progressively lowered the 1,500m World record by more than a minute from 5:20 to 4:16.31 – and by the age of twenty-four.

There were other successes too. Sam Herrington had won gold and silver medals at the AAA Under-seventeen Championships at Sheffield. The sixteen year old threw the discus 54.42m to win the national title by a margin of three metres and was runner-up in the shot putt with 15.60m. Scott Simpson maintained an unbeaten record in UK league and cup matches that season when he won the pole vault in the final BAL Division one fixture at Wigan.

In early September, the club won the UK Young Athletes Boys Auxiliary Final for the first time in twenty-one years. In a tight and exciting conclusion, a total of ten event wins contributed towards a ten points margin of victory over Croydon, who had been in the lead with only two events remaining.

Team Captain Sam Herrington led by example and achieved a throws double, despite suffering from a leg injury. He also won a silver medal in the hammer competition.

Edward Dunford won a record ninth English Schools' title at the Don Valley Stadium in Sheffield. He scored 6,932 points at the boys' senior decathlon to defend the title that he had won at Derby in 2002. Edward had won an unprecedented six English Schools' multi-events and three hurdles titles. He also held the English Schools' multi-event records in the two younger age groups.

Jade Surman added the ESSA junior girls pentathlon to the long jump title, which she had won in July.

Two young Stags mounted the Flanders Cup podium in Belgium. Jonathan Moore was a clear victor of the men's long-jump competition with a marginally wind-assisted leap of 7.80m and a legal 7.60m. Scott Simpson won the pole vault with a 5.01m clearance.

Birchfield gained their sixth Midland Men's Six-Stage Road Relay Championship by the considerable margin of three minutes and nine seconds. There was a double cause of celebration when the second team won the 'B' competition. They placed thirteenth out of the ninety-four teams to complete the race.

During September there had been a special announcement by Kelly Sotherton on her athletics future. She was ready to give up her day job in a bid to fulfil her Olympic dream. The multi-talented athlete had twice gone close to achieving the qualifying mark needed to compete in the heptathlon event in Athens in 2004. Her fine run of form had come as she juggled the demands of training with her full-time employment with banking giants HSBC. Now she was prepared to commit herself totally to maximising her potential. Kelly had given another glimpse of that during the month when she scored an impressive 6,037 in the French city of Talence.

Her coach Charles van Commenee declared: 'Kelly is not yet the complete heptathlete but the long term looks promising, particularly as she is about to receive lottery funding. She scored more than 6,000 points twice this season, which is an improvement of more than 250 points on her best score last year.'

In October Denise Lewis added dimension to the focus on Athens 2004 by confirming that she had returned to her Midlands roots in order to prepare for the defence of her Olympic title. 'If I've counted correctly, there are 317 days to go until Athens and I cannot afford to be lazy for a single one', stated the thirty-one year old. She would once again team up with Charles van Commenee, the coach who led her to success in Sydney.

They would be based at the High Performance Centre at the Alexander Stadium, with its state-of-the-art equipment, complete with full medical and physiotherapy support. The facilities were a massive advance on the more basic ones the Wolverhampton schoolgirl had to use as she developed into the UK's most successful combined events athlete throughout the 1990s.

Du'aine Ladejo passes on his skills.

Denise had taken a break after Sydney to start a family with her partner, Belgian sprinter Patrick Stephen. She had returned to action in the summer of 2003 and led the Great Britain team to victory in the European Cup of Combined Events in Estonia before finishing fifth in the World Championships in Paris.

'Time management is crucial. It always has been with so many events but it's more so now as a mum. I'll be training in the morning, sleeping in the afternoon and training some evenings. It's a pattern I've been used to for years.'

Charles van Commenee added: 'Let there be no misunderstanding – Denise is on a mission to retain her title. I have confidence we can work together again and I'll be seeing her twice a day, six days a week.'

There was an entertaining twist for the club at the climax of the year. An impressive display of power and consistency earned Du'aine Ladejo the accolade of Superstars Champion in the final screened by BBC TV. The thirty-two year old defeated the Scottish skier Alain Baxter by four and a half points, with another 400m runner Jamie Baulch third, a further two points adrift.

Du'aine accomplished his childhood dream with victory in the 100m sprint; a hat-trick of runners-up places in swimming, football and kayak; and third places in the gymnasium tests and tennis.

Thirty-Seven: Glory Leg

Kelly Sotherton was one of several leading club athletes who began Olympic year by flying off on New Year's Day for three weeks warm weather training in South Africa. Denise Lewis, Ashia Hansen, Nathan Morgan and Jonathan Moore would also be based at Stellenboch.

Kelly had begun to feel the benefit of training with Denise Lewis under the tutelage of Charles van Commenee at the High Performance Centre at the Alexander Stadium. She reported: 'I feel much stronger, physically and mentally, than I did three months ago. One big difference is that I get two hours more sleep in the morning to allow my body to recover from doing two training sessions a day rather than one. Charles says that I am beginning to look like a proper athlete rather than a gangly runner. He is a fantastic coach to have, a real hard task master who cracks the whip.'

'I can't think of any other athlete in Britain who trains with a current Olympic Champion. Denise is a great role model to watch and learn from. Denise and I get on very well together. She encourages me and I do the same for her.'

A week after Denise and Kelly, Mark Lewis-Francis and Christian Malcolm jetted off to Stellenboch. The decision to form a partnership was made by the coaches of the two athletes, Steve Platt and Jock Anderson. Speaking at the Alexander Stadium on the eve of their departure Steve Platt declared: 'Jock and I have been good friends for a long time and we both felt that Mark and Christian would be good for one another. Whilst Christian is competitive at 100m, he is more of a 200m runner. Jock and I believe that Mark can help Christian's flat speed and Christian can help improve Mark's speed endurance.'

In colder climes, Tim Werrett in only his second cross-country race since the previous January, after winning two England vests for fell running, exceeded expectations when he placed twelfth in a time of 41:24 at the Midland Cross Country Championships. The thirty-two-year-old Walsall postman had been a Birchfield Harrier since 1987. He utilised his experience to begin steadily before working his way through the field. Martin Whitehouse, after being in the leading group in the early stages, eventually finished twenty-first in 42:04. Tom Penfold, who won the bronze medal in the junior men's race, achieved the best performance of the day in a black vest.

Helen Karagounis accomplished three important goals in the Norwich Union Indoor International match against Russia, Sweden, Italy and a World Select in Glasgow. The European Under-twenty-three 400m Champion clocked a World Indoor Championships qualifying time – and an indoor personal best by more than half a second – in scoring Great Britain's second victory of the day to the delight of a capacity crowd in the Kelvin Hall. The twenty-two-year-old Stagbearer powered off the last bend to overtake Natalya Lavshuk of Russia in the last twenty metres and win in 53.31.

A decade after winning the European 400m titles indoors and out, Du'aine Ladejo finished third in the distance in 47.88. He then ran a spectacular glory leg to send the crowd home happy after the final event of the match. After accepting the baton in fourth place in the 4 x 400m relay, the Stag clocked 46.9, lunging into second place in the last couple of strides.

Phil Hinch moved up a gear to win the final Birmingham First Division Cross Country League race at Leek in February. Three weeks previously, the twenty-six-year-old former Army Champion had broken a rib when he collided with a telephone junction box while training in Edgbaston.

Despite the damaged rib still being sore when he breathed deeply, Phil went out hard from the gun and was one of a quartet of runners to break clear of the 150-strong field. After a protracted contest in which the lead changed hands several times, Phil and Kidderminster's Matt Vaux-Harvey sprinted shoulder to shoulder to the finish. The timekeepers gave them identical times of 28:39 for the tough 9.5km, course but the Stag just snatched victory. Tim Werrett moved through the field to sixth in 29.43 and helped the Stags record their second team victory of the winter by one point from Loughborough University. This performance advanced the Stags from fourth to second place overall in the thirteen clubs' league table for the 2003/4 season.

Indoors, Denise Lewis enjoyed mixed fortunes at the AAA Championships and World Trials. She won a silver medal in the shot with 14.59, and placed third in her 60m hurdles heat after hitting one of the early hurdles. Denise summarised: 'I've regained a lot of the strength that I lost in the last couple of years but I am not throwing with speed yet. It was the first time that I have used blocks in the hurdles and it showed. In the 60m you cannot afford to let the girls get away.'

Helen Karagounis clocked a personal best time of 52.86 to add the AAA Indoor 400m silver medal to her collection. Helen fought off a spirited challenge from the defending champion, Wigan's Jenny Meadows.

Bobby Aloyius, who placed fourth for India in the 2002 Commonwealth games, completed a hat-trick of AAA silver medals for the Birchfield ladies when she cleared 1.83m in the high jump.

Nineteen-year-old Jonathan Moore was runner-up in the long jump with a distance of 7.38m.

Kelly Sotherton improved her indoor long jump personal best by eighteen centimetres to 6.38m when she placed fourth in the European Indoor Cup long jump in Leipzig. Great Britain's number two in both heptathlon and long jump in 2004, Kelly was having her first competition after returning from training in South Africa.

The Norwich Union Grand Prix at the NIA produced its usual quality field. In her first competition since she won the World Indoor title on the same run-up the previous March, Ashia Hansen put the 8,000 spectators through more agonies before a golden outcome. The multi-titled champion had three fouls before leaping 14.47m with her fourth and final attempt.

Mark Lewis-Francis catapulted to second in the world that year by winning his heat in 6.53 seconds. This was close to his best-ever time of 6.51 when Mark won a World Indoor bronze at Lisbon in 2001. In the final he came through with his last-gasp surge to finish fifth in 6.63. 'I am a very happy guy at the moment. All the false starts made me nervous, which is why I didn't run well in the final. This is all about the outdoors for me. I have no plans to run in the World Indoor Championships.'

Kelly Sotherton was third in the long jump with 6.23m in the third round, after a keen contest with the Spanish jumper Montaner. Marion Jones improved throughout the event and won with a 6.75m leap.

Five days after he broke forty-eight seconds for the first time to win the Birmingham Games 400m, nineteen-year-old Dan Cossins improved by a margin of sixty-three hundredths of a second when he was runner-up on his Grand Prix debut. The powerful young Stag flew out of his blocks and got to the bell first in a time of 21.8. Although he was overtaken by Adam Potter, the teenager hung on to stop the clock in a career-best time of 47.10. This was a quarter of a second faster than the former World Champion Jamie Baulch achieved in the other race.

In the fresh air, and despite a lack of competition over the previous year because of injury, Julian Moorhouse finished thirteenth out of 750 finishers at the National Cross Country Championships. These were held over an extremely demanding 12km course at Temple Newsam in Leeds.

The Olson sisters, who had recently become Birchfield Harriers when they relocated from Ashford in Kent, won their respective AAA Indoor junior pole vault competitions at the NIA. Natalie, aged twenty, won the under-twenty competition on countback after both she and Rachel Gibbins cleared 3.60m. Natalie's younger sister Hannah, at the age of fifteen, lifted the under-seventeen title with a 3.70m clearance to complete a distinctive family double.

Alex Williams and Daniel Fagan, who are both coached by Andy Paul, dominated the 200m sprints. Alex, who made his international debut at the 2003 European Junior Championships in Finland, defeated a high quality field to take the junior crown in a time of 21.55. He had won his semi-final in a career-best time of 21.43 to go sixth on the UK all-time age rankings. Daniel scorched to number three on the UK under-seventeen all-time list with a winning time of 21.77. This was an improvement of more than half a second – and a dozen positions in the rankings.

Amy Harris completed a nap hand for the club when she won the AAA under-seventeen long jump title double with a best distance of 5.87m, after winning the outdoor version the previous summer. The sixteen-year-old schoolgirl had achieved a clean sweep of domestic honours having won the British and English Schools' titles in July 2003.

Andrew Thomas improved by a third of a metre to take home a silver medal from a tight junior shot putt contest with a 17.43m effort.

Helen Karagounis experienced mixed emotions on her debut at the World Indoor Championships in Budapest. The twenty-two-year-old Birchfield Harrier qualified for the semi-final when she placed third in the first heat in 52.66. Helen chopped a further thirteen hundredths of a second from her indoor best time when she placed fifth in a high quality semi-final in a time of 52.53. The Stagbearer reported: 'It was a bit quick on the first 200 metres in the semi-final but I am pleased with my performances here. I have achieved two personal best performances in two races so I can't complain too much about that.'

There was frustration when the 4 x 400m relay squad paid the penalty for resting both Helen and Catherine Murphy. They failed to qualify for the final of the competition.

Allan Meddings had another sprint double in the over-seventy-five group at the inaugural World Indoor Masters Athletics Championships in the German town of Sindelfingen. A month after his seventy-sixth birthday, Allen clocked 30.93 to win the 200m on the second day of competition. A leg injury cast doubt on his participation over the shorter distance. Allan recalled: 'I was in agony but managed to get through my heat and semi-final. I ran badly but did enough to win the 60m sprint.'

Mike Fox completed a golden hat-trick for the Stags when he won the World Masters over-seventy 800m title. Denis Withers added to the medal haul with a bronze medal in the over-seventy-five 3km race walk. More than 2,500 competitors from fifty-seven countries took part in this inaugural championship.

Mike Fox leads the over–sixty-five Euro Vets, 800m.

In his first season as a senior athlete, Edward Dunford finished in the bronze medal position at the AAA Indoor heptathlon. The nineteen year old added seven points to his best ever score to finish with 5,169 points. Three of his best disciplines were a 1.95m clearance in the high jump, 8.33 for the 60m hurdles and a 14.14m shot putt.

Eliud Kibet Kirui delighted his friends in Birmingham when achieved a top six placing in the men's 4km race at the World Cross Country Championships in Brussels. The twenty-two-year-old Kenyan led the World Championship for the first two kilometres and withstood a late challenge to become his country's first scorer when he stopped the clock in 11:45. Kirui had been ever-present in the 2002 British Athletics league season. He was unbeaten over the 3,000m steeplechase and lost only once over 5,000m.

Birchfield Harriers began the Spring road relay season by finishing runners-up at the Warwickshire Open Road Relays Championship in Sutton Park. Rachel Cook, Amanda Wright Allen and Josie Grey completed the 3 x 2.75 miles course in 48:02. This was within twenty-nine seconds of the winners, Coventry Godiva.

Despite the non-availability, through illness, of two of their former international runners, Amanda Wright Allen and Cath Mijovic, Birchfield placed fourth in the Midland Women's Six-Stage Road Relay at Sutton Park.

A greatly depleted men's team finished seventh in the Midland Twelve-Stage Road Relay.

Jade Surman created a small piece of athletics history by becoming the first champion to successfully defend their individual 'All Rounder' title at the UK Sports Hall Finals at the NIA.

In a nail-biting conclusion, five points separated the leading five competitors from all over England. Jade retained her crown, just one point more than Lucy Sergeant from Essex (278–277). Jade commented: 'I struggled in the long jump today, usually one of my strongest events and had two 'no-throws' in the shot putt. There was a lot of pressure on me to retain my title and I am really pleased to win.'

Above left: Jade Surman.

Above right: Mickey Bushell.

Thirteen-year-old Mickey Bushell, who was born with lumbar sacral agenesis congenital paraplegia, successfully defended his London Wheelchair Marathon Under-fourteen title.

'It was raining before the start of my race, but I hardly noticed it as my heart was racing. I could hear the crowds cheering even before I came out of the tunnel. It sounded like a plane taking off. It was really loud! But it gave me a real boost. The wind eased a bit, and it got easier to push. When I rounded the corner into the Mall I could see the finish line in the distance. I sprinted the hardest I could all the way to the finish line. The crowds were fantastic, they cheered and shouted me all the way to the end. When I crossed the line they gave me my medal and told me I was the winner of the eleven to thirteen boys' category for the second year. Even though the course was wet and windy, I was very happy not only to have finished but to win my age group again.'

Sixteen-year-old Kevin Ward improved by two and a half minutes on his performance the previous year to finish third overall in the wheelchair competition.

Phil Hinch was the most high-profile Stag in the television coverage of the London Marathon as he encouraged and paced Birhan Dagne, the English National Cross Country Champion. The Ethiopian-born runner was to finish second amoung British woman after leading the UK challenge for all but the final two crucial miles. The experience had whetted Phil's appetite and he was keen to race the London Marathon on a further occasion: 'It was a fantastic experience. The crowd was very supportive to all the runners. I definitely want to run there again'.

In July, and two years after snapping his patella tendon whilst competing in the 2002 AAA Junior Championships, Jonathan Moore made a triumphant return to Bedford. The twenty-one year old established an AAA Under-twenty-three Championship best performance for the long jump with a wind-assisted leap of 7.75m, despite cold and wet conditions. Afterwards Jonathan said: 'I know that I am getting close to eight metres again. I just need to be faster going into the last four strides.'

An impressive throw of 49.72m in the sixth and final round, not only gave Becky Bartlett the AAA Junior javelin title, but secured the nineteen year old a place in the Great Britain team for the World Junior Championships later that month.

In the Norwich Union Grand Prix at Gateshead, Daniel Caines battled hard to finish a close second in the men's 400m. In miserable weather conditions, Daniel crossed the line in a season's best of 45.29. This was inside the Olympic 'A' standard for Athens. Helen Karagounis finished seventh in the women's 400m race in a season's best of 51.91.

Allan Meddings accomplished yet another sprint double in the over-seventy-five age group at the British Masters Athletics Federation Championships at the Alexander Stadium to add to his raft of major titles. The seventy-six year old battled into a head wind in the home straight to win the 100m by three seconds in a time of 14.55 and followed this the next day with a comprehensive 200m victory in 30.36 seconds. Allen then made a special announcement: 'I will do the Europeans and call it a day.'

Meanwhile, the former World Veterans sprint record holder Ron Taylor made his return to competition to be crowned the British Masters Over-seventy Champion in a time of 13.39.

Fifty-seven-year-old Bob Care was the best of the race walkers when he covered the 3,000m in 13:59.4. This time was faster than competitors in the younger age groups.

At the end of the month Ashia Hansen was able to report on the career-threatening patella tendon injury suffered on 9 June at the European Cup Final in Poland. 'As you can see I have been allowed to dispense with my crutches but I still need a brace to support my knee. The operation went well and I am being well looked after.'

The Stags finished the month strongly to place third in Division One at Plaistow, East London. The four fixtures series had begun disappointingly with sixth place in the first match at Wood Green in early May, before getting much worse with last place at Hendon a week later. This meant that the club were uncharacteristically in the relegation zone in seventh place.

The fight-back in the second half of the season began with second place in the home fixture at the Alexander Stadium on 3 July before a visit to London on 31 July ensured Birchfield Harrier's status in the top three of British athletics.

The result maintained team manager Dave Lawrence's proud record of never finishing outside the top four in his twenty-four years at the helm of Birmingham's most successful sporting club. Belgrave Harriers won the match to clinch the title for a record eighth successive year.

In early August, Denise Lewis and Kelly Sotherton helped their team finish second in the UK Women's League Division One match in Manchester. The duo flew north from London after competing in the Friday night Norwich Union Grand Prix long jump competition at Crystal Palace.

Denise placed second in the shot with 14.87m and was third in the 100m in 14.00 seconds. Kelly accomplished 'B'-string double victories with a 13.21m putt and 13.81 in the hurdles.

The defending champions, Sale, won with 235 points to clinch their fifth successive league title. Birchfield scored 195 to defeat Trafford AC by one point and advance one place to finish fourth in the final league table.

Jade Surman defeated the best young athletes in the UK to win the AAA under-seventeen heptathlon title at the Alexander Stadium. Although she was bottom age in the under-seventeen age group and will be able to defend her title yet again – fifteen-year-old Jade scored 4,818 points to add another AAA age-group medal to her collection.

At the other extreme of the age scale, Allan Meddings bowed out of international athletics with a brace of silver medals in the over-seventy-five category in the European Veterans Finals in the Danish city of Aarhus. His times were 14.30 and 29.63 respectively. Allen intended to continue to train and to pass on his experience and coaching experience as requested to all ages.

Another Stag, Mike Fox, was runner-up in the over-seventy 800m in 2:34.37 and third in the 400m in a time of 67.47.

August meant the Athens Olympics, of course, the event of the sporting year, and for one young Stag – the event of his lifetime.

First we go to Olympia, some 200 miles south-west of Athens, and the men's shot putt competition. After leading the morning's qualification session by a margin of a half a metre with 21.15m, Adam Nelson won his second Olympic silver medal. Sixth in the throwing order, Adam opened with a throw of 21.16m. It was to be his only legal throw of the event, and would hold up as the first-place throw until the end of the competition. As Adam waited for his own final putt, 2002 European Champion Yuriy Bilonog of the Ukkaine matched the American with a throw of 21.16m. This put him in the lead because his second-best throw had been better than Adam, who had no legal second mark at that point. Adam stepped into the circle for his final attempt and unleashed what looked to be a possible winning throw – only to have it declared foul.

His status as the world's most consistent shot putter, having won two Olympic and three World Championship silver medals, would initially do little to comfort Adam for missing out on the top step of the podium by the narrowest of margins.

Denise Lewis arrived at the games as a defending Olympic Champion. Ten years previously she had decorated a young Kelly Sotherton with gold after the English Schools' Championship. Kelly had told Denise that day: 'One day I will be there with you.' After four events on the first day, Kelly was in the silver medal position on 3,869 points. Denise was in ninth place on 3,688 and heading for the massage table to be treated for cramp. Sweden's Carolina Kluft led with 4,109 and had one hand on Denise's crown.

After the 100m hurdles and high jump in the morning session, Kelly was already joint-second behind Kluft. Denise had dropped to fourteenth spot having failed to better 1.73m in the high jump, this after Denise had taken her heat of the 100m hurdles in a season's best of 13.40 and been placed sixth overall – one spot ahead of Kelly, whose high-jumping was superior.

Kelly's jump of 1.85m surpassed her previous best of 1.78m, and seemed to quell some of the doubt articulated by Charles van Commenee about her ability to transfer previous form into the challenges of the Olympic arena.

'I was a bit disappointed with the 200 metres because I've been running faster than that in training', reported Kelly. She ran 23.57 to Denise's 25.42. 'But we only had a twenty-minute turnabout after the shot putt, so there wasn't long to get my composure. I was very happy with my throwing because normally it puts me back down to about tenth or eleventh place.' Kelly threw 13.29m, against Denise's 15.33. 'All in all I've had a pretty good day.'

At the end of the second day Kelly was to initially suffer mixed emotions. She finished with Olympic bronze, just eleven points behind silver medallist Austra Skujyte. Kelly would have overtaken her had she gone two seconds faster in the 800m. Kelly could only manage 37.19m in the javelin when she was in the silver medal position.

Happy landings for Kelly.

'I went out to get the silver medal so I'm actually disappointed', said a breathless Sotherton afterwards. 'I only did one personal best over the two days and my javelin was poor. But I got a bronze medal and I don't believe it. I can't believe the enormity of an Olympic bronze. I had a dream of a medal, but this is a surprise. It's been a tough two days and I'm absolutely knackered. All it feels like at the moment is as if I've won bronze in a national championships – but I'm sure it will sink in soon.'

While Kelly sealed her emergence that season, Carolina Kluft's golden performance confirmed her status as the best all-round female athlete in the world. She finished 517 points clear.

Once Kelly had composed herself, she found time to speak to the club's President and Press Officer Tom McCook on the telephone. Her first question was: 'How did we get on in the Cup Final?' The Olympic heptathlon bronze medallist admitted that she had wondered how her club back home was faring several times between her events in Athens.

Tom was able to confirm that the club had won the Jo Smith Trophy on the very day that Kelly was achieving her step onto the Olympic podium. It had been a nail-biting conclusion to the Jubilee Cup Final at Bedford.

In a good all-round performance, Birchfield had achieved a nap hand of victories, the same number of second places, and significantly no less than nine third place finishes – including both women's relays.

So it was a double dose of good news for Kelly who was able to analyse her feelings in greater depth to the President. 'If someone had suggested a year ago that I would win an Olympic medal, I would have laughed at them. My mother and other members of my family have helped me financially for the last ten months, which I appreciate greatly. I was a bit of a softy competitively before Charles van Commenee became my coach. He does not give praise lightly but patted me on the back after my high jump. I ran a fast 600 metres time-trial in Cyprus earlier this month and Charles felt that I could have run quicker than I did in the last event in Athens. However, my legs felt like concrete when I lined up on the start line for the 800 metres on Saturday night. Charles likes to goad me into improving and I proved him wrong by getting a medal this time. I am really pleased that Denise is to carry on because she is my training partner. Denise has had a difficult year through injuries. She has been an inspiration to many people in our sport and for women.'

If Kelly had produced a surprise – what came as the climax of the games was suitably described by BBC Sport: 'Gold medals are always precious but they take on a different hue when they come out of the blue.'

After the performances of Britain's male athletes in Athens, few expected them to come up trumps on the final day of track and field action. Just when it looked like they would finish without an Olympic medal of any colour for the first time in history, the 4 x 100m relay team recorded one of the most spectacular victories of the Games.

Mark Lewis-Francis.

The United States quartet looked unbeatable. With 100m champion Justin Gatlin, 200m champion Shawn Crawford and three-time World Champion Maurice Greene in their line-up, they were by far the quickest team. Even the fourth member, Coby Miller, had dipped below ten seconds in the US trials in July.

In stark contrast, the records of the British squad were far less impressive. Only Jason Gardener had officially run under ten seconds – and that was back in 1999. As for Darren Campbell, he had been troubled by a hamstring injury while Marlon Devonish had failed to even earn selection in the individual 200m. Finally, Mark-Lewis Francis had concerns about his form in recent months.

Also taking into account the poor record of the British in recent relay races, it was easy to understand why few gave them any chance of success. Yet, eighty minutes after Kelly Holmes had taken her place in British Athletics history by adding the 1,500m gold to her 800m title, the impossible happened.

The young Stag Mark Lewis-Francis held off the USA's Maurice Greene on the glory leg to win a stunning gold medal.

Jason, Darren, Marlon and Mark were faultless with their baton changes as they stunned the pre-race favourites.

Britain clocked 38.07 with the USA one hundredth of a second behind, and Nigeria taking the bronze. The USA bid stumbled with a poor change between Justin Gatlin and Coby Miller. It still required that sensational effort from Mark Lewis-Francis, who had failed to reach the final in the individual 100m, to stay ahead of the fast-finishing Greene, the 100m bronze medallist and former Olympic Champion. It was the first British Olympic relay gold medal since 1912.

Time stood still for just a split second inside the Olympic Stadium as the crowd tried to comprehend what they had just witnessed. When Mark started to leap around like a madman before being swamped by his teammates, reality began to sink in.

Britain had been almost disqualified from the semi-final after a poor third baton change but Mark insisted their team bond drove them to victory: 'With the team spirit that we had we knew we could come back stronger and we proved everyone wrong.'

He concluded: 'I can go home with my head held high even though my individual race didn't go to plan. I am an Olympic Champion, it is the greatest thing to ever happen to me in my life.'

It is the perfect symmetry on which to conclude; a glorious past and a glorious future.

Birchfield Harriers Records and Statistics:

The authors are indebted to the work of the National Union of Track Statisticians (N.U.T.S.) from whose lists many of these statistics are drawn. In the case of women who competed under both maiden and married names, the name by which she is better known is used. Hence, Judy Livermore/Simpson is Judy Simpson, and Daphne Arden/Slater is Daphne Arden.

Olympic Games

Representatives   Men   Women

1896 ATHENS

1900 PARIS

1904 ST LOUIS

1908 LONDON
  Vic Loney, 1,500m
  Arthur Robertson, 3-mile team race, steeplechase

1912 STOCKHOLM
  Fred Hulford, 800, 1,500m

1920 ANTWERP
  Joe Blewitt, 5,000m, 3,000m team race
  Walter Freeman, cross-country
  Charles Clibbon, 10,000m

1924 PARIS
  Bert Macdonald, 3,000m team race
  Harry Houghton, 800m
  Eddie Webster, 10,000m, cross country
  Syd Newey, Steeplechase
  David Slack, Decathlon
  James Dalrymple, Javelin
  Cyril Ellis, 1,500m

1928 AMSTERDAM
  Joe Blewitt, 5,000m, 3,000m team race
  Cyril Ellis, 1,500m
  Harry Houghton, 800m
  Billy Green, 400m
  Fred Light, 5,000m
  Jack Hambidge, 200m

1932 LOS ANGELES

1936 BERLIN
  Godfrey Brown, 400m, 4x400m relay   Audrey Brown, 100m, 4x100m relay

1948 LONDON
  Sydney Cross, Triple Jump   Gladys Clarke, Javelin

FLEET AND FREE

1952 HELSINKI

Winifred Jordan, 100m

1956 MELBOURNE
Mike Rawson, 800m
Mike Farrell, 800m
John Salisbury, 400m, 4x400m relay

Carole Quinton, 80m hurdles

1960 ROME
Peter Radford, 100m, 4x100m relay
Nick Whitehead, 4x100m relay
Malcolm Yardley, 400m, 4x400m relay
Robbie Brightwell, 400m, 4x400m relay

Carole Quinton, 80m hurdles,
4x100m relay
Diane Leather, 800m

1964 TOKYO
Robbie Brightwell, 400m, 4x400m relay
John Cooper, 400m hurdles, 4x400m relay
Peter Radford, 100m, 4x100m relay
Howard Payne, Hammer
John Morbey, Long Jump

Daphne Arden, 100m, 4x100m relay

1968 MEXICO
John Cooper, 400m hurdles
Howard Payne, Hammer
Howard Davies, 400m
John Sherwood, 400m hurdles, 4x400m relay
Stuart Storey, 110m hurdles

Pat Jones, 80m hurdles
Pat Lowe, 800m
Sue Reeve, Pentathlon

1972 MUNICH
Ian Stewart, 5,000m
Dave Cropper, 800m
Geoff Capes, Shot Put
Howard Payne, Hammer
Ray Smedley, 1,500m
John Sherwood, 400m hurdles
Bill Tancred, Discus

Pat Lowe, 800m
Ruth Martin-Jones, Long Jump
Jean Roberts (*Australia*), Shot Put

1976 MONTREAL
Ainsley Bennett, 200m, 4x400m relay
Ian Stewart, 5,000m
Aston Moore, Long Jump

Sue Reeve, Long Jump
Mary Stewart, 1,500m

1980 MOSCOW

Sue Reeve, Long Jump

1984 LOS ANGELES
Phil Brown, 400m, 4x400m relay
Eric McCalla, Triple Jump
Robert Weir, Discus & Hammer

Judy Simpson, Heptathlon

1988 SEOUL
Phil Brown, 400m, 4x400m relay
Stewart Faulkner, Long Jump
Derek Redmond, 400m, 4x400m relay

Judy Simpson, Heptathlon

1992 BARCELONA
Derek Redmond, 400m

Sally Ellis, Marathon
Lorraine Hanson, 400m
Clova Court, Heptathlon

1996 ATLANTA
Robert Weir, Discus

Denise Lewis, Heptathlon, Long Jump
Katharine Merry, 200m

2000 SYDNEY
Daniel Caines, 400m, 4x400m relay
Karl Keska, 10,000m
Robert Weir, Discus
Glen Smith, Discus
Adam Nelson (*USA*), Shot Put

Denise Lewis, Heptathlon
Katharine Merry, 400m, 4x400m relay

2004 ATHENS
Daniel Caines, 400m
Mark Lewis-Francis, 100m & 4x100m relay
Adam Nelson (*USA*), Shot Put
Bobby Aloysius (India), High Jump
Tiombe Hurd (*USA*), Triple Jump

Denise Lewis, Heptathlon
Kelly Sotherton, Heptathlon
Helen Karagounis, 4x400m relay

World Championships

Representatives   Men

Women

1983 HELSINKI
Ainsley Bennett, 4x400m relay
Phil Brown, 400m, 4x400m relay.
Robert Weir, Discus

Judy Simpson, Heptathlon

1987 ROME
Lincoln Asquith, 4x100m relay
Phil Brown, 400m, 4x400m relay
Derek Redmond, 400m, 4x400m relay

Judy Simpson, Heptathlon

1991 TOKYO
Derek Redmond, 400m, 4x400m relay

Lorraine Hanson, 400m, 4x400m relay
Clova Court, Heptathlon
Sally Ellis, Marathon

1993 STUTTGART
Robert Weir, Discus

Katharine Merry, 200m
Clova Court, Heptathlon, 100m hurdles

1995 GOTHENBURG
Robert Weir, Discus

Denise Lewis, Heptathlon
Lorraine Hanson, 4x400m relay

1997 ATHENS
Robert Weir, Discus

Katharine Merry, 200m
Michelle Thomas, 4x400m relay
Denise Lewis, Heptathlon

1999 SEVILLE
Nathan Morgan, Long Jump
Robert Weir, Discus
Glen Smith, Discus

Katharine Merry, 400m
Helen Frost, 4x400m relay
Denise Lewis, Heptathlon

2001 EDMONTON
Mark Lewis-Francis, 100m
Mike Openshaw, 5,000m
Robert Weir, Discus
Adam Nelson (*USA*), Shot Put

Helen Frost, 4x400m relay

2003 PARIS
Mark Lewis-Francis, 100m, 4x100m relay

Denise Lewis, Heptathlon

Daniel Caines, 400m,4x400m relay
Adam Nelson (*USA*), Shot Put

Helen Karagounis, 4x400m relay

European Championships

1934 TURIN

1938 PARIS
Godfrey Brown, 400m, 4x400m relay

Audrey Brown, 100m, 4x100m relay
Dorothy Cosnett, High Jump, Long Jump
(The women's championships were held in Vienna)

1946 OSLO

Winifred Jordan,100m, 200m, 4x100m relay

1950 BRUSSELS

Sydney Cross, Triple Jump

1954 BERNE
Fred Green, 5,000m

Diane Leather, 800m

1958 STOCKHOLM
Robbie Brightwell, 200m
Peter Radford, 100m, 4x100m relay
John Salisbury, 400m, 4x400m relay

Diane Leather, 800m
Carol Quinton, 80m hurdles
Averil Williams, Javelin

1962 BELGRADE
Robbie Brightwell, 400m, 4x400m relay
Berwyn Jones, 100m, 4x100m relay
John Morbey, Long Jump
Peter Radford, 100m, 4x100m relay

Daphne Arden, 100m, 4x100m relay

1966 BUDAPEST
John Sherwood, 400m hurdles, 4x400m relay

Daphne Arden, 100m, 4x100m relay

1969 ATHENS
Howard Payne, Hammer
John Sherwood, 400m hurdles
Ian Stewart, 5,000m
Bill Tancred, Discus

Thelwyn Bateman, 1,500m
Pat Lowe, 800m, 4x400m relay
Sue Reeve, Pentathlon

1971 HELSINKI
Geoff Capes, Shot Put
Howard Payne, Hammer
John Sherwood, 400m hurdles
Peter Stewart, 1,500m

Pat Lowe, 800m, 4x400m relay

1974 ROME
Ainsley Bennett, 200m
Howard Payne, Hammer
Ray Smedley, 1,500m

Blondelle Thompson, 100m hurdles

1978 PRAGUE
Aston Moore, Triple Jump

Sue Reeve, Long Jump
Mary Stewart, 1,500m

1982 ATHENS
Phil Brown, 400m, 4x400m relay

Judy Simpson, Heptathlon

1986 STUTTGART
Phil Brown, 400m, 4x400m relay   Judy Simpson, Heptathlon
Derek Redmond, 400m, 4x400m relay

1990 SPLIT
Phil Brown, 4x400m relay   Lorraine Hanson, 400m
Stewart Faulkner, Long Jump   Clova Court, Heptathlon

1994 HELSINKI
Robert Weir, Discus   Katharine Merry, 200m, 4x100m relay
                                                  Clova Court, 100m hurdles
                                                  Denise Lewis, Long Jump

1998 BUDAPEST
Karl Keska, 5,000m   Michelle Thomas, 4x400m relay
Nathan Morgan, Long Jump   Katharine Merry, 200m
Robert Weir, Discus   Denise Lewis, Heptathlon

2002 MUNICH
Daniel Caines, 400m, 4x400m relay   Ashia Hansen, Triple Jump
Karl Keska, 10,000m   Helen Karagounis, 4x400m relay
Robert Weir, Discus   Helen Frost, 4x400m relay

Empire and Commonwealth Games

Representatives

1930 HAMILTON
Bob Sutherland (*Scotland*), 3 miles, 6 miles

1934 LONDON
Ralph Brown, 440yds hurdles   Gladys Lunn, 800yds, Javelin
Joseph Heath, Javelin   Margaret Cox, Javelin
Stanley Wilson, Javelin

1938 SYDNEY

                                    Winifred Jordan, 440 and 660yds relays
                                                  Gladys Lunn, Javelin

1950 AUKLAND

1954 VANCOUVER
Fred Green, 3 miles

1958 CARDIFF
Robbie Brightwell, 220yds   Iris Mouzer, Shot Put
Denis Field, Triple Jump   Carole Quinton, 80m hurdles
Mike Farrell, 880yds   Averil Williams, Javelin
Mike Rawson, 880yds
Peter Radford, 100yds, 4x110yds
John Salisbury, 440yds, 4x440yds
Nick Whitehead (*Wales*), 110yds, 220yds, 4x110yds
John Woolley (*Wales*), Long Jump

1962 PERTH
Robbie Brightwell, 440yds, 4x440yds   Daphne Arden 100yds, 220yds, 4x110yds
Berwyn Jones, 100yds, 4x110yds
Howard Payne, Hammer
Peter Radford, 100yds, 220yds, 4x110yds
Nick Whitehead (*Wales*), 100yds, 220yds, 4x110yds

1966 KINGSTON

John Morbey, Long Jump
Howard Payne, Hammer
John Sherwood, 440yds hurdles

Daphne Arden, 100yds, 220yds, 4x110yds relay
Pat Lowe, 880yds

1970 EDINBURGH

Geoff Capes, Shot Put
Howard Payne, Hammer
Chris Perry, Steeplechase
John Sherwood, 400m hurdles & Long Jump
Ian Stewart (*Scotland*), 5,000m
Peter Stewar (*Scotland*), 1,500m
Niall McDonald (*Scotland*), Hammer

Pat Lowe, 800m
Sue Reeve, Pentathlon
Ruth Martin-Jones (*Wales*), Pentathlon

1974 CHRISTCHURCH:

Howard Payne, Hammer
John Sherwood, 400m hurdles
Ian Stewart (*Scotland*), 5000m, 10,000m
Bill Tancred, Shot Put, Discus

Gloria Dourass (*Wales*), 800m
Pat Lowe, 800m
Ruth Martin-Jones (*Wales*), Long Jump, 4x100m relay
Mary Stewart (*Scotland*), 1,500m

1978 EDMONTON

Aston Moore, Triple Jump

Ruth Martin-Jones (*Wales*), Pentathlon
Sue Reeve, Long Jump
Mary Stewart, 1,500m
Jackie Zaslona (*Wales*), Javelin

1982 BRISBANE

Phil Brown, 400m, 4x400m relay
John Graham (*Scotland*), Marathon
Aston Moore, Triple Jump & Heptathlon
Ray Smedley, Marathon
Robert Weir, Hammer, Discus

Gill Dainty, 1,500m
Judy Simpson, 100m hurdles

1986 EDINBURGH

Lincoln Asquith, 4x100m relay
Phil Brown, 400m, 4x400m relay
John Graham (*Scotland*), Marathon
Rob Harrison, 1,500m
Aston Moore, Triple Jump

Gill Dainty, 1,500m
Judy Simpson, Heptathlon

1990 AUCKLAND

Phil Brown, 400m
Shane Peacock, Hammer
Stewart Faulkner, Long Jump

Judy Simpson, Heptathlon
Sally Ellis, Marathon

1994 VICTORIA

Robert Weir, Discus
Kevin Brown, Discus

Geraldine McLeod, 200m & 4x100m relay
Clova Court, 100mH & Hepathlon
Denise Lewis, Long Jump & Heptathlon

1998 KUALA LUMPAR

Karl Keska, 5,000m
Bradley Donkin, 800m
Ian Gillespie (*Scotland*), 5,000m
Robert Weir, Discus
Glen Smith, Discus

Denise Lewis, Heptathlon
Clova Court, Heptathlon
Michelle Thomas, 400m, 4x400m relay

2002 MANCHESTER

Mark Lewis-Francis, 100m, 4x100m relay
Daniel Caines, 400m & 4x400m relay

Helen Karagounis, 400m, 4x400m relay
Helen Frost, 400m, 4x400m relay

Nathan Morgan, Long Jump
Robert Weir, Discus
Glen Smith, Discus
Chris Baillie (*Scotland*), 110m hurdles
James Hillier (*Wales*), 400m hurdles

Zoe Derham, Hammer
Tamsin Stephens (*N. Ireland*), 100m hurdles
Lesley Brannan (*Wales*), Hammer
Bev Hartigan, Marathon
Ashia Hansen, Triple Jump
Kelly Sotherton, Heptathlon
Bobby Aloysius (India), High Jump

Medal Winners at major International Championships
Olympic Games:

Gold — Arthur Robertson, 3 miles team race 1908
Godfrey Brown, 4x400m relay 1936
Mark Lewis-Francis, 4x100m relay 2004

Denise Lewis, Heptathlon 2000

Silver — Arthur Robertson, Steeplechase 1908
Godfrey Brown, 400m 1936
Joe Blewitt, 3,000m team race 1920
Bert Macdonald, 3,000m team race 1924
John Cooper, 400m hurdles 1964
John Cooper, 4x400m relay 1964
Robbie Brightwell, 4x400m relay 1964
Phil Brown, 4x400m relay 1984
Adam Nelson (USA), Shot Put 2000
Adam Nelson (USA), Shot Put 2004

Bronze — Peter Radford, 100m 1960
Peter Radford, 4x100m relay 1960
Nick Whitehead, 4x100m relay 1960
John Sherwood, 400m hurdles 1968
Ian Stewart, 5,000m 1972

Katharine Merry, 400m 2000
Kelly Sotherton, Heptathlon 2004

World Championships:

Gold — Derek Redmond, 4x400m relay 1991

Silver — Phil Brown, 4x400m relay 1987
Derek Redmond, 4x400m relay 1987
Adam Nelson (USA), Shot Put 2001
Adam Nelson (USA), Shot Put 2003
Mark Lewis-Francis, 4x100m relay 2003

Denise Lewis, Heptathlon 1997
Denise Lewis, Heptathlon 1999

Bronze — Phil Brown, 4x400m relay 1983
Ainsley Bennett, 4x400m relay 1983

European Championships:

Gold — Godfrey Brown, 400m 1938
Robbie Brightwell, 400m 1962
Mike Rawson, 800m 1958
Ian Stewart, 5,000m 1969
John Salisbury, 4x400m relay 1958
Derek Redmond, 4x400m relay 1986
Denise Lewis, Heptathlon 1998
Daniel Caines, 4x400m relay 2002

Pat Lowe, 4x400m relay 1969

Silver — Godfrey Brown, 4x400m relay 1938
Peter Radford, 4x100m relay 1958
John Salisbury, 400m 1958

Winifred Jordan, 100m 1946
Winifred Jordan, 200m 1946
Diane Leather, 800m 1954

Robbie Brightwell, 4x400m relay 1962
Phil Brown, 4x400m relay 1982

Diane Leather, 800m 1958
Carole Quinton, 4x100m relay 1958
Pat Lowe, 800m 1971

Bronze   Godfrey Brown, 4x100m relay 1938
Peter Radford, 100m 1958
Berwyn Jones, 4x100m relay 1962
Daniel Caines, 400m 2002

Daphne Arden, 4x100m relay 1962
Judy Simpson, Heptathlon 1986
Katharine Merry, 4x400m relay 1998

Empire & Commonwealth Games:

Gold   Peter Radford, 4x110yds relay 1958
Peter Radford, 4x110yds relay 1962
Howard Payne, Hammer 1962
Howard Payne, Hammer 1966
Howard Payne, Hammer 1970
Ian Stewart, 5,000m 1970
John Sherwood, 400m hurdles 1970
Robert Weir, Hammer 1982
Phil Brown, 4x400m relay 1982
Phil Brown, 4x400m relay 1986
Robert Weir, Discus 1998
Nathan Morgan, Long Jump 2002
Daniel Caines, 4x400m relay 2002

Gladys Lunn, 880yds 1934
Gladys Lunn, Javelin 1934
Sue Reeve, Long Jump 1978
Mary Stewart, 1,500m 1978
Judy Simpson, Heptathlon 1986
Denise Lewis, Heptathlon 1994
Denise Lewis, Heptathlon 1998
Ashia Hansen, Triple Jump 2002

Silver   Fred Green, 3 miles 1954
John Salisbury, 4x440yds relay 1958
Robbie Brightwell, 440yds 1962
Robbie Brightwell, 4x440yds relay 1962
Howard Payne, Hammer 1974
Lincoln Asquith, 4x100m relay 1986

Winifred Jordan, 660yds relay 1938
Carole Quinton, 80m hurdles 1958
Daphne Arden, 4x110yds relay 1962
Daphne Arden, 4x110yds relay 1966
Pat Lowe, 800m 1970
Gill Dainty, 1,500m 1982
Judy Simpson, Heptathlon 1982
Helen Karagounis, 4x100m relay 2002
Helen Frost, 4x100m relay 2002

Bronze   Ralph Brown, 440yds hurdles 1934
Mike Rawson, 880yds 1958
Nick Whitehead (Wales), 4x110yds relay 1962
Bill Tancred, Discus 1970
John Sherwood, 4x400m relay 1970
Aston Moore, Triple Jump 1978
Aston Moore, Triple Jump 1982
Phil Brown, 400m 1986
Robert Weir, Discus 1994
Robert Weir, Discus 2002

Gladys Lunn, Javelin 1938
Winifred Jordan, 440yds relay 1938
Averil Williams, Javelin 1958
Ruth Martin-Jones (Wales), Long Jump 1974
Karen Pugh, Discus 1986
Judy Simpson, Heptathlon 1990

British Empire v. USA

A series of 11 matches began in 1920 and ended in 1964. All meetings were staged shortly after an Olympic Games, with the exception of one in 1930 which followed the first Empire Games in Hamilton, Ontario.

1920 LONDON (Queens Club)

1924 LONDON (Stamford Bridge)
4 x 1 mile relay. British Empire 2nd: 17:47.6mins
(W. Porter, Cyril Ellis, Bert Macdonald, H. Johnston)

4 x 2 laps Steeplechase. British Empire 8:14.2mins - 2nd
(W.F. Boardman, F. Blackett, W. Tatham, E. Montague)

3 miles team race: 6 runners 4 to count.
Eddie Webster: 9th in race (non counter)

4 x 880yds. British Empire 1st 7:56.8mins
(E. Mountain, D. Oldfield, Harry Houghton, H. Stallard)

Javelin Throw. Aggregate of teams of 3. Empire 2nd – 448ft 11ins
Jock Dalrymple: 126ft 7in.

1928 LONDON (Stamford Bridge)
4 x 1 mile. Empire 1st – 17:22.6mins
(Docherty, Starr, Whyte, Cyril Ellis)

3 miles team race: 6 runners – 4 scorers
Fred Light: Empire 1st scorer, 2nd in race.

1930 CHICAGO (Soldier Field)
3 miles team race: 6 runners – 4 scorers
Robert Sutherland: 5th – 4th scorer for Empire

1932 SAN FRANCISCO

1936 LONDON (White City)
4 x 440yds. Empire 1st
(W. Roberts, W. Fritz, G. Rampling, Godfrey Brown)

1948 LONDON (White City)

1952 LONDON (White City)
3 miles team race: 5th Fred Green 14:04mins

1956 SYDNEY
4 x 880yds. Empire 7:42.2mins – 2nd
(Mike Rawson, Mike Farrell, B. Hewson, D. Johnson)

Medley Relay. Empire 3:22.6mins – 1st
(John Salisbury, Cockburn, Hogan, Butchart)

1960 LONDON (White City)
Hammer. Howard Payne 194ft 2ins – 4th

4 x 110yds. Empire 40.1 – 2nd
(Peter Radford, D. Jones, S. Anteo, T. Robinson)

4 x 440yds. Empire 3:07.1 – 2nd
(T. Tobacco, K. Gosper, Robbie Brightwell, Milka Singh)

Non–scoring women's events
80m Hurdles
Carole Quinton, 10.9 – 1st (equalled British record)

4 x 110yds. Empire 46.1 – 2nd
(Carole Quinton, D. Hyman, J. Smart, M. Bignal)

1964 OSAKA (USA v. Commonwealth v. Japan)
4 x 400 Empire 3:08.3mins – 2nd
(Graham, Warden, Vassella, John Sherwood)

Hammer
Howard Payne 59.75m – 4th

Women
4 x 100m. Empire 46.9 – 2nd
(Piotrowski, D. Hyman, Daphne Arden, Black)

Club Records

Senior Men

100m	10.04	Mark Lewis-Francis	July 5 2002	St Denis (France
200m	20.42	Ainsley Bennett	Sept 12 1979	Mexico City
400m	44.50	Derek Redmond	Sept 2 1987	Rome
800m	1:46.01mins	Rob Harrison	June 14 1986	Bratislava
1,500m	3:35.74mins	Rob Harrison	May 26 1986	Cwmbran
1 mile	3:53.85mins	Rob Harrison	July 15 1986	Nice
3,000m	7:46.83mins	Ian Stewart	May 26 1976	Crystal Palace
5,000m	13:18.06mins	Ian Gillespie	July 16 1997	Hechtel (Belgium)
10,000m	27:44.09mins	Karl Keska	Sept 25 2000	Sydney
Marathon	2:09:28hrs	John Graham	May 23 1981	Rotterdam
110m hurdles	13.96	Steve Buckeridge	May 31 1986	Lisbon
400m hurdles	49.03	John Sherwood	Oct 15 1968	Mexico City
3,000m St	8:38.67mins	John Hartigan	June 21 1986	Crystal Palace
High Jump	2.23m	Mark Lakey	Aug 29 1982	Amsterdam
Long Jump	8.26m	Nathan Morgan	July 20 2003	Hamburg
Triple Jump	17.01m	Eric McCalla	Aug 3 1984	Los Angeles
Pole Vault	5.36m	Scott Simpson	Aug 10 2003	Cwmbran
Shot Put	21.26m	Adam Nelson	Aug 2003	Paris
Discus	65.11m	Glen Smith	July 18 1999	Barking
Hammer	75.08m	Robert Weir	Oct 3 1982	Brisbane
Javelin	65.78m	Nigel Bevan	July 31 1999	Birmingham
Decathlon	7643pts	Tom Leeson	Sept 8 1985	Arles (France)
4x100m	39.86	Asquith, Campbell, Bennett, Rosswess	Aug 16 1987	Birmingham
4x400m	3:07.38mins	Basyni 48.0, Caines 46.0 Yiend 47.0, Ladejo 46.2	Aug 16 2003	Bedford

Senior Women

100m	11.34	Katharine Merry	June 25 1994	Birmingham
200m	22.76	Katharine Merry	July 25 2000	Barcelona
400m	49.59	Katharine Merry	June 11 2001	Athens
800m	2:01.36mins	Gill Dainty	Aug 31 1983	Koblenz
1,500m	4:06.00mins	Mary Stewart	June 24 1977	Middlesborough
1 mile	4:31.65mins	Gill Dainty	June 26 1982	Oslo
3,000m	8:59.65mins	Gill Dainty	July 20 1983	Luxembourg
10,000m	33:10.25mins	Shireen Barbour	July 5 1986	Oslo
Marathon	2:33:24hrs	Sally Ellis	Apr 23 1989	London
100m hurdles	13.04	Clova Court	Aug 9 1994	Helsinki
400m hurdles	56.70	Lorraine Hanson	Aug 13 1989	Birmingham
High Jump	1.92m	Judy Simpson	Aug 8 1983	Helsinki
Long Jump	6.69m	Sue Reeve	June 10 1979	Furth
	6.69m	Denise Lewis	July 30 2000	Talence (France)
Shot Put	16.38m	Jean Roberts	Apr 9 1972	Birmingham
Discus	55.90m	Jean Roberts	Jan 15 1974	Melbourne
Javelin (pre-1999)	56.50m	Denise Lewis	Aug 11 1996	
Javelin (1999 style)	51.13m	Denise Lewis	Aug 19 2000	Bedford
Heptathlon	6831pts	Denise Lewis	July 30 2000	Talence (France)
4x100m	44.52	Maylor, Davies Wilson, Merry	June 4 2000	Gateshead
4x400m	3:36.35mins	Waldo, Hanson Levermore, Stanton	Aug 10 1991	Gateshead

Indoor All-Time Best Performances

60m

6.51	Mark Lewis-Francis	Lisbon	March 11 2001
6.54	Michael Rosswess	Paris	March 11 1994
6.62	Lincoln Asquith	Cosford	Jan 23 1988
6.75	Michael Tietz	Birmingham	Feb 6 1999
6.77	Curtis Browne	Birmingham	Feb 3 1996
6.77	Nathan Morgan	Birmingham	Feb 6 1999
6.81	Ainsley Bennett	Cosford	Jan 26 1980

(Lincoln Asquith registered 5 timings inside 6.70, his best 10 timings average 6.69)

100m

10.34	Mark Lewis-Francis	Perry Barr	Feb 6 2003

200m

20.62	Daniel Caines	Vienna	Mar 1 2002
21.26	Richard Knowles	Birmingham	Jan 16 2000
21.63	Ben Lewis	Birmingham	Jan 19 2002
21.68	Lincoln Asquith	Birmingham	Feb 26 1993
21.77	Julian Thomas	Birmingham	Jan 26 2003
21.78	Phil Brown	Berlin	Feb 3 1979
21.8	*Ainsley Bennett*	*Cosford*	*Jan 29 1982*

400m

45.43	Daniel Caines	Birmingham	Mar 16 2003
46.43	Ainsley Bennett	Budapest	Mar 6 1983
46.84	Richard Knowles	Birmingham	Jan 29 2000
46.87*	Mark Thomas	Lincoln	Mar 1 1986
	Phil Brown	Cosford	Mar 9 1985
47.32	Derek Redmond	Ghent	Jan 26 1992
	Brad Yiend	Birmingham	Mar 1 2003

*(Assessment: 440yds in 47.11)

600yds

1:11.6mins	Mike Rawson	Boston	Feb 7 1959

600m

1:18.92mins	Colin Szwed	Cosford	Mar 13 1982
1:19.5mins	John Goodacre	Cosford	Mar 1 1978

800m

1:49.63mins	John Goodacre	San Sebastian	Feb 12 1977
1:49.7+mins	Colin Szwed	Sentfenburg	Feb 27 1982

+(oversized track)

1,500m

3:42.8mins	Ray Smedley	Cosford	Feb 17 1973
3:43.53mins	Alan Salter	Cosford	Jan 30 1982
3:44.46mins	Ian Gillespie	Birmingham	Feb 20 1993

1 mile

4:00.30mins	Alan Salter	Cosford	Mar 13 1982
4:02.6mins	Peter Stewart	Cosford	Feb 1 1969
4:03.4mins	Ian Stewart	Kansas City	Jan 24 1970

3,000m

7:49.86mins	Ian Gillespie	Birmingham	Feb 23 1997
7:50.0mins	Ian Stewart	Cosford	Jan 29 1970
7:53.6mins	Peter Stewart	Sofia	Mar 14 1971

7:54.43mins	Ray Smedley	Gothenburg	Mar 10 1974
7:58.22mins	Alan Salter	Cosford	Mar 13 1987
7:58.65mins	John Hartigan	Budapest	Feb 8 1987
7:59.79mins	Ross Copestake	Cosford	Jan 26 1985
7:59.88mins	Ashworth Laukam	Cosford	Jan 26 1985

60m hurdles

7.77	Steve Buckeridge	Cosford	Feb 4 1989
7.78	Chris Baillie	Glasgow	Jan 26 2003
7.79	Alan Tapp	Cosford	Jan 25 1986
7.80	David Humphrys	Cosford	Feb 17 1990
8.09	Tom Leeson	Cosford	Jan 11 1986
8.10	Edward Dunford	Sheffield	Feb 7 2004
8.0	*Stuart Storey*	*Cosford*	*Feb 22 1969*

Pole Vault

5.31m	Scott Simpson	Glasgow	Feb 23 2002

Long Jump

8.05m	Stewart Faulkner	Seville	Feb 27 1990
7.38m	Nathan Morgan	Budapest	Feb 10 2001
7.74m	Aston Moore	Cosford	Jan 10 1981
7.73m	John Morbey	New York	Feb 22 1964
7.51m	Jonathan Moore	Birmingham	Feb 20 2004
7.50m	Trevor Sinclair	Vittel	Feb 4 1984
7.50m	Kevin Liddington	Cosford	Mar 19 1989

Women
60m

7.34	Katharine Merry	Glasgow	Jan 23 1994
7.36	Geraldine McLeod	Birmingham	Feb 3 1996
7.43	Sarah Oxley	Birmingham	Jan 12 2002
7.44	Samantha Davies	Birmingham	Jan 13 2001
7.47	Clova Court	Birmingham	Feb 19 1994
7.5	Ashia Hansen	Birmingham	Jan 25 1998
7.52	Donna Maylor	Neubrandenburg	Mar 4 2000
7.4	*Daphne Arden*	*Stuttgart*	*Mar 22 1963*

200m

22.83	Katharine Merry	Birmingham	Feb 14 1999
23.30	Sarah Oxley	Birmingham	Jan 13 2002
23.82	Geraldine McLeod	Birmingham	Jan 27 1996
24.08	Ena Waldo	Birmingham	Mar 15 1992
24.09	Kelly Sotherton	Birmingham	Feb 23 2003
24.22	Clova Court	Birmingham	Feb 4 1996
24.29	Helen Karagounis	Cardiff	Feb 29 2004
24.50	Michelle Thomas	Birmingham	Jan 16 2000
24.69	Debby Bunn	Berlin	Feb 3 1979
	Helen Frost	Birmingham	Jan 30 2000

300m

39.17	Geraldine McLeod	Birmingham	Jan 3 1994
39.26	Suzanne Guise	Cosford	Mar 12 1988
38.8	*Michelle Thomas*	*Birmingham*	*Jan 30 1999*
39.3	*Ena Waldo*	*Cosford*	*Feb 27 1988*

400m

50.53	Katharine Merry	Birmingham	Feb 18 2001
52.53	Helen Karagounis	Budapest	Mar 6 2004
53.62	Michelle Thomas	Birmingham	Feb 14 1999

54.14	Kelly Sotherton	Birmingham	Mar 2 2003
54.54	Suzanne Guise	Cosford	Jan 23 1988
55.39	Janet Levermore	Glasgow	Jan 27 1991
54.6+	*Elizabeth Eddy*	*Senftenburg*	*Feb 17 1978*

(+oversized track)

600m

1:31.2mins	Suzanne Guise	Cosford	Mar 24 1990

800m

2:04.7mins	Mary Stewart	San Sebastian	Feb 12 1977
2:06.2mins	Gill Dainty	Senftenburg	Feb 27 1982
2:07.9mins	Gloria Rickard	Cosford	Dec 8 1973

1,000m

2:45.11mins	Gill Dainty	Sherbrooke	Feb 7 1982
2:48.0mins	Gloria Rickard	Cosford	Jan 8 1972

1,500m

4:08.1mins	Mary Stewart	Dortmund	Feb 19 1977
4:17.6mins	Gill Dainty	Cosford	Jan 24 1981

3,000m

9:09.6mins	Mary Stewart	Cosford	Mar 20 1976
9:37.4mins	Thelwyn Bateman	Cosford	Jan 12 1980

60m hurdles

8.12	Clova Court	Glasgow	Feb 12 1994
8.21	Judy Simpson	Sindelfingen	Feb 1 1985
8.29	Kerry Robin-Millerchip	Cosford	Jan 23 1988
8.30	Denise Lewis	Birmingham	Feb 8 1997
8.36	Tamsin Stephens	Sheffield	Feb 8 2004
8.41	Blondel Caines	Cosford	Feb 11 1988
8.55	Kelly Sotherton	Cardiff	Mar 23 2003

High Jump

1.85m	Judy Simpson	Sindelfingen	Feb 1 1985
1.84m	Claire Summerfield	Cosford	Jan 23 1987

World Indoor Championships
Representatives

1987	Indianapolis		
1989	Budapest	Michael Rosswess	60m
1991	Seville	Michael Rosswess	60m
1993	Toronto	Clova Court	60m hurdles
1995	Barcelona	Michael Rosswess	60m
1997	Paris	Richard Knowles	4x400m relay
		Katharine Merry	200m
		Clova Court	60m hurdles
		Michelle Thomas	4x400m relay
1999	Maebashi (Japan)		

2001	Lisbon	Mark Lewis-Francis	60m
		Daniel Caines	400m and 4x400m
		Du'aine Thorne-Ladejo	4x400m
		Adam Nelson (*USA*)	Shot Putt
2003	Birmingham	Mark Lewis-Francis	60m
		Daniel Caines	400m and 4x400m

World Indoor Medal Winners:

Gold	Daniel Caines	400m	2001
Silver	Daniel Caines	400m	2003
	Adam Nelson (USA)	Shot	2001
Bronze	Mark Lewis-Francis	60m	2001
	Daniel Caines	4x400m relay	2003

European Indoor Championships

The championships in the 1960s were called European Indoor Games. The first official championships were those held in Vienna in 1970. From then they were held annually until 1990 when it was decided to move to biennial championships to be held on alternate years to the World Indoor Championships.

1966	Dortmund		
1967	Prague		
1968	Madrid		
1969	Belgrade	Ian Stewart	3,000m
		Sue Reeve	Long Jump
1970	Vienna		
1971	Sofia	Peter Stewart	3,000m
1972	Grenoble		
1973	Rotterdam		
1974	Gothenburg	Ray Smedley	3,000m
		Mary Stewart	1,500m
		Ruth Martin-Jones	Long Jump
1975	Katowice	Ian Stewart	3,000m
		Mary Stewart	1,500m
1976	Munich	Sue Reeve	Long Jump
		Ray Smedley	3,000m
1977	San Sebastian	Ray Smedley	3,000m
		Mary Stewart	1,500m
		Sue Reeve	Long Jump
1978	Milan	Sue Reeve	Long Jump
1979			
1980	Stuttgart		

1981	Grenoble	Gill Dainty	1,500m
1982	Milan		
1983	Budapest	Ainsley Bennett	400m
1984	Gothenburg		
1985	Athens		
1986	Madrid		
1987	Lievin		
1988	Budapest	Mark Thomas	400m
		Steve Buckeridge	60m hurdles
1989	The Hague	Michael Rosswess	60m
		Steve Buckeridge	60m hurdles
		Stewart Faulkner	Long Jump
1990	Glasgow	Rob Harrison	1,500m
		Stewart Faulkner	Long Jump
		Sylvia Black	3,000m walk
1992	Genoa	Michael Rosswess	60m
1994	Paris	Michael Rosswess	60m
		Clova Court	60m hurdles
1996	Stockholm	Denise Lewis	Long Jump
1998	Valencia		
2000	Ghent	Daniel Caines	400m
		Richard Knowles	4x400m relay
2002	Vienna	Mark Lewis-Francis	60m
		Daniel Caines	200m
		Ashia Hansen	Triple Jump

Medals				
Gold	Ian Stewart	3,000m	1969
	Peter Stewart	3,000m	1971
	Ian Stewar	3,000m	1975
	Mary Stewart	1,500m	1977
Silver	Sue Reeve	(Long Jump)	1969
	Ainsley Bennett	400m	1983
	Mark Lewis-Francis	60m	2002
	Ashia Hansen	(Triple Jump)	2002
Bronze	Ray Smedley	3,000m	1976
	Sue Reeve	(Long Jump)	1978
	Michael Rosswess	60m	1992

European Junior Championships

This competition effectively began with a meeting in Warsaw in September 1964. It was followed by meetings in Odessa (1966) and Leipzeig (1968) but the first to be granted official status was held at the Colombe Stadium in Paris 11-13 September 1970.

1970	Paris	John Boggis	3,000m
1973	Duisberg	Ainsley Bennett	200m, 4x100m
		Mary Stewart	1,500m
1975	Athens	Aston Moore	Long Jump, Triple Jump
1977	Donetsk	Colin Szwed	800m
1979	Bydgoszcz	Phil Brown	4x100m relay
		Trevor Sinclair	Long Jump
		Alan Salter	3,000m
		Linda Callow	4x400m relay
1981	Utrecht	Phil Brown	4x100m relay
1983	Schwechat	Lincoln Asquith	100m, 200m, 4x100m relay
		Derek Redmond	400m
		Karen Pugh	Discus
1985	Cottbus		
1987	Birmingham	Stewart Faulkner	Long Jump
1989	Varazdin	Kevin Liddington	Long Jump
		Katharine Merry	100m, 200m
1991	Thessaloniki	Katharine Merry	200m, 400m
		Denise Lewis	Heptathlon
1993	San Sebastian	Darius Burrrows	5,000m
		Katharine Merry	100m, 200m, 4x100m relay
1995	Nyiregyhaza (Hun)		
1997	Ljubljana		
1999	Riga	Mark Lewis-Francis	100m, 4x100 relay
		Donna Maylor	100m
		Helen Thieme	400m and 4x400m relay
		Zoe Derham	Hammer
2001	Grosseto	Mark Lewis-Francis	100m, 4x100m relay
		Jonathan Moore	Triple Jump
2003	Tampere (Fin)	Jonathan Moore	Long Jump

Medal Winners

Gold	Aston Moore	Triple Jump	1975
	Lincoln Asquith	100m	1983
	Mark Lewis-Francis	100m	2001
	Katharine Merry	200m	1993
Silver	John Boggis	3,000m	1975
	Phil Brown	4x100m relay	1979
	Stewart Faulkner	Long Jump	1987
	Katharine Merry	100m	1993

| Bronze | Lincoln Asquith | 200m | 1983 |
| | Lincoln Asquith | 4x100m relay | 1983 |

World Junior Championships
Competitors

1986	Athens		
1988	Sudbury (Can)	Stewart Faulkner	Long Jump
1990	Plovdiv (Bul)	Jason John	100m
		Katharine Merry	100m, 4x100m relay.
1992	Seoul		
1994	Lisbon	Darius Burrows	5,000m
1996	Sydney	Nathan Morgan	Long Jump
1998	Annecy (France)		
2000	Santiago (Chile)	Mark Lewis-Francis	100m, 4x100m relay
		Donna Maylor	100m, 4x100m relay
		Helen Thieme (Karagounis)	4x400m relay
2002	Kingston (Jam)		

Medal Winners

Gold	Mark Lewis-Francis	100m	2000
	Mark Lewis-Francis	4x100m	2000
	Helen Thieme	4x400m	2000

Silver

| Bronze | Nathan Morgan | Long Jump | 1996 |

World Youth Championships
Representatives

1999	Bydgoscz	Mark Lewis-Francis	100m
		Donna Maylor	100m
2001	Debrecen (Hun)		
2003	Sherbrooke (Can)	Andrew Thomas	(Discus)
		Sam Herrington	(Discus)

Medal Winners

| Gold | Mark Lewis-Francis | 100m | 1999 |

Veteran Men: Records (manual or automatic timing)

100m	11.4	Barrington Williams	July 9 1997	Burton
200m	23.2	Barrington Williams	Sept 20 1997	Birmingham
400m	48.74	Darrell Maynard	Aug 22 2002	Potsdam
800m	1:52.70mins	Darrell Maynard	Aug 17 2002	Potsdam
1,500m	4:02.91mins	John Potts	June 15 1990	Birmingham
1 mile	4:30.0mins	John Potts	Aug 26 1989	Sutton Coldfield
3,000m	8:50.5mins	John Potts	July 22 1987	Cheltenham

5,000m	15:10.20mins	Mike Cadman	July 29 1999	Chester-le-Street
10,000m	33:09.1mins	Mike Cadman	July 4 1999	Solihull
110m hurdles	23.6	Chris Weir	July 24 1993	Telford
400m hurdles	70.9	Chris Weir	July 24 1993	Telford
3,000m S	10:49.0mins	Chris Weir	Aug 14 1993	
High Jump	1.60m	Joe Reece	Aug 6 1995	Exeter
Pole Vault	2:60m	Joe Reece	June 26 1994	Solihull
Long Jump	7.48m	Barrington Williams	June 1 1998	Birmingham
Triple Jump	13.85m	Barrington Williams	July 6 1996	Birmingham
Discus	63.03m	Robert Weir	July 21 2001	Bedford
Javelin	41.56m	John Murphy	June 10 1990	Solihull
Hammer	70.88m	Howard Payne	June 29 1974	Warsaw
3K Walk	12:46.1mins	Bob Care	May 23 1990	Birmingham
5K Walk	22:09.8mins	Bob Care	June 10 1990	Solihull
10K Walk	47:22.0mins	Bob Care	Aug 14 1994	Solihull

Veteran Women

100m	11.69	Clova Court	May 29 1995	Bedford
200m	23.63	Clova Court	Aug 23 1997	London
300m	44.1	Ann Haywood	Apr 13 1997	Redditch
400m	58.1	Gloria Rickard	July 25 1981	Wolverhampton
800m	2:18.5mins	Gloria Rickard	July 26 1981	Wolverhampton
1,500m	5:00.7mins	Natalie Adkins	May 14 1998	Burton
3,000m	10:21.2mins	Sally Ellis	Aug 8 1993	Birmingham
5,000m	18:09.68mins	Natalie Adkins	July 27 1997	Birmingham
1 hour	13,567m	Christine Rollason	Aug 3 1997	Leamington
80m hurdles	16.5	Carol Morris	Aug 19 1990	Solihull
100m hurdles	13.14	Clova Court	July 26 1997	Budapest
High Jump	1.55m	Marina Semanova	July 31 1999	Birmingham
Long Jump	5.72m	Clova Court	June 1 1997	Sheffield
Triple Jump	7.13m	Carol Morris	June 17 1992	Telford
Shot	14.44m	Clova Court	May 25 1995	Bedford
Discus	24.70m	Lyn Orbell	May 6 1995	Glasgow
Javelin	52.26m	Clova Court	Sept 24 1997	London
1,500m walk	8:27.6mins	Beryl Randle	Sept 8 1988	Warley
2000m walk	9:01.5mins	Sylvia Black	July 21 1993	Telford
3,000m walk	14:20.1mins	Sylvia Black	July 19 1997	Birmingham
5,000m walk	23:26.72mins	Sylvia Black	July 12 1997	Birmingham

Veteran World Championships
Medal Winners

Gold	Toronto	1975	Howard Payne	M40	Hammer
	Miyasaki	1993	Allan Meddings	M65	100m
	Gateshead	1999	Allan Meddings	M70	100m
	Gateshead	1999	Allan Meddings	M70	200m
Silver	Turku	1991	John Potts	M45	500m
	Miyazaki	1993	Allan Meddings	M65	200m
	Buffalo	1995	Bob Care	M45	5K walk
Bronze	Buffalo	1995	Allan Meddings	M65	100m
	Buffalo	1995	John Potts	M50	1,500m
	Gateshead	1999	Mike Fox	M65	800m
	Gateshead	1999	Allan Meddings	M70	4x100m relay

AAA Champions

1989		Phil Brown		400m
		Stewart Faulkner		Long Jump

1990	Stewart Faulkner	Long Jump
1991	Derek Redmond	400m
1993	Robert Weir	Discus
1994	Kevin Brown	Discus
1996	Robert Weir	Discus
1997	Robert Weir	Discus
1998	Robert Weir	Discus
	Karl Keska	5,000m
1999	Robert Weir	Discus
2000	Robert Weir	Discus
2001	Nathan Morgan	Long Jump
	Glen Smith	Discus
2002	Mark Lewis-Francis	100m
	Robert Weir	Discus
2003	Daniel Caines	400m

WAAA Champions

1994	Katharine Merry	100m
	Katharine Merry	200m
	Clova Court	100m hurdles
1996	Denise Lewis	Long Jump
1997	Katharine Merry	200m
1998	Katharine Merry	200m
	Denise Lewis	Long Jump
1999	Katharine Merry	400m
2001	Sarah Reilly	200m
2002	Ashia Hansen	Triple Jump
2003	Helen Karagounis	400m

Birchfielders setting or equalling British Records

Men
100yds

9.4	Peter Radford	Wolverhampton	May 30 1959
9.4	Peter Radford	Wolverhampton	May 28 1960

Automatic timing

9.84	Peter Radford	Cardiff	July 19 1958
9.81	Peter Radford	Cardiff	July 19 1958
9.80	Peter Radford	Cardiff	July 19 1958
9.62	Peter Radford	London	July 16 1960

100m

10.31	Peter Radford	Paris	Sept 13 1958

200m

20.8	Peter Radford	Paris	Sept 14 1958
20.5	Peter Radford	Wolverhampton	May 28 1960 (World record)
Automatic timing			
21.25	Peter Radford	Rome	Sept 2 1960
21.12	Peter Radford	Rome	Sept 2 1960
21.04	Peter Radford	Rome	Sept 3 1960

220yds

21.0	Peter Radford	Birmingham	Oct 4 1958
21.0	Peter Radford	Oxford	Apr 28 1958
21.0	Peter Radford	Cambridge	May 3 1960
20.5	Peter Radford	Wolverhampton	May 28 1960 (World record)
Automatic timing			
21.54	Robbie Brightwell	Cardiff	July 22 1958
21.47	Peter Radford	Cardiff	July 22 1958

300m

32.99	Ainsley Bennett	London	July 20 1974

400m

48.35	Godfrey Brown	Berlin	Aug 6 1936
47.31	Godfrey Brown	Berlin	Aug 7 1936
46.68	Godfrey Brown	Berlin	Aug 7 1936
46.31	Robbie Brightwell	Rome	Sept 3 1960
46.25	Robbie Brightwell	Rome	5 Sept 1960
46.13	Robbie Brightwell	Tokyo	Oct 17 1964
45.79	Robbie Brightwell	Tokyo	Oct 18 1964
45.75	Robbie Brightwell	Tokyo	Oct 19 1964
44.82	Derek Redmond	Oslo	July 27 1985
44.50	Derek Redmond	Rome	Sept 1 1987

440yds

47.7	Godfrey Brown	Cambridge (USA)	July 10 1937
47.6	Godfrey Brown	London	Aug 1 1938

880yds

1:52.2mins	Godfrey Brown	Princeton (USA)	July 17 1937

1,000yds

2:11.2mins	Cyril Ellis	London	Sept 7 1927 (World Record)

1,000m

2:27.8mins	Cyril Ellis	Manchester	July 30 1927

1,500m

3:39.0mins	Ian Stewart	London	Sept 1 1969
3:39.0mins	Peter Stewart	Warsaw	Sept 12 1970
3:38.22mins	Peter Stewart	London	July 15 1972

1 mile

3:55.3mins	Peter Stewart	London	June 10 1972

2 miles

8:26.8mins	Peter Stewart	London	Sept 5 1972
8:22.0mins	Ian Stewart	Stockholm	Aug 14 1972

3 miles

13:32.2mins	Fred Green	London	July 10 1954 (World record)

5,000m

15:01.2mins	Arthur Robertson	Stockholm	Sept 13 1908 (World Record)
13:22.8mins	Ian Stewart	Edinburgh	July 25 1970

3,000m Steeplechase

9:57.6mins	Eddie Webster	Glasgow	Aug 6 1927

2-mile Steeplechase

10:46.0mins	Fred Ward	Coventry	July 22 1922
10:23.2mins	Eddie Webster	Northampton	Aug 9 1924

400m hurdles

51.0	John Cooper	London	Aug 14 1963
50.5	John Cooper	Volgograd	Sept 29 1963
50.57	John Cooper	Tokyo	Oct 14 1964
50.40	John Cooper	Tokyo	Oct 15 1964
50.19	John Cooper	Tokyo	Oct 16 1964
49.37	John Sherwood	Mexico City	Oct 14 1968

440yds hurdles

51.1	John Cooper	London	July 11 1964
51.10	John Sherwood	London	July 9 1966
50.94	John Sherwood	London	July 15 1967

4x200m

1:28.1mins	Radford-Whitehead-Salisbury-Brightwell	Birmingham	July 18 1959

Long Jump

7.23m	John Morbey	London	Aug 23 1963

Triple Jump

16.68m	Aston Moore	London (CP)	June 23 1978

Shot

19.56m	Geoff Capes	London	Apr 26 1972
19.75m	Geoff Capes	Helsinki	July 26 1972
19.82m	Geoff Capes	Helsinki	July 26 1972
20.18m	Geoff Capes	Helsinki	July 26 1972
20.27m	Geoff Capes	London	July 14 1973

Discus

57.96m	Bill Tancred	Loughborough	Mar 29 1972
59.02m	Bill Tancred	Loughborough	April 7 1972
59.22m	Bill Tancred	Oxford	April 26 1972
59.42m	Bill Tancred	London	May 10 1972
59.58m	Bill Tancred	London	May 10 1972
59.80m	Bill Tancred	Loughborough	June 3 1972
60.56m	Bill Tancred	Loughborough	June 7 1972
61.94m	Bill Tancred	Loughborough	June 7 1972
61.96m	Bill Tancred	Warley	May 27 1973
62.10m	Bill Tancred	London	Aug 11 1973
62.92m	Bill Tancred	London	Aug 12 1973
63.98m	Bill Tancred	Loughborough	Oct 13 1973
64.32m	Bill Tancred	Woodford	Aug 10 1974

(Also, 64.94 at unsanctioned meeting, Loughborough, 21 July 1974)

Hammer

65.28m	Howard Payne	Portsmouth	Aug 7 1968
65.68m	Howard Payne	Portsmouth	Sept 14 1968

65.98m	Howard Payne	Mexico City	Oct 5 1968
68.06m	Howard Payne	Mexico City	Oct 16 1968
68.20m	Howard Payne	Warley	June 20 1970
68.82m	Howard Payne	London	July 11 1970
69.24m	Howard Payne	Solihull	Sept 26 970
75.08m	Robert Weir	Brisbane	Oct 3 1982

Javelin

56.82m	Jock Dalrymple	London	June 28 1924

Decathlon

4789pts	David Slack	Paris	July 11/12 1924

Women

100yds

10.6	Daphne Arden	London	July 4 1964

220yds

23.6	Daphne Arden	London	July 4 1964

400m

56. 3	Diane Leather	Budapest	Oct 1 1955

440yds

56.6	Diane Leather	London	Aug 21 1954

800m

2:22.8mins	Gladys Lunn	Birmingham	July 26 1930
2:18.2mins	Gladys Lunn	London	Aug 16 1930
2:08.9mins	Diane Leather	Berne	Aug 26 1954
2:08.6mins	Diane Leather	Bordeaux	Sept 4 1955
2:07.7mins	Diane Leather	Moscow	Sept 11 1955
2:06.9mins	Diane Leather	Prague	Sept 14 1955
2:06.8mins	Diane Leather	London	Aug 23 1957
2:06.6mins	Diane Leather	Stockholm	Aug 24 1958

880yds

2:34.6mins	Phyllis Hall	Paris	Aug 20 1922
2:18.2mins	Gladys Lunn	London	Aug 16 1930
2:09.0mins	Diane Leather	London	June 19 1954

1,000m

3:33.8mins	Phyllis Hall	London	Aug 11 1922
3:25.0mins	Phyllis Hall	Paris	Aug 20 1922
3:04.4mins	Gladys Lunn	London	May 16 1931
3:00.6mins	Gladys Lunn	Birmingham	June 25 1934
2:39.42mins	Mary Stewart	London	May 25 1976

1,500m

4:30.0mins	Diane Leather	Hornchurch	May 16 1957
4:29.7mins	Diane Leather	London	July 19 1957

1 Mile

5:23.0mins	Gladys Lunn	London	July 18 1936
5:20.8mins	Gladys Lunn	Dudley	May 8 1937
5:17.0mins	Gladys Lunn	London	Aug 7 1937
5:02.6mins	Diane Leather	London	Sept 30 1953
5:00.2mins	Diane Leather	Birmingham	May 26 1954

4:59.6mins	Diane Leather	Birmingham	May 29 1954
4:50.8mins	Diane Leather	London	May 24 1955
4:45.0mins	Diane Leather	London	Sept 21 1955
4:36.1mins	Mary Stewart	London	May 18 1977

80m Hurdles

11.07	Carole Quinton	Rome	Aug 31 1960
11.07	Carole Quinton	Rome	Aug 31 1960
10.99	Carole Quinton	Rome	Sept 1 1960

100m Hurdles

14.3	Pat Jones	Cardiff	Sept 10 1966
13.0	Blondel Thompson	Warsaw	June 29 1974

Automatic timing

14.15	Sue Reeve	Athens	Sept 17 1969
13.75	Sue Reeve	Edinburgh	July 21 1970

Javelin

29.88m	Gladys Lunn	Handsworth	Aug 13 1932
32.60m	Gladys Lunn	Schaerbeek	Aug 15 1934
32.98m	Gladys Lunn	Redditch	May 6 1935

Pentathlon

3832pts	Sue Reeve	Warley	May 31 1969
4141pts	Sue Reeve	Vlaardingen	June 7/8 1969

Heptathlon

4898pts	Ruth Martin-Jones	Birmingham	Sept 23/24 1978
6259pts	Judy Simpson	Athens	Sept 9/10 1982
6347pts	Judy Simpson	Sofia	Sept 10/11 1983
6623pts	Judy Simpson	Stuttgart	Aug 29/30 1986

5,000m Walk

25:09.2mins	Betty Jenkins	Warley	Sept 16 1972

1 mile Track walk

7:38.4mins	Beryl Randle	London	June 19 1954

Winners of the BOURNVILLE MILE
An invitation one mile race for the Bournville Bowl, an impressive ornamental trophy donated by the Cadburys Chocolate firm and run on grass in May at the firm's sports ground. Runners who won the race three times were allowed to keep the trophy and the record shows Cadburys had to provide replicas. Three time winners were Ellis (twice), Eeles, Hawkley and Green.

1926	Eddie Webster (Birchfield)	4:28.8mins
1927	Cyril Ellis (Birchfield)	4:22.8mins
1928	Stan Ashby (Godiva)	4:21.8mins
1929	Cyril Ellis (Birchfield)	4:21.4mins
1930	Cyril Ellis (Birchfield)	4:31.4mins
1931	Cyril Ellis (Birchfield)	4:23.0mins
1932	Cyril Ellis (Birchfield)	4:23.2mins
1933	Cyril Ellis (Birchfield)	4:20.2mins
1934	Bernard Eeles (Southgate)	4:22.8mins
1935	Bernard Eeles (Southgate)	4:20.6mins
1936	Bernard Eeles (Southgate)	4:22.0mins
1937	Ron Draper (Hinkley)	4:21.0mins
1938	Jim Alford (Roath)	4:15.4mins
1939	Sydney Wooderson (Blackheath)	4:12.0mins
1946	Bill Hawkley (Bromsgrove)	4:35.8mins
1947	Bill Hawkley (Bromsgrove)	4:27.0mins
1948	Bill Hawkley (Bromsgrove)	4:16.8mins
1949	Fred Green (Birchfield)	4:22.1mins
1950	Bill Hawkley (Bromsgrove)	4:20.6mins
1951	Fred Green (Birchfield)	4:27.4mins
1952	Fred Green (Birchfield)	4:16.0mins
1953	Colin Simpson (S.Heath)	4:21.0mins
1954	Fred Green (Birchfield)	4:17.6mins
1955	Frank Wyatt (Bristol)	4:19.2mins

ROBERT WEIR gained his first British vest throwing the hammer at the GB v. GDR match in Dresden on June 14, 1981, and his last on September 21, 2002, in the discus at the IAAF World Cup in Madrid. This span of 21 years is the longest of any male GB T&F internationalist except for walker Chris Maddocks who has a span of 22 years of international appearances.

PETER RADFORD improved the UK (auto timing) record for 100yds three times on the same day. At the 1958 Commonwealth Games in Cardiff the second round heats, semi-finals and final were all held on Saturday July 19 and Peter, representing England, successively ran times of 9.84, 9.81 and 9.80.

Hammer thrower HOWARD PAYNE was aged 43 when he threw a personal best of 70.88m on June 29 1974. This stood as a British veterans record for 30 years. His total of 61 GB vests is a record number for any Birchfielder.

At the time of writing the club's longest standing record was set by JOHN SHERWOOD when he was 3rd in the 400 hurdles in 49.02 at the 1968 Olympics. In this race, as the winner David Hemery crossed the line BBC commentator David Coleman astonished British statisticians with the words, 'Who cares who's third?'

When IAN STEWART (born January 15, 1949) ran 1,500m in 3:39.0mins on September 1st 1969 in the GB v. France match he became the youngest ever holder of the British record for 1 mile or 1,500m. On September 12 1970 in Warsaw, PETER STEWART ran exactly the same time (manual timing) in winning the 1,500m at the GB v. Poland match. For nearly two years the brothers were joint holders of the British 1,500m record.

The first Birchfielder to compete in an Olympic event was VIC LONEY who won his heat of the 1,500m in London in 1908. The club's first medal winner was ARTHUR ROBERTSON who took a gold in the 3 Miles Team Race and a silver in the Steeplechase, also at the 1908 Games. Birchfield's first woman Olympian was AUDREY BROWN in Berlin in 1936. She was also the first medal winner, a silver in the 4x100m relay.

To date, and not including those who have appeared in more than one Games, 71 Birchfielders have competed in the Olympics: 49 men and 22 women. SUE REEVE is the only one to make three Games, those of 1968, 1976 and 1980. In Mexico in 1968 at 17 she was the youngest British T&F competitor at the Games, and of course the youngest of all Birchfield Olympians.

The bronze medal KATHARINE MERRY received after finishing 3rd in the 400m at the Sydney Olympics proved to be slightly damaged. She complained and received another one, so returned home with two bronzes – 'One's for my mother', she said.   When PETER STEWART won the AAA mile championship in 1972 his medal was presented by Sir Roger Bannister. It had to be exchanged, the one he received on the podium was for the pole-vault.

The first Birchfielder to represent two countries was ERNEST MASSEY who ran for Wales in the International cross-country championship in 1909, England in 1910 and Wales again in 1914. First Empire Games representative was ROBERT SUTHERLAND who ran in the 3 and 6 miles races for Scotland in Hamilton, Ontario, in 1930, but the first medal winner was RALPH BROWN who was 3rd in the 440yds hurdles at the Games in London in 1934.

A problem for present day historians is discovering the first names of athletes who competed at a time when only initials were used. In this area the work of the National Union of Statisticians cannot be praised too highly. Thus, we are now able provide full names of all Birchfield's representatives at major international championships. The name that came to light recently and closes the list is that of J.C.W. (JOSEPH) HEATH who was 5th in the javelin at the 1934 Empire Games.

WAL MONK was one of the few athletes of the 1920s to be accorded a first name in meeting programmes because his brother William also competed so an entry from a W. Monk needed clarification.

Bibliography

The History of Birchfield Harriers 1877-1988, Professor W.O. Alexander and Wilfred Morgan, Club publication.
History of the English Speaking Peoples, Part Work, Purnell.
Centenary History of the AAA

Magazines:
Athletics Weekly
Athletics Today
Sport and Play
The Athletic Field and Swimming World
Great Barr Observer, Central Independent Newspapers Archives, Tamworth

Reports:
Annual Reports, Birchfield Harriers
Press Officer's reports, Tom McCook, Birchfield Harriers
Archive, The Alexander Stadium, Birmingham

Websites:
www.wenlock-olympian-society.org.uk
www.infed.org/christianeducation/muscular-christianity.html
www.olympics.org.uk/olympicmovement/modernhistory.asp
www.observer.guardian.co.uk
www.newsrole/bbc.co.uk

Photographs/Illustrations

Central Independent Newspapers, Tamworth courtesy of Neil Rose, Sports Editor
Mark Shearman (athleticsimages@aol.com)
Club archives and clubhouse display
David Sprason
Derek Carruthers, Barry Stephenson, Ian Somerville www.speedwayswapshop.co.uk

Long Service

Throughout their long history Birchfield Harriers have been extremely fortunate to have attracted and retained individuals who have worked tirelessly in many capacities to serve our club. Some of the notable people who have carried on this tradition since the publication of the last club history in 1988 include the following: -

Brian Abbey, Ainsley Bennett, Dave Billiard, Norma Blaine, Barbara Broadfield, John and Maureen Bullen, Darrell Bunn, Ivy and John Clarke, Eddy Cockayne, Pauline Churchill, Robin Davis, Betty Downes, Ken Etheridge, Mo Graham, Pauline Hadley, Tony Hadley, Don Hitchman, Keith Holt, Brian Holyfield, Vernice Jeffers, Dave Lawrence, Marianne Lingen, Tom McCook, Adrian Miles, Maurice Millington, Wilf Morgan, Lyn Orbell, Beryl Randle, Janet, Stuart and Andy Paul, Steve Platt, Mike Rawson, Kevin Reeve, Terry Roberts, Dave Skelcher, Robin Simpson, David Sprason, Peter Stewart, Vic Stokes, Roy Tilling, Geoff Warr and Jan Yarnall.

In paying tribute to the foregoing, we also gratefully acknowledge the support of their partners and families for allowing them the time to contribute so much effort for the benefit of our club and it's members.

Index

ALEXANDER W.W. 13, 14, 15, 16, 25, 35, 36, 41
ALEXANDER SPORTS GROUND 11, 35, 36, 38, 39, 40, 46, 51
ALEXANDER STADIUM 61, 188, 189
AMATEUR ATHLETIC CLUB 8
ARDEN DAPHNE 53, 55
ASQUITH LINCOLN 64, 65, 67, 68, 69, 70, 71, 72, 79
ASTON HALL AND PARK 10, 11, 12, 13
ATHENS 1997 123-124
ATHENS 2004 PS.194-196
ATLANTA 1996 112-113
AUCKLAND 1990 82-83
AUSTIN GEOFF 44
BAILLIE CHRIS 149, 159
BARBER EUNICE 150, 151, 155, 161, 168
BARBOUR SHIREEN (née SAMY) 78, 91, 98, 103, 107
BARCELONA 1992 93-94
BEMAN JACK 29, 30, 31, 32, 33, 34, 35, 36, 37, 38, 40, 41
BENNETT AINSLEY 63, 67, 70, 79
BENTLEY SARAH 112, 115, 130, 138, 143
BIRCHALL ROB 115, 117, 127, 128, 139, 142, 143, 144, 145, 159, 172, 173, 181, 182, 183
BIRMINGHAM 2003 184
BLADES CANDACE 141
BLEWITT JOE 26, 27, 28, 29, 30, 31, 32, 33, 34, 35, 36, 37, 38
BOULDSTRIDGE MIKE 131, 154, 182
BRAUN SABINE 123, 124, 130, 139, 150
BRENNAN DEBORAH 162, 163, 167, 187
BRIGHTWELL ROBBIE 47, 53, 54, 55, 56
BROWN GODFREY 41, 42, 43, 104
BROWN KEVIN 85, 100, 147
BROWN PHIL 62, 63, 64, 65, 66, 67, 68, 69, 70, 71, 72, 75, 78, 79, 83, 83
BROWNE CURTIS 84, 85, 86, 92, 168
BUDAPEST 1998 138-139
BUNN DARRELL 102, 112, 113, 119, 121, 123, 132, 138, 139, 146, 147
BURROWS DARIUS 90, 98, 99, 100, 102, 103, 108, 114, 115, 116, 121, 127, 128, 131, 154, 173, 182
BUSHELL MICKEY 184, 193
CAINES DANIEL 144, 152, 153, 164, 165, 166, 167, 174, 176, 178, 180, 181, 184, 185, 186, 187, 193
CARE BOB 193
CHRISTIE LINFORD 76, 77, 85, 87, 88, 91, 92, 98, 99, 100, 101, 104, 105, 109, 128, 137, 144.147
CLARKSON MATT 114, 127, 130, 131, 137, 142
COOPER JOHN 54, 55, 56
De COURBETIN, BARON PIERRE 18, 19
COURT CLOVA 78, 79, 84, 87, 89, 92, 93, 94, 95, 97, 98, 99, 100, 101, 102, 104, 106, 109, 110, 111, 113, 114, 117, 118, 119, 125, 133, 136, 138, 139, 142
CRAM STEVE 173
DAINTY GILL 62, 63, 64, 66, 70, 71, 78, 103, 181
DALRYMPLE JOCK 32, 34, 36, 37, 40
DANIELS DARREN 110, 114, 131
DAVIES SAMANTHA 133, 137, 142, 152
DUNFORD EDWARD 128, 147, 163, 168, 176, 181, 183, 187, 188, 192
EDMONDS STEVE 130, 131, 154
EDMONTON 2001 171
ELLIS CYRIL 36, 37, 38, 40
ELLIS SALLY 74, 78, 77, 86, 87, 88, 89, 93, 100, 103, 107, 115
EVERETT DANNY 142
FARRELL MIKE 47, 48, 49, 54, 181
FAULKNER STEWART 72, 73, 75, 76, 78, 80, 81, 83, 84, 86, 111
FLEMMING JANE 71, 82, 83, 102, 119
FOX MIKE 191, 192, 194
FREEMAN CATHY 86, 156, 160, 178
FREEMAN WALTER 26, 27, 28, 29, 30, 31, 32, 34, 35
FROST HELEN 120, 138, 146, 148, 149, 158, 177, 180, 181
GEORGE WALTER 13
GILLESPIE IAN 114, 115, 117, 121, 126, 127, 132, 135, 136
GOTHENBURG 1995 106
GRAHAM JOHN 64, 66, 67, 71, 81, 82, 181
GREEN BILLY 35, 36, 37, 38, 40, 41, 50
GREEN FREDDIE 46, 48
HADLEY TONY 62, 75, 78, 108, 121, 131
HANSEN ASHIA 170, 173, 174, 175, 176, 177, 178, 180, 181, 184, 189, 190, 193
HANSON LORRAINE 78, 79, 80, 84, 85, 88, 92, 94, 106, 110, 113, 119, 120, 122, 125, 133, 136, 138, 139, 186
HARRISON ROB 70, 84
HARTIGAN BEV 103, 105, 107, 110, 112, 116, 130
HELSINKI 1994 102
HIRSCH MARK 130, 131, 154
HORNBY EMMA 112, 113, 126, 134, 139, 155
HOUGHTON HARRY 31, 33, 35, 36, 38, 40
HULFORD FREDDIE 21
INDOOR FACILITIES- HIGH PERFORMANCE CENTRE 172, 173, 183, 188, 189
JOHN JASON 74, 84, 86, 91, 108, 109, 110, 124, 131
JORDAN RACHAEL 115, 118, 130, 144
KARAGOUNIS HELEN (née THIEME) 147, 152, 155, 160, 162, 163, 168, 169, 170, 171, 176, 177, 178, 179, 180, 185, 186, 189, 190, 191, 193
KESKA KARL 92, 110, 121, 134, 135, 136, 137, 138, 141, 153, 154, 162, 180, 187
KIRUI EILUD 169, 180, 181, 192
KNOWLES RICHARD 117, 120, 122, 124, 145, 146, 155, 168, 172
KRUGER FRANTZ 140, 177, 178
KUALA LUMPUR 1998 140-142
LADEJO DU'AINE 155, 158, 169, 170, 186, 189, 190
LAW JOEY 13, 14
LAWRENCE DAVE 74, 80, 100, 110, 111, 125, 159, 171, 193
LEATHER DIANE 48, 49, 181
LEWIS BEN 118, 126, 127, 168, 169
LEWIS DENISE 74, 89, 95, 100, 101, 104, 106, 108, 109, 110, 111, 112, 113, 114, 118, 119, 120, 121, 123, 124, 125, 128, 129, 130, 131, 132, 133, 135, 136, 138, 139, 141, 146, 149, 150, 151, 155, 156, 157, 159, 161,

162, 163, 164, 168, 170, 171, 174, 175, 185, 186, 187, 189, 190, 194
LEWIS-FRANCIS MARK 118, 125, 126, 132, 137, 140, 144, 146, 148, 157, 158, 159, 160, 162, 163, 164, 167, 168, 170, 173, 174, 175, 176, 177, 183, 184, 185, 186, 187, 190, 196
LISBON 2001 166
LUNN GLADYS 36, 40, 41, 43, 182
LYONS DENNIS 20, 22, 36, 38, 41
MAYLOR DONNA 137, 142, 148, 149, 155, 160
MBANGO FRANCOISE 178, 181, 184
McCALLA ERIC 62, 65, 67, 68, 69, 71, 72
McLEOD GERALDINE 78, 87, 92, 94, 95, 97, 102, 109, 111, 113
McCOOK JAMES 103, 121, 154
McCOOK TOM 56, 57, 182, 195
MEDDINGS ALLAN 96, 105, 191, 193, 194
MERRY KATHARINE 73, 74, 77, 78, 79, 80, 81, 84, 86, 88, 90, 92, 93, 94, 95, 96, 97, 99, 100, 101, 105, 108, 110, 114, 117, 118, 122, 124, 125, 128, 133, 134, 136, 137, 138, 139, 144, 147, 148, 149, 150, 152, 155, 156, 160, 164, 165, 168, 178, 181, 185, 186
MILES PAUL 133
MILLINGTON MAURICE 99, 127, 131, 154, 162
MITCHELL GEORGE 87, 90
MONK WAL 26, 27, 28, 30, 31, 34, 35
MOORE ASTON 62, 64, 65, 66, 67, 70, 155, 180, 181
MOORE JONATHAN 155, 160, 169, 170, 176, 180, 181, 185, 188, 189, 190, 193
MOORHOUSE JULIAN 127, 128, 133, 142, 146, 154, 183, 190
MORGAN NATHAN 132, 134, 136, 137, 138, 146, 147, 148, 167, 169, 170, 171, 176, 178, 179, 187, 189
MUNICH 2002 178-180
NEBIOLO, DR.PRIMO 104

NELSON ADAM 102, 139, 156, 162, 163, 166, 169, 181, 187, 194
NELSON-NEALE DORETTE 66, 95
O'CALLAGHAN PAUL 127, 130, 131, 142, 148, 154
OLIVER HARRY 15, 16
OLUBAN MICHAEL 74, 76, 99, 107
OPENSHAW MIKE 165, 166
ORBELL LYN 152, 183
PARIS 2003 185-187
PAYNE HOWARD 47, 66, 85, 91, 96
PEACOCK SHANE 81, 85, 90
PENNY BROOKS, DR. WILLIAM 18, 19
PLATT STEVE 128, 164, 189
PROKHOROVA HELENA 161
PUGH KAREN 63, 65, 69, 71, 72
PUGSLEY JUSTIN 130, 142, 144, 145
PYATYICH ANNA 176
QUINTON CAROLE 52
RADFORD PETER 47, 48, 50, 51, 52, 55, 105, 181
RANDLE BERYL 95, 181
RAWSON MIKE 47, 48, 49, 50, 54, 55, 105, 144, 162
REEVE SUE 62, 63, 64, 181, 185
REDMOND DEREK 69, 72, 75, 78, 79, 81, 82, 84, 85, 88, 89, 90, 92.93, 94, 96, 105
REID BOB 45
REILLY SARAH (née OXLEY) 118, 124, 125, 148, 149, 170, 173
ROBERTSON ARTHUR 22, 23
ROSSWESS MICHAEL 74, 75, 76, 77, 80, 85, 87, 88, 89, 90, 91, 92, 97, 98, 99, 100, 105, 106, 107, 109, 111
ROWE DEBBIE 118, 148, 149, 170, 176
SAZONOVICH NATASHA 112, 139, 161
SEVILLE 1999 149-151
SHERWOOD JOHN 55
SHEVYN MIKE 114, 130, 131, 154
SHOUAA GARDA 112, 119, 150
SIMPSON JUDY (née LIVERMORE) 65, 66, 68, 71, 73, 74, 75, 82, 83, 89, 91, 119
SMEDLEY RAY 62, 63, 64, 65, 66
SMITH GLEN 101, 134, 136, 138,

145, 147, 149, 150, 159, 162, 169, 170, 171, 172, 175, 176, 186
SNOOK WILLIAM 14, 16
SOTHERTON KELLY 164, 171, 174, 181, 183, 184, 185, 186, 188, 189, 190, 194, 195
SPEEDWAY RACING 38, 39, 46, 54
STANTON RALPH 24, 28, 29, 30, 31, 32
STEWART IAN 47, 55, 57, 58, 59, 61, 90, 92, 108, 116, 153, 166, 175
STEWART MARY 57, 59, 60, 61, 62, 63, 67, 68, 69, 70, 181
STEWART PETER 57, 58, 59, 70, 181
STUTTGART 1993 97
SURMAN JADE 172, 176, 183, 184, 186, 188, 192
SYMONDS ANDY 89, 99, 130, 131
THOMAS MICHELLE 95, 117, 118, 119, 120, 124, 125, 136, 139, 142, 144, 148, 152
TILLING ROY 125, 182
TOKYO 1991 89
UDALL CARL 115, 116, 117, 127, 128
UNDERWOOD ADAM 21
VAN COMMENEE CHARLES 151, 155, 161, 163, 174, 186, 188, 189, 194
VICTORIA BC 1994 102, 141
WARREN CARL 116, 127, 128, 130, 131, 137, 142, 143, 144, 145, 154
WEBSTER EDDIE 30, 31, 32, 33, 34, 35, 36, 37, 38, 40, 41, 45
WEIR ROBERT 63, 64, 65, 66, 67, 68, 96, 97, 100, 101, 102, 106, 110, 111, 114, 120, 121, 122, 125, 134, 136, 138, 140, 141, 147, 156, 159, 162, 168, 169, 170, 171, 177, 178, 179
WEST SCOTT 90, 98, 99, 100
WHARTON ARTHUR 14, 15
WILLIAMS BARRINGTON 76
WLODARCZYK URSZULA 112, 123, 139, 157
WRIGHT FRANK 24, 31, 34, 38, 41, 42
YIEND BRAD 155, 171, 187
YOUNG JOHN 50

If you are interested in purchasing other books published by Tempus, or in case you have difficulty finding any Tempus books in your local bookshop, you can also place orders directly through our website

www.tempus-publishing.com